T0215663

Pro Apache NetBeans

Building Applications on the Rich Client Platform

Ioannis Kostaras
Constantin Drabo
Josh Juneau
Sven Reimers
Mario Schröder
Geertjan Wielenga

Apress®

Pro Apache NetBeans: Building Applications on the Rich Client Platform

Ioannis Kostaras
The Hague, South Holland, The Netherlands

Constantin Drabo
Ouagadougou, Burkina Faso

Josh Juneau
Chicago, IL, USA

Sven Reimers
Salem, Germany

Mario Schröder
Berlin, Germany

Geertjan Wielenga
Amsterdam, The Netherlands

ISBN-13 (pbk): 978-1-4842-5369-4
https://doi.org/10.1007/978-1-4842-5370-0

ISBN-13 (electronic): 978-1-4842-5370-0

Managing Director, Apress Media LLC: Welmoed Spahr
Acquisitions Editor: Jonathan Gennick
Development Editor: Laura Berendson
Coordinating Editor: Jill Balzano

Cover image designed by Freepik (www.freepik.com)

Distributed to the book trade worldwide by Springer Science+Business Media New York, 233 Spring Street, 6th Floor, New York, NY 10013. Phone 1-800-SPRINGER, fax (201) 348-4505, e-mail orders-ny@springer-sbm.com, or visit www.springeronline.com. Apress Media, LLC is a California LLC and the sole member (owner) is Springer Science + Business Media Finance Inc (SSBM Finance Inc). SSBM Finance Inc is a **Delaware** corporation.

For information on translations, please e-mail rights@apress.com, or visit http://www.apress.com/rights-permissions.

Apress titles may be purchased in bulk for academic, corporate, or promotional use. eBook versions and licenses are also available for most titles. For more information, reference our Print and eBook Bulk Sales web page at http://www.apress.com/bulk-sales.

Any source code or other supplementary material referenced by the author in this book is available to readers on GitHub via the book's product page, located at www.apress.com/9781484253694. For more detailed information, please visit http://www.apress.com/source-code.

Printed on acid-free paper

Dedicated to our families who have silently supported us in our adventures as authors. More specifically:

Ioannis Kostaras:

To my lovely wife Katerina; my adorable little son Nikolaos-Ioannis; and my parents, Nikolaos and Zinovia

Constantin Drabo:

I dedicate this book to my lovely mother, my brother Emmanuel, and sister Denise, my spouse Mariam, and my little son Johann. Finally, to these special persons: Geertjan Wielenga and Malo Sadouanouan

Josh Juneau:

To my wife Angela; and my children, Katie, Jake, Matt, Zach, and Luke

Sven Reimers:

To my beloved wife Isabelle

Mario Schröder:

To my wife Fridah

Geertjan Wielenga:

To my wife Hermine

Table of Contents

x

About the Authors

Ioannis (John) Kostaras graduated from the Informatics Department at the University of Athens. He also holds a Master of Science degree in Telecommunications and Information Systems from the Electronics Systems Engineering Department of Essex University, and a Master of Arts degree in Management Studies also from Essex University. Ioannis is a software architect/senior software engineer in an international organization located in The Hague, Netherlands, developing real-time critical distributed systems, and has been a Java developer since JDK 1.0 was released. One of the many applications he has written for the industry, developed in the NetBeans Rich Client Platform, was awarded the 2012 Duke's Choice Award. He is also a member of the NetBeans Dream Team and an Apache NetBeans contributor. Apart from Java, he "speaks" other languages, such as C/C++, Python, Ruby, and Erlang, to name a few; and he codes them using his favorite IDE, NetBeans. He has written a number of articles in JavaCodeGeeks, and in the NetBeans wiki, and runs an online course for Java in Greek in the Mathesis platform, teaching the latest Java and Apache NetBeans to audiences speaking Greek. Finally, but not least, he is a co-organizer of JCrete, the hottest Java unconference, on the island of Crete.

Constantin Drabo earned a Master's Degree from the Université de Picardie Jules Verne (France) in Internet Technologies. He is a software engineer in the National Treasury of Burkina Faso, and is a part-time teacher at the Université Nazi Boni of Bobo-Dioulasso, where he teaches on Java/Java EE and the Human/Machine Interface. He participates in the Java Community Process (JCP) through his contribution to JSR 381 (Visual Recognition). Constantin is a member of the NetBeans Dream Team, and creator of the FasoJUG Java User Group. He is currently studying for his PhD in Machine Learning in Medical Systems.

Josh Juneau has been developing software and database systems for several years. Database application development and sophisticated web apps have been the focus of his career since the beginning. Early in his career, he became an Oracle database administrator and adopted the PL/SQL language for performing administrative tasks and developing applications for the Oracle database. In an effort to build more complex solutions, he began to incorporate Java into his PL/SQL applications, and later developed standalone and web applications with Java. Josh wrote his early Java web applications utilizing JDBC to work with back-end databases. Later, he incorporated frameworks into his enterprise solutions, including Java EE, Spring, and JBoss Seam. Today, he primarily develops enterprise web solutions utilizing Java EE. He is an avid contributor to Oracle's *Java Magazine*, speaks at conferences and Java user group events, contributes to the Chicago Java User Group, and is an Apache NetBeans committer and a Java Champion.

Sven Reimers is based at Lake Constance in Southern Germany where he works as a systems engineer for Airbus Defence and Space creating next-generation ground segment software for space systems. He has more than 20 years' experience building complex distributed software systems, and more than 20 years' experience with Java. In 2009, Reimers was the winner of the Duke's Choice Award in the Network Solutions category for ND SatCom's Satellite Communication Management Software. He is part of the Apache NetBeans PMC, an author at OpenJFX, a regular speaker at conferences, as well as leader and founder of JUG Bodensee. For his long-term commitment to Java, the Java community, and his contributions to the Java ecosystem, Reimers was named a Java Champion in 2014.

Mario Schröder earned a Master's Degree in Civil Engineering from the University of Rostock in Germany. However, he discovered his passion for computer science during his studies and made programming and software development into his profession. He started working with Java professionally in 2001. He is a certified Java Programmer, iSAQB-Software Architect, and ISTQB-Tester. His first contact with NetBeans was in 2004. He was a member of the NetCat team for Version 7.2, has contributed patches to the platform, and has developed several plugins.

Geertjan Wielenga is the Apache NetBeans PMC Chair and a product manager at Oracle for Oracle JET, which is Oracle's free and open source front-end JavaScript technology stack. He lives and works in Amsterdam. He is a Java and JavaScript technology enthusiast, advocate, trainer, speaker, and writer. He studied law at the University of Natal in Pietermaritzburg, South Africa. In early 1996, he started working as a technical writer for a software technology organization in the Netherlands and, after having worked at various other software organizations in the Netherlands, he moved to Vienna, Austria, and worked as a technical writer for the documentation of Coca-Cola's ERP system. In 2004, he moved to Prague, Czech Republic, to work on NetBeans IDE, again as a technical writer. He discovered that NetBeans IDE is a unique product, project, and ecosystem and became inspired and continually enthused by the open source ecosystem around NetBeans IDE, the technologies around it, and the central role that the NetBeans community plays in them. He is happy and proud of the role NetBeans IDE has played in its many years of existence and its continued development in the Apache Software Foundation.

About the Technical Reviewer

 **Kevin Farnham** has developed software for high-volume data analysis and mathematical modeling since the 1980s. He has been site editor and lead blogger for technology websites at Oracle, Intel, and O'Reilly Media.

Kevin has served as technical editor and reviewer for dozens of software engineering books.

Acknowledgments

Authoring a book is like departing for an adventure. Even though you make a plan, you don't know how long it is going to take, how big the waves will be, and what new land you are going to explore. Like Odysseus, we seek our Ithaca and the way is not always easy – it is full of adventures and exciting indeed – but rewarding in the end.

This book is our adventure into an IDE we all love and continue to work with. So before anybody else, we would like to acknowledge and thank this little team from the University of Prague who had the fancy idea of creating NetBeans, its never-tired Product Manager, Geertjan Wielenga, as well as all the people that have contributed one way or another, all these years, to make this IDE a necessity for all of us.

We would also like to thank the Apress team for their patience and support in a multi-author community book that has not always been easy to manage and coordinate, their persistent comments leaving nothing to chance, and scrutinizing every sentence of the drafts. However, any errors that may still exist are the responsibility of the authors.

Finally, but not least, we would like to thank our families for bearing with us during our adventure, when we were spending many hours behind a computer's screen, trying to explain as best as we could the many NetBeans topics you will find in this book, as well as writing example programs that would give more value to its readers.

Introduction

Pro Apache NetBeans provides a detailed overview of the latest additions to NetBeans IDE, like support for JShell, the Jigsaw Module System, and Local Variable Type Inference, focusing on what this new version brings to developers. It also describes new features in NetBeans Platform, that is, the framework the NetBeans IDE has been built upon.

The book is a practical, hands-on guide providing a number of step-by-step recipes that help you take advantage of the power in the latest Java (and other) software platforms, and it gives a good grounding in using NetBeans IDE for your projects. This book has been written by the Apache community members who have been using the IDE and actively contributing and developing Apache NetBeans as an open source project.

Pro Apache NetBeans consists of three parts. The first part describes how to use the IDE as well as the new features that it brings to support the latest Java versions. The second part describes how you can extend NetBeans by creating plugins or writing your own standalone applications using the Rich Client Platform. The third part describes how you can contribute to develop your favorite IDE further, becoming part of the open source team that is driving future developments in the toolset.

In more detail, Chapter 1, "What Is NetBeans," provides a gentle introduction to NetBeans. It explains what NetBeans is and what it is not, its history, all the way to its new home, the Apache Software Foundation, being its second biggest project. It also provides an introduction of the many programming languages and tools that NetBeans supports, and it introduces you to many other things that are explained in more detail in the rest of the book.

Chapter 2, "Getting Started with NetBeans," provides an overview of the NetBeans IDE, which will help new users to become familiar with its User Interface, the various windows, and it introduces you to how to build your first Java project. It also provides useful tricks and tips to help you speed up your productivity.

Chapter 3 provides an overview of the new features that Apache NetBeans IDE, since version 9.0, provides for Java versions 9–12 and other programming languages. It describes support for JShell, the Jigsaw Module System, HttpClient and Local Variable Type Inference, as well as improvements for PHP.

Chapter 4 describes how to develop desktop applications. These are standalone applications running, typically, locally on your machine without the need of a web or an application server. The chapter explains there are three ways to develop Java GUI desktop applications: using the Abstract Window Toolkit (AWT), Swing, or JavaFX. NetBeans provides a very powerful visual editor that you can use to build your GUI with dragging and dropping components onto forms (panels). The chapter also guides you through the steps for developing your own desktop application.

Chapter 5 describes how to build Enterprise (or Web) applications. Contrary to desktop applications, these require a web or application server to serve HTML pages. Java EE support has been included with Apache NetBeans since release 11.0. Full support for Maven web applications and Java EE technologies such as Enterprise JavaBeans (EJB), Contexts and Dependency Injection (CDI), and JavaServer Faces (JSF) allows developers the convenience of auto-completion, code fragments, and easy syntax recognition. After finishing this chapter, you will have a basic understanding of the conveniences provided by Apache NetBeans for full stack Java EE development.

Chapter 6, "Debugging and Profiling Applications," explains in detail the powerful debugger and profiler of Apache NetBeans. If debugging makes your code right, profiling will make it run fast. Things like breakpoints, debugging multi-threaded code, CPU and memory profiling, snapshots, etc., are explained in this chapter.

Part II of the book describes the NetBeans Platform (or Rich Client Platform), that is, the framework or libraries that the NetBeans IDE has been built upon. With this knowledge you can better understand the NetBeans source code that will allow you to fix bugs, or extend it by writing your own plugins. Or you can use it to develop your own desktop applications faster than using Swing.

Chapter 7, "Mastering the Core Platform," introduces the reader to the core APIs of the NetBeans Platform, namely, the NetBeans module system, the FileSystem, and the Lookups. NetBeans provides its own module system to modularize applications, which supports the use of OSGi. A comparison with Java's module system, Jigsaw, is provided in this chapter. NetBeans also provides its own libraries to access the filesystem. A comparison with NIO.2, introduced in Java 7, is provided. Finally, the Lookups are a very powerful tool to build loosely coupled applications. A comparison with Java 6 ServiceLoader is also provided.

Chapter 8, "Mastering the User Interface," teaches the reader the GUI components of the NetBeans Platform, namely the Window system, the Action system, the Node System, and the Explorer Views and Property Sheets, all reducing the time you need to develop powerful UIs.

In Chapter 9, the reader applies what s/he has learned so far by porting a desktop application to NetBeans RCP. The development is done in three steps: (1) Build a "static" visual prototype of the user interface; (2) Build a "dynamic" prototype of the application, coding user interface events and associated business logic and creating customized UI components as needed; and (3) Code the persistence logic.

Chapter 10, "Learning the Extras of the Platform," describes many of the other APIs provided by the NetBeans Platform, such as the Dialogs API, the Visual Library and the Palette, the Status Bar and Notifications, the progress bar, the QuickSearch and the Output window, etc.

Chapter 11 teaches you how to extend NetBeans by writing a plugin for it. You will learn step by step how to develop a plugin for Hyperledger, an open source effort to advance blockchain technologies, hosted by the Linux Foundation.

Part III gives you an overview of the new home that hosts NetBeans, the Apache Foundation; its infrastructure to support open source projects like the various tools that allow issue tracking, testing, documentation, etc.; and gives you all the information you need to become a contributor of Apache NetBeans.

Chapter 12 describes the Apache NetBeans Process. After a short history, it explains how the migration of source code was achieved from Oracle to Apache, the various NetBeans versions under Apache as an incubator project, and the graduation to a top-level Apache Project.

Chapter 13 describes the Apache Infrastructure and the various tools that the Apache Software Foundation provides for its projects for issue/bug reporting, wikis, websites, etc.

Chapter 14 describes the NetCAT program. The *Net*Beans IDE *C*ommunity *A*cceptance *T*esting program is very important for the quality of the product. A typical NetCAT program takes around two months of activities. The chapter explains how each NetBeans version is tested by the community before it is released. You can easily participate in this program and execute tests, thus helping to improve your favorite IDE.

Chapter 15, provides an overview of the NetBeans source code, its architecture, its various modules, and their dependencies. It describes how to download and build the NetBeans source code, load it in NetBeans IDE, and debug it. Finally, this chapter encourages you to contribute to the NetBeans source code by fixing bugs and committing your changes to a baseline.

PART I

Using Apache NetBeans

CHAPTER 1

What Is Apache NetBeans

It isn't often that a technology sweeps the world and ends up being a relevant piece of the technological universe for over 20 years. However, the Java language is one of the few that has. The Java programming language was originally developed in 1995 by Sun Microsystems, and it has grown into a massive ecosystem over the years. The Java Virtual Machine (JVM) is a virtual computer that is defined by a specification, and the Java programming language can be used to program applications that run on the JVM. A JVM can be installed on just about any computer or hardware device that is available on the market. As such, the JVM is installed on millions of devices worldwide, and there have been dozens of different programming languages built on top of the JVM that compile down to Java byte code, allowing developers to utilize different language syntax to run on the JVM. What does this mean? Well, frankly it means that the JVM and Java are everywhere, and one can use a multitude of languages to program applications that will run just about anywhere. Java is an ecosystem that started in 1995, and it will be around long into the future.

As developers on one of the most prominent development platforms, folks can develop applications in a number of different ways. It is possible to develop Java code in a text editor, compile and run it via a terminal using the `java` executable, and then be on your way. It is also possible to create libraries of files and projects all via the terminal, without the use of any specialized tools for development. However, although it can be done, development without a code editor or a "development environment" including a project-based system, can be cumbersome, and Apache NetBeans is one of the most popular development environments for the Java Platform that helps to make development easy. Although Apache NetBeans is a great development tool, it is much more than just an editor. Apache NetBeans is a comprehensive development tool with support for several languages; it is a development platform for creating rich client applications; and it is a vibrant open source community with members from around the globe.

3

© Ioannis Kostaras, Constantin Drabo, Josh Juneau, Sven Reimers, Mario Schröder, Geertjan Wielenga 2020
I. Kostaras et al., *Pro Apache NetBeans*, https://doi.org/10.1007/978-1-4842-5370-0_1

The Journey to Apache NetBeans

In 1996, a student project was started under the guidance of the Faculty of Mathematics and Physics at Charles University in Prague. This student project aimed to make the development of Java much easier, providing a syntax editor for the code that would help to reduce errors and speed up development time when programming. It allowed one to compile and build entire projects with just a few clicks of a button. This project was originally named Xelfi, and in 1997 a company was formed around the project and it was renamed to NetBeans IDE. Sun Microsystems liked the project so much, that they purchased it in 1999 and open sourced the NetBeans IDE a year later.

After Sun Microsystems purchased Apache NetBeans, the user base and community began to thrive. Primarily developed and maintained by Sun Microsystems at the time, the community was able to provide patches, enhancements, and so forth since the IDE was open source. However, the overall road map and direction of NetBeans was controlled by the commercial entity. That wasn't necessarily a bad thing, as it helped to foster the IDE and the Java ecosystem as a whole, since NetBeans was being targeted toward both beginners and experienced Java developers alike.

NetBeans was part of the portfolio that Oracle had purchased from Sun Microsystems in January of 2010. As part of that portfolio, Oracle strived to drive NetBeans forward as the first IDE that would support the latest features of Java SE and Java EE alike. Oracle also strove to make NetBeans an IDE for many languages; they even hired Python and Ruby developers to help foster the JVM counterparts of those languages, Jython and JRuby respectively. As part of that initiative, NetBeans IDE gained support for these languages via the use of separately installed NetBeans modules. Since NetBeans was developed as a modular IDE, it was easy to add functionality as time went on, without increasing the footprint of the core IDE.

Oracle did a great job of moving NetBeans forward: it was still an open source IDE, and the community also played an important role. However, Oracle still drove the road map, and it was not very straight forward to become involved contributing code to NetBeans under the Oracle open source process. The NetBeans community has developed conferences organized around the IDE. Many have developed modules to extend the IDE. Even more have given talks or written tutorials about NetBeans features. The next step in the evolution of the IDE was to make contribution easier, and to give the IDE road map and sources to the community.

Oracle donated the NetBeans IDE sources and tutorials to Apache in the fall of 2016. Even though Oracle donated the IDE to Apache, it still remains very much involved in the development of Apache NetBeans, but the community now controls the road map. Contributing to Apache NetBeans is now as easy as creating a GitHub Pull Request. Since the donation, Apache NetBeans has changed its release cadence so that its releases are now more closely targeting the Java release cycle. Apache NetBeans still continues to be the first IDE to support the latest flavors of the JDK, and the community is as vibrant as ever.

Installing Apache NetBeans

There are a couple of different ways to install Apache NetBeans onto your machine, depending upon your uses. For those who are interested in modifying Apache NetBeans, the IDE can be built from source after cloning the Git repository. For those who are simply interested in utilizing Apache NetBeans as a development tool, the archive can be downloaded and extracted, and then the executable can be invoked. This section will briefly explain how to install by extracting Apache NetBeans. If you are interested in building from source, please refer to Chapter 14.

The initial requirement for utilization of Apache NetBeans is the installation of a Java Development Kit. Apache NetBeans supports JDK 8 and 11. The JDK must be installed in order to build the IDE from source or to run the IDE. To download Apache NetBeans, visit the downloads area at `https://netbeans.apache.org/download/` and obtain the most recent release. The downloads page includes links to obtain the sources or binaries for each of the releases. It also contains information about building the IDE from source. To download the binaries, click on the "Binaries" link, and then the "Apache Download Mirrors" page will be displayed. Choose a download mirror and click to obtain the archive.

Once the archive has been downloaded, extract within a folder. The extracted archive should resemble that in Figure 1-1. The executable is contained within the bin directory.

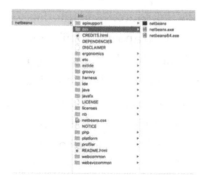

Figure 1-1. *Apache NetBeans Installation*

If more than one Java installation exists, edit the `etc/netbeans.conf` file accordingly and add the `JAVA_HOME` that should be used for running Apache NetBeans. To run Apache NetBeans, double-click the executable for the corresponding workstation's platform, which resides within the `bin` directory.

Note   To learn how to build Apache NetBeans from source, please refer to Chapter 14.

Integrated Development Environment

Apache NetBeans is most widely known as an Integrated Development Environment (IDE). That is why it is commonly referred to as NetBeans IDE. Originally made to be a development environment for Java, the breadth of Apache NetBeans IDE has grown immensely over the years into a development tool for many different languages. As of the release of Apache NetBeans 10, the IDE contains first-class support for a variety of languages, including Java, PHP, and JavaScript. Support not only means that the editor contains nice syntax coloring or keyword highlighting, but it also typically contains features such as automatic indentation as per language standards, auto-completion for keywords and code fragments, and in some cases also automated rebuilds of projects for an easy debugging and development life cycle. The source code editor makes it easy to jump to different portions of code using keyboard shortcuts and mouse clicks. The editor font, color, etc., can be modified within the Apache NetBeans preferences.

Did I mention debugging? Yes, the development environment also contains a full debugger for various languages, including the ability to set breakpoints, review variable values during live debugging, and perform hot code refreshes. The development environment also contains a full-fledged performance tuning solution for Java applications. One can use the performance tools to run an application and pinpoint code issues or threads that may be causing problems.

When it comes time to build a project, few build frameworks that are as widely used as Apache Maven. The Apache NetBeans IDE contains outstanding support for Apache Maven, making a sometimes daunting build framework easy to use. If one chooses to utilize XML directly for pulling in Maven dependencies, then the XML editor is there to assist through the process, but if one would rather simply type in required dependencies and have them automatically added, then that is another option.

One of the most important pieces of the development process is workflow and team collaboration. The NetBeans IDE contains first-class support for version control systems such as Git and Subversion, making collaboration a breeze. It is possible to clone Git repositories, update code, commit changes, and push to remote repositories right within the IDE. It is also easy to compare differences between files using the DIFF comparison tool.

Over the next few sections, we will go through some of the basic Apache NetBeans IDE features for some of the most common use cases.

Java Code Editor

First and foremost, Apache NetBeans IDE is a world-class Java editor. The editor contains a number of features to assist developers, making all aspects of application development more productive. Although this section highlights Java code editing features specifically, it should be noted that many of these same features are available for other languages, such as JavaScript and PHP.

Code completion provides developers with a boost by making code easier to write with less keystrokes, and also because it is great for typing those method names and variables that you don't quite remember. The code completion is automatically invoked by pressing CTRL-Space while typing. Doing so will cause a drop-down menu to appear, which includes a number of code suggestions for continuing your current line of code. The code suggestions are context-based, providing meaningful suggestions for the current code at the top of the list, and less meaningful suggestions toward the bottom.

Of course, code completion is configurable, so it can be made to automatically open the code completion drop-down menu while typing or when typing certain characters. By default, when a "." character is typed, context-based suggestions will appear, which can be beneficial for easily completing method names and so forth.

Code templates and snippets are handy for inserting segments of skeleton code, as needed, making it easier to complete logic. Templates can be invoked by clicking on a suggestion icon or by typing various strings of code such as "sout". When "sout" is typed and then the spacebar is pressed, the code "System.out.println("")" is expanded, leaving the cursor within the parentheses to continue typing. One can define custom code snippets for code that is often used. There are also refactoring options for automatically completing simple boilerplate code, such as creating getters and setters, without coding at all.

Java SE Applications

Apache NetBeans was originally built for development of Java Standard Edition (Java SE) applications: that is, a Java application that contains one or more Java classes, a starting point, and an action or graphical user interface that provides functionality for a user. Traditional Java development requires Java classes to be compiled before they can be executed. Compiling and execution of an application typically occurs via a command prompt or terminal, utilizing the javac compiler and the java command to execute resulting class files. What's more, if an application consists of more than one class file or resource, then it must be packaged into a *Java Archive (JAR)* before it is executed. Performing these tasks manually can be time consuming and cumbersome. Why not automate these minuscule tasks so that the developer can spend more time creating, rather than performing routine tasks? That is the original intention of Apache NetBeans IDE ... to make development easier and more productive by reducing the number of required routine tasks.

Note   Prior to installing Apache NetBeans, be sure to have a JDK installed. If you are planning to develop Java EE/Jakarta EE applications, be sure to install the version of the JDK that you will be using for the container to which the application is deployed. Once installed, the netbeans_jdkhome configuration variable, located within etc/netbeans.conf, should be assigned the path to the JDK you are using to run Apache NetBeans.

Let's walk through the development of a simple "Hello World" Java application and introduce some of the core features of Apache NetBeans IDE. To begin, open Apache NetBeans and create a new project by choosing "File" ➤ "New Project" or selecting the "New Project" icon in the toolbar.

Next, within the "New Project" dialog, choose the "Java" category from the *Categories* pick list, and then select "Java Application" from the *Projects* pick list. A *New Java Application* dialog will appear (Figure 1-2), and a **Project Name**, **Project Location**, and **Project Folder** can be provided. Type "HelloApacheNetBeans" as the project name.

Next, select a location on your computer in which to store the project files. Apache NetBeans allows one to provide a common area for storing third-party libraries, but skip that for now, and ensure "Create Main Class" is checked, maintaining the default *Main Class* name. Click "Finish" to create the project.

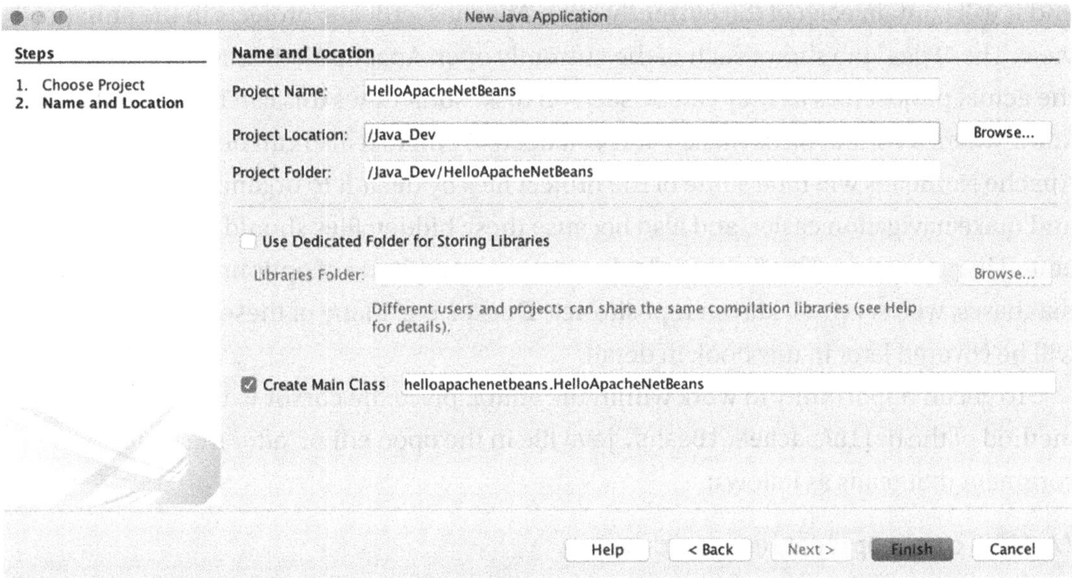

Figure 1-2. New Java Application Dialog

Apache NetBeans will open the HelloApacheNetBeans main class in the editor, and you will see that the project has been added to the left-hand navigator (Figure 1-3). When the project menu in the left-hand navigator is expanded, a single source file named HelloApacheNetBeans.java is displayed within the package helloapachenetbeans, and the default JDK that is registered with Apache NetBeans can be seen under the Libraries node. The HelloApacheNetBeans.java file is opened in the source editor by default.

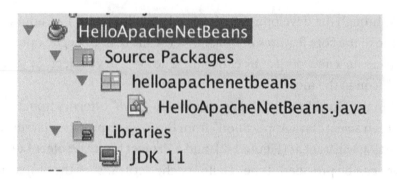

Figure 1-3. *Project Menu*

The project is displayed in an enhanced format, making it easy to navigate the project files and see project dependencies. At the top of the left-hand navigator, there are tabs for "Project," "Files," and "Services." The "Project" tab is displayed by default, and it will contain each of the currently open Apache NetBeans projects in the enhanced view. The "Files" tab shows each of the currently open Apache NetBeans projects using the actual project files as they can be seen on disk. Sometimes this can be useful if you know where a certain file is placed and you need to edit it. It also can be useful because Apache NetBeans will hide some of the project files by default to organize the project and make navigation easier, and also because these hidden files should not need to be edited in most cases. The "Services" tab contains a multitude of options for working with databases, web services, Maven repositories, Docker, etc. Many of these various services will be covered later in this book in detail.

To get an opportunity to work within the editor, place the cursor within the `main()` method of the `HelloApacheNetBeans.java` file in the open editor, after the code comment that reads as follows:

```
// TODO code application logic here
```

Press the return button to start a new blank line, and begin typing: `System.out.println("Hello Apache NetBeans");` While typing, auto-completion options are presented to make coding easier. In fact, by simply typing `sout` and pressing the tab button, the line will be auto-completed using a code template. Type the string "Hello Apache NetBeans" within the `println()` method. The code should look like that below:

```java
public static void main(String[] args) {
  // TODO code application logic here
  System.out.println("Hello Apache NetBeans");
}
```

Within the project navigator, the right-click provides many additional options, as it brings up the contextual menu. Most of these options will be covered later in the book, but for now right-click on the HelloApacheNetBeans project within the project navigator and select "Clean and Build." Doing so removes any compiled code from disk, and performs a build including any external dependencies for the project. Next, right-click on the project name and click "Run." Below the editor resides a number of tabs, and one of them is the "Output" tab. When the project is run, the "Output" tab should display the following:

```
run:
Hello Apache NetBeans
BUILD SUCCESSFUL (total time: 0 seconds)
```

Java Web Applications

Java web applications typically have a number of processes that need to be coordinated in order to develop and test. For instance, most web applications need to be deployed to an application server container of some kind, and many access a database. Apache NetBeans allows for easy development, deployment, and testing of Java web applications by allowing one to maintain all of these separate processes within one place. What's more, it contains a debugger mode that will easily allow one to deploy an application in debug mode and then step through breakpoints to help troubleshoot issues. See Chapter 5 for more details on the debugger.

Java web applications typically contain a number of different code and styling files, and the Apache NetBeans code editor is capable of editing just about any file. The code editor supports many different languages with features such as syntax highlighting, auto-completion, and error marking. When working with web applications especially, having the ability to edit different types of files within the same editor is essential. The Apache NetBeans plugin portal also provides the ability for developers to create third-party extensions for the IDE, making the possible supported files and options for expansion unlimited. For instance, there are third-party plugins available for many application server containers, allowing special functionality to be made available for these servers. See Chapter 11: Writing a Plugin for NetBeans for more details.

There are multiple options for developing web applications within Apache NetBeans. Each option contains a different project type. There are three options available under the "New Project" dialog's "Java Web" category: Web Application, Web Application with Existing Sources, and Web Free-Form Application. The "Web Application" is typically used to create a new web application project using Apache Ant for a build system. Such a project would require the developer to manually handle resources using Apache Ant. The "Web Application with Existing Sources" allows one to create a project from an existing Apache Ant-based web application. There are other available options for creating web applications utilizing the "Java EE" and "Maven" categories. Typically, older style Java Enterprise applications can be created from the options within the "Java EE" category. The "Maven" category provides options for creating Java EE projects using the Apache Maven build system. If unsure where to start, the safest and most modern style of web application project can be created by choosing the Maven "Web Application" project.

Note   If using Apache NetBeans release prior to 11.0, you will need to install the "Java EE" plugin in order to create a new web application project. In release 11.0+, the plugin is integrated within the IDE.

Let's walk through the development of a simple "Hello World" web application. First, open the "New Project" dialog and choose "Java Web" category, followed by the "Web Application" project type. Once selected, the "New Web Application" dialog will be displayed. Name the web application "HelloWorldWeb," and choose a good location for the project (Figure 1-4).

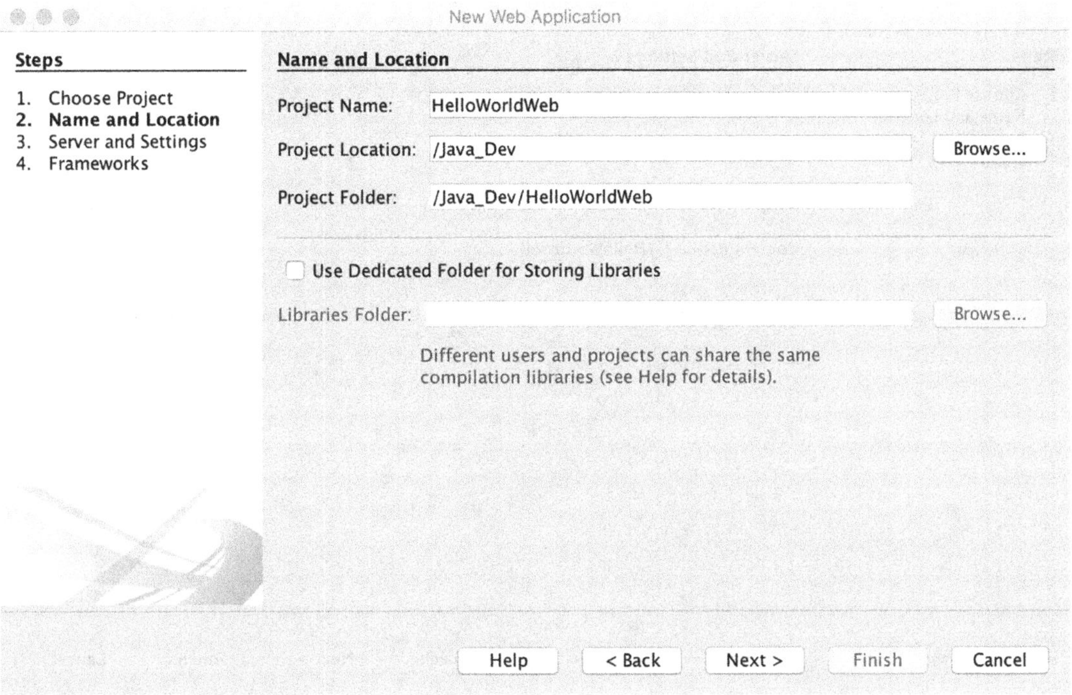

Figure 1-4. *New Web Application Dialog*

Click next, and then select an application server and "Java EE Version" to support. In this case, the "Payara 5.183.1" server is selected (see section on how to add a new server to Apache NetBeans), and "Java EE 7 Web" is selected as the **Java EE Version**. Leave the **Context Path** as is (Figure 1-5).

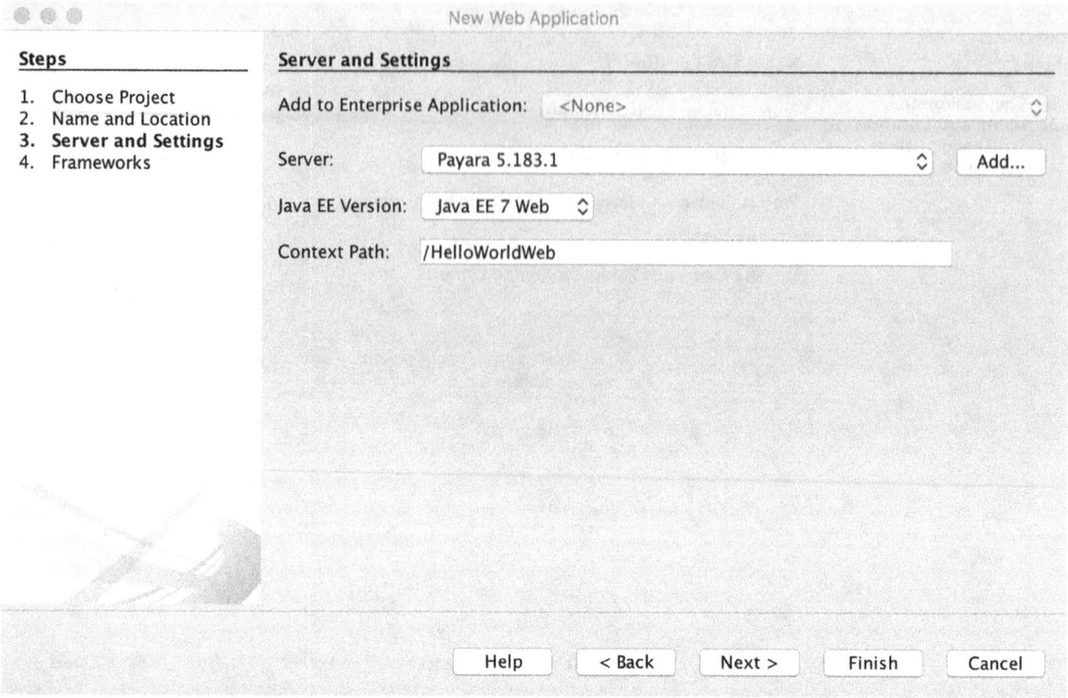

Figure 1-5. *Server and Settings*

The final section to the "New Web Application" wizard is the **Frameworks** dialog. In this section, if you'd like to use a particular Java Web framework, you could select it here to add any required dependencies and configuration files for the chosen framework. In this case, do not select anything and simply click "Finish." The project will appear within the "Projects" navigator in the left-hand menu, and the index.html file for the project will open within the editor. The project contains the following nodes: "Web Pages," "Source Packages," "Libraries," and "Configuration Files," as seen in Figure 1-6.

Figure 1-6. Java Web Project Structure

At this point, the project is ready to be deployed to the designated application server, and that can be done by right-clicking on the project and choosing "Run." By selecting "Run," the designated application server will start and the application will be compiled and deployed. The editor that contains the HTML file will provide options for editing HTML, and if a CSS or JavaScript file is created, then the editor will provide options that are specific to those types of files. Of course, all of the features that are available for Java SE projects are also available for Java Web projects.

PHP and Other Languages

Although Apache NetBeans was originally created for the development of Java applications, over the years the community has added support for a number of other languages. One such language that has outstanding support in Apache NetBeans is PHP. Another well-supported language is JavaScript. In Apache NetBeans 10, PHP gained full support within the IDE, so features such as multi-catch exception handling, nullable types, context sensitive lexer, etc., are available. The code editor contains PHP-specific features, such as hints for void return types, hints for incorrect non-abstract methods, suggestions for strict types declaration, etc. There is also support for an HTML forms palette to aid in development of PHP web forms.

To create a PHP project, there are a few options placed under the "New Project" ➤ "PHP" category. The options are as follows: "PHP Application," "PHP Application with Existing Sources," and "PHP Application from Remote Server." The first option allows one to create a PHP project from scratch, providing flexibility for debugging and running the project. The second option, "PHP Application with Existing Sources," allows one to import an existing PHP project into a standard IDE project and begin working with it right away. The third option allows one to download a remote project, for which a standard IDE project is created. The third option also automatically configures the newly created standard IDE project such that it will automatically upload local changes to the remote server.

Maven Support

The most prevalent build system for Java applications is Apache Maven. Therefore, it is no surprise that Apache NetBeans has first-class support for this build system. The IDE contains various starter projects that are based upon the Apache Maven project format. Any Maven project can be opened in Apache NetBeans IDE, and immediately it will be recognized so that development can begin.

To open an existing Maven project within Apache NetBeans, simply browse to the project using the file explorer and open. The IDE will automatically detect the language type and open a project utilizing the template that pertains to the selected project. For instance, if a Java SE Maven project is opened, then the Java SE Apache NetBeans project template will be utilized.

Using Maven, project dependencies are downloaded and added to the resulting archive file when a project is built. Therefore, when the "Build with Dependencies" option is utilized in Apache NetBeans, Maven does just that. It is also easy to add dependencies to a project by right-clicking the "Dependencies" node within the project navigator and selecting "Add Dependency" (Figure 1-7).

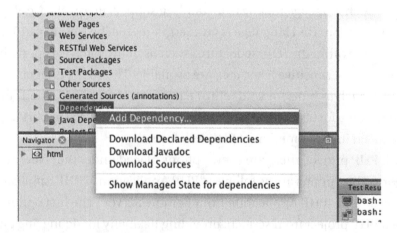

Figure 1-7. *Add Maven Dependency*

After clicking the "Add Dependency..." option, the "Add Dependency" dialog appears, allowing one to easily search for dependencies found in remote or local Maven repositories (Figure 1-8). When a dependency is added to the project, the associated project POM file is modified to include it, so that the user does not have to manually modify the XML.

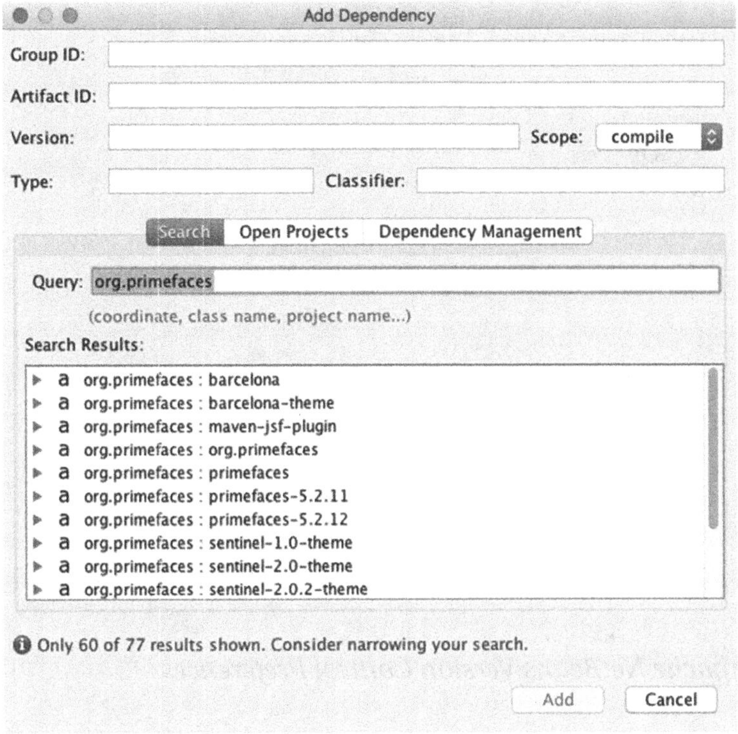

Figure 1-8. *Add Dependency dialog*

Other Maven support features include the ability to integrate SureFire tests within Maven builds; utilizing Apache Maven as build systems for various project types including other JVM languages, ApacheNetBeans plugins, etc.; and easy editing of POM files with auto-completion for dependencies.

Collaboration

The Apache NetBeans IDE helps teams work easily together using integrated support for version control systems (VCS) such as Git, Mercurial, and Subversion. The IDE contains first-class support for these VCS, as each Apache NetBeans project can be managed separately from within the IDE. Prior to integrating with either of the VCS, the system of choice must be installed on the same workstation as Apache NetBeans. The Apache NetBeans Preferences "Team" ➤ "Versioning" tab can then be used to manage the VCS of choice (Figure 1-9).

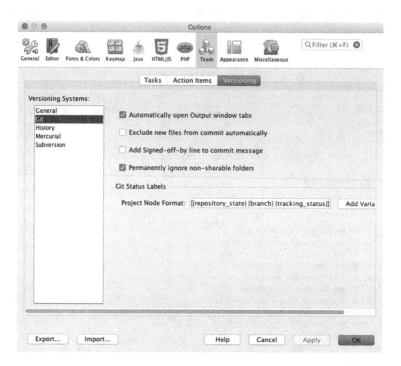

Figure 1-9. *Apache NetBeans Version Control Preferences*

The next couple of paragraphs will outline the Apache NetBeans Git support. However, the same level of support is available for Mercurial or Subversion as well. The "Team" menu provides options for creating new or browsing existing repositories (Figure 1-10).

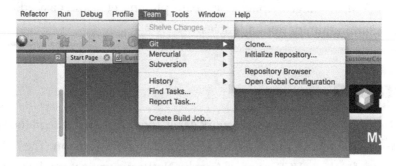

Figure 1-10. *Apache NetBeans Team Menu*

The "Open Global Configuration" option provides the ability to manage the global `.gitconfig` file directly within the editor, as seen in Figure 1-11.

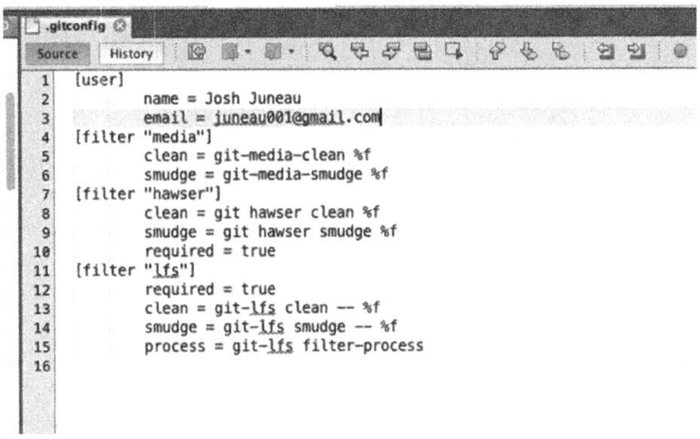

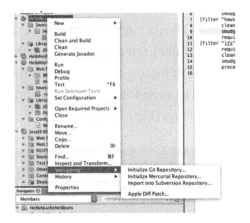

Figure 1-11. *Managing Global Git Configuration File*

There are also VCS options available within the contextual menu by right-clicking an Apache NetBeans project. Options include the ability to initialize a repository (Figure 1-12), and a host of available options are available for working on the VCS repository for projects that have already been initialized and have a repository (Figure 1-13).

Figure 1-12. *Initializing a Repository for an Apache NetBeans Project*

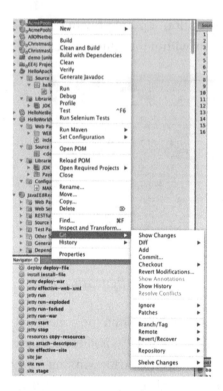

***Figure 1-13.** Git Options for Initialized Project*

The IDE contains an integrated Push/Pull system for the VCS, so if a project contains files that have been modified and differ from the HEAD, then the text for those files turns green. It is then easy to perform a DIFF comparison between the HEAD and currently selected file, and commit changes to a repository simply by choosing options within the contextual menu and using the dialogs (Figure 1-14).

***Figure 1-14.** Comparing Files Using DIFF*

Apache NetBeans covers many more version control features. To see more information about such features, please refer to online resources for using Git with Apache NetBeans: `https://netbeans.apache.org/kb/docs/ide/git.html` or Mercurial: `https://netbeans.org/kb/docs/ide/mercurial.html` just to name a few.

Profiling, Debugging, and Refactoring

The Apache NetBeans IDE contains excellent profiling, debugging, and refactoring abilities. The profiler allows one to dig into the internals of application method calls to pinpoint troublesome areas. The Telemetry profiler screen provides an overview of CPU and Garbage Collector, Memory, Garbage Collection, and lastly, Threads and Classes. The CPU and Garbage Collector chart allows drilling in to specific times to find CPU and GC Time, Memory provides Heap Size and Used Heap, Garbage Collection displays Surviving Generations, and the Threads and Classes chart shows just that, the number of threads and loaded classes (Figure 1-15).

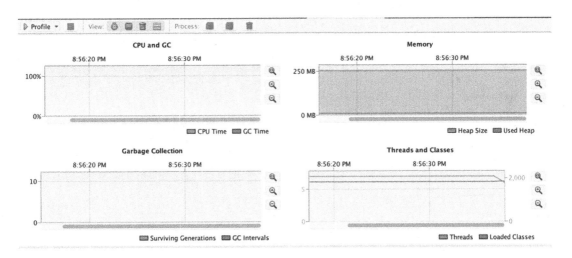

Figure 1-15. *Telemetry Display*

Process buttons invoke certain functions, such as garbage collection at-will. Method profiling allows one to profile all classes, project classes, or selected classes only. The user interface makes it easy to drill into single method calls to pinpoint problems (Figure 1-16).

Name		Total Time ▼		Total Time (CPU)	
▼ ⬚ Thread-5		24,568 ms	(100%)	75.7 ms	(100%)
▼ helloapachenetbeans.TestSleepMethod.**run** ()		24,568 ms	(100%)	75.7 ms	(100%)
⏱ java.lang.Thread.**sleep[native]** (long)		24,492 ms	(99.7%)	0.0 ms	(0%)
▶ java.io.PrintStream.**println** (int)		75.7 ms	(0.3%)	75.7 ms	(100%)
⏱ Self time		0.0 ms	(0%)	0.0 ms	(0%)
▶ ⬚ main		228 ms	(100%)	10.3 ms	(100%)
▶ ⬚ Reference Handler		0.0 ms	(-%)	0.0 ms	(-%)
▶ ⬚ Finalizer		0.0 ms	(-%)	0.0 ms	(-%)
▶ ⬚ Common-Cleaner		0.0 ms	(-%)	0.0 ms	(-%)
▶ ⬚ process reaper		0.0 ms	(-%)	0.0 ms	(-%)
▶ ⬚ DestroyJavaVM		0.0 ms	(-%)	0.0 ms	(-%)

Figure 1-16. Methods Profiler

The object profiler enables sorting of objects by size, and double-clicking an object will take you directly to the sources (Figure 1-17).

Name	Live Bytes ▼		Live Objects	
byte[]	51,842,264 B	(66.5%)	254,905	(34.7%)
java.util.HashMap$Node	6,062,240 B	(7.8%)	189,445	(25.8%)
java.lang.String	6,048,360 B	(7.8%)	252,015	(34.3%)
char[]	3,823,472 B	(4.9%)	248	(0%)
long[]	3,024,568 B	(3.9%)	1,648	(0.2%)
java.util.HashMap$Node[]	2,940,784 B	(3.8%)	929	(0.1%)
int[]	2,763,928 B	(3.5%)	1,783	(0.2%)
java.lang.Class	251,880 B	(0.3%)	2,079	(0.3%)
java.lang.Object[]	182,320 B	(0.2%)	3,596	(0.5%)
java.nio.HeapCharBuffer	110,928 B	(0.1%)	2,311	(0.3%)
java.lang.reflect.Method	76,032 B	(0.1%)	864	(0.1%)
java.util.concurrent.ConcurrentHashMap$Node	65,216 B	(0.1%)	2,038	(0.3%)
java.util.HashMap	50,688 B	(0.1%)	1,056	(0.1%)
java.lang.invoke.LambdaForm$Name	38,016 B	(0%)	1,188	(0.2%)
java.lang.String[]	37,112 B	(0%)	1,309	(0.2%)
java.lang.invoke.MemberName	35,808 B	(0%)	746	(0.1%)
java.lang.Class[]	35,696 B	(0%)	1,346	(0.2%)
java.util.LinkedHashMap$Entry	35,400 B	(0%)	885	(0.1%)
java.lang.Integer	22,976 B	(0%)	1,436	(0.2%)
java.util.concurrent.ConcurrentHashMap$Node[]	21,296 B	(0%)	71	(0%)
java.lang.invoke.MethodType$ConcurrentWeakInternSet$WeakEntry	20,640 B	(0%)	645	(0.1%)

Figure 1-17. Object Profiler

These features just scratch the surface of the Apache NetBeans profiler. The debugger allows one to set breakpoints in code, and then execute the code (locally or deployed to server), and step through the code to help debug and find the cause of issues. Once a breakpoint is set in the code, the debugger will stop execution at the breakpoint, and the IDE will display the values of variables at that time (Figure 1-18).

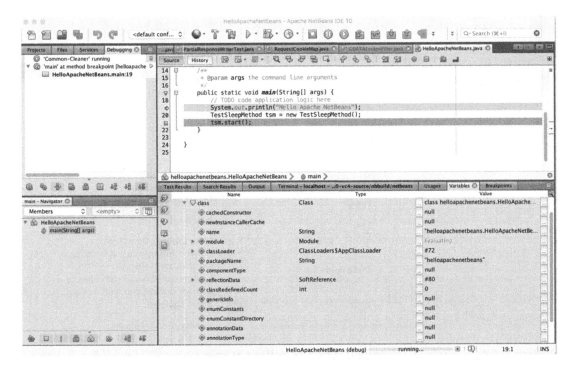

Figure 1-18. *Apache NetBeans Debugger*

The debugger also allows one to set watches on variables, enabling the code execution to stop when a variable contains a specified value. There is also a snapshot option that allows snapshots to be taken at specified times so that code can be monitored as it is executing. If developing a JavaFX or Swing graphical user interface, there is a visual debugger that allows viewing of component properties, components within a container, and more. Please refer to Chapter 5 to learn more about the debugger and profiler.

Another key component of an IDE is the ability to refactor code. Apache NetBeans allows one to change the name of code files, automatically add code such as getters and setters, change method parameters, and more (Figure 1-19).

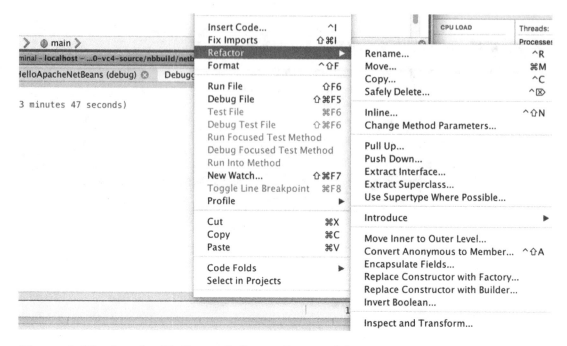

Figure 1-19. Apache NetBeans Refactor Context Menu

Apache NetBeans Platform

Apache NetBeans is much more than an IDE for applications. The IDE is built on a platform designed specifically for the purpose of creating rich client desktop applications ... the NetBeans Platform. As it turns out, the platform is extremely extensible and can be very useful for developing any number of desktop-based applications for the Java Platform. In fact, there are many successful applications that have been built upon the NetBeans Platform ranging from entire desktop applications to useful utilities. The NetBeans Platform also enables one to easily build modules that can be installed to extend Apache NetBeans IDE. The IDE itself contains project templates that can be used for building applications and modules that utilize the NetBeans Platform.

To develop a NetBeans module, open the "New Project" dialog and select the "NetBeans Modules" category (Figure 1-20). There are a number of options from which to choose for creating a NetBeans module, ranging from development of a single module, to a module library, to an entire NetBeans Platform Application.

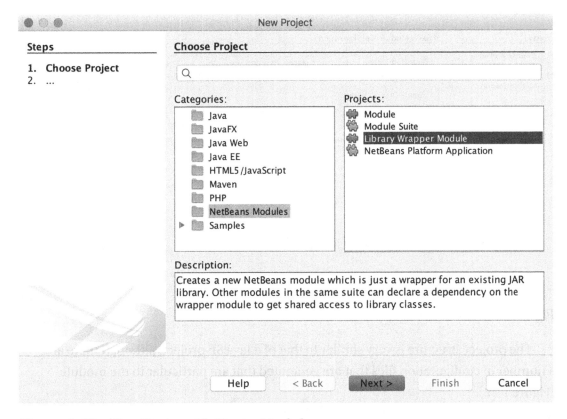

Figure 1-20. *New Project: NetBeans Modules*

Development of Standalone Apache NetBeans Modules

In many cases, developers wish to build extensions to the Apache NetBeans environment. There have been many dozens of useful NetBeans modules created by developers in the community. Such modules extend the IDE to incorporate new and/or enhanced functionality. Extensions can encapsulate almost any functionality. For instance, a module can be used for adding new language support to the IDE, or for extending existing functionality such as adding enhanced Git support. Whatever it may be, Apache NetBeans modules are easy to develop using the project templates.

To get started, select the "NetBeans Modules" ➤ "Module" project type. Once selected, the new module can be created as a "Standalone" module or it can be added to a "Module Suite." On the next panel, a "Code Name Base" must be specified. The "Code Name Base" is much the same as a base package name (Figure 1-21). A package localizing bundle can also be specified, as well as the option to generate the module as an OSGI module.

New Module

Steps	Basic Module Configuration
1. Choose Project 2. Name and Location 3. **Basic Module Configuration**	

Code Name Base: org.apache.netbeansbook

(e.g. "org.yourorg.modulename")

Module Display Name: module1

Localizing Bundle: org/apache/netbeansbook/Bundle.properties

☐ Generate OSGi Bundle

Help   < Back   Next >   Finish   Cancel

Figure 1-21. *New Module Wizard*

The project structure is very similar to that of a Java SE project, although there are a number of configuration files that are generated that are particular to the module (Figure 1-22).

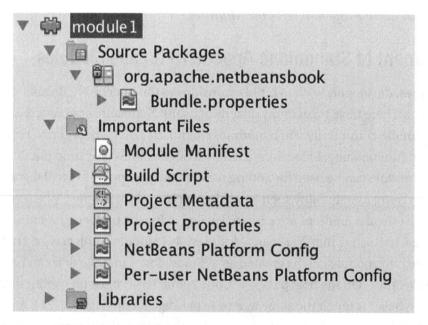

Figure 1-22. *NetBeans Module Structure*

The module will create an NBM file, which can later be added as an extension to NetBeans IDE. The module can also be deployed as a NetBeans plugin for distribution.

Development of Applications Built on the NetBeans Platform

The NetBeans Platform allows developers to architect-rich client applications utilizing a skeleton framework that provides many under the cover features for free. The platform allows development of Java Swing applications in a fraction of the time that it would take to develop one from scratch. The platform includes features such as state saving and life-cycle management, standardized UI toolkit, window system; and all of these features are easy to implement out of the box.

When developing on the NetBeans Platform, the IDE allows for easy debugging into modules or platform applications. As such, this makes it easy to rapidly create stable user interfaces that utilize a standard architecture. Since the platform provides many essential client-side application APIs out of the box, you can be certain that all standard NetBeans Platform applications behave in a consistent manner.

Apache NetBeans Community

Apache NetBeans has a vibrant community consisting of several online resources, frequent conference speakers and sessions, and a rich history of documentation and tutorials. The Apache NetBeans community has been around since the early 2000s, and it has grown tremendously over the years from a small core group to an entire open source community.

Mailing Lists and NetCAT

One of the most basic and informative ways to become a part of the Apache NetBeans community is to join the mailing lists. The lists are frequently used to post questions and to discuss new and existing features for the IDE. The lists are also useful for learning how an open source community functions, as there are always seasoned experts on the lists ready to assist. To join the Apache NetBeans mailing lists, visit the following webpage:

```
https://netbeans.apache.org/community/mailing-lists.html
```

Prior to an Apache NetBeans release, the impending release must be tested to ensure full functionality. One of the phases of Apache NetBeans testing is the NetCAT program. NetCAT is a community of testers that are each assigned to test different portions of the

IDE. The IDE functionality is broken up into different NetCAT organizational groups. Each group meets periodically online to formulate plans for testing, and each tester completes test cases using an online form. Becoming a NetCAT tester can provide you with more knowledge of the Apache NetBeans IDE and allow you to give back to the community by helping to weed out issues. Learn more about joining NetCAT using the link mentioned for the Apache NetBeans mailing lists.

Tackle an Issue

One of the most important ways that one can contribute to the Apache NetBeans ecosystem is to find an issue on the Apache NetBeans JIRA (issue tracker) and repair it. This is easy to do by simply creating a fork of the Apache NetBeans GitHub repository, and then making the necessary code updates to repair the issue within the fork. Once the issue has been repaired, changes within the fork can be added back to the Apache NetBeans GitHub repository by submitting a Pull Request. To learn more about contributing code to Apache NetBeans, please refer to Chapters 14 and 15.

CHAPTER 2

Getting Started with NetBeans

When you want to quickly develop an application, you can use *Apache NetBeans IDE* to simplify your tasks. In this chapter, you will discover the layout of the editor along with some tips that will help you to have some control over your code and speed up development.

Default Layout and Purpose

Each window in the IDE appears as a tab in the pane or position where it resides. Additionally, the IDE's window system enables you to arrange windows anywhere in the IDE by dragging and dropping to any of the window positions shown in the layout of Figure 2-1.

© Ioannis Kostaras, Constantin Drabo, Josh Juneau, Sven Reimers, Mario Schröder, Geertjan Wielenga 2020
I. Kostaras et al., *Pro Apache NetBeans*, https://doi.org/10.1007/978-1-4842-5370-0_2

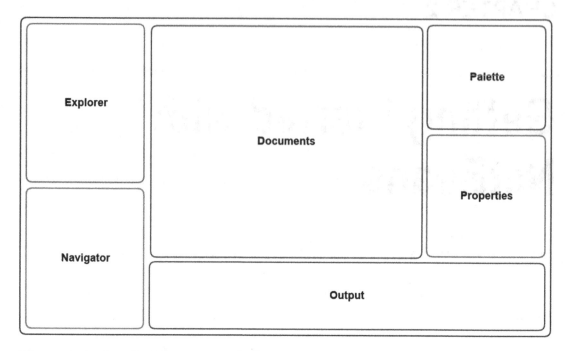

Figure 2-1. *Apache NetBeans Default Layout Windows positions*

The following sections cover some of the specific windows that you will see for each of the positions in Figure 2-1. For example, the *Explorer window position* can show projects, or files, or services, all depending upon the context of what you are doing at a given time.

Explorer Window

The Explorer window position is used by all windows that provide access to user objects. These windows include the projects window, files window, services window, and the tasks window.

Projects Window

The *Projects Window* (**Ctrl+1** or **Cmd+1**) displays project sources. It displays the logical view of one or more projects. Each project or view is represented by a node, with a specific icon depending on the project type (e.g., a Java application node is presented differently from a JavaFX application node) as shown in Figure 2-2.

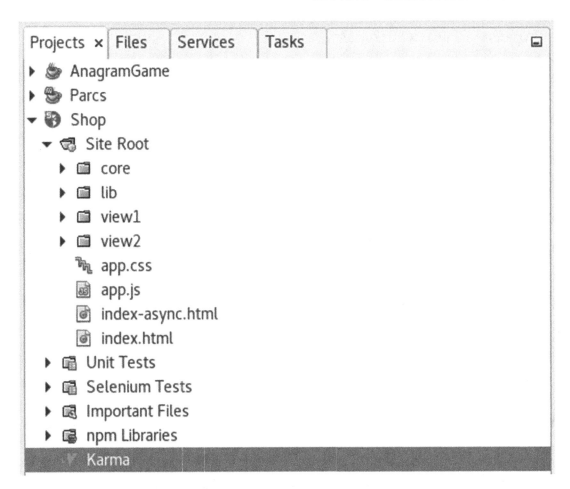

Figure 2-2. *Projects Window with different types of projects*

Right-clicking on each node invokes a pop-up menu listing commands that you can run on that node. The pop-up menu provides project commands to compile, build, run, etc. You can also execute the main file of a Java project by selecting the project and pressing the *F6* shortcut key.

Files Window

The *Files Window* (**Ctrl+2** or **Cmd+2**) displays the directory-based view of a project, including files and folders that are not displayed in the Projects window. Right-clicking on each node invokes a menu that has commands to create new files or directories, and also copy, cut, and paste actions. Figure 2-3 shows an example of a project structure.

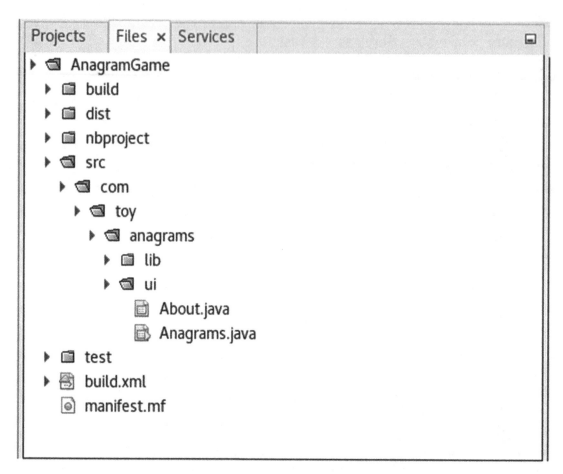

Figure 2-3. *Directory-based structure of a project in Files Window*

Services Window

The *Services Window* (**Ctrl+5** or **Cmd+5**), shown in Figure 2-4, displays the logical view of runtime resources such as servers, databases, web services, Docker containers, issue trackers, and the tasks repository, which are registered with Apache NetBeans IDE.

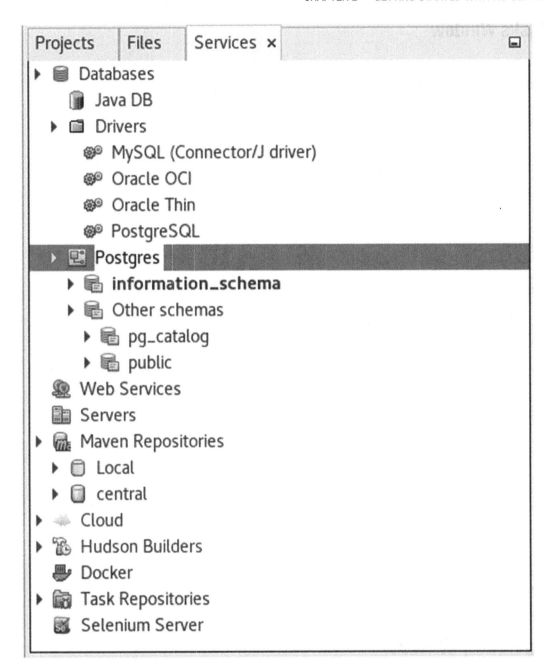

Figure 2-4. *Services Window*

Tasks Window

The *Tasks Window* (**Ctrl+Shift+6** or **Cmd+Shift+6**) is conceived for the inventory of
tasks registered in a task's repository such as JIRA, Bugzilla, and so forth. Figure 2-5
shows an example of a Tasks Window.

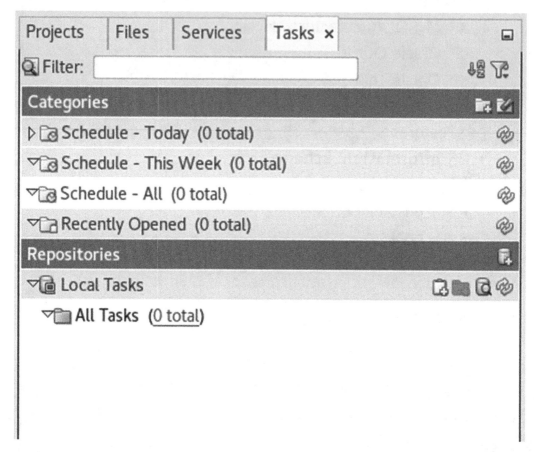

Figure 2-5. *Tasks Window*

Navigator Window

The *Navigator Window* (**Ctrl+7** or **Cmd+7**) provides a compact view of the currently
selected file and simplifies navigation between different parts of the file. For a Java file,
the window displays members (constructors, properties, and attributes) and Beans
Patterns as shown in Figure 2-6.

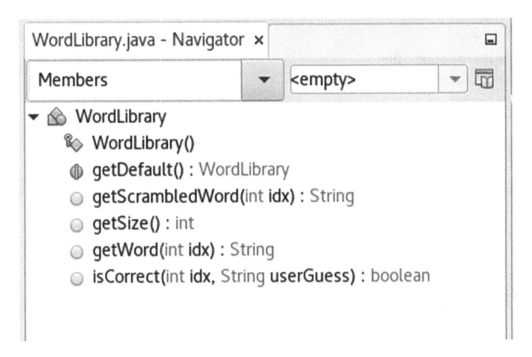

Figure 2-6. *Navigator Window*

The Navigator Window also displays Maven goals in the event the project is a Maven-based application. Figure 2-7 shows an example, a list of Maven goals for a Maven application. In the case of Maven, you are able to execute a goal by double-clicking its node.

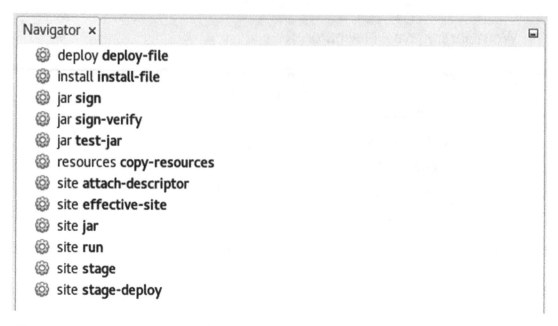

Figure 2-7. *Maven goals displayed in a Navigator Window*

Editor Window

Document windows are normally displayed in the *Editor Window position*. With Document windows you are able to edit Java program files and other source files. You are also able to execute commands from the *Java Platform Shell*, because the Java 9 shell's command-line interface has been also integrated within a Document Window.

Source Editor

The *Source Editor* is the part of the IDE layout that is used the most. It is the place to write your source code or design graphic user interfaces for Java or other types of application.

The *Java Source Editor* is comprised of tabs: the *Source view* (where the user writes code), the *Design view* (where the user designs forms), and the *History view* (displays the modification history of the file). All three tabs are shown in Figure 2-8, and you can see in the figure that the user is editing some Java source code.

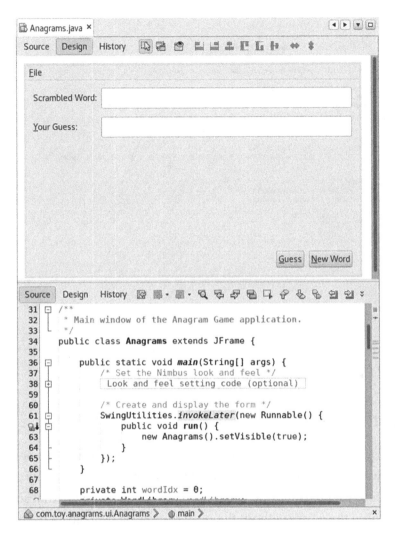

Figure 2-8. *Source Editor for a Java File*

The Source Editor helps you achieve coding tasks more quickly. thanks to many interesting features such as code completion, code templates, refactoring, and syntax coloring.

The Source Editor is not limited to just Java code. It can be used for several other language file types. The Source Editor offers features that apply to the specific type of file the user is working on (for example, Java, JSP, HTML, etc.).

Figure 2-9 shows the Source Editor being used to edit an HTML file.

```
Source   History  🔲 🔲 ▾ 🔲 ▾ 🔍 💾 🗇 📇 🔲 🗲 🔖 🗞 🖉 🗞 ● 🔲 ᴬᵇᶜ <                                        ⊞
 1      <!DOCTYPE html>
 2      <!--[if lt IE 7]>       <html lang="en" ng-app="myApp" class="no-js lt-ie9 lt-ie8 lt-ie7"> <![endif]-->
 3      <!--[if IE 7]>          <html lang="en" ng-app="myApp" class="no-js lt-ie9 lt-ie8"> <![endif]-->
 4      <!--[if IE 8]>          <html lang="en" ng-app="myApp" class="no-js lt-ie9"> <![endif]-->
 5      <!--[if gt IE 8]><!-->  <html lang="en" ng-app="myApp" class="no-js"> <!--<![endif]-->
 6      <head>
 7        <meta charset="utf-8">
 8        <meta http-equiv="X-UA-Compatible" content="IE=edge">
 9        <title>My AngularJS App</title>
10        <meta name="description" content="">
11        <meta name="viewport" content="width=device-width, initial-scale=1">
12        <link rel="stylesheet" href="lib/html5-boilerplate/dist/css/normalize.css">
13        <link rel="stylesheet" href="lib/html5-boilerplate/dist/css/main.css">
14        <link rel="stylesheet" href="app.css">
15        <script src="lib/html5-boilerplate/dist/js/vendor/modernizr-2.8.3.min.js"></script>
16      </head>
17      <body>
18        <ul class="menu">
19          <li><a href="#!/view1">view1</a></li>
20          <li><a href="#!/view2">view2</a></li>
21        </ul>
22
23        <!--[if lt IE 7]>
24          <p class="browsehappy">You are using an <strong>outdated</strong> browser. Please <a href="http://brow
         <![endif]-->
26
27        <div ng-view></div>
28
         <div>AngularJS seed app: v<span app-version></span></div>
30
31        <!-- In production use:
32        <script src="//ajax.googleapis.com/ajax/libs/angularjs/x.x.x/angular.min.js"></script>
33        -->
34        <script src="lib/angular/angular.js"></script>
35        <script src="lib/angular-route/angular-route.js"></script>
36        <script src="app.js"></script>
37        <script src="view1/view1.js"></script>
```

Figure 2-9. *HTML code source in HTML Editor*

Java Platform Shells

The Java Platform Shell (see Figure 2-10) is an interesting use case of the Source Editor window. The Java Platform is the place where you can write code snippets and interact with the JShell interpreter. You can edit source code but also execute that source code directly from within the editor without the need to create a Java file with a `main()` method.

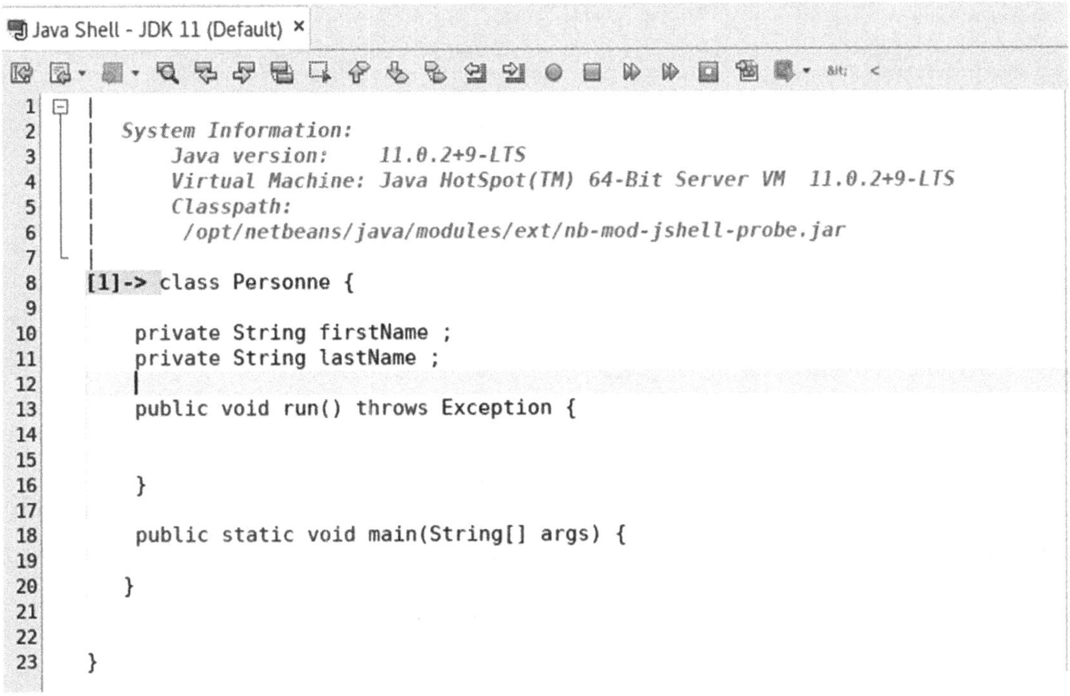

🗊 Java Shell - JDK 11 (Default) ×

```
 1
 2        System Information:
 3            Java version:     11.0.2+9-LTS
 4            Virtual Machine: Java HotSpot(TM) 64-Bit Server VM  11.0.2+9-LTS
 5            Classpath:
 6             /opt/netbeans/java/modules/ext/nb-mod-jshell-probe.jar
 7
 8    [1]-> class Personne {
 9
10        private String firstName ;
11        private String lastName ;
12        |
13        public void run() throws Exception {
14
15
16        }
17
18        public static void main(String[] args) {
19
20        }
21
22
23    }
```

Figure 2-10. *Java Shell Editor*

Output Window

The *Output Window position* (**Ctrl+4** or **Cmd+4**) can dock multi-tabbed windows to display messages from the Apache NetBeans IDE. The *Output Window* is displayed automatically after an execution succeeds (Figure 2-11), when compilation errors have occurred, when you debug your application, or in other cases where output needs to be presented to you.

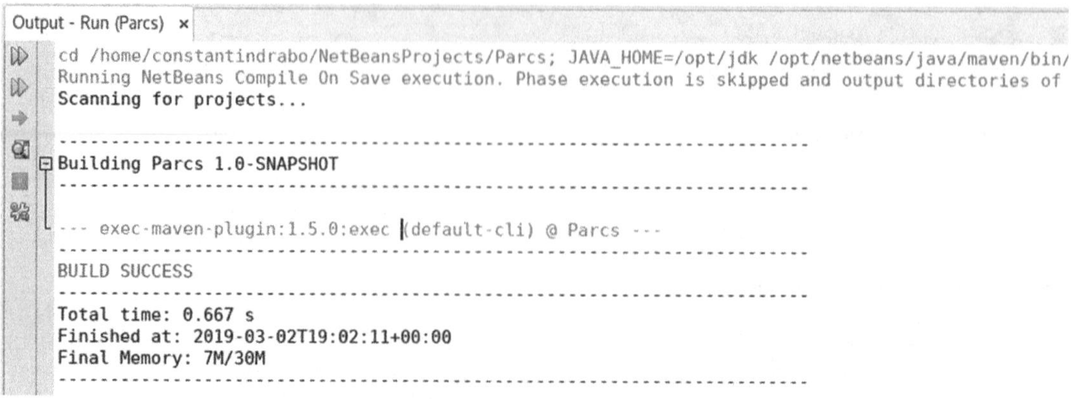

```
Output - Run (Parcs)  ×

  cd /home/constantindrabo/NetBeansProjects/Parcs; JAVA_HOME=/opt/jdk /opt/netbeans/java/maven/bin/
  Running NetBeans Compile On Save execution. Phase execution is skipped and output directories of
  Scanning for projects...

  ------------------------------------------------------------------------
  Building Parcs 1.0-SNAPSHOT
  ------------------------------------------------------------------------

  --- exec-maven-plugin:1.5.0:exec (default-cli) @ Parcs ---
  ------------------------------------------------------------------------
  BUILD SUCCESS
  ------------------------------------------------------------------------
  Total time: 0.667 s
  Finished at: 2019-03-02T19:02:11+00:00
  Final Memory: 7M/30M
  ------------------------------------------------------------------------
```

Figure 2-11. *Output Window after an execution succeeds*

When errors occurred during compilation, the Output Window displays the errors with hyperlinks to their location in the source code. Figure 2-12 shows a typical error listing.

```
run:
Exception in thread "AWT-EventQueue-0" java.lang.NullPointerException
        at com.toy.anagrams.ui.Anagrams.<init>(Anagrams.java:77)
        at com.toy.anagrams.ui.Anagrams$1.run(Anagrams.java:63)
        at java.desktop/java.awt.event.InvocationEvent.dispatch(InvocationEvent.java:313)
        at java.desktop/java.awt.EventQueue.dispatchEventImpl(EventQueue.java:770)
        at java.desktop/java.awt.EventQueue$4.run(EventQueue.java:721)
        at java.desktop/java.awt.EventQueue$4.run(EventQueue.java:715)
        at java.base/java.security.AccessController.doPrivileged(Native Method)
        at java.base/java.security.ProtectionDomain$JavaSecurityAccessImpl.doIntersectionPrivilege(ProtectionDomain.java:85)
        at java.desktop/java.awt.EventQueue.dispatchEvent(EventQueue.java:740)
        at java.desktop/java.awt.EventDispatchThread.pumpOneEventForFilters(EventDispatchThread.java:203)
        at java.desktop/java.awt.EventDispatchThread.pumpEventsForFilter(EventDispatchThread.java:124)
        at java.desktop/java.awt.EventDispatchThread.pumpEventsForHierarchy(EventDispatchThread.java:113)
        at java.desktop/java.awt.EventDispatchThread.pumpEvents(EventDispatchThread.java:109)
        at java.desktop/java.awt.EventDispatchThread.pumpEvents(EventDispatchThread.java:101)
        at java.desktop/java.awt.EventDispatchThread.run(EventDispatchThread.java:90)
```

Figure 2-12. *Output Window when an error occurred*

When a program requires user input, a new tab appears in the Output Window.

Terminal Window

Apache NetBeans IDE offers a *Terminal Window*, which is also displayed in the Output Window position, which allows you to interact with the operating system. Click on the menu **Window ➤ IDE Tools ➤ Terminal** to open this window. You can run operating system commands and scripts as shown in Figure 2-13.

```
Terminal - constantindrabo@localhost:~ ×
[constantindrabo@localhost parcs]$ ls
Animals.java  Personne.java
[constantindrabo@localhost parcs]$ cd
[constantindrabo@localhost ~]$ ls
Android              Bureau     Downloads       IdeaProjects  Modèles  NetBeansProjects  Téléchargements
AndroidStudioProjects Documents 21mgestionequipement Images         Musique  Public            Vidéos
[constantindrabo@localhost ~]$
```

Figure 2-13. *Executing commands from the Terminal Window*

Palette Window

The *Palette Window* (**Ctrl+Shift+8** or **Cmd+Shift+8**) contains all the components that help in Rapid-Application Development (RAD). The behavior of the Palette is associated with the editor, and the list of components differs from one type of editor to another. Figure 2-14 shows the contents of the Palette when the Design view is dealing with a Java form (left) and an html form (right)

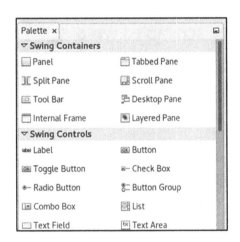

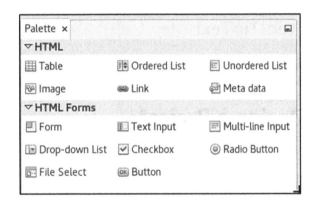

Figure 2-14. *Palette Window for Java form and html form*

Properties Window

Elements (nodes) in *Projects, Files, Services, Documents,* or *Navigator* windows have properties that can be viewed in the *Properties* window as shown in Figure 2-15. These elements can be Java classes, Swing components, and so on.

You can click a property to modify its value field. Note that not all properties can be modified (for example, *File Size, Modification Time,* etc.). A value field can be an input box, or it can be a list of values.

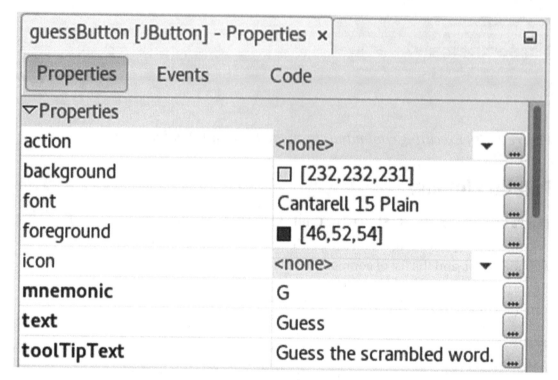

Figure 2-15. *An example of a Property sheet*

Design a Project

Apache NetBeans offers you the ability to design an application using one of the popular build automation tools: *Ant* or *Maven* or *Gradle*. The following sections show examples of each of these cases.

Set Up an Ant-Based Project

By default, the Apache NetBeans IDE uses Ant as a build automation tool. Following are the steps to create a new project using Ant:

1. To create a project, choose **File ➤ New Project** (Ctrl+Shift+N) or click on the **New Project** toolbar icon (a folder with a green plus sign at top left). The *New Project* wizard appears as shown in Figure 2-16.

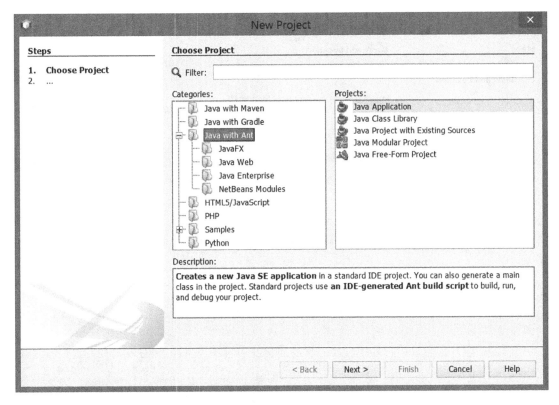

Figure 2-16. *New Project wizard*

2. Select the *Java with Ant* category. A number of project templates is
   displayed on the right side such as *Java Application, Java Modular
   Project,* etc. Select a project template; choose *Java Application* if
   you are following along with the current example. Then click **Next**.

3. The next step is shown in Figure 2-17. Here you can provide the
   Project Name, the directory where the application will be stored
   (Project Location), as well as the class that will contain the main( )
   method. Fill in the fields as shown in Figure 2-17. Then click **Finish**.

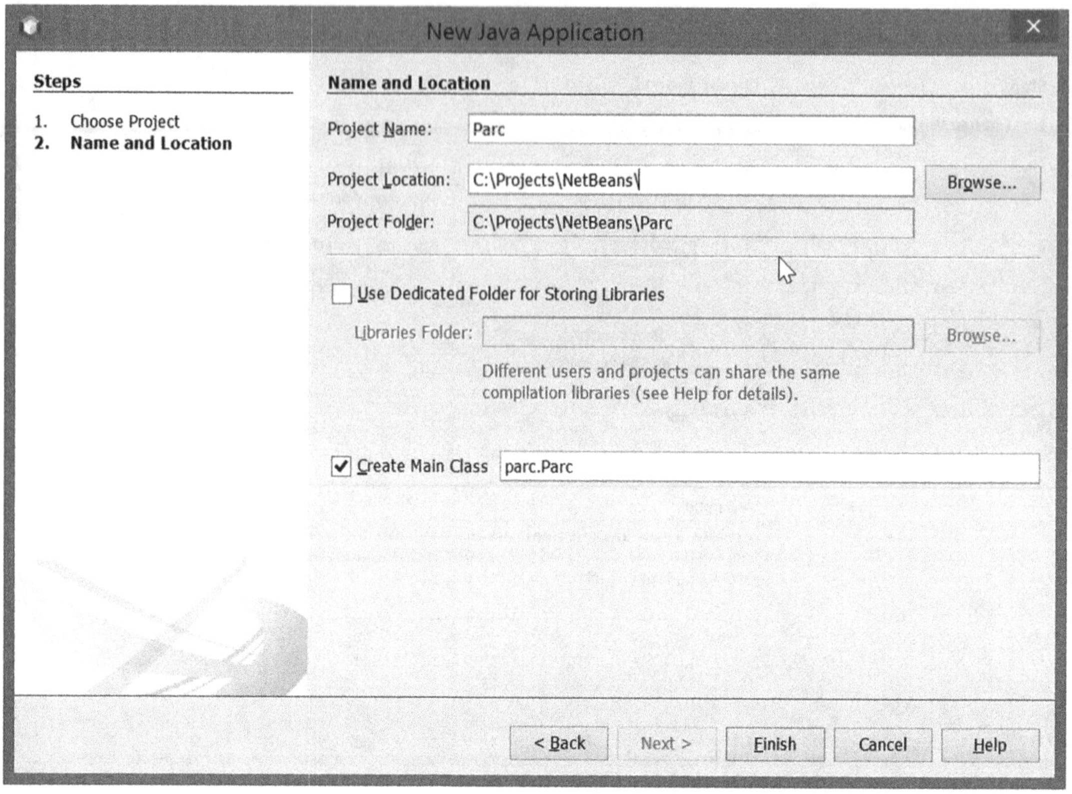

Figure 2-17. *Provide the project name and location in step 2 of the wizard*

You have created a new Java project. The Java Application template sets up a basic Java project and includes a main class as shown in Figure 2-18.

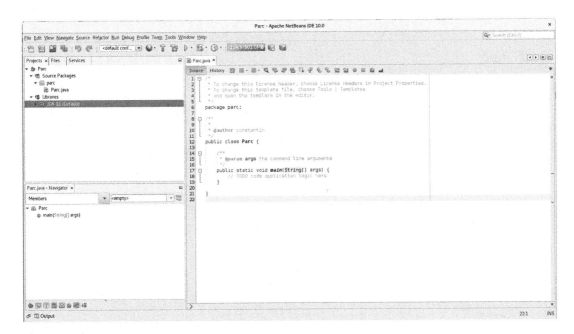

Figure 2-18. *A new Java Application created*

The new application contains the *Ant build file.* You can display that build file through the *Files* tab. When selecting the *Ant manifest,* the *Navigator Window* displays the build targets as shown in Figure 2-19.

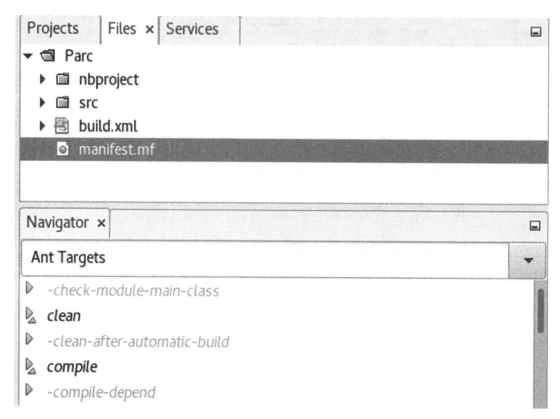

Figure 2-19. *Ant build file and targets*

Set Up a Maven-Based Project

Maven is a very popular build automation tool that dominates the Java ecosystem. Apache NetBeans supports Maven naturally (i.e., integrated inside the IDE, not as a plugin like in other IDEs). You can set up a new project using Maven by performing the following steps:

1. Create a Maven project by choosing **File ➤ New Project** (Ctrl+Shift+N), or by clicking the **New Project** toolbar icon (▧). The *New Project* wizard opens as shown in Figure 2-20.

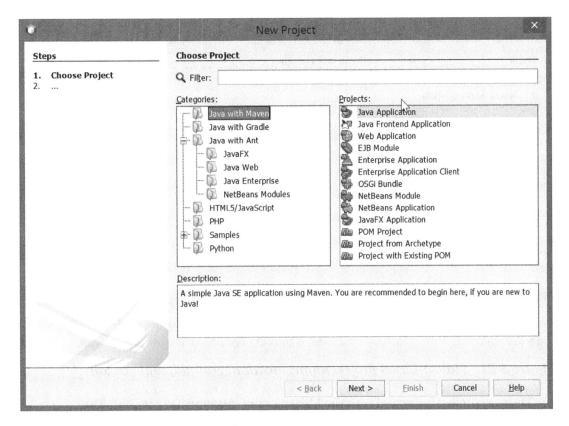

Figure 2-20. *New Project wizard*

2. Select the *Java with Maven* category to display the available project templates (see Figure 2-20). Choose *Java Application* for the current example, and click **Next**.

3. In the next step (see Figure 2-21), you can provide the *project name* and *location* as well as the Maven coordinates (*groupid, version,* and *package*). When you are done, click **Finish**.

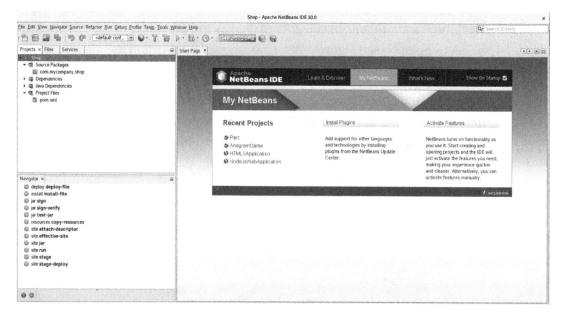

Figure 2-21. *Maven-based project name, location, groupid, and version*

The new project is created with the Maven's configuration file pom.xml. The Navigator Window in Figure 2-22 displays the *goals* (each set of predefined commands).

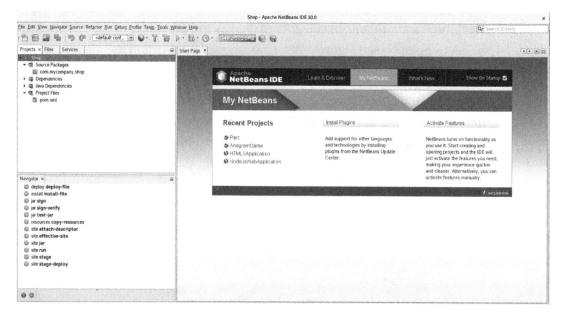

Figure 2-22. *A new Maven-based project*

Set Up a Gradle-Based Project

Gradle is the new player on the game. It was created to ease some of the hassles of Maven, like, for example, the long *pom* files. Similar to the above, to create a new Gradle-based project, create a new project and select the *Java with Gradle* category as shown in Figure 2-23 (NetBeans might activate the feature if it is the first time that it is being used).

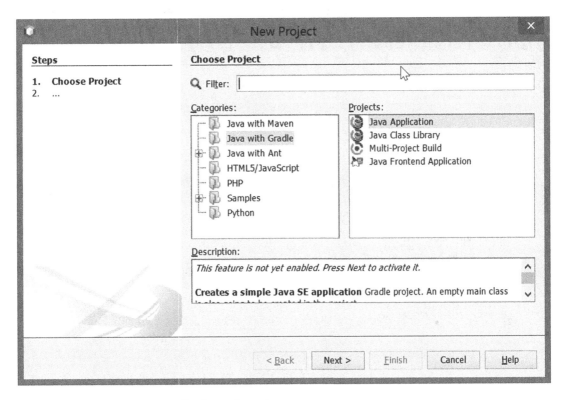

Figure 2-23. *A new Gradle-based project*

Pressing **Next**, complete the various fields like project name and location; and the optional group, version, description, etc., of the second step of the wizard and click **Finish** in order to see your new Gradle project created.

Speed Up Your Application Coding

The Apache NetBeans IDE has plenty of rich features that allow you to speed up your coding tasks. The IDE has default features such as code completion, syntax highlighting, code templates, and so on that you can use and modify by changing various settings.

Intelligent Code Completion

Code completion is the most exciting and most-used feature of the IDE. It is specific to the Source Editor, and it is available for the majority of the supported languages (Java, HTML, PHP, and so on).

There are two ways to open the code completion pop-up dialog box (shown in Figure 2-24): by pressing `Ctrl+Space` or by typing the dot (`.`) character inside the editor.

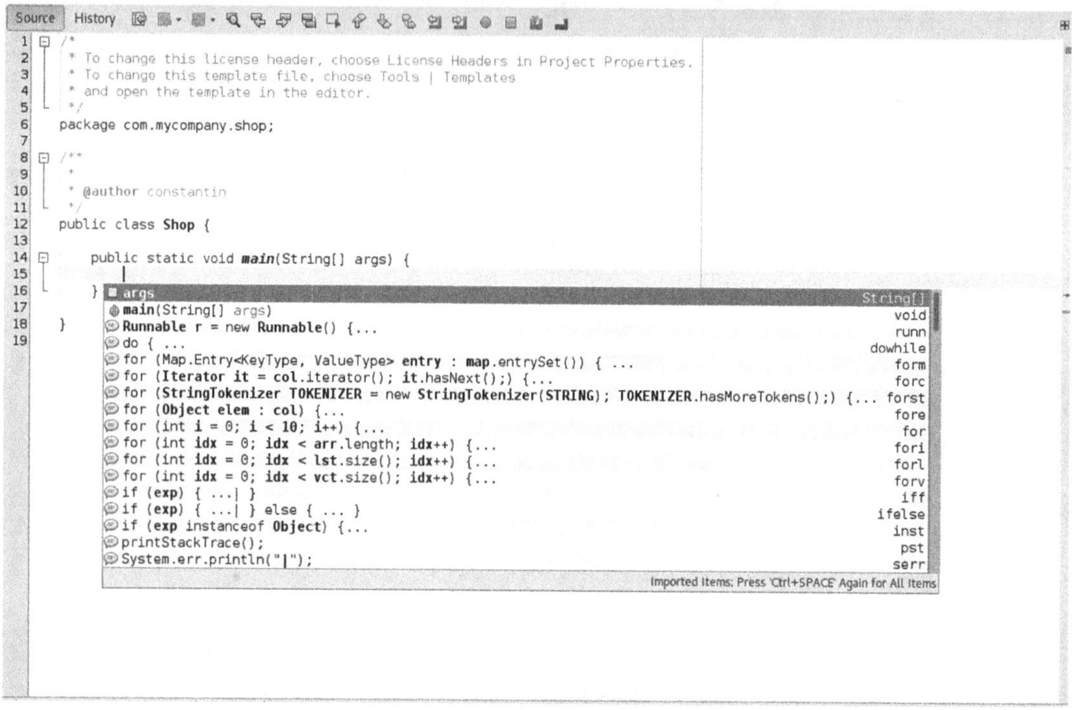

Figure 2-24. *Code completion in the Java editors*

The code completion feature is smarter than it has never been. For example, if you want to call a variable, a class, or a method, the auto pop-up code completion dialog will list all the elements defined and help you to easily choose the one you need by typing the first character of the element's name.

There is also *camel case completion*. Instead of typing all the characters, you can type just the capital letters of the word you're interested in. Then press `Ctrl+Space` and the camel case completion feature will complete the full name of the element.

You also have access to Javadoc for an element. Put the cursor on an element name and press Ctrl+Space as shown in Figure 2-25. You'll see a dialog open with the Javadoc for the element you've selected.

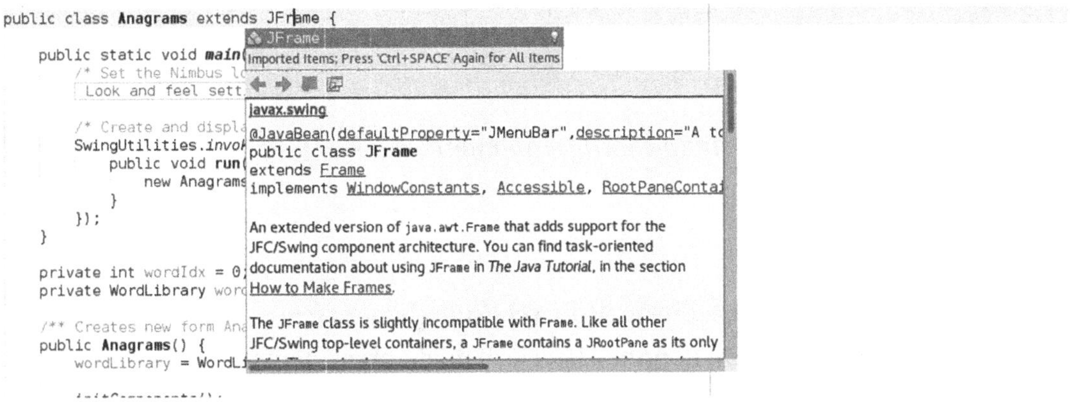

Figure 2-25. *Javadoc pop-up window*

The IDE also provides keyword completion. In this case the editor checks the context and suggests the most relevant keywords. Figure 2-26 shows an example, and you can see how the editor sees that you are specifying a class definition and offers you the opportunity to either extend another class, or to implement an interface.

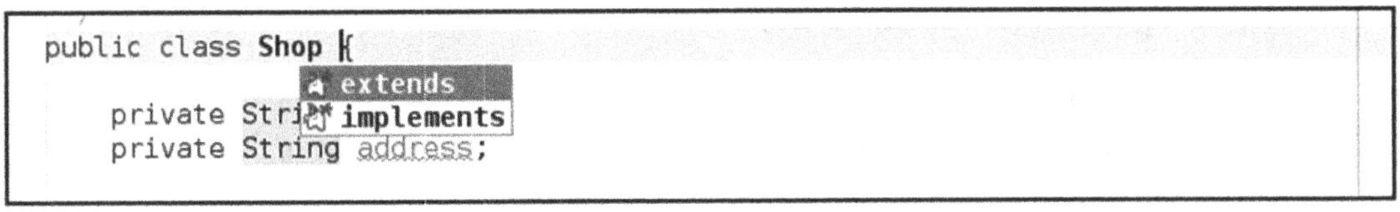

Figure 2-26. *Keyword completion*

Hints

Hints are excellent guides when typing code. Hints provide suggestions on how to fix errors and complete whatever statement or expression you are typing. The editor displays small *light bulbs* in the IDE's left-hand margin for the lines of code for which hints are available (see Figure 2-27). Click on a bulb, and one or more hints appear.

```
16    public class AnimalRepository {
17
18 ⊟      public static void main(String[] args) {
19            File  file   = new File("/home/constantin/animal.txt");
           BufferedReader buffer  =  new BufferedReader(new FileReader(file));
21    ┌──────────────────────────────────────────────────┐
       │ 💡 Add throws clause for java.io.FileNotFoundException   │  null){
23    │ 💡 Surround Statement with try-catch                       │
24    │ 💡 Surround Block with try-catch                           │
25    └──────────────────────────────────────────────────┘
```

Figure 2-27. *Hint to solve surrounding statement issue*

Refactoring

Sometimes you want to change the name of a specific element (class, variable, method) in a project, but this can have a domino effect as it might break dependencies, that is, other elements that depend on that name. Instead of modifying each file that uses that name, you can use the *refactoring* feature. Refactoring an element will replace the old name of each occurrence by the new name.

Say, for example, that you would like to rename a class from *Animals* to *Animal.* Here are the steps to getting the IDE to do the work for you:

1. Put the cursor on the class name in the Source Editor and press Ctrl-R, or right-click and select **Refactoring ➤ Rename** from the pop-up menu (see Figure 2-28).

2. Check **Apply Rename on Comments**, if you wish that the modification will be applied also to occurrences in comments.

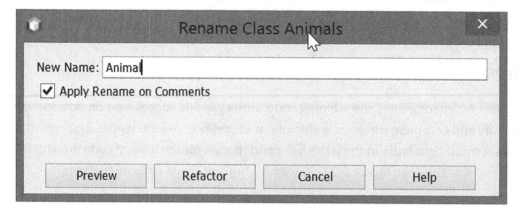

Figure 2-28. *Rename class refactor window*

3. Type the new name of the class and press **Preview** to preview all
    the occurrences or **Refactor** to apply the rename without preview.
    The IDE will present you with both versions of your source file, as
    shown in Figure 2-29.

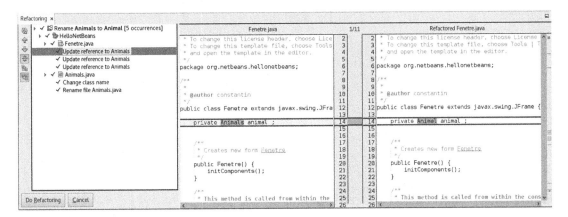

Figure 2-29. *Preview Refactoring occurrences*

4. Does everything look good? Then press **Do Refactoring** to apply
    the modifications. Otherwise press **Cancel**.

Comparing Files

The editor offers a "diff" feature to deal with the problem of finding differences
between two files. For example, say that you have two *Animal* class definitions, each
one in a separate package. Do the following to see whether those definitions are the
same or different:

1. Open both class files in the Source editor.

2. Right-click on one of the source files in the *Projects window* and
    select **Tools ➤ Diff to...** A dialog box appears displaying a list with
    the files that open in the Editor.

3. Select the second file from the Files Open in Editor list to display
    the results of the diff operation. Figure 2-30 shows how green
    backgrounds are used to indicate lines of code that are present in
    one file, but missing from the other.

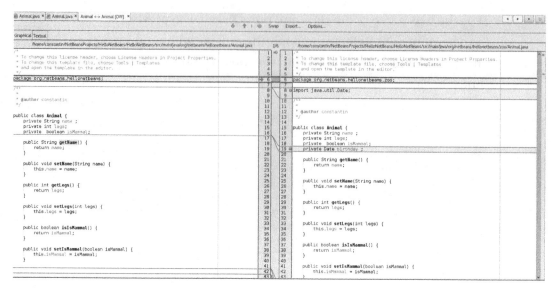

Figure 2-30. *Differences between two files*

Generating Code

You can generate pieces of code when coding a Java application. The IDE offers some alternatives: by using the *Code Completion* feature, or from the *Code Generation* pop-up menu, or by using the *Refactoring* features. The code completion feature can be used to add code snippets in a Java class body. For example, the feature can help to generate the accessors in a class for which you have defined properties that you wish to make available to other classes.

Figure 2-31 shows how to create a setter function in the class `Animal` for the `name` attribute. If the pop-up menu doesn't appear, type `Ctrl+space`.

```
11      /
12    public class Animal {
13
14        private String name;
15        private int legs;
16        private boolean isMammal;
17        private String territory;
18
        .set|
20        @ setIsMammal(boolean isMammal) - generate  void
21        @ setLegs(int legs) - generate            void
22        @ setName(String name) - generate         void
23    }  @ setTerritory(String territory) - generate void
24            Imported Items; Press 'Ctrl+SPACE' Again for All Items
```

Figure 2-31. *Generate code snippets with code completion*

Use the *Code Generation* pop-up menu by clicking inside the editor and pressing `Alt-Insert` (or choosing **Source ➤ Insert code**). It helps, for example, to generate a constructor as shown in Figure 2-32.

Figure 2-32. *Code Generation pop-up menu*

Thanks to this feature you can easily generate the body of class with extreme speed. It generates getters and setters, `toString()`, `equals()` and `hashCode()` methods, overrides methods from the superclasses, etc., in only a few clicks.

The option **Add property** creates with one action both a field and its accessors. Below is a sample of inputs for the *Add Property* dialog box (Figure 2-33).

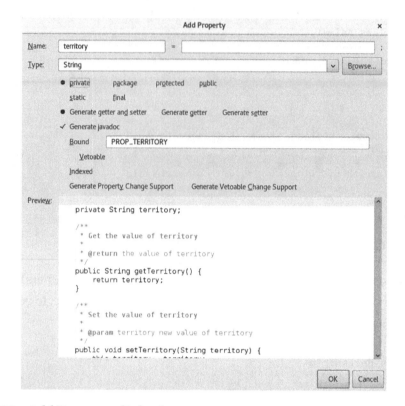

Figure 2-33. *Add Property dialog box*

The second alternative to generate accessors is by choosing **Refactor ➤ Encapsulate**. The IDE displays the *Encapsulate Fields* dialog box (see Figure 2-34).

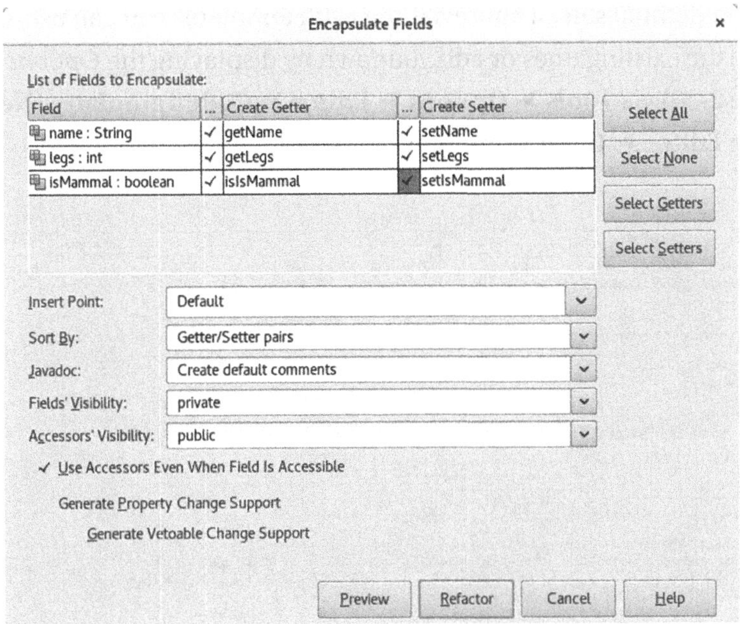

Figure 2-34. *Encapsulate Fields dialog box*

Select one or more fields or select all the fields by pressing the **Select All** button. Then press **Refactor** to encapsulate the fields (i.e., generate the accessors with the visibility you selected).

Using Code Templates

The IDE helps with predefined pieces of code provided through code templates. Code templates are abbreviations of long code snippets.

To access a code template, type the abbreviation and hit `Ctrl+Space`. Doing so will expand the full code as shown in Figure 2-35. There you can see that I typed the keyword `while`. Then when I pressed `Ctrl+Space`, NetBeans suggested several templates with code snippets beginning with that same keyword.

Figure 2-35. *Code template for while*

There are predefined sets of abbreviations with templates you can use, or you may customize the existing ones or add your own by displaying the *Options* dialog box (see Figure 2-36) via **Tools ➤ Options ➤ Editor ➤ Code Templates** (**NetBeans ➤ Preferences ➤ Editor ➤ Code Templates** on Mac).

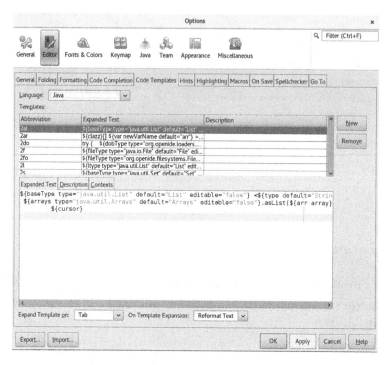

Figure 2-36. *Code Templates window*

Splitting Windows

It often happens that we want to look at different source files simultaneously. You can easily look at two files by *splitting* the Source Editor. Having at least two source files open, click on the tab of a file and then drag it to the far left, far right, or bottom of the Source Editor window. Release the mouse button when the red outline that appeared around the tab when you started dragging changes to a rectangle indicating the placement of the split window. Figure 2-37 shows the result.

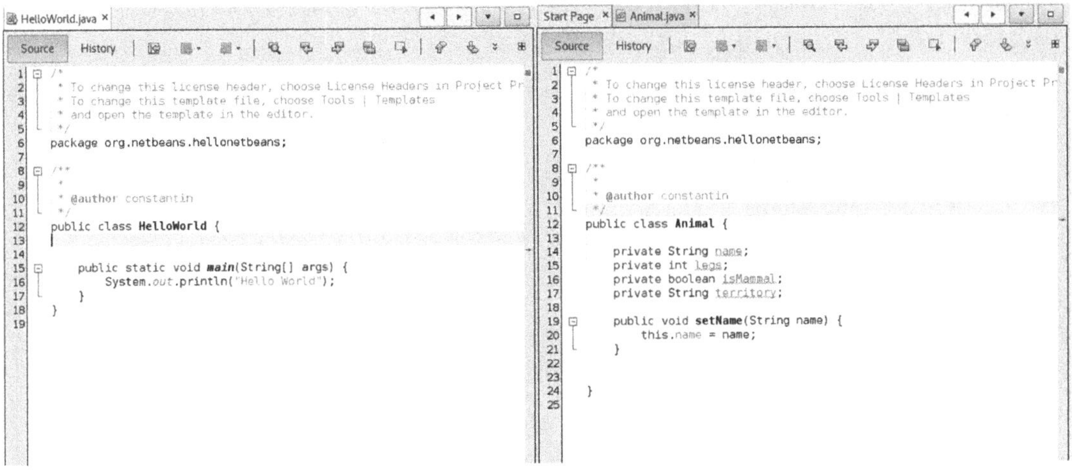

Figure 2-37. *View of two files simultaneously*

Splitting windows is applicable to a single source file, too. Below there are four ways to split a source file into two views:

- On the right side of each editor window, above the vertical scrollbar, there is a small plus icon that you can drag to split the window horizontally or vertically.

- Use the menu action **Window ➤ Configure Window ➤ Split Document ➤ Horizontally or Vertically**.

- Right-click the file's tab and select **Clone.**

- Right-click the file's tab and select **Split ➤ Vertically** or **Split ➤ Horizontally.**

Figure 2-38 shows the same source file being edited in two views. The advantage of such an edit is that you can have one view positioned on, say, a class definition in order to remind yourself of what the class is about while you are writing code later in the document that refers to the class. That is one of many reasons why you might want to view the same file in two or more tabs.

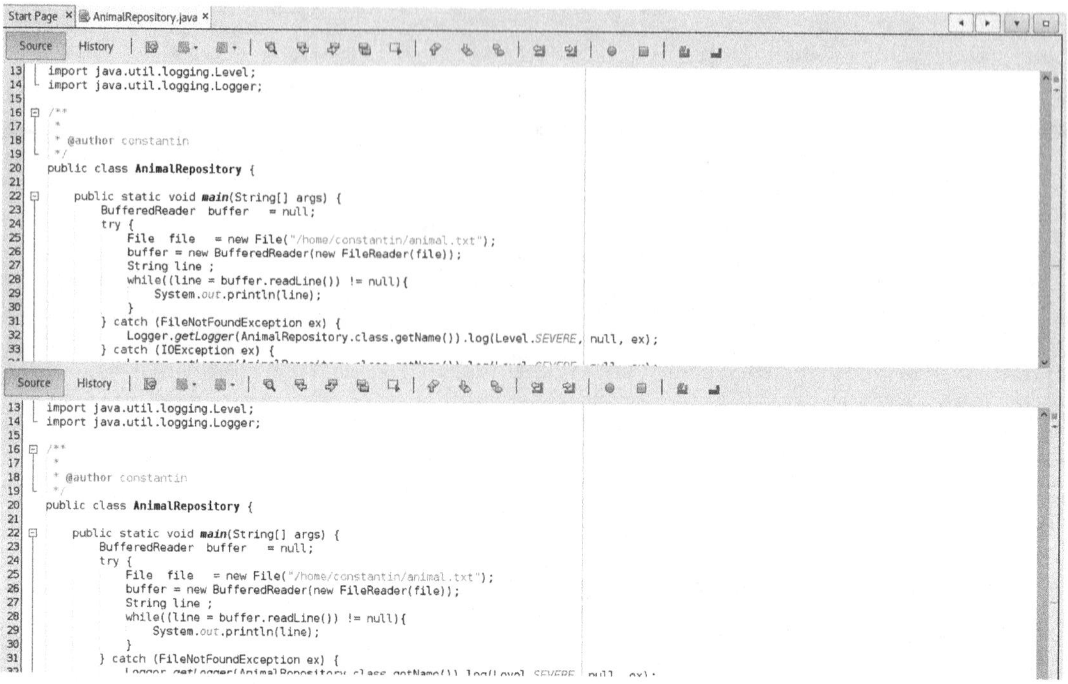

Figure 2-38. *A single file split in two views*

Enriching Your IDE

You can change the default setting of the IDE and also enrich it with additional features through plugins. To install a plugin, open the *Plugins* dialog box (**Tools ➤ Plugins**) as shown in Figure 2-39. Then choose which of the plugins that interest you and press **Install** (installation requires an Internet connection but you may also install downloaded plugins with the *Downloaded* tab).

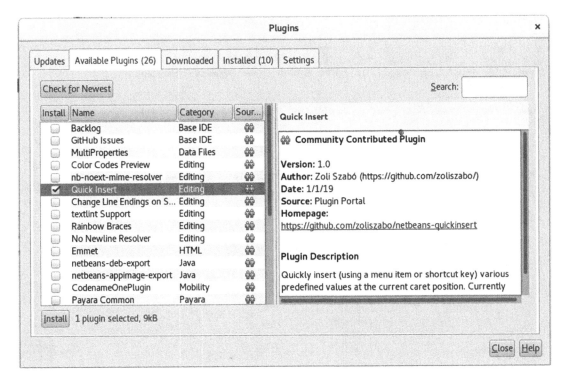

Figure 2-39. *Plugins dialog box*

The *Options* dialog box (**Tools ➤ Options** or **NetBeans ➤ Preferences** on Mac) is a multi-tabbed window that enables you to change any of the IDE's configuration settings. The Options dialog box is the place, for example, to change the editor's fonts and colors, the Java coding general configuration, the code completion behaviors, etc. Figure 2-40 shows an example of an editor formatting configuration.

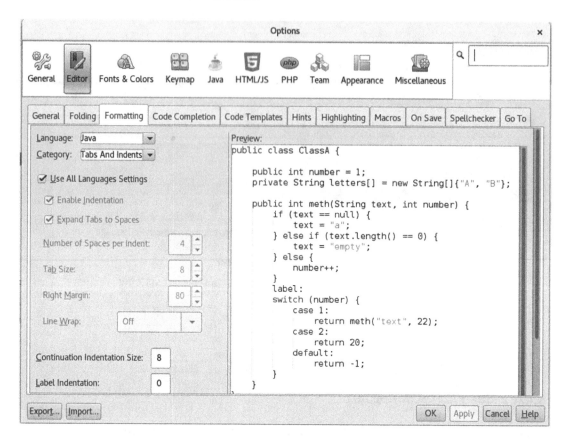

Figure 2-40. *Options dialog box*

Conclusion

This chapter gave an introduction to the main features of the Apache NetBeans IDE. We saw the IDE's layout with the default windows positions (Editor, Explorer, Navigator, Output, Properties, Palette); we saw how to create a Java Application project using Ant, Maven or Gradle, as well as tips to make you more productive. You are now equipped with knowledge that is good enough to further explore Apache NetBeans in the next chapters.

CHAPTER 3

Apache NetBeans: New Features

The Apache NetBeans IDE has made a number of advances since the release of NetBeans 8.2, the last release under Oracle Corporation. The release cadence has stayed closely in-line with the release cadence of Java, and therefore, there has been a number of releases in a short period of time since open sourcing of the IDE. Apache NetBeans 9 focused on modularity support and JShell. Release 10 contained new features such as JDK 11 support and PHP. Apache NetBeans 11 targeted JDK 12 support, Java EE, and Gradle support.

Note It is important to note that in order to utilize support for a particular JDK release feature, you must be running Apache NetBeans on the same JDK release or a greater JDK release. One can easily set Apache NetBeans to run under a different version of the JDK by setting the `netbeans_jdkhome` property within the `netbeans/etc/netbeans.conf` configuration file.

In this chapter, we will take a brief tour covering some of the most important new features of these past few releases. This chapter will not take a deep dive into these features, as the intention is to provide a quick overview. However, many of the features mentioned in this chapter contain larger sections elsewhere in this book, which go into much more detail.

© Ioannis Kostaras, Constantin Drabo, Josh Juneau, Sven Reimers, Mario Schröder, Geertjan Wielenga 2020
I. Kostaras et al., *Pro Apache NetBeans*, https://doi.org/10.1007/978-1-4842-5370-0_3

Apache NetBeans 9.0

The significant new features of Apache NetBeans 9.0 included modularity support, local variable type inference, and JShell. In this section, we will provide a brief look into each of these features, giving you a quick look at their usage.

Jigsaw (Modularity) Support

Perhaps the largest new feature of the JDK in its entire lifetime has been the release of the Java Modularity system, better known as Jigsaw. The modularity system in the Java Platform allows one to break down applications into modules, rather than as one large monolithic application.

As part of the module system, the Modulepath has taken precedence over the CLASSPATH. The Modulepath was added to Apache NetBeans in order to provide support for modules, along with compatibility for those applications that still make use of the CLASSPATH.

A standard Java SE project can be made into a module by adding a module-info. java file to its default package. The Apache NetBeans IDE has full support for module-info.java, including auto-completion. There is also an Ant-based project type known as the Java Modular Project. This project type can be used to create a modular application, consisting of a number of modules. To begin, open the **New Project** wizard, and choose the **Java with Ant** category, then choose **Java Modular Project**.

Local Variable Type Inference

Local variable type inference brings the **var** keyword to the Java language. This allows the developer to declare a var type, while the compiler infers the type from the other local variables in the code. The Apache NetBeans IDE contains a number of features to assist developers in the use of local variable type inference. There are a number of "hints" added to the editor to help signify when code has been typed that would support a changeover to utilize local variable type inference. Hints can be clicked upon to instantly make the suggested changes.

For instance, there is a hint to *Replace explicit type with 'var'*, and vice versa. There are also hints to split compound declarations. It is all baked into Apache NetBeans, making code easier to read and manage.

JShell

The JShell was a long overdue feature of the Java language, as many modern languages nowadays have a REPL (Read Eval Print Loop) utility packaged with the distribution. The Java language gained a REPL in JDK 9, and it is known as JShell. This tool provides auto-completion and basic development/testing capabilities. It also allows one to execute Java dynamically on the fly, evaluating statements and blocks of code without compilation. The Apache NetBeans IDE contains support for JShell by providing an instance of the REPL within the editor pane for quick access. To open JShell, use the **Tools ➤ Open Java Platform Shell** menu option. Once selected, an editor window will open the JShell utility for the Java Platform on which Apache NetBeans is running.

Note   You must be running Apache NetBeans on JDK 9 or greater in order to utilize the JShell utility.

Once in the JShell editor, the utility can be used just as it is from the command line. That is, one can execute Java statements or blocks without enclosing them into a Java class. Moreover, Java code can be executed without compilation. This makes the JShell editor perfect for performing testing. See Figure 3-1.

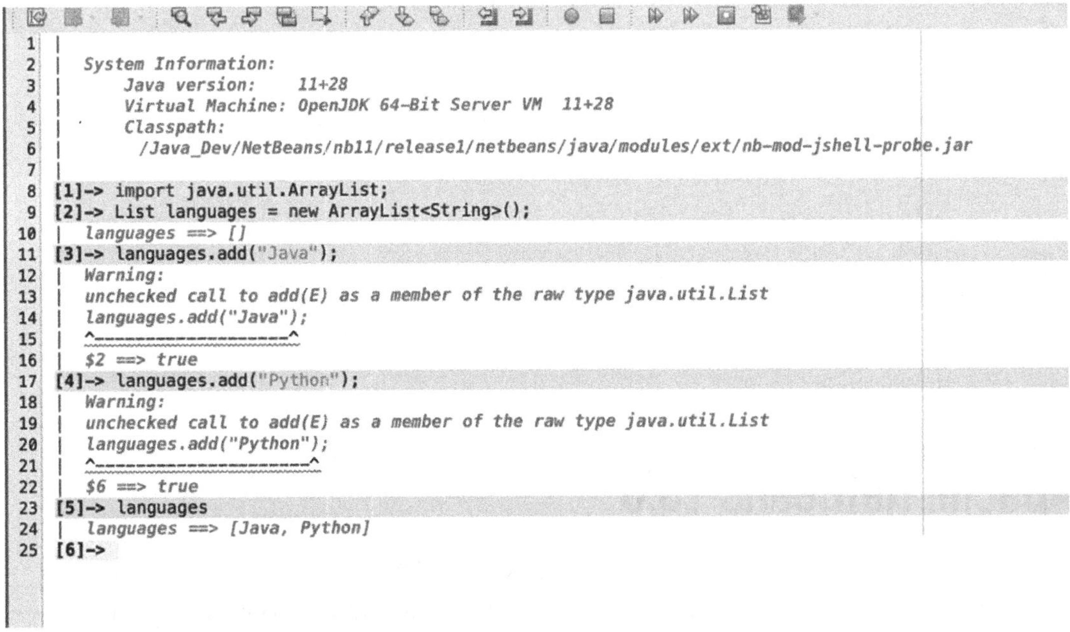

Figure 3-1. *Apache NetBeans JShell Editor*

Utilizing JShell from within Apache NetBeans has some great benefits. When working within the editor, one can test code and then press the **Save to Class** button to save the code into a Java class with one click. JShell can also be configured into Ant-based Java SE applications as an agent, allowing JShell to be invoked by the application. The preferences pane of Apache NetBeans includes options for configuring JShell history, auto-open the JShell, and modifying the JDK used for JShell. See Figure 3-2.

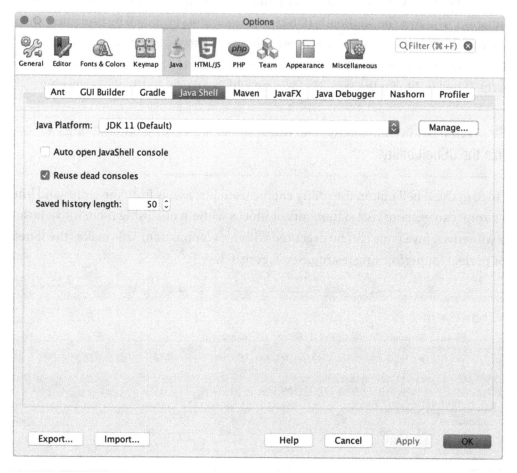

Figure 3-2. *JShell Support*

Apache NetBeans 10.0

The Apache NetBeans 10.0 release included a couple of major enhancements, those being JDK 11 and PHP support. In this section, we will take a brief look at each of these features so that you can begin to explore them in their entirety.

JDK 11 Support

JDK 11 was the first Long Term Support (LTS) release of Java since the new release cycle had been introduced. This release included some great new features, which are fully supported in Apache NetBeans. JDK 11 has a number of new features, ranging from new `String` methods to the new HTTP client. Apache NetBeans contains full support for these features.

Taking a look at the new Java `String` method support, the IDE will auto-complete the newly added methods. In the screenshot below (Figure 3-3), you can see the new `repeat()` functionality.

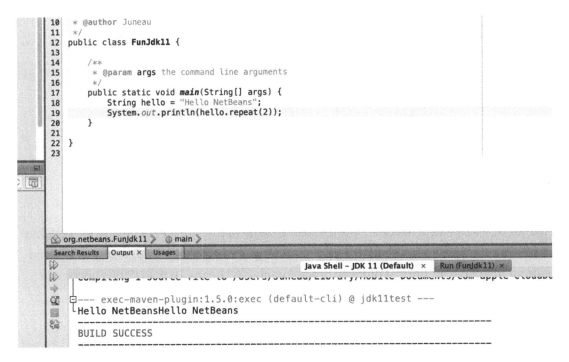

Figure 3-3. *JDK 12 Support*

The IDE also has complete support for the new HTTP client. As the next screenshot demonstrates (Figure 3-4), the `HttpClient` can be utilized within a Java SE class, and the IDE includes full auto-complete support while coding.

```
 8  import java.net.http.HttpClient;
 9  import java.net.http.HttpResponse;
10  import java.net.http.HttpRequest;
11  import java.net.http.HttpResponse.BodyHandlers;
12  import java.net.URI;
13
14  /**
15   *
16   * @author Juneau
17   */
18  public class FunJdk11 {
19
20      /**
21       * @param args the command line arguments
22       */
23      public static void main(String[] args) {
24          HttpClient client = HttpClient.newHttpClient();
25          HttpRequest request = HttpRequest.newBuilder()
26                  .uri(URI.create("http://openjdk.java.net/")).build();
27          client.sendAsync(request, BodyHandlers.ofString()).thenApply(HttpResponse::body).thenAccept(System.out::println).join();
28      }
29
30  }
31
```

```
org.netbeans.FunJdk11  )  main  )  request  )
Search Results   Output – Run (FunJdk11)  x   Usages
        &#183;  <a href="http://www.oracle.com/us/legal/privacy/">Privacy</a>
        &#183;  <a href="http://www.oracle.com/us/legal/third-party-trademarks/third-party-trademarks-078568.htm
    var sc_project=2527440;
    var sc_invisible=1;
    var sc_partition=24;
    var sc_security="d832a704";
    var sc_remove_link=1;
    </SCRIPT><script type="text/javascript" src="https://www.statcounter.com/counter/counter_xhtml.js" async="yes
    ------------------------------------------------------------
    BUILD SUCCESS
    ------------------------------------------------------------
    Total time: 3.374 s
    Finished at: 2019-06-16T00:10:40-05:00
    Final Memory: 7M/30M
```

Figure 3-4. *HttpClient Support*

PHP

The Apache NetBeans IDE contains full support for PHP 7.0, 7.1, 7.2, and 7.3. This enables one to create a new PHP project using some of the latest PHP advances. PHP has been a part of Apache NetBeans for years, but only up through PHP 7.0 was it supported without installing additional plugins. Since Apache NetBeans 10.0, PHP has become a part of the standard distribution. See Figure 3-5.

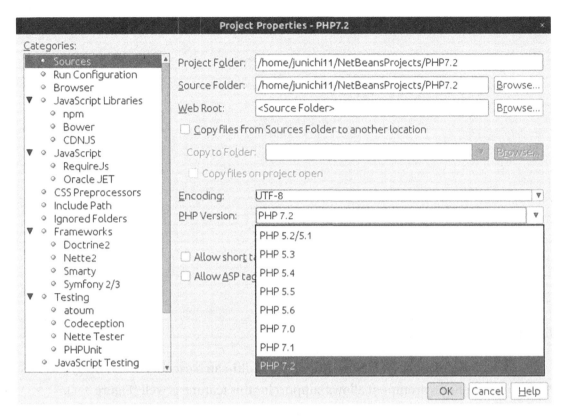

Figure 3-5. *PHP New Project Dialog*

The Apache NetBeans editor supports such features as the "void" type in PHP, as well as any of the other PHP enhancements through PHP 7.3. For instance, there is support for allowing a trailing comma in function calls. This may help in the case where a comma is accidentally forgotten or perhaps a list may continue to grow at some point. See Figure 3-6.

```php
<?php
// Function Calls
$array1 = ['baz'];
$array2 = ['qux'];
$merged = array_merge(
    $array1,
    $array2,
    ['foo', 'bar'],
);

// Method & Closure Calls
$foo = new Foo(
    'constructor',
    'foo',
);

$foo->bar(
    'method',
    'bar',
);

$bar(
    'closure',
    'bar',
);

// Language Constructs
unset(
    $param1,
    $param2,
);
```

Figure 3-6. *Trailing Comma Support*

Another newer feature of PHP is support for multi-catch exception handling, and the Apache NetBeans environment allows support for this feature as well (Figure 3-7).

```php
<?php

class ExceptionType1 extends Exception {
    public function something1() {
    }
}

class ExceptionType2 extends Exception {
    public function something2() {
    }
}

try {
    // Some code...
} catch (ExceptionType1 | ExceptionType2 $ex) {
    echo $ex->getMessage();
} catch (\Exception $e) {
    echo $e->getMessage();
}
```

Figure 3-7. *PHP Multi-Catch Exception Handling*

The life of a PHP developer can also be made easier by making use of the native debugger. One can set a breakpoint on a line of code and run the debugger, then the application will run and once the breakpoint is reached, the editor will be opened to the breakpoint, enabling the developer to debug variable values and states at that point in time.

All of these advancements in PHP support make Apache NetBeans one of the foremost IDEs for developing in PHP.

Apache NetBeans 11.0

The Apache NetBeans 11.0 release includes full support for Java EE and Gradle, as well as support for JDK 12 features.

JDK 12 Support

The Java release cadence is allowing for a new release of the JDK every six months. As such, the Apache NetBeans release cycle should allow the IDE to continue to include the support for the most recent JDK. That said, JDK 12 support has been added to Apache NetBeans 11.0, including a preview of switch expression support, and support for compact number formatting. This includes hints such as the "convert to rule switch" for the new `switch` support.

Java EE Support

Up through Apache NetBeans 10.0, if one wished to utilize Java EE features, the modules needed to be enabled via the Apache NetBeans 8.2 update center. This is because Java EE support was not yet part of the Apache NetBeans distribution. The full enterprise cluster has been transferred to become part of the Apache NetBeans distribution with Apache NetBeans 11.0. This means that out of the box, the Apache NetBeans distribution includes full support for Java EE, without the requirement to download and install any additional modules.

Not only does Apache NetBeans 11.0 include support for Java EE, but it also includes support for Jakarta EE 8 via the Java EE 8 support that has been added in Apache NetBeans 11.1. The new support allows one to create a new Maven-based Jakarta EE/Java EE project using Java EE 8. It also allows one to install Java EE 8-compliant application server containers and manage them via the IDE, such as GlassFish 5.1.

Gradle

Another feature that required enablement in previous Apache NetBeans releases was Gradle support. As part of Apache NetBeans 11.0, Gradle support has been made first-class, so it works out of the box. Gradle projects can now be opened out of the box, and a Gradle Task Navigator has been integrated, allowing one to run tasks using a double-click. This also allows one to make use of Gradle supported unit test frameworks, and make use of run, debug, and test … even with single methods.

Conclusion

The Apache NetBeans IDE continues to progress with each release, supporting newer releases of the JDK and adding enhancements to make the IDE more useful to a broader spectrum of developers. If you have any features that you would like to see added to Apache NetBeans, please join the community and contribute your ideas. Now you are ready to develop desktop applications.

CHAPTER 4

Developing Desktop Applications

Apache NetBeans has excellent support for developing desktop applications. By desktop applications, we mean applications that do not require a web or application server (even though one can be used in the back end), are installed in the user's machine, and provide a richer Graphical User Interface (GUI) than the browser.

Historically, *Abstract Window Toolkit (AWT)* was the first GUI library released with JDK 1.0. The AWT is part of the Java Foundation Classes (JFC), the standard API for providing a GUI for a Java program. AWT's components (or widgets) are "heavyweight" or native, which means that their look and feel (L&F) depended on the platform they were running (when run on Windows, a button would look like a Windows button; when run on MacOSX, like a MacOSX button etc.). AWT was multi-threaded, had only basic support of GUI components, and could run in the browser without the need for a plugin.

Swing was released with JDK 1.2 and was a replacement of AWT. Swing was developed to provide a more sophisticated set of "lightweight" GUI components (written entirely in Java and therefore platform independent) than the earlier Abstract Window Toolkit (AWT) ones. Swing provides a look and feel that emulates the look and feel of several platforms, and also supports a pluggable look and feel that allows applications to have a look and feel unrelated to the underlying platform. Swing follows a single-threaded programming model; all GUI related code is executed in the *Event Dispatch Thread (EDT)*. Additionally, the framework provides a layer of abstraction between the code structure and the graphic presentation of a Swing-based GUI.

JavaFX (`https://openjfx.io/`) is the most recent GUI library provided by Java to build rich GUIs or *Rich Internet Applications* (*RIAs*) that can run across a wide variety of devices. JavaFX abstracts the UI presentation (typically declared in an XML file – `.fxml`) from the actual logic (action events, etc.). This way one can use *Cascading Style Sheets* (*CSS*) to decorate the GUI without the need to recompile the application. JavaFX 1.0.2

© Ioannis Kostaras, Constantin Drabo, Josh Juneau, Sven Reimers, Mario Schröder, Geertjan Wielenga 2020
I. Kostaras et al., *Pro Apache NetBeans*, https://doi.org/10.1007/978-1-4842-5370-0_4

was released in 2008. As of JDK 7u6 it has been integrated in the JDK. JavaFX 8 was included in JDK 8; however, as of JDK 11, JavaFX has again been separated from the JDK. JavaFX is actively maintained by Gluon (https://gluonhq.com/). While JavaFX is intended to be a replacement of Swing, both will stay on the market for quite some time.

Apache NetBeans Support for Desktop Applications

The Apache NetBeans IDE provides several tools to simplify the process of building GUIs as shown in Figure 4-1.

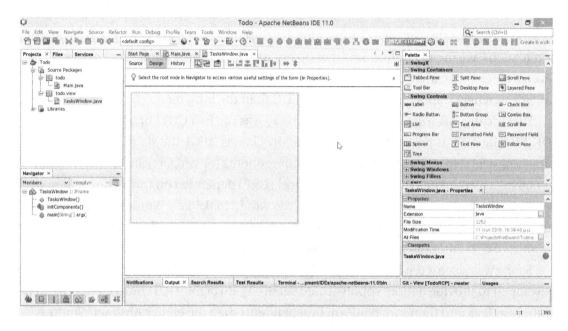

Figure 4-1. *Apache NetBeans GUI Development tools*

- **GUI Builder**: this is where you design the GUI of your application. The GUI Builder, or *Matisse*, enables you to lay out forms by placing components where you want them and by providing visual feedback in the form of guidelines.

- **Navigator window**: displays a tree hierarchy of all components contained in the currently opened form. These can be visual components and containers, such as buttons, labels, menus, panels, etc., as well as nonvisual components such as timers and data sources.

- **Palette window**: contains groups of components or widgets that can be added to forms by drag and drop. The palette window can be customized to display its contents as icons only, or as icons with component names. With the help of the *Palette Manager* you add new components to the palette.

- **Properties window**: allows changing the properties for the currently selected component, such as the displayed text, its size, etc. It also allows adding/modifying events and bindings.

Apache NetBeans supports development of desktop applications using either AWT, Swing, or JavaFX. The visual design capabilities are among NetBeans' strongest features. Building prototypes of the application's UI helps end users to state their requirements, and that's one of the reasons visual GUI builders became so popular.

Typically, you create a new Java Application and then you add GUI components using wizards or by dragging and dropping widgets from the Palette.

Before you proceed, either open an existing Java Application NetBeans project, or create a new *Java Application* project, as shown in Figure 4-20, by selecting the **File ➤ New Project** menu item and clicking **Next**. In step 2 of the wizard, provide a project name and choose a suitable project location (anywhere in your hard disk) as shown in Figure 4-21. Then click **Finish**. Last, select the project or the *Source Packages* of the project in the *Projects* tab, and click on **File ➤ New File** as explained in the following sections.

AWT Support

Developing in AWT is very rare nowadays, and so it will not be covered in this book. However, we shall briefly describe Apache NetBeans' support for AWT. You may create a number of AWT forms as shown in Figure 4-2. You open this wizard by clicking on the menu **File ➤ New File**.

- **Applet Form**: creates a new `java.applet.Applet`. *Applets* are small applications that can run inside a (Java-enabled) browser.

- **Dialog Form**: creates a new `java.awt.Dialog` within an application or Applet. Dialogs can be *modal* (the dialog is blocking the application waiting for user input) or *modeless* (the dialog is not blocking the application waiting for user input).

- **Frame Form**: creates a new form that is based on `java.awt.Frame` and is usually used as the top-level window within an application.

- **Panel Form**: creates a `java.awt.Panel` that can be added inside AWT containers such as `Frames`, `Dialogs`, or `Applets`.

Once you have added one of the above forms into your application, the Design editor appears in NetBeans along with the Palette. Figure 4-3 shows the available widgets you can drag and drop onto the AWT form. AWT forms support different layouts, which you can set by right-clicking on the form and selecting **Set Layout** from the pop-up menu.

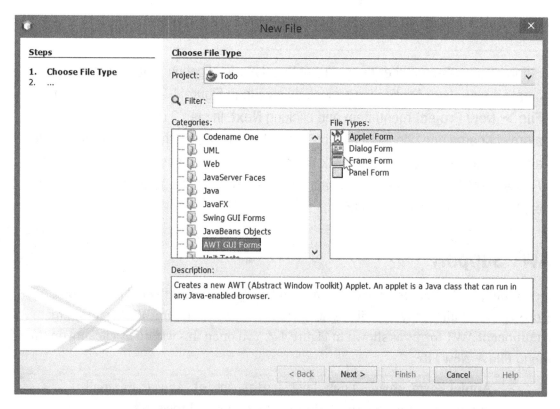

Figure 4-2. *AWT GUI Forms*

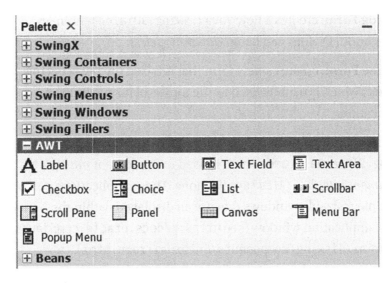

Figure 4-3. *AWT GUI widgets*

Swing Support

Similar to AWT, the *New File* wizard offers you the choices shown in Figure 4-4.

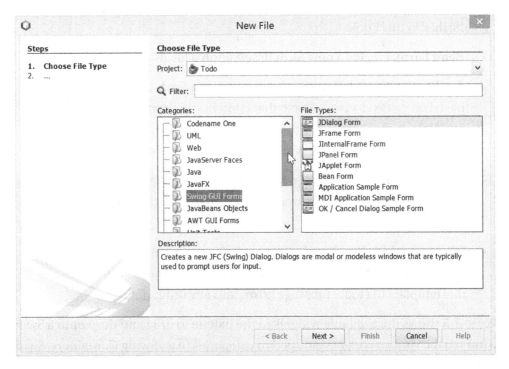

Figure 4-4. *Swing GUI Forms*

- **JDialog Form**: creates a new `javax.swing.JDialog` within an application. Dialogs can be *modal* or *modeless*.

- **JFrame Form**: creates a new form that is based on `javax.swing.JFrame`, which is usually used as the top-level form within an application.

- **JInternalFrame Form**: creates a new form that is based on `javax.swing.JInternalFrame`, which is used to implement *multiple document interface (MDI)* applications. These applications contain multiple resizable windows that are all displayed within the bounds of the application window (see `https://docs.oracle.com/javase/tutorial/uiswing/components/internalframe.html`).

- **JPanel Form**: creates a `javax.swing.JPanel` that can be used within Swing containers such as `JFrames` and `JDialogs`.

- **JApplet Form**: creates a Swing applet that can be run from within a browser window that has the necessary Java Swing plugin. As applets have fallen out of favor and have been replaced by other technologies such as HTML5 and JavaScript, we won't discuss them further in this book.

- **Bean Form**: creates a new form based upon a JavaBean component.

- **Application Sample Form**: creates a skeleton form application based on `javax.swing.JFrame` that contains the standard **File**, **Edit**, and **Help** menus created within the form. This can be a very useful starting point for the main window of your application.

- **MDI Application Sample Form**: same as the previous skeleton form application, but it allows adding `JInternalFrames` to create an MDI application.

- **OK / Cancel Dialog Sample Form**: creates a sample dialog (either modal or modeless) containing **OK** and **Cancel** buttons. You can use this template to create message boxes and any other dialogs.

Figure 4-5 shows the available widgets in the palette to drag and drop onto a Swing form. You see the various widgets grouped in categories (e.g., Swing Containers, Swing Controls, Swing Menus, Swing Windows, and Swing Fillers).

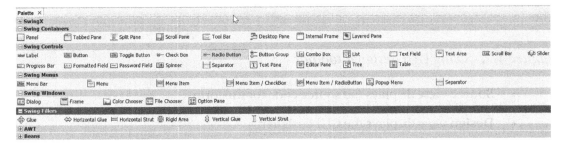

Figure 4-5. *Swing GUI widgets*

The Apache NetBeans visual editor allows you to develop your GUIs by using drag and drop of components (or widgets) from the palette onto it. Just right-click inside the JFrame and select the **Set Layout** menu item (see Figure 4-6). You'll see the default choice is not a traditional Swing/AWT layout manager; it's something named *Free Design*. This means you are using the *Matisse* visual GUI builder, which was introduced in NetBeans 5. *Matisse* configures the JFrame to use the GroupLayout layout manager developed in the SwingLabs java.net project.

Figure 4-6. *Swing layouts*

Aligning Components

To help us lay out controls within a form, Apache NetBeans provides a toolbar (see Figure 4-7) along the top of the design view, containing tools to align and preview forms.

Figure 4-7. *Swing GUI designer toolbar*

- **Source view** displays the source code for the form.

- **Design view** displays the GUI designer.

- **History** displays the source code local history and can be useful if you need to revert to previous versions.

- **Selection mode**: allows components to be selected.

- **Connection mode**: allows creating connections between two components so that an event on one component can trigger an event on another component.

- **Preview design**: allows previewing how the form will be displayed at runtime.

- **Align Left In Column**: allows multiple components to be left-aligned.

- **Align Right In Column**: allows multiple components to be right-aligned.

- **Center Horizontally**: allows multiple components to be centered horizontally.

- **Align Top In Row**: allows multiple components to be top-aligned.

- **Align Bottom In Row**: allows multiple components to be bottom- aligned.

- **Center Vertically**: allows multiple components to be centered vertically.

- **Change Horizontal Resizability**: resize the selected component horizontally rather than being anchored to the left and right of other components.

- **Change Vertical Resizability**: resize the selected component vertically rather than being anchored to the top and bottom of other components.

Matisse also allows a group of selected components to be centered down the axis of the first selected component. Horizontal and vertical centering are available. Multiple components must be selected; then all are centered on the widest selection. Another option allows centering components horizontally and vertically in their parent container. We shall see some examples later in this chapter.

Anchoring Components

As the name implies, anchoring a component to a position means that the component will stay in that position relative to other components or boundaries even if its container is resized.

When we anchor a component, we are basically saying that when we resize the form, we want the component to stay aligned with another component. So, for example, if we anchor a JLabel to the bottom right of a JFrame, when we expand the JFrame, the label will stay at the bottom right. To indicate that a widget is anchored to another object, Apache NetBeans displays a dotted horizontal or vertical line, ending at the boundary that the component is anchored to. If a component is not anchored on a particular edge, a zigzagged line is displayed indicating that the location of the component may expand in the specified direction. In Figure 4-8, the JLabel is anchored to the bottom right of the frame. There is, therefore, a dotted line between the label and the bottom and right edges of the JFrame and a zigzagged line between the left and top edges of the JFrame.

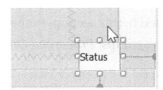

Figure 4-8. *Anchoring a label*

You may also right-click on the widget and select **Anchor ➤ (Left, Right, Top, Bottom)** from the context menu.

Resizing Components

When we resize a form, anchored components move along to stay in their position while the form is resized, but they are not resized themselves.

If we want to allow a component to resize when a form is resized, we must specify that the component can auto-resize. Right-click on the component and select the **Auto-Resizing** menu item and choose either *Horizontal* or *Vertical* (or both). Figure 4-9 shows the JLabel of Figure 4-8 that can be auto-resized both horizontally and vertically. You now notice that both zigzagged lines have been transformed to dotted lines.

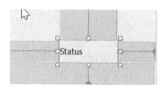

Figure 4-9. *Auto-resizing a label*

You may also double-click on each of the surrounding empty spaces and define the exact size of the space using the *Edit Layout Space* dialog box.

To set two or more widgets to the same size, select them, right-click any one of them, and choose **Set the Same Size ➤ Set Width** (or **Same Size ➤ Set Height**) from the contextual menu.

Properties

The *Properties* window is broken down into three categories:

- **Properties** tab (see Figure 4-10): editable properties for the selected component can be edited in this section. Properties are usually grouped in the following groups: *Properties, Other Properties, Layout,* and *Accessibility*.

- **Events** tab (see Figure 4-11): allows defining what actions are performed on a component when certain events (for example, mouse click, key pressed, etc.) are triggered. For example, to define an actionPerformed() on a button, click on the drop-down menu next to the actionPerformed event (a small black down arrow); a pop-up is displayed, suggesting a name for the event handler. This name consists of the name of the widget being edited, together with the name of the event. Upon selecting the name for the event handler, NetBeans automatically opens up the *Source* window, placing the caret ready for entering the event handler code. You will notice that the source code editor contains areas that cannot be edited. This is necessary because this code is automatically generated by the GUI Builder, and changing this code manually might break this binding between the code and the GUI designer. Finally, click on the **...** button in the GUI designer to add, remove, or rename an event handler.

- **Code** tab (see Figure 4-12): allows providing custom code snippets for a component, for example, any pre/post initialization code, etc.

Note   Older versions of NetBeans (before the donation to Apache) had also a *Binding* tab. This has, unfortunately, been removed from Apache NetBeans due to licensing issues and due to the fact that JSR 295 (`https://jcp.org/en/jsr/detail?id=295`) has not become official. Take a look at this JIRA item (`https://issues.apache.org/jira/browse/NETBEANS-530`) for more information.

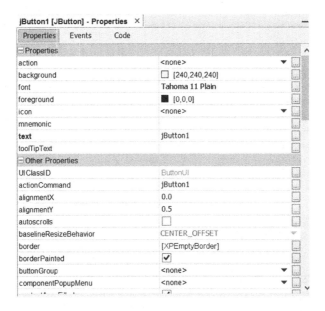

Figure 4-10. Properties window

You can modify a property in one of three ways:

- By directly editing its value,

- By using the drop-down menu (if one exists),

- By using the custom editor (via the ... button).

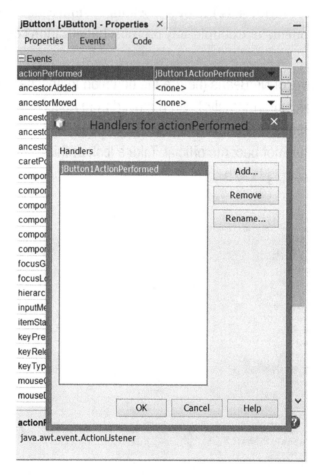

Figure 4-11. *Events*

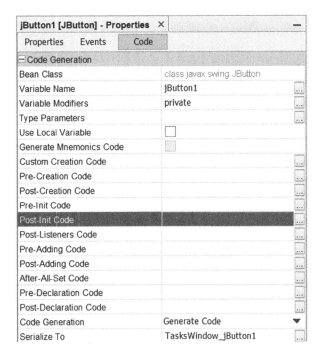

Figure 4-12. *Custom code*

Connection Tool

Apache NetBeans provides an easy way to make connections between components, using the *Connection Mode* button (see Figure 4-7). Clicking on that button, NetBeans will display a message asking to select the component that will generate the event:

Upon selecting the source component, NetBeans displays a message, asking to select the component that will receive the event:

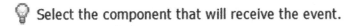

Upon selecting a component to receive the event, NetBeans will display the *Connection Wizard* window of Figure 4-13.

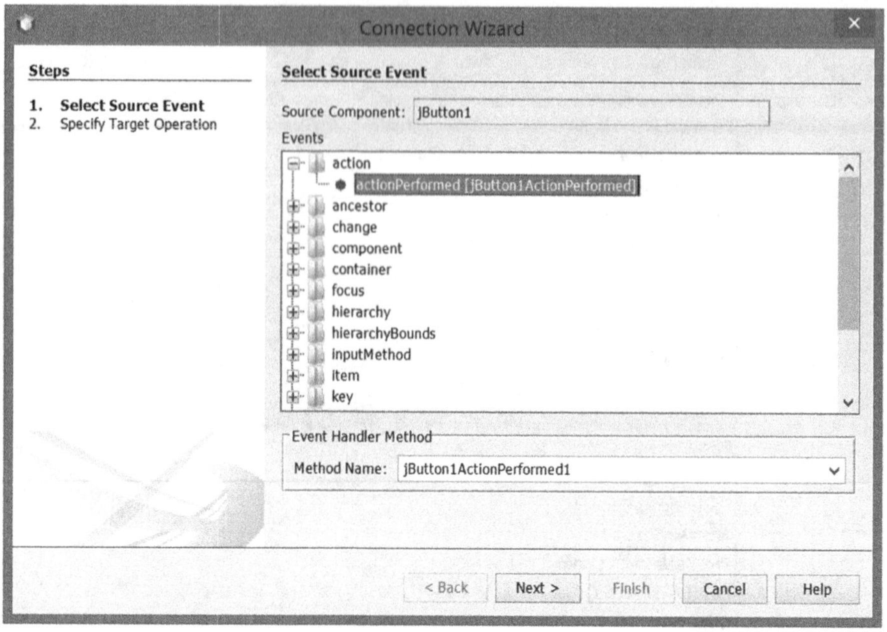

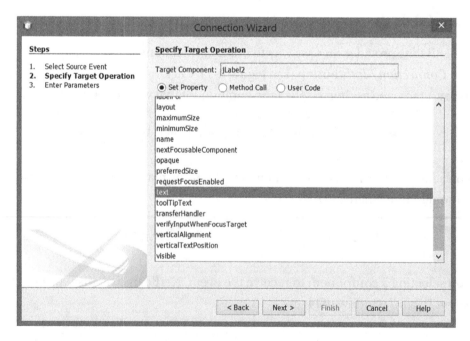

Figure 4-13. *Connection wizard step 1*

Select the source event, click **Next,** and specify the target operation (see Figure 4-14).

Figure 4-14. *Connection wizard step 2*

In the next step, you need to enter how the target will be modified (see Figure 4-15).

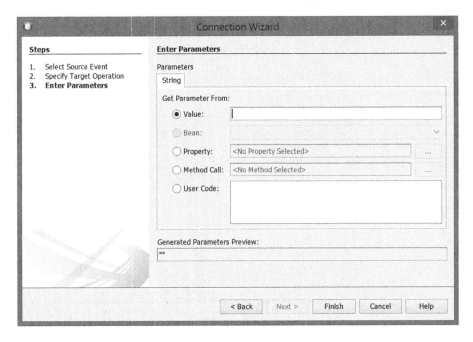

Figure 4-15. *Connection wizard step 3*

To view an example project that illustrates Swing forms, create a new project (menu **File ➤ New Project**), choose the *Samples/Java* category and the *GUI Form Examples* file type. The generated project contains three examples of Swing forms (Antenna, ContactEditor, and Find) that give you some ideas of the capabilities that Apache NetBeans IDE provides to design GUIs. The *Anagram Game* under the same category is another example.

JavaFX Support

Apache NetBeans allows you to create JavaFX projects by clicking on **File ➤ New Project** menu item. You may create Ant-based or Maven-based JavaFX projects. Select **Java with Ant ➤ JavaFX** category and choose one of the available JavaFX projects as shown in Figure 4-16. Or select the **Java with Maven** category and choose **JavaFX Application** project. In the first case, you can create a JavaFX application developing the GUI using Java code, or use an FXML file to script the GUI widgets of your application. You may also create an application that mixes Swing and JavaFX components.

Once you have created your JavaFX application, you may add additional JavaFX classes of FXML files by using the **File ➤ New File** wizard as shown in Figure 4-17.

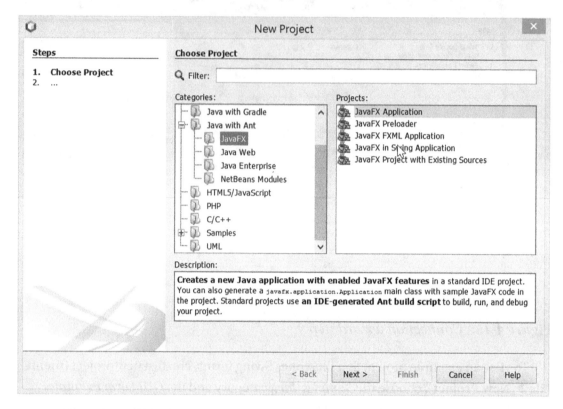

Figure 4-16. *JavaFX Project types*

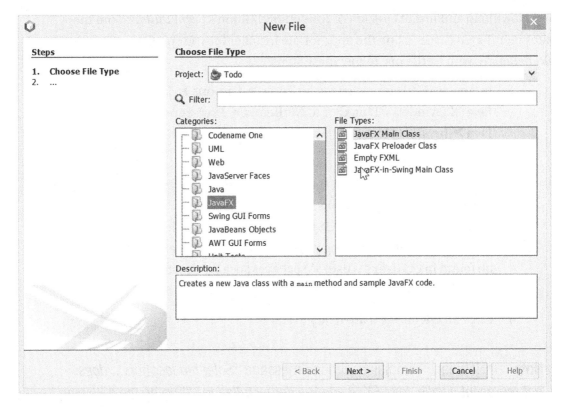

Figure 4-17. *JavaFX file types*

Apache NetBeans doesn't provide a GUI designer for JavaFX applications, like the Matisse GUI builder for Swing. One can, however, integrate *SceneBuilder* with NetBeans. *SceneBuilder* (see Figure 4-18) allows you to build JavaFX applications graphically. Oracle has stopped support of the SceneBuilder, which latest version is 2.0 (`http://www.oracle.com/technetwork/java/javase/downloads/javafxscenebuilder-info-2157684.html`). *Gluon* (`https://gluonhq.com/products/scene-builder/`) has taken over support and development of *SceneBuilder*. We shall see shortly how to set up Apache NetBeans to use *SceneBuilder*.

Sven Reimer's *Monet* (`http://plugins.netbeans.org/plugin/55434/monet-the-javafx-scene-builder-integration`) plugin is an attempt to run *SceneBuilder* from within NetBeans to build the GUI of JavaFX applications the same way as when you use Matisse to build the GUI of your Swing applications.

Download and install Oracle's or (preferably) Gluon's *SceneBuilder* from the sites mentioned earlier using the appropriate installer for your platform. To integrate *SceneBuilder* with NetBeans, follow these steps:

1. In Apache NetBeans, navigate to **Tools ➤ Options ➤ Java ➤ JavaFX** (Windows/Linux) or to **NetBeans ➤ Preferences ➤ Java ➤ JavaFX** (MacOSX), and click **Activate** if JavaFX support is not yet activated.

2. After activation is finished, set the *Scene Builder Home* to be the Gluon directory (e.g., this is the path to /Applications/SceneBuilder.app in MacOS). Some Windows installers install *SceneBuilder* without asking you for a directory. *SceneBuilder* can be found in C:\Users\<User>\AppData\Local\SceneBuilder or in C:\Program Files\SceneBuilder.

3. Click on **OK** and you are ready to start.

Note   If NetBeans complains with the message "*Selected location ... does not represent a valid Java FX Scene Builder installation*," then do the following workaround.

1. Navigate to the directory where *SceneBuilder* was installed,

2. Enter app folder,

3. Make a duplicate of SceneBuilder.cfg to SceneBuilder. properties in the same folder.

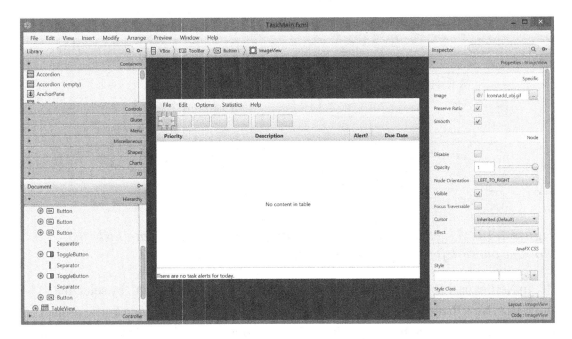

Figure 4-18. *Gluon SceneBuilder*

Developing a Swing Application

We shall develop the GUI for a Personal Information Manager (PIM) desktop application
that allows you to organize your tasks. This application will be further developed in
part 2. The *Todo* application is composed of a tasks list main window and a task-editing
dialog box. A rough sketch for both is shown in Figure 4-19. We shall build a dynamic
prototype of the *Todo* application using Swing. In the next section, we shall rebuild the
dynamic prototype using JavaFX.

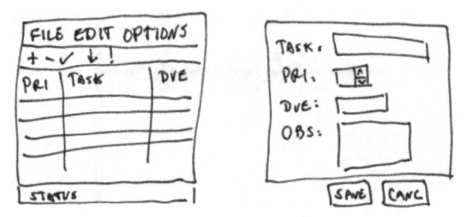

Figure 4-19. *A sketch of the Todo application user interface (main tasks list window on the left and task-editing form on the right)*

In NetBeans, create a new Java Application as shown in Figure 4-20, by selecting the **File ➤ New Project** menu item. In step 2 of the wizard, provide Todo as the project name and choose a suitable project location (anywhere in your hard disk) as shown in Figure 4-21. Then click **Finish**. Apache NetBeans creates the project containing a Java package named after the project name and a class named Main inside package todo.

Design the Main Tasks List Window

Create a new package by right-clicking on the todo package, selecting **New ➤ Java package** from the pop-up menu and giving the package name todo.view.

Now right-click the todo.view package icon and choose **New ➤ Other** (or choose **File ➤ New File** from the main menu), then select the *Swing GUI Forms* category and the *JFrame Form* file type (see Figure 4-4) and click **Next.**

In the next step of the wizard, type TasksWindow as the class name and press **Finish**. The IDE opens the visual form editor, as shown in Figure 4-1; notice also the location of the *Projects, Navigator,* and *Properties* windows; the *Palette* and the *editor* area.

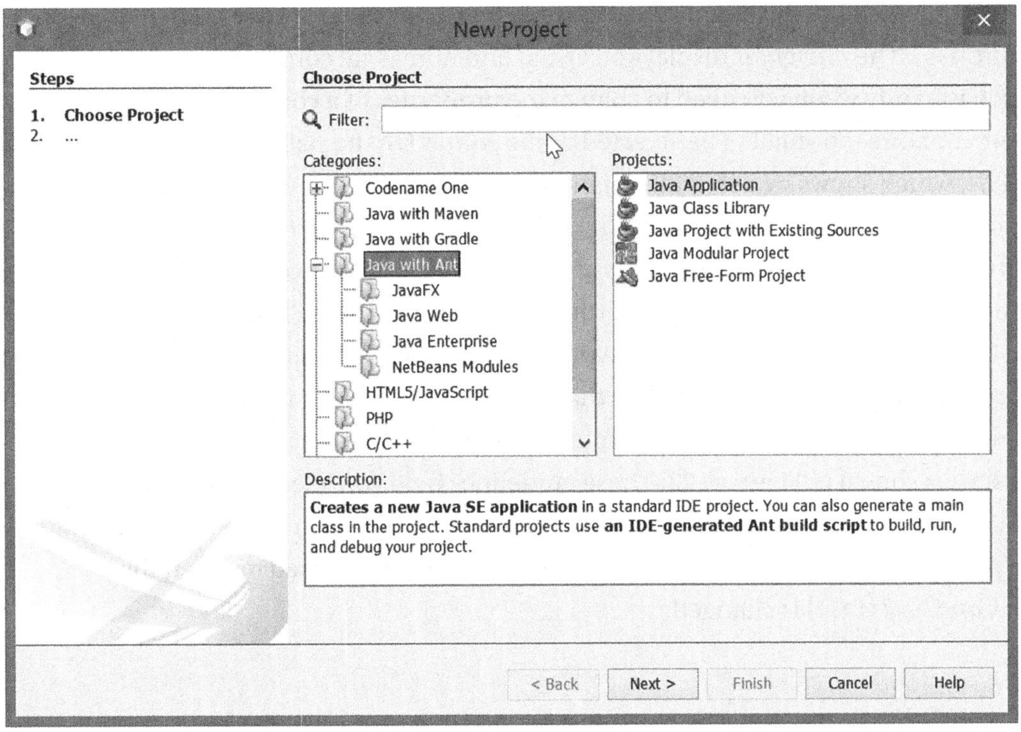

Figure 4-20. *Create a new Java Application project*

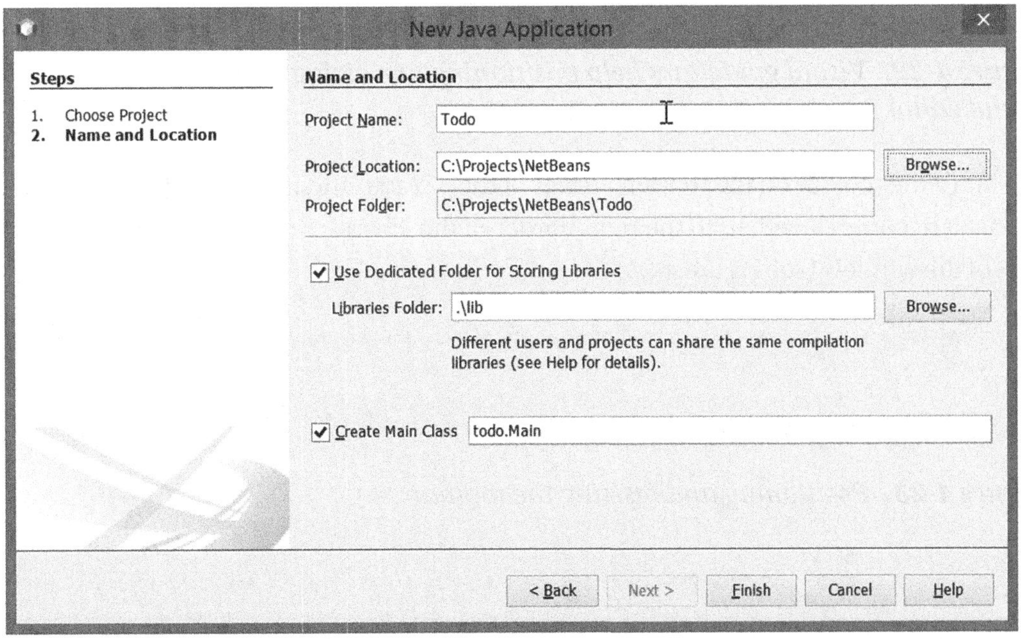

Figure 4-21. *In step 2 of the wizard, provide the project name and location*

An orange frame highlights the selected component (the JFrame content pane in Figure 4-1). The *navigator* displays all visual and nonvisual components of the JFrame, which is handy when you need to change the properties of a component hidden by another or one too small to be selected in the *editor*. On the right you see the *component palette*, which shows by default the standard Swing components (you can also add third-party JavaBeans by right-clicking on it and choosing *Palette Manager*), as well as the *Properties* windows. *Properties* are categorized to ease access to the ones most commonly used, and changed properties have their names highlighted in bold.

Let's create the GUI of our prototype. From the palette, drag the *toolbar* icon and drop it over the JFrame. You'll notice that a placeholder for the toolbar follows the mouse pointer, and that the visual editor displays guidelines when it's close to the edges of the JFrame, as shown in Figure 4-22. These guidelines help you keep controls aligned and spaced out inside the container. Matisse generates the layout constraints to maintain the positioning of each component when the container is resized or when the *Look and Feel* (L&F) is changed.

Figure 4-22. *Visual guidelines help positioning and sizing controls in the visual editor*

Move the toolbar on the top-left corner of the JFrame, and then drag the right border so that it becomes attached to the right border of the JFrame, thus filling up all the top part of the window (see Figure 4-23).

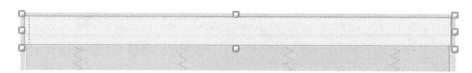

Figure 4-23. *Positioning and resizing the toolbar*

Repeat the process to insert a JLabel attached to the bottom of the JFrame. This label will be used as the *status bar* for the tasks window. Then add a JScrollPane, filling up the area between the JToolbar and the JLabel.

Now try resizing the JFrame content pane. The JToolbar, JLabel, and JScrollPane should resize to keep the borders attached to the JFrame's corners and to each of the other borders.

You may give more descriptive names to the variables of the various widgets, by right-clicking on each of them in the *Navigator* window and selecting **Change Variable Name** from the pop-up menu. From the same context menu, you can modify the widget's displayed text by selecting **Edit Text** action.

Next, let's add a JTable inside the JScrollPane and create the toolbars' buttons in order for the TasksWindow to start resembling the sketch of Figure 4-19.

You may use the icons provided together with the sources of this book. Copy the icons folder inside the *Source Packages* of the *Todo* project.

Non-Java files inside the *Source Packages* folder will be added by Apache NetBeans to the resulted application jar file that will be created inside the dist folder, and the application will be able to refer to them as *classpath* resources, no matter where the jar file is installed on the user machine. As a bonus, the application code doesn't have to worry about platform-specific details like path separators and drive letters.

To add a button to the toolbar, drag it from the palette onto the toolbar. Clear the *text* property and click on the ... button of the *icon* property to display the editor shown in Figure 4-24. Choose the appropriate package (icons) and the appropriate icon file.

Note   I use a convention to name the various widgets, called the *Hungarian notation*, which you are free to follow or not. In front of every widget's variable name, I add three letters that describe the widget. For example, I use btn for buttons, lbl for labels, tbl for tables, etc. As you can see in Figure 4-24, I have named the first button as btnAddTask.

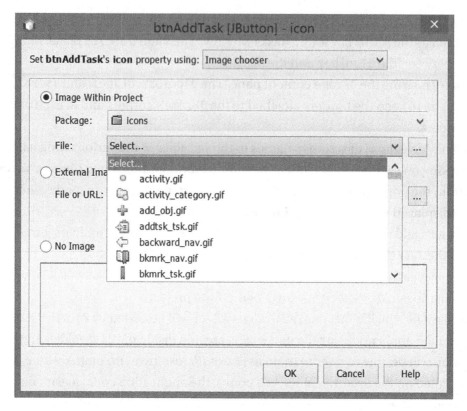

Figure 4-24. *Icon property editor*

NetBeans also provides a customizer to define the JTable's model property. Make sure to select the JTable widget from the *Navigator* window (and not the JScrollPane) and click on the ... button of its *model* property. The dialog box of Figure 4-25 appears. I have edited the columns to look like the application we wish to develop. However, this customization is only useful for prototyping, as in the real application the model will be created from real (Task) objects. Typically, the customization of JTables will require the development of custom Java classes like cell renderers and editors, column models, etc.

Finally, we need a menu bar. Go on and drag a *Menu Bar* widget from the palette on the top of the form. Use the *Navigator* window or click directly on the Menu Bar on the GUI designer to add the menus, as shown in Figure 4-26 (left as an exercise to the reader). You can choose between JMenuItem, JCheckBoxMenuItem, JRadioButtonMenuItem, JMenu, and JSeparator. You can also add *mnemonic*s by setting this property for the menu item (and/or the *accelerator* property). The *accelerator* is a key stroke that calls the action directly (e.g., F11 key in Figure 4-26). The *mnemonic* is a key stroke that accesses the menu item using the keyboard in combination with the `Alt` key. For example, you can access the `File` menu (not the underlying `F`) by pressing `Alt+F`.

tblTasks [JTable] - model
Set tblTasks's model property using: Table model customizer
Table Model
Table Settings
Default Values
Specify Title and Column Types Here:
Column
Title
Type
Editable
1
Priority
Integer
2
Description
String
3
Alert
Boolean
4
Due Date
String
Insert
Delete
Move Up
Move Down
Rows: 4
Columns: 4
OK
Reset to Default
Cancel
Help

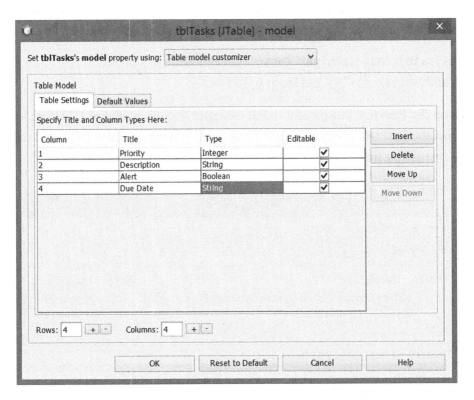

Figure 4-25. *JTable model customizer*

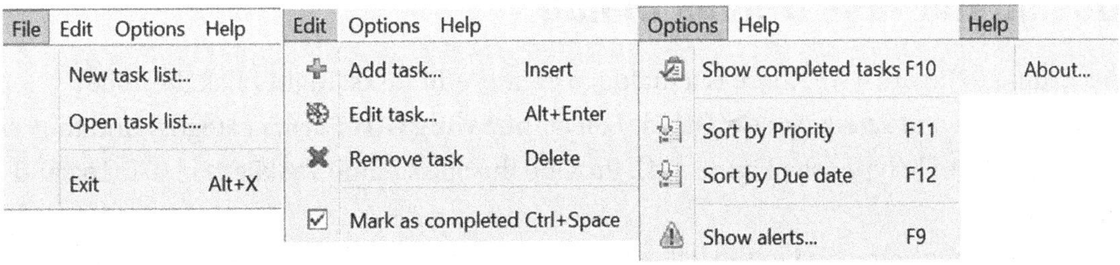

File Edit Options Help
New task list...
Open task list...
Exit Alt+X
Edit Options Help
Add task... Insert
Edit task... Alt+Enter
Remove task Delete
Mark as completed Ctrl+Space
Options Help
Show completed tasks F10
Sort by Priority F11
Sort by Due date F12
Show alerts... F9
Help
About...

Figure 4-26. *Complete menus for the TasksWindow form*

Click outside the form in *Design* view, then select the *[JFrame]* tree node (under *Form TasksWindow* tree) from the *Navigator* window, and change its *title* property to TasksWindow. You may also define an icon image to be used when the window is minimized (click on the *iconimage* property, click the **...** button and add a line like this):

```
new javax.swing.ImageIcon(getClass().getResource(
"/icons/addtsk_tsk.gif")).getImage()).
```

Click on the **Preview** button of the GUI designer's toolbar (Figure 4-7) in order to view how the TasksWindow will behave during runtime (see Figure 4-27). You can navigate the menus, interact with the JTable; the Preview is quite powerful.

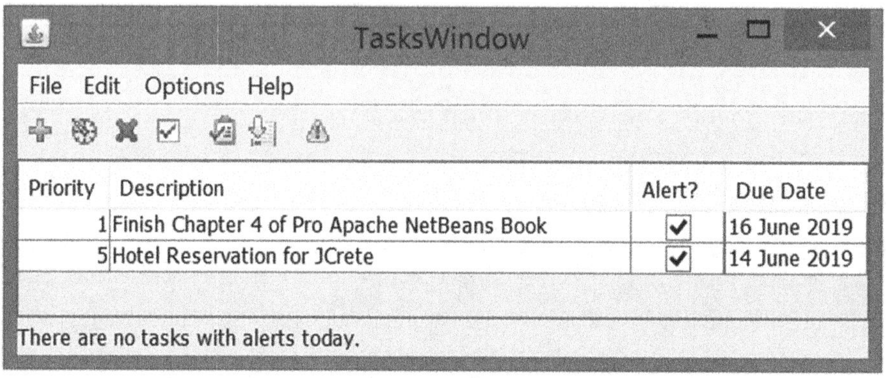

Figure 4-27. *The TasksWindow in Preview*

Design the Task Details Dialog

According to Figure 4-19, there is a dialog to create/edit tasks. Right-click the todo. view package and select **New ➤ Other**. Select the **Swing GUI Forms** category and the **JDialog Form** file type (see Figure 4-4). Provide the class name TaskDetailsDialog and press **Finish**.

Add a JLabel attached to the left, top, and right borders of the dialog, with no spacing; it will serve as a message area for validation errors and the like. Rename it to lblMessageArea (right-click it in the *Design* view, then select **Change Variable Name** from the pop-up menu) and set its *opaque* property and the *background* color so that it looks like a band at the top of the dialog. Also add an EmptyBorder (*border* property) so there's empty space around the text and the band's borders.

Next add three JLabels for the *description, priority,* and *due date* fields (edit the text labels to *Description, Priority,* and *Due Date* respectively and rename the variables to lblDescription, lblPriority, lblDueDate respectively). Attach all three to the left of the JDialog internal area (the drawing area). Leave some spacing between the components and the border. Resize the two shorter labels to attach their right borders to the right border of the larger one. Then select the three labels (with Shift + click) and change the *horizontalAlignment* property to RIGHT.

Then add a JTextField next to the *Description* label (rename it to txtDescription) and a JSpinner (rename it to spPriority) next to the *Priority* label. Make sure that the guidelines keep the label and the field baseline aligned. The JSpinner does not provide any property to set a preferred or minimum width, while the JTextField uses the *column* property for this. However, you can resize the JSpinner and Matisse will set the component's preferred size in pixels.

Note Sizing GUI components in pixels is not guaranteed to work well in different platforms, or if your users change the default Swing Look and Feel (L&F). Use this Matisse feature with care!

We need to restrict the task priority between 1 and 10. Select the JSpinner widget, and in the *Properties* window, first click on the ellipsis (**...**) button for the *value* property, choose **Custom code** from the combo box, and set spPriority.setValue(**1**). Then click on the *Code* button and select the ellipsis (**...**) button for the *Post Creation Code* property. Enter the code as shown in Figure 4-28 and click **OK**. Go to the *Source* view, right-click inside the editor, and **Fix Imports** to resolve the errors.

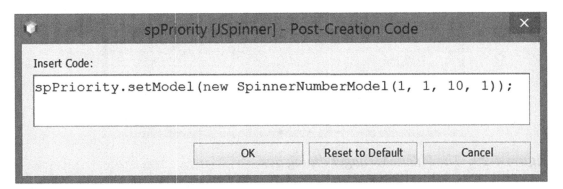

Figure 4-28. *The PaletteManager dialog box*

For the due date, we can use a JFormattedText to save the date, but we shall see how to use a Date Picker Swing component instead. There are a number of available solutions, for example: *JDatePicker* (https://sourceforge.net/projects/jdatepicker/), *JDateChooser* (http://plugins.netbeans.org/plugin/658/jdatechooser-1-2), *LGoodDatePicker* (https://github.com/LGoodDatePicker/LGoodDatePicker) and the not maintained anymore *SwingX JXDatePicker* from SwingLabs (http://www.java2s.com/Code/Jar/s/Downloadswingxall165jar.htm). Unfortunately, none of them stores the picked date using the latest java.time.LocalDateTime. We will see how to integrate *SwingX JXDatePicker* from SwingLabs (it is left as an exercise to integrate any of the others if you wish). Download it and extract it to a folder on your machine.

Right-click on the palette and select the *Palette Manager* from the context menu (see Figure 4-29).

Figure 4-29. *The PaletteManager dialog box*

Click on **New Category** button and give the name *SwingX*. Click the **Add from JAR** button, select the swingx-all-1.6.5.jar, from the location you downloaded previously, and click **Next**. In the next step, select all the available components and click **Next**. In the final step, choose the *SwingX* category you created earlier and click **Finish**. You just added a new category in the *Palette* that contains all the *SwingX* components.

Drag the JXDatePicker component on the TaskDetailsDialog form next to the *Due Date* label. Mainly, this is it. I let you explore the API of the widget to find out how to set the date format, if you are not happy with the default one, and how to get/set the date value.

Tip   OK, now that you learned the hard way, I must confess that there is an easier way. Once you have added the jar file of your library (e.g., swingx-all-1.6.5.jar) to your project (inside *Libraries* in the *Projects* tab), just expand the jar file, navigate to the class that is your widget, and drag it to your form. You don't need to add the widget beans to the palette. For example, dragging org.desktop.swingx.JXDatePicker.class on the TaskDetailsDialog form has the same effect as dragging it from the palette.

To aid accessibility, it's a good practice to set the *labelFor* property on a JLabel to describe which component the label is for. This can greatly enhance the performance of screen readers and other accessibility software.

Add a JLabel (label: Obs:, name: lblObs), a JScrollPane (name: spObs) and inside it add a JTextArea (name: txtaObs), a JCheckBox (text: Completed Task, name: chkCompleted), and four JButtons (text: Save, name: btnSave, text: Cancel, name: btnCancel, text: Clear, name: btnClear, text: Remove, name: btnRemove). The final TaskDetailsDialog form should look like the one in Figure 4-30.

Good UI design makes all buttons from a logical group the same size. Just select all desired buttons (actually you can select any control you want) and right-click any of the selected buttons. Then select **Same Size ➤ Same Width** and **Same Size ➤ Same Height** check-box menu items. The drawing area will indicate that the controls were configured to always have the same size.

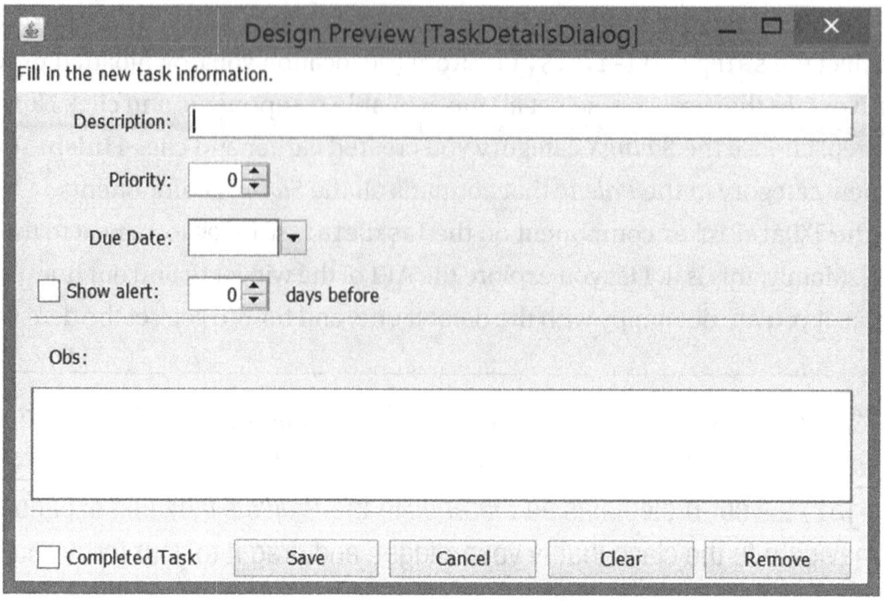

Figure 4-30. *The TaskDetailsDialog*

As an example of the **Connection mode** button, connect the *Clear* button with the txtDescription text field; when the *Clear* button is pressed (actionPerformed() event), the txtDescription.text property is called and clears its value. The above actions are translated to the code of Listing 4-1.

Listing 4-1. btnClearActionPerformed() method

```
private void btnClearActionPerformed(java.awt.event.ActionEvent evt) {
    txtDescription.setText("");
}
```

To complete our prototype, we need to add code to display the TaskDetailsDialog from the main window. Double-click the btnAddTask on the toolbar and make the changes shown in Listing 4-2 (alternatively, you may select it, click on the *Events* button in the *Properties* window, and select the down arrow in *actionPerformed* property).

Listing 4-2. AddTask actionPerformed() method

```java
public class TasksWindow extends javax.swing.JFrame {
    private final JDialog dlgTaskDetails = new TaskDetailsDialog(this, true);

    /**
     * Creates new form TasksWindow
     */
    public TasksWindow() {
        initComponents();
        dlgTaskDetails.pack();
    }

    private void btnAddTaskActionPerformed(java.awt.event.ActionEvent evt) {
        dlgTaskDetails.setVisible(true);
    }
}
```

> **Note**   Apache NetBeans also added an action listener to the `btnAddTask` component under the hood (inside `initComponents()` method) so that this method would be invoked at the correct time.

You may add similar methods for `TasksWindow.mnuAddTask` (don't forget the *DRY* principle and do some refactoring here) and `TaskDetailsDialog.btnClose`. Finally, you need to implement the `main()` method as shown in Listing 4-3.

Listing 4-3. Main.main() method

```java
public static void main(String[] args) {
    TasksWindow tasksWindow = new TasksWindow();
    tasksWindow.pack();
    tasksWindow.setVisible(true);
}
```

Our *Todo* prototype application is now complete, ready to be shown to your customers to get useful feedback before you begin implementing it.

As a final step, you can ask Matisse to automatically internationalize the application's UI. This means that for each resource that would normally be internationalized by hand, Matisse automatically adds the value supplied in the UI designer to a resource bundle. This is done for all UI elements. The visual localization feature works in harmony with automatic internationalization. Just right-click the root form node (TasksWindow) in the *Navigator* window, locate the **Design Locale** combo box in the *Properties* window (see Figure 4-31), and then select a locale or add a new one (see Figure 4-32). Check the **Automatic Internationalization** check box in the *Properties* window, too. Once the **Design Locale** is selected, you can now simply edit the text in the UI as if normally editing a form. The localization for the *Design Locale* takes place automatically with the values entered into the UI. The locale can be changed and the form reedited to set the values for the newly selected locale. It is as simple as it sounds to create a fully internationalized UI with Apache NetBeans (see Figure 4-33) to satisfy your customers throughout the globe.

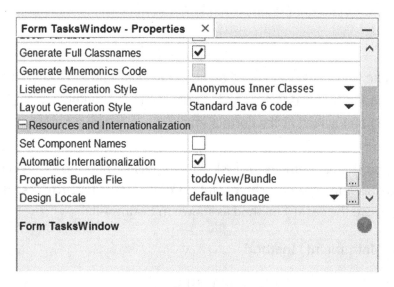

Figure 4-31. *Automatic Internationalization*

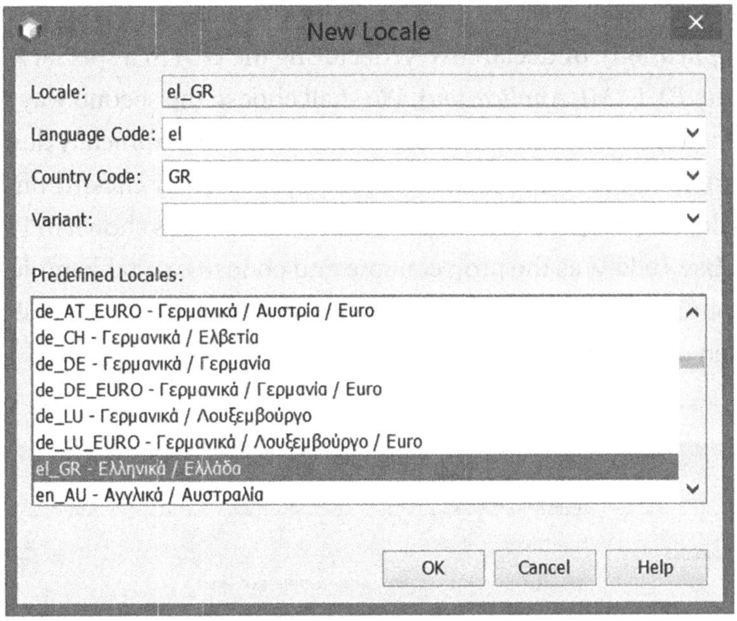

Figure 4-32. *New Locale dialog box*

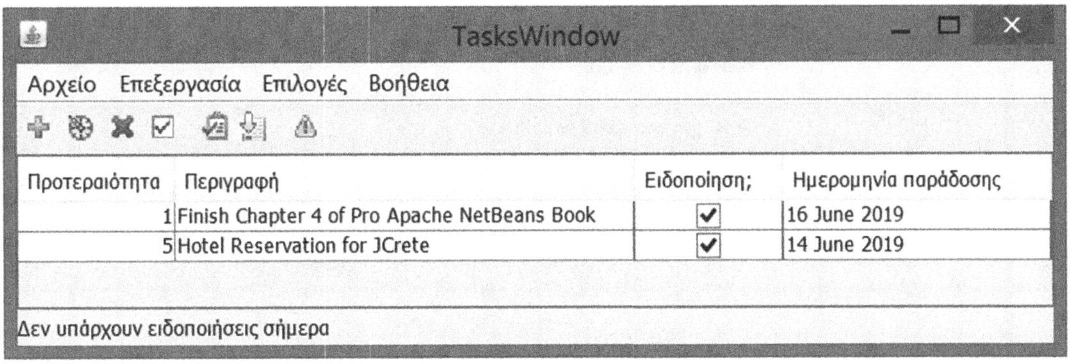

Figure 4-33. *Automatic internationalization of your UI*

Developing a JavaFX Application

We shall develop the *Todo* application of Figure 4-19 in JavaFX, too. We shall use a
JDK with integrated JavaFX such as JDK 8 or 10. We shall see how to develop JavaFX
applications with JDKs without JavaFX later.

There are two ways to develop a JavaFX application, either programmatically, using Java (*JavaFX Application*); or declaratively, declaring the GUI in a special XML format, called FXML (*JavaFX FXML Application*). We shall choose the second way here, which has also the advantage that you can use the *SceneBuilder* to graphically design the GUI.

Let's get started. Create a new *JavaFX FXML Application* by clicking on **File ➤ New Project**, selecting the **Java with Ant ➤ JavaFX** category as shown in Figure 4-16, and click **Next**. Use TodoFX as the project name and choose a suitable project location (anywhere in your hard disk). Modify the rest of the dialog box entries as shown in Figure 4-34. Then click **Finish**.

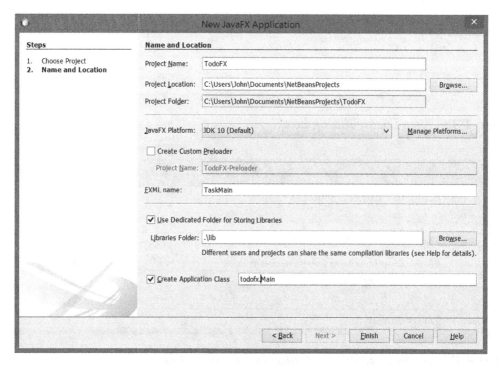

Figure 4-34. *New JavaFX application wizard*

The *TodoFX* project's layout is shown in Figure 4-35.

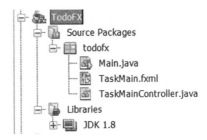

Figure 4-35. *New JavaFX application wizard*

You can easily identify Main, the .fxml file that represents the main view (the tasks list in our case) and the respective TaskMainController. NetBeans saves you development steps by creating all these for you. You don't need to create the view and the controller separately; they are created in a single step! Run the project; you should see a similar application like in Figure 4-36.

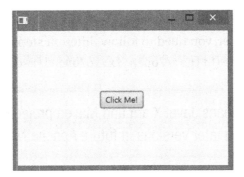

Figure 4-36. *Sample JavaFX application*

Apache NetBeans has created a full-blown sample JavaFX application for you. Double-click on TaskMain.fxml; the file will open inside *SceneBuilder* (see Figure 4-37).

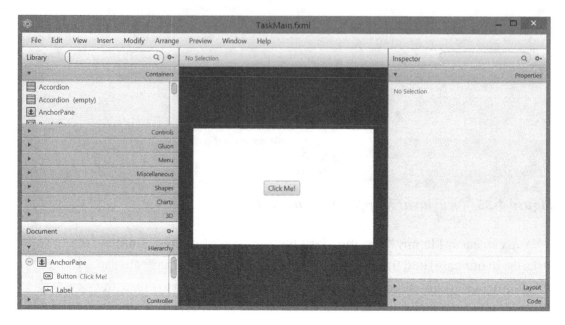

Figure 4-37. *SceneBuilder open from NetBeans*

If you need to create a JavaFX project using a JDK that doesn't include JavaFX, like, for example, JDK 11 and later, you need to follow different steps as described in the *JavaFX and NetBeans* article (`https://openjfx.io/openjfx-docs/#IDE-NetBeans`).

Note   The Apache NetBeans JavaFX ant and Maven projects will be fixed to work correctly with JDK 11 and later versions in future Apache NetBeans versions.

With *Scenebuilder* you can quickly design your GUI by using a simple drag and drop of widgets, in a similar way that Matisse allows you to build Swing GUIs.

As this is not a book about JavaFX though, if you wish to develop *TodoFX* application, please follow this tutorial (`http://wiki.netbeans.org/TodoFX`).

Conclusion

In this chapter you learned how to develop Java Desktop Applications using the Apache NetBeans IDE. NetBeans allows you to build desktop applications using either AWT, or Swing or JavaFX. To develop Swing applications, Apache NetBeans provides a very advanced GUI Builder that has the code name *Matisse*. We saw the capabilities of Matisse and actually saw how to build a prototype application with it.

For more information about how to use the Matisse GUI Builder please refer to Chapter 11 of the "Developing Applications with NetBeans IDE" (`https://docs.oracle.com/netbeans/nb82/netbeans/NBDAG/toc.htm`) guide.

We also saw how we can integrate the *SceneBuilder* with NetBeans in order to develop JavaFX applications. Apache NetBeans provides GUI builders to build web applications, too. But let's wait until the next chapter.

CHAPTER 5

Apache NetBeans Java EE Development

Java EE support has been included with Apache NetBeans since release 11.0. Prior to this release, Java EE support had to be added to Apache NetBeans 9.0+ as a plugin, since it was still licensed under Oracle. If the plugin was added, the functionality for developing, debugging, and maintaining Java EE was the same in Apache NetBeans 9.0 as it is in release 11.0 and beyond. The support provides the ability to add application server containers that can be managed from within the IDE. Full support for Maven web applications and Java EE technologies such as Enterprise JavaBeans (EJB), Contexts and Dependency Injection (CDI), and JavaServer Faces (JSF) allows developers the convenience of auto-completion, code fragments, and easy syntax recognition. The bottom line is that Apache NetBeans is a tremendous tool for development of Java EE applications ... both older and modern.

In this chapter, we'll take a look at the support, in detail, that Apache NetBeans provides for Java Enterprise development. You will learn how to manage containers from within the IDE, develop back-end business logic, and Java Persistence API (JPA) queries. In the end, you will have a basic understanding of the conveniences provided by Apache NetBeans for full stack Java EE development.

Configuring Server Containers

Before you can associate application projects with a container for deployment or testing, you must register one or more application server containers for use by Apache NetBeans. It is a good idea to register a container with Apache NetBeans even in the case where you are developing microservices that will be deployed to a container,

© Ioannis Kostaras, Constantin Drabo, Josh Juneau, Sven Reimers, Mario Schröder, Geertjan Wielenga 2020
I. Kostaras et al., *Pro Apache NetBeans*, https://doi.org/10.1007/978-1-4842-5370-0_5

such as Payara Micro or Wildfly. Note that it is good practice to only configure application server containers for development purposes within Apache NetBeans, and not for deployment to production containers.

To add a local or remote application server container to Apache NetBeans, perform the following tasks:

1. Navigate to the **Services** window and right-click on the **Servers** menu selection. Click **Add Server**, as shown in Figure 5-1.

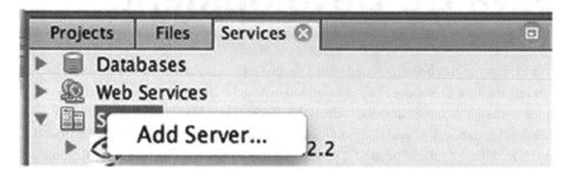

Figure 5-1. *Add Application Server Container to Apache NetBeans IDE*

2. When the Add Server Instance dialog appears, choose the server type that you wish to add (Figure 5-2).

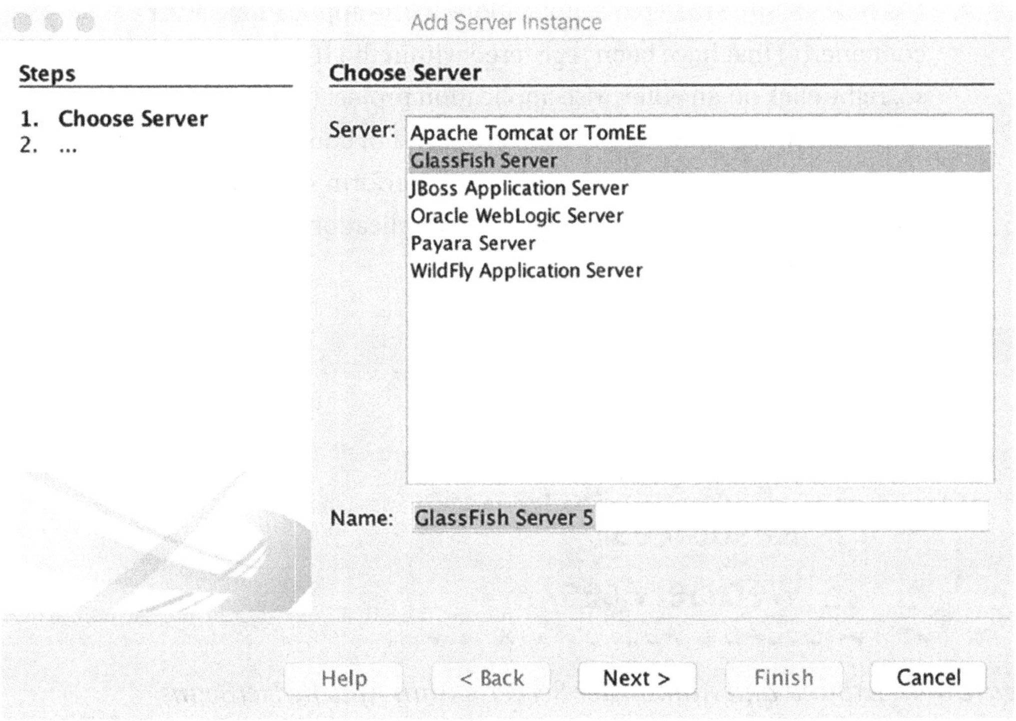

Figure 5-2. *Add Server Instance*

3. On the next screen, enter the path to the application server installation that you would like to configure within Apache NetBeans (Figure 5-3). Once you have chosen the location, click the Finish button.

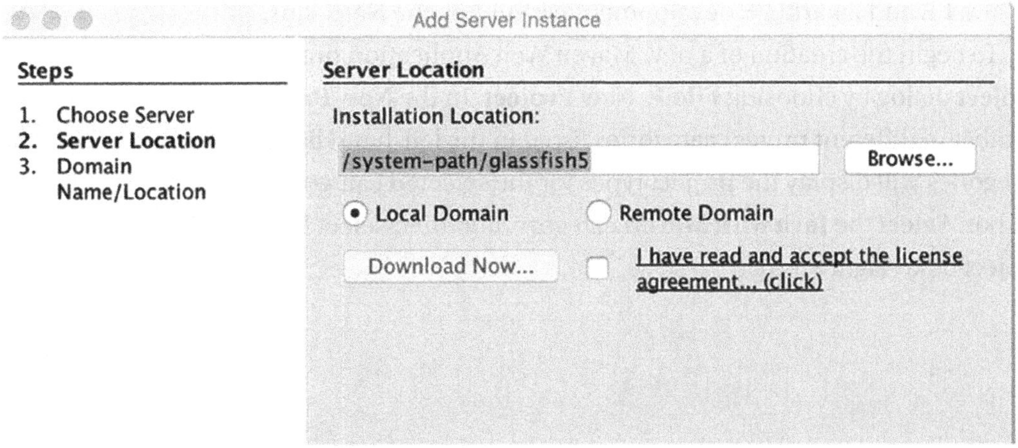

Figure 5-3. *Set Server Location*

4. It is now possible to deploy applications to the application server container(s) that have been registered within the IDE. To do so, right-click on an enterprise application project (Maven Web Application, etc.) and then specify the server of choice within the project properties. Note that you can also perform some basic application server tasks by selecting the application server from within the Servers window (Figure 5-4).

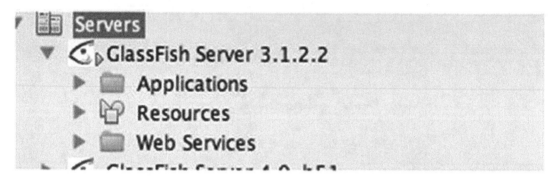

Figure 5-4. *Expand and Administer Server within Apache NetBeans*

Creating a Maven Web Application

There are a variety of configurations from which to choose for the creation of Java Enterprise projects within Apache NetBeans. This chapter covers the creation of Maven Web Applications in detail, which is the de facto standard and default project selection for Java EE and Jakarta EE development within Apache NetBeans.

To begin the creation of a new Maven Web Application project, open the **New Project** dialog by choosing **File ➤ New Project**. In the **New Project** dialog, you will see a number of different project categories listed in the left-hand list box. Selecting one of the categories will display the project types for the selected category within the right-hand list box. Select the **Java with Maven** category, and then select **Web Application** as the project type (Figure 5-5).

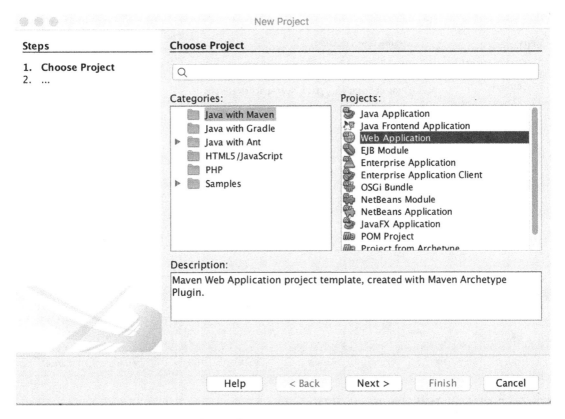

Figure 5-5. *New Maven Web Application*

Note   The **Java with Maven** category allows the creation of projects using the old-style Java EE and J2EE configurations such as **EJB Module** and **Enterprise Application**. In most cases, these projects are no longer being used for creating new applications. However, they remain supported by Apache NetBeans.

After a project type is chosen and **Next** is clicked, the **New Web Application** dialog will open. Enter a project name and location, as shown in Figure 5-6. Once finished, choose **Next**.

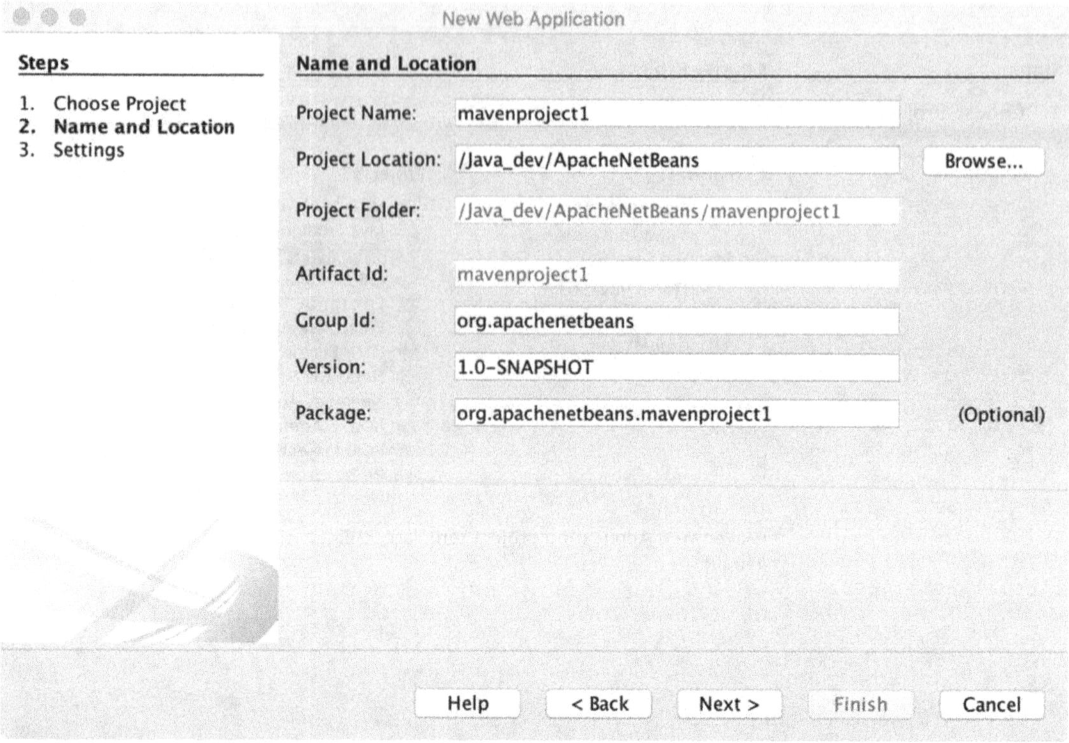

Figure 5-6. *New Web Application Dialog*

In the Server and Settings screen, choose the application server container that you wish to use for development purposes (see Configuring Application Servers in NetBeans), along with the Java EE version that you wish to use. If you plan to use CDI, then select the designated check box (Figure 5-7).

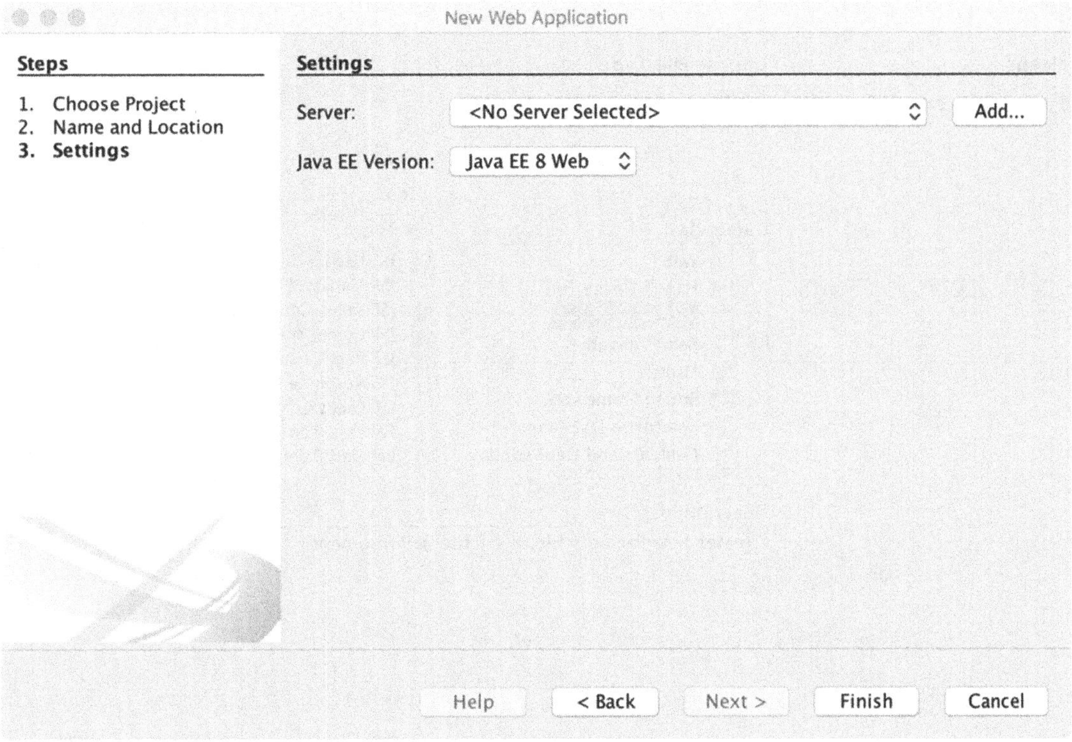

Figure 5-7. *Setting the Application Server Container*

Developing JSF Applications

Utilizing the Apache NetBeans IDE, it is easy to develop JSF applications due to the wizards and file recognition. In this section, we will walk through the development of a JSF application from a standard Maven Web Application project. Therefore, if you haven't done so already, utilize the information in the previous section to create a bare-bones project.

Creating JSF Application Files

If you wish to create JSF views, then right-click on the **Web Pages** node, and if you wish to create a Java source file for JSF, right-click on the **Source Packages** node. Right-clicking on the appropriate node ensures that the files are generated within the correct project area. From within the context menu, choose **New**, and then **Other...** in order to open the New File dialog. Within the dialog, choose JavaServer Faces from the "Categories" list box to open the JSF file types within the left-side list box (Figure 5-8). In this example, right-click on **Web Pages** and create a new JSF Page.

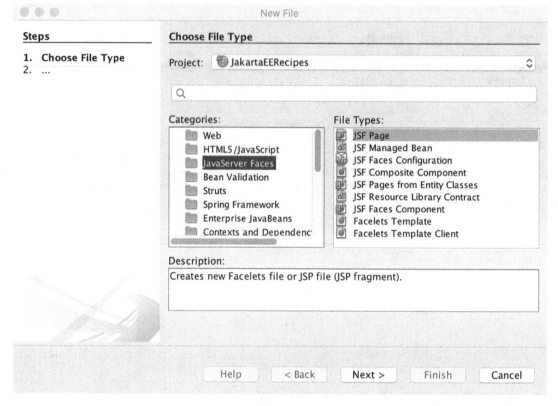

Figure 5-8. *Create JSF File*

The JSF file types include the following options:

- JSF Page

- JSF Managed Bean (This creates a CDI Controller when using Java EE 7+)

- JSF Faces Configuration

- JSF Composite Component

- JSF Resource Library Contract

- JSF Pages from Entity Classes

- JSF Faces Component

- Faces Template

- Faces Template Client

Note   As of Java EE 7+ and Jakarta EE 8, you should not be creating JSF Managed Beans any longer. This is because the JSF Managed Bean technology is being deprecated in favor of CDI beans. Therefore, the JSF Managed Bean option creates a CDI Controller.

After clicking **Next**, the JSF Page file selection opens a dialog that can be used to generate a new JSF Page (Figure 5-9). The dialog allows one to choose a file location and name, and it also contains the ability to apply different options for the page type. The page type options include Facelets (default), JSP File, or JSP Segment. The examples throughout this chapter use the Facelets page type.

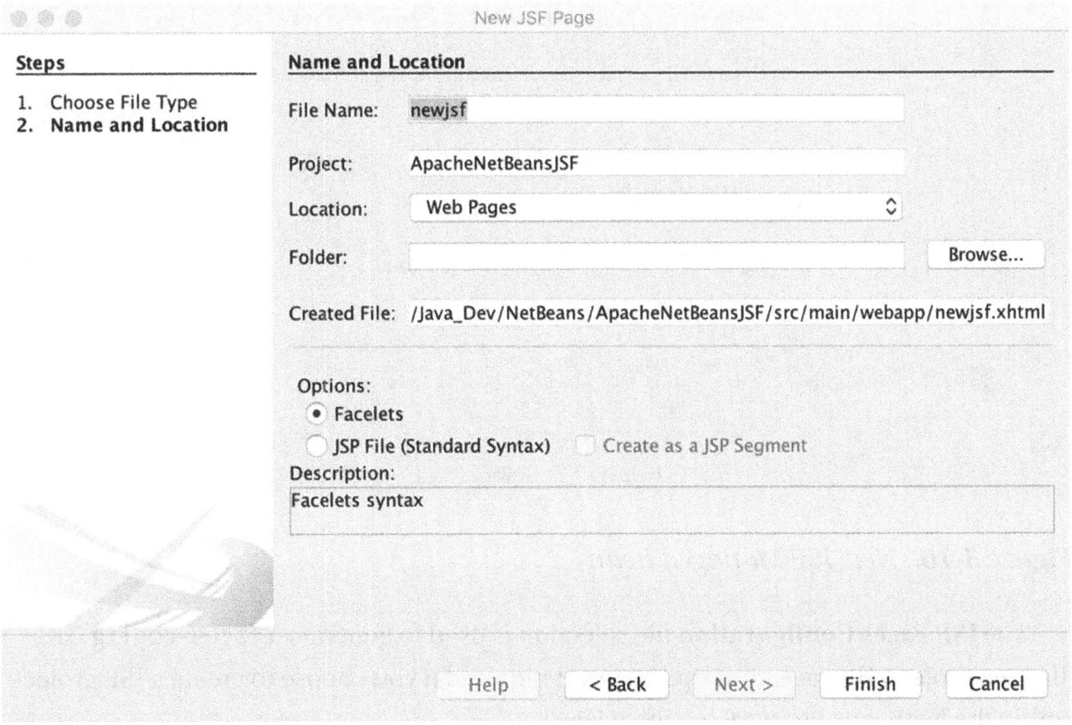

Figure 5-9. *New JSF Page Dialog*

The JSF Managed Bean file selection opens a dialog that allows one to generate a CDI Managed Bean controller class (Figure 5-10). The dialog provides the ability to add the bean data to the `faces-config.xml` file, if desired, as well as choose the scope of the bean.

Note   The `faces-config.xml` (JSF Faces Configuration) file is not generated by default, as it is not a required file for a JSF project. However, it can be added using the **Other...**, JavaServer Faces context menu.

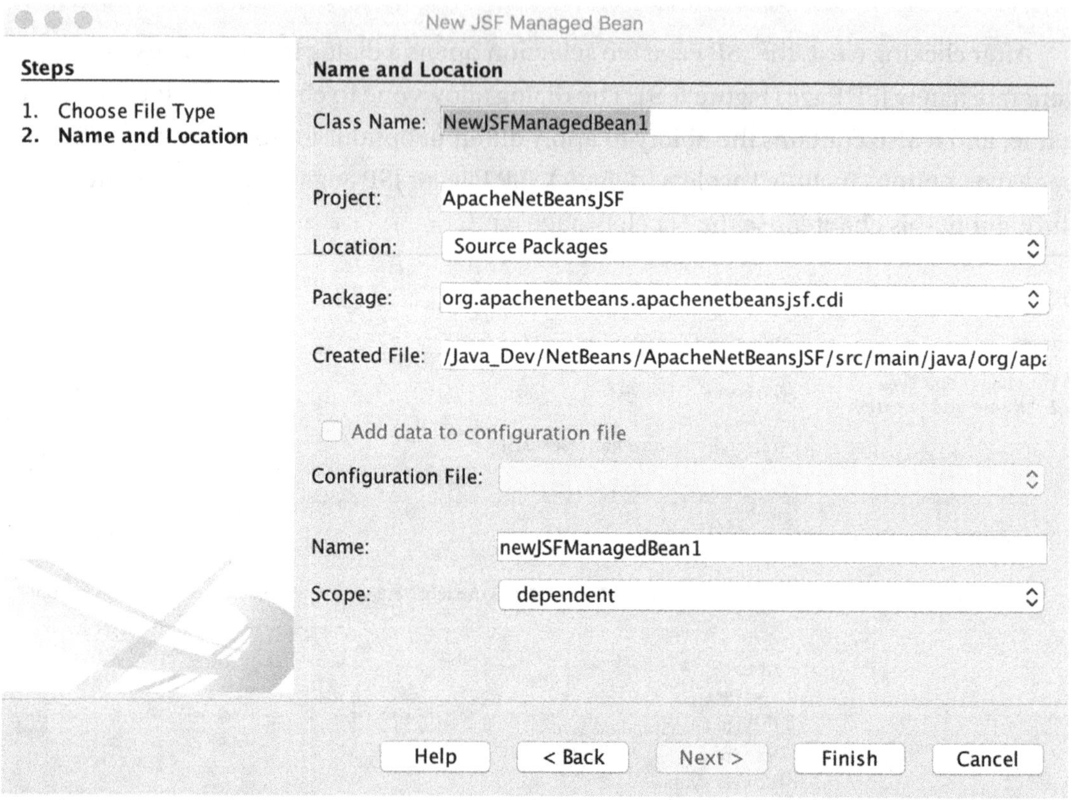

Figure 5-10. *New JSF Managed Bean*

The **JSF Faces Configuration** file selection is used to generate a `faces-config.xml` file for a project. However, this option is not required if you choose to create a JSF project within the NetBeans Project Creation wizard.

The **JSF Composite Component** file selection opens a dialog that can be used to create a composite component file. The dialog does not provide many options other than the ability to choose a file location and name. The generated file contains the skeleton of a composite component, as listed in the following lines:

```
<?xml version='1.0' encoding='UTF-8' ?>
<!DOCTYPE html PUBLIC "-//W3C//DTD XHTML 1.0 Transitional//EN"
"http://www.w3.org/TR/xhtml1/
DTD/xhtml1-transitional.dtd">
<html xmlns="http://www.w3.org/1999/xhtml"
xmlns:cc="http://xmlns.jcp.org/jsf/composite">
  <!-- INTERFACE -->
  <cc:interface>
  </cc:interface>
  <!-- IMPLEMENTATION -->
  <cc:implementation>
  </cc:implementation>
</html>
```

The **JSF Pages from Entity Classes** file selection can be quite powerful in that it allows you to choose an Entity Class from which to generate one or more JSF pages, resulting in the page(s) being bound to the entity class for generation and update of those entity records. In order to use this option, the project must contain at least one entity class.

Developing Entity Classes

The Apache NetBeans IDE provides facilities to help develop Entity Bean classes, either manually or based upon a selected database table. To access the entity class wizards, right-click a project's *Source Packages* folder to open the context menu, and then choose **New ➤ Other** to open the **New File** dialog. Once it is open, choose the *Persistence* category from the left-side list box to display the file types in the right-side list box (Figure 5-11).

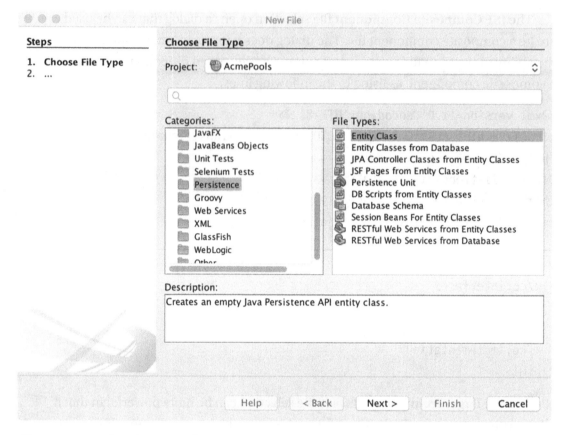

Figure 5-11. *Persistence File Types*

The *Entity Class* file type allows you to generate a blank entity class. The *Entity Classes from Database* file type allows you to create entity class(es) based upon the selected database tables. In doing so, all of the requisite code for mapping the entity class(es) to the selected database tables are automatically generated for you.

Using Java Persistence Query Language (JPQL)

Apache NetBeans includes a feature that allows one to query a database utilizing the Java Persistence Query Language (JPQL) syntax. This can be quite helpful for those who are using JPQL in their EJB session beans or RESTful web services. To utilize the JPQL query tool, expand an Apache NetBeans web project that contains a `persistence.xml` configuration file in the project's *Configuration Files* directory. Then perform the following steps:

1. Right-click the `persistence.xml` configuration file to open the context menu.

2. Click **Run JPQL Query** to open the tool (Figure 5-12), type the query, and click the **Run** button on the upper right-hand side of the query editor.

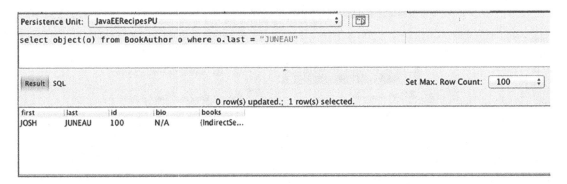

Figure 5-12. *JPQL Tool*

Note   To add a persistence.xml configuration file for JPA configuration, right-click on the project and choose: **Other...**, **Persistence**, **Persistence Unit**.

Deploying and Debugging

The Apache NetBeans IDE makes the development life cycle for enterprise applications very easy. To deploy and test a Maven Web Application, ensure that a local application server container target that is registered within Apache NetBeans is set correctly within the "Run" tab of the project properties. Once set, a project can be deployed by right-clicking on the project and choosing "**Run**" from the contextual menu. Once chosen, the project WAR file is deployed to the target application server if everything is compiled correctly, and the application is opened in the default browser.

Note   A different default browser can be configured for each project within
Apache NetBeans by selecting the browser in the toolbar (Figure 5-13).

Figure 5-13.   *Choosing Default Browser*

To debug a project, right-click on the project and choose "**Debug**" from the
contextual menu. This will cause the target application server container to start in
"Debug" mode, and the project WAR file will be deployed accordingly. When the
application server is started in debug mode, breakpoints can be set within the project
and watches can also be configured, just as is the case with standard Java SE applications.
Please refer to Chapter 6 for more details on debugging and profiling applications.

Other Java EE Support Features

The Apache NetBeans 11.0 IDE contains support for a number of file types to aid the
development of Java EE applications. There have been a number of wizards covered
previously in this chapter, and in this section, we will take a brief look at some of the file
support.

By right-clicking on a project package, then choosing "**New**" ➤ "**Other**" the "*New File*" dialog appears. This dialog contains a number of categories, including "Web," "HTML5/JavaScript," "Bean Validation," and "Contexts and Dependency Injection" to name a few. Inside each of these categories are a number of file options. Each of the supported file types includes auto-complete for the syntax, color coding, and nice formatting.

Perhaps the most widely used category is the "Web" category. In this category are the following file types (geared toward front-end development):

- JSP

- JSF

- Servlet

- Filter

- Web Application Listener

- WebSocket Endpoint

- HTML

- XHTML

- Cascading Style Sheet

- JavaScript

- Json

- Tag Libraries

Some of the file types will be placed into the "Web Pages" folder of a web project, while others will create Java source files or XML configuration. Each of the file types in this section are geared toward front-end development.

Other file type categories that are geared toward enterprise development include the following:

- HTML/JavaScript

- JavaServer Faces

- Bean Validation

- Struts

- Spring Framework

- Enterprise JavaBeans

- Contexts and Dependency Injection

- Selenium Test

- Persistence

- Web Services

- GlassFish

- WebLogic

- Other

Summary

The Apache NetBeans IDE includes exceptional support for Java EE applications. It is easy to build a Java EE project from the ground up, with options for generating front-end, back-end, and configuration files. By adding a container for deployment, the IDE allows for easy debugging and deploy-on-save options. Apache NetBeans helps boost productivity for beginner and advanced enterprise developers alike.

CHAPTER 6

Debugging and Profiling

Debugging and profiling are probably the two most important things, besides writing code, for which you can use Apache NetBeans. Debugging is the art of figuring out problems and their root causes. Apache NetBeans provides a very feature-rich debugging environment from multiple sessions to multiple languages. If debugging makes your code right, profiling will make it run fast. Apache NetBeans contains one of the most advanced profiling engines for memory and CPU profiling based on the JFluid technology developed by Sun Microsystems. Although Apache NetBeans supports debugging for a lot of different programming languages and project types, this chapter focuses on support for the JVM and the Java Language.

Debugging
Getting Started

Starting a debugging session is simple. As an example, we use the Anagram Game sample provided by NetBeans. Just select *New Project*, go to the *Samples* category expand *Java* in the tree, and select *Anagram Game* in the *Project* list. Once you have it opened, just press the *Debug Project* button in the toolbar or use the menu item from the context menu of the project node. Besides just running a project in the debugger, Apache NetBeans also supports attaching a debugger to a running process. There are different attachment modes: *ProcessAttach*, *SocketAttach*, or *SocketListen*. Depending on the installed plugins, it will be possible to select different debuggers as well; for example, gdb if C++ plugins are available.

The dialog for attaching a debugger is shown in Figure 6-1.

© Ioannis Kostaras, Constantin Drabo, Josh Juneau, Sven Reimers, Mario Schröder, Geertjan Wielenga 2020
I. Kostaras et al., *Pro Apache NetBeans*, https://doi.org/10.1007/978-1-4842-5370-0_6

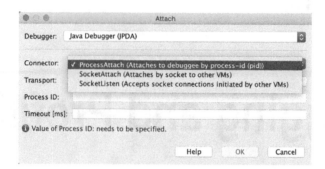

Figure 6-1. *Attach debugger to running process*

Once the debugger is running, Apache NetBeans automatically shows two additional views, the *Debugging* view and the *Variables* view. The *Debugging* view is used to display all threads running (or paused) in the debugged process. The *Variables* view displays information about variables in the actual context, once the debugger stops. An example of NetBeans showing the initial debugger experience can be seen in Figure 6-2.

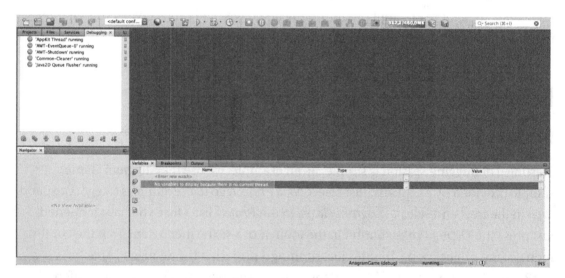

Figure 6-2. *Initial debugging experience*

Note   If any of the screenshots show windows that are not immediately visible to you, this is typically caused by window presets differing from the default (e.g., caused by usage of your IDE). To open the necessary window, just select *Window* from the main menu and select the corresponding item from the *Debugging* submenu.

In addition to the two views, Apache NetBeans shows the *Debug* toolbar. This toolbar provides access to all the necessary actions to control the debugging session. Besides the toolbar, all actions can also be triggered via the *Debug* main menu item or selected ones using the keyboard. All buttons to control the debugging workflow can be seen in Figure 6-3.

Figure 6-3. *Debugging toolbar*

The actions from left to right are the following:

- **Finish Debugger Session (⇧-F5)**. Ends the debugging session by either detaching from or killing the debugged process, depending on the mode the debugger is used in.

- **Pause Debugger Session**. Suspends all running threads of the debugged process.

- **Continue Debugger Session (F5)**. Resumes all paused threads.

- **Step over (F8)**. Moves the execution pointer to the next line.

- **Step over Expression (⇧-F8)**. Moves the execution pointer one expression further.

- **Step into (F7)**. Moves the execution pointer one stack-level down, that is, steps into the method call in this line. If multiple method calls are available, the exact method call can be selected.

- **Step out (⌘+F7)**. Moves the execution pointer one stack-level up, that is, steps out from the actual method debugged.

- **Run to Cursor (F4)**. Moves the execution pointer to the line that the cursor is positioned on.

- **Apply Code Changes**. Compiles the code in the active editor tab and pushes the changed code to the JVM. In addition, the execution pointer may be moved up the stack, to accommodate the new code.

- **Toggle Pause in GraalVM Script**. Schedules a suspend with regard to the Truffle multi-language integration. To use this action, NetBeans must run on GraalVM.

- **Take GUI Snapshot**. Takes a snapshot of the current state of the Swing component graph for interactive inspection and modification.

The last thing needed to have a real debugging session is a *Breakpoint*. A breakpoint defines where the debugger will automatically suspend the thread, which happens to run past the defined breakpoint. The simplest way to create a new breakpoint is to either click into the gutter of the editor on the correct line, or press ⌘-**F8** (in Mac) or Ctrl+F8 (on Windows/Linux) with the cursor being on the line where the debugger should suspend the execution. The same actions can be taken to remove a breakpoint, that is, the action triggered is called *Toggle Breakpoint*. Once a breakpoint is created, it is marked in the gutter with a special symbol. This can be seen in Figure 6-4.

```
70
71  ⊟        /** Creates new form Anagrams */
72  ⊟        public Anagrams() {
              wordLibrary = WordLibrary.getDefault();
74
75            initComponents();
76            getRootPane().setDefaultButton(guessButton);
77            scrambledWord.setText(wordLibrary.getScrambledWord(wordIdx));
```

Figure 6-4. *Debugging toolbar*

The Debugging View

Starting with the simple breakpoint shown in Figure 6-4, we start a new debugging session, and as expected, the debugger stops at line 73 in the Anagrams class. The debugging view will show by default the suspended thread with call stack information, as can be seen in Figure 6-5.

Figure 6-5. *Debugging view*

On the bottom of the view are a couple of buttons to control the behavior of the view (options). From left to right, they are:

- **Show less**. Toggles which threads are shown in the view. By default, only the suspended threads are shown, but you can toggle between all threads and suspended threads only using this button.

- **Show thread groups**. Toggles the visibility of thread groups, which switches the list-style view to a tree-style view and groups the visible threads by their thread group.

- **Show suspend/resume table**. Toggles the visibility of the column on the right-hand side of the view, displaying the actual state of the thread, that is, paused or running.

- **Show system threads**. Toggles the visibility of system threads. By default, system threads are hidden.

- **Show monitors**. Toggles the display of monitors (locks) obtained by a thread. By default, monitors are not shown.

131

- **Show qualified names**. Toggles the display of full qualified class names. This can be helpful to identify where a specific class showing up in the displayed stack is really coming from.

- **Sort by suspended / resumed state**. Toggles sort ordering of the thread list according to their state.

- **Sort by name**. Toggles sort ordering of thread list according to their name.

- **Sort by default**. Switches to default sort order (sorted by name).

Besides the options that are available to configure the view, the view also allows interaction with the threads. The first thing to control is thread state. By clicking on the buttons shown on the right-hand side of the view, running threads can be suspended and suspended threads can be resumed. This may be helpful once the application really requires multiple threads during debugging, and it is necessary to suspend the threads as needed to ensure correct application state. In addition, multiple threads often stop at breakpoints, which are currently not interesting (but still required to be active). Using these controls, those threads can be resumed.

Another interesting technique is to investigate the state at different frames in the call stack. The active frame is highlighted in bold (as shown in Figure 6-5) and can be changed by either double-clicking onto another stack frame entry or by using the context menu item *Make Current* of a stack frame.

The context menu of a stack frame has an additional interesting feature. Besides just inspecting the stack at a different frame, the menu item *Pop To Here* allows it to unwind the stack up to the selected stack frame. This is a nice little helper, since it allows retrying code fragments – especially if they do not modify the state.

If the context menu is invoked not directly on the call stack entries, you get some additional helper actions. Two of them are straightforward, *Resume All Threads*, and *Suspend All Threads*, but the third is more interesting. The *Check for Deadlock* tool is very useful for addressing tricky multi-threaded situations, where deadlocks are often difficult to detect and debug.

There is more hidden in the *Debugging* view, but we look into this later in the context of multi-session debugging.

Now let's start stepping through the code. Stepping into code will take us to the WordLibrary. Apache NetBeans will automatically open a new tab to show the source code of the WorldLibary class and stops again. This situation is shown in Figure 6-6.

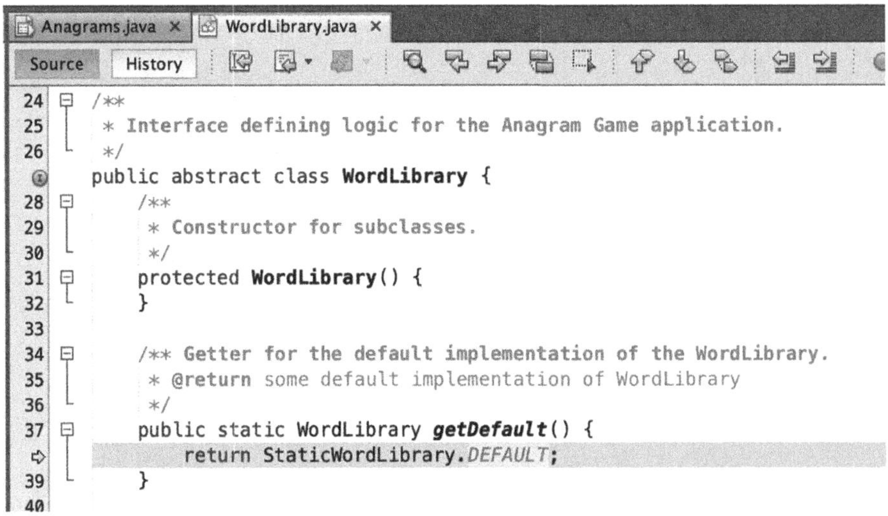

Figure 6-6. *Multiple editor tabs for debugging*

Expression Evaluation

Now let's assume we are interested in what StaticWordLibrary.DEFAULT is all about. Hovering with the mouse over DEFAULT, a tooltip shows up displaying basic information as seen in Figure 6-7.

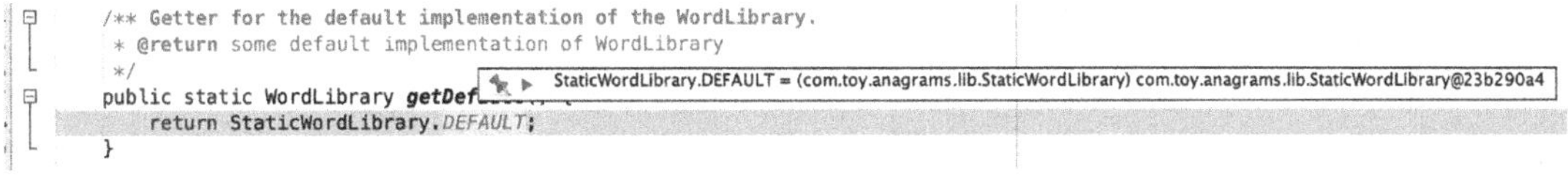

Figure 6-7. *Tooltip for evaluation*

If we want to know more details, just click on the little arrow in front of the text, and you will get a structured view of the object evaluated by hovering. You can drill deeper by following the displayed tree structure and can finally see the words used, as shown in Figure 6-8.

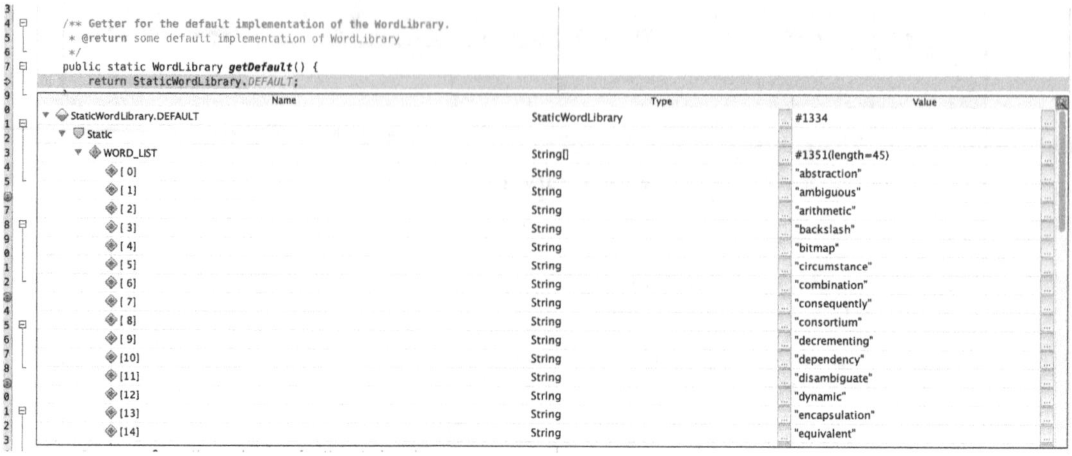

Figure 6-8. *Tooltip for evaluation (expanded)*

This type of evaluation allows for a fast drill down into details of an object state. It can even be used to change the state. Just click in the right colum (value) for a field with a simple type, for example, `String`, and type a new value and hit **Enter**. This will change the value of the field to the entered value.

Another helpful shortcut is the possibility to highlight a piece of code and get a tooltip with the result. Step further through the code until you reach the `StaticWordLibrary` again and the debugger stops for you in line 147. Now select the `SCRAMBLED_WORD_LIST(idx)` and hover with the mouse. A tooltip shows up as can be seen in Figure 6-9.

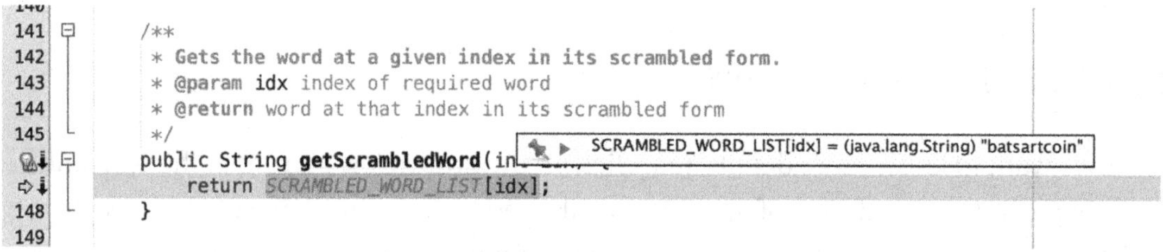

Figure 6-9. *Tooltip for expression evaluation*

If you look close enough, there is a pin shown before the arrow icon. Clicking the pin (symbol/icon) pins the expression evaluation into the source code. So, whenever you come back to the file, the expression is automatically reevaluated by the debugger, and the result is shown and kept current. A pinned evaluation expression is shown in Figure 6-10.

```
158    /**
159     * Checks whether a user's guess for a word at the given index is correct.
160     * @param idx index of the word guessed
161     * @param userGuess the user's guess for the actual word
162     * @return true if the guess was correct; false otherwise
163     */
        public boolean isCorrect(int idx, Strin┌─ getWord(idx) = (String) "abstractions" ··· ⊙ ×
            return userGuess.equals(getWord(idx));
166    }
```

Figure 6-10. *Pinned expression evaluation*

In addition to the expression evaluation as part of the source code editor, there is
a special view, which can be opened using **⌘+F9** (on Mac) or Ctrl+F9 (on Windows/
Linux) or from the main menu in the *Debug* menu. It displays an area where you can
enter arbitrary code, which can be evaluated by either pressing CTRL-⏎ or clicking on
the button on the lower-right corner. The arbitrary code example can be a complex code
snippet covering multiple lines. The result of the evaluation is shown in the *Variables*
view in Figure 6-11.

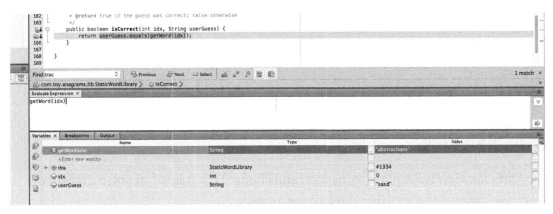

Figure 6-11. *Evaluate Expression and Variables view*

The code editor area is aware of the actual debugging context, that is, it offers
completion for visible fields and methods from the context and even supports code
completion during writing code. In case you need some code snippet you already used
before, there is a button in the upper-right corner showing the last-used code snippets
from the *Evaluate Expression* view.

The code snippets evaluated cannot only be used to read data but also write changes
back to the debugged application. This can be very helpful if it is necessary to change the
state of a debugged application, for example, after applying a code fragment, to ensure

a correct retry of the code. A complete history of the evaluated expressions can also be seen in the *Evaluation Result* view shown in Figure 6-12.

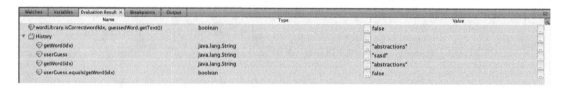

Figure 6-12. *Evaluation Result view*

In contrast to the *Evaluation Result* view that shows multiple results all at the same time, the *Variables* view in Figure 6-11 shows only the latest evaluated expression on top of all other information.

Let's have a more detailed look at this view, as shown in Figure 6-13.

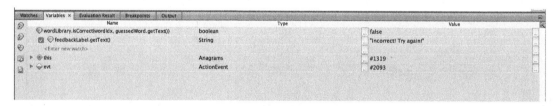

Figure 6-13. *Variables view*

Variables View

The *Variables* view is the place to inspect (and change) the state of all objects reached during debugging. It is split into three major areas.

First, the evaluation result of the code snippet from the *Evaluate Expression* view is shown (pinkish icon).

Second, there is a list of watches shown (blue icon). *Watches* are a kind of persistent shortcut to simple evaluation results, for example, some special field that is some levels down the hierarchy in the list of variables that can be made statically visible, despite the variable list refreshing during debugger context changes, for example, leaving a class during debugging. If you temporarily do not need the watches to be updated anymore, it is possible to disable each watch by deselecting the check box in front of the displayed watch.

Third, the list of variables, for example, *this* and *local variables*, is shown (green icon). Like other views, the *Variables* view can also be customized. The customization can be done by using one of the buttons on the left-hand side of the view. From top to bottom:

- **Show Evaluation Result inside Variable View**. Toggles the visibility of the result from evaluating the code snippet in the *Evaluate Expression* view in the *Variables* view.

- **Show Watches inside Variables View**. Toggles the visibility of the defined watches in the *Variables* view.

- **Create new Watch**. Opens up a dialog, which allows the user to enter an expression to be watched. The text field supports code completion to allow for a faster creation of the watch with less typing.

- **Open Formatter Options**. Opens the preferences window (options window) allowing the user to define how objects of a special type will be rendered in the *Variables* view.

- **Show values as visual property editors, when available**. If a property editor is available (registered) in the IDE for the type of the variable (field), the property editor is used for rendering / editing of the type instead of the defined formatter logic.

As an alternative, a watch can also be created by double-clicking on the label *"<Enter new watch>"*. The text field showing up supports code completion as well, as can be seen in Figure 6-14.

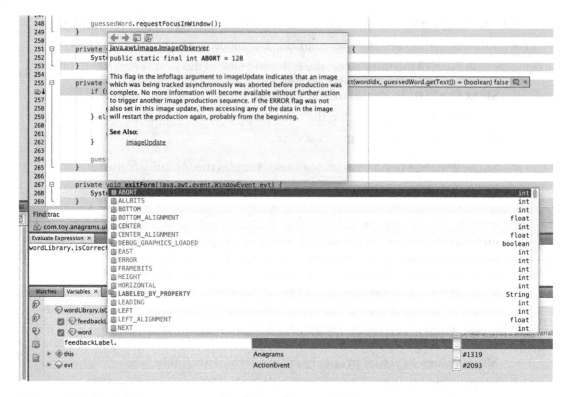

Figure 6-14. *Adding new watch with code completion*

The context menu on the different items in the *Variables* view helps with further interactions:

- **Delete**. Deletes a watch: either fixed, pinned, or default watch.

- **Delete All**. Deletes all watches.

- **Create Fixed Watch**. Creates a watch, which is not based on the actual context but on the global context.

- **Edit**. Opens up a dialog, which allows changing the expression to be watched. The text field supports code completion to allow for a faster creation of the watch with less typing.

- **Show Pinned Watches**. Shows all watches created by pinning down an expression evaluation in the source code view.

- **New Watch**. Opens up a dialog, which allows the user to enter an expression to be watched. The text field supports code completion to allow for a faster creation of the watch with less typing.

- **Go to Type Source**. Opens the source code attached to the type in an editor tab. If there is no source code available, a disassembled substitute is shown.

- **View as**. Toggles the view component to use a table or a tree table for displaying the data.

- **Show references**. Opens a *Heap Walker* view to inspect the actual reference network of the selected variable.

- **Mark Object**. Attaches a label to an object to help identify that object during the further debugging process.

- **Show Only Rows where**. Filters out rows from the view based on the type of the variable. Different filter types are available.

With all these possibilities, the *Variables* view is a very powerful tool to help you understand the state of your application. This view is accompanied in Apache NetBeans with a couple of other views that support the debugging process from different perspectives. The first one that we take a deeper look at is the *Watches* view.

Watches View

The *Watches* view is a spcialized view, which is dedicated only to the display of and interaction with the *watches* feature (which has already been described as part of the *Variables* view). An example view is shown in Figure 6-15.

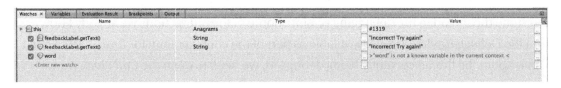

Figure 6-15. *Watches view*

The major difference to the *Variables* view is that the *Variables* view provides mixed information where the *Watches* view focuses solely on displaying watches. All interactions with watches described in the *Variables* view section are available here as well:

- **Show Pinned Watches**. Shows all watches created by pinning down an expression evaluation in the source code view.

- **New Watch**. Opens up a dialog, which allows the user to enter an expression to be watched. The text field supports code completion to allow for a faster creation of the watch with less typing.

- **Create fixed watch**. Creates a watch, which is not based on the actual context but on the global context.

Threads View

The *Threads* view is a simplified version of the *Debugging* view. It shows all the threads of the debugged process by name in a tree view, grouped by their thread groups. An example of the view is shown in Figure 6-16.

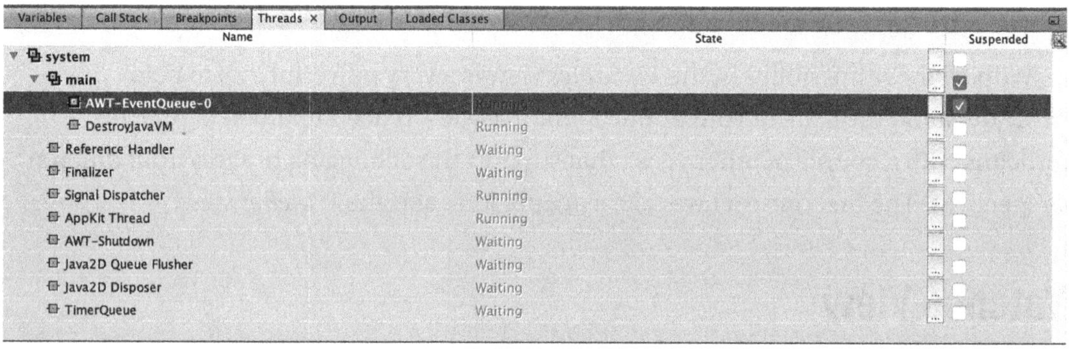

Figure 6-16. *Threads view*

Additional columns show a description of the thread state and if the thread is suspended by the debugger. The column showing the suspended state can also be used to suspend or resume the thread in the debugging session. Some of the interactions we already know from the *Debugging* view are also available as part of the context menu for thread. If we need details about the thread currently being debugged, we need to open the *Call Stack* view.

Call Stack View

The *Call Stack* view is the other half of the *Debugging* view as a separate view. It shows the call stack of the debugged thread and allows the same kind of interaction on the stack frames that are available in the *Debugging* view, that is, *Make Current, Pop To Here*. Typically during a debugging session, the *Debugging* view is sufficient for all things around thread management and control, so that the separate views for call stacks and threads are not used. The call stack display is shown in Figure 6-17.

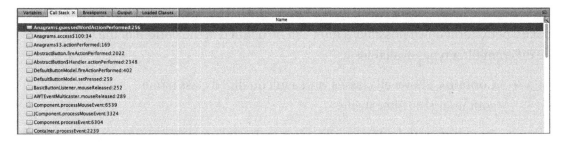

Figure 6-17. *Call Stack view*

A lot of the debugging features and techniques we discussed so far are centered around threading and evaluation of values. One other feature that is far less known is the possibility to do a heap walk during the debugging session. A heap walk is a debugging technique to investigate the content of the heap starting from either a single instance (as displayed in the *Variables* view) or a heap histogram showing how many instances (with total size) of which type (class) are part of the heap. Such a histogram can be shown by opening the *Loaded Classes* view.

Loaded Classes View

The *Loaded Classes* view displays for all loaded classes a histogram based on the number of instances of each class. This is a simple starting point for analyzing the composition of the heap. The view displays the instance number as an absolute value and as a percentage of all instances. The table is by default sorted by the absolute instance count as can be seen in Figure 6-18.

Class Name		Instances [%]	Instances ▼
char[]		■	9.351 (18,7%)
java.lang.**String**		■	9.300 (18,6%)
java.util.**HashMap$Node**		■	3.495 (7%)
java.lang.**Class**		▌	2.457 (4,9%)
java.util.**Hashtable$Entry**		▌	2.111 (4,2%)
java.util.concurrent.**ConcurrentHashMap$Node**		▌	1.698 (3,4%)
java.lang.**Object[]**		▌	1.681 (3,4%)
java.lang.ref.**SoftReference**		▌	1.142 (2,3%)
java.lang.ref.**Finalizer**		▌	1.058 (2,1%)
java.util.concurrent.**ConcurrentHashMap**		▌	990 (2%)
sun.font.**CFont**		▌	919 (1,8%)
sun.font.**Font2DHandle**		▌	919 (1,8%)
java.lang.**Integer**		▌	843 (1,7%)

Figure 6-18. *Loaded Classes view*

Due to the nature of such a heap histogram, the list of classes can be really long. To make a better drill down possible, a filter can be defined at the bottom of the table. There are different filter types available:

- **Contains**. Shows all classes with a full qualified class name containing the filter string.

- **Does not contain**. Shows all classes with a full qualified class name not containing the filter string.

- **Regular Expression**. Shows all classes with a full qualified class name matching the filter string as a regular expression.

- **Subclass of**. Shows all classes that are a subclass of the entered class. The class needs to be entered with the full qualified class name.

Once the filter is active, a red **x** is shown on the right-hand side of the filter text field. It can be used to clear the filter. On the far right-hand side is a kind of spinner control, which gives access to previously entered filter strings.

For each row displaying a class from the heap, there is a context menu with the following actions:

- **Show in Instances View**. Opens the Instances view if it is closed in an editor tab and displays the instances of the selected class.

- **Show Only Subclasses**. Enables the subclass filter capability based on the selected class.

- **Go to Source**. Opens the source for the selected class in an editor tab. If the tab is already available, it will be activated and shown.

Trying to analyze the heap content starts with a good filter for the histogram; typically look for your own classes first and figure out what the object graph for this instance is. This analysis is done using the *Instances* view.

Instances View

The *Instances* view is at the heart of the heap analysis (heap walking). The major thing shown in this view is a list of the different instances of one class. By selecting one instance from the list in the upper-left tree, the other three components get updated. The lower-left one shows a value representation of the instance, for example, the character sequence for a `String`. The upper right-hand side is the structured view of the instance, that is, it allows you to view all fields with the values recursively by digging through the tree. The lower right-hand side shows where the actual instance is used. This is the reference chain, which can be followed up to figure out which object is holding onto your precious instance. All these details can be seen in Figure 6-19.

Figure 6-19. *Instances view*

If you want to see details of an instance that is shown as part of the fields list, open the context menu and select *Show Instance*. This switches the *Instances* view to render the instance list of the same type as the selected instance in the fields list and preselects the instance in the instances list. This allows for a quick drill into the hierarchy of objects.

Now that we already know how to deal with threads, memory, and evaluations in Apache NetBeans during debugging sessions, we still need to figure out how to deal with breakpoints.

Breakpoints

Breakpoints are a crucial feature for debugging, because they allow to stop the debugged process at arbitrary places in the code. Breakpoints in Apache NetBeans can be managed and displayed across source files using the *Breakpoints* view. Besides viewing breakpoints as an unstructured list, breakpoints can be grouped into custom or predefined, for example, by programming language, *Breakpoint Groups*. One breakpoint can belong to one custom group and can be moved from one group to another if needed. Before we dive deeper into those details, let's start with creating some new breakpoints.

There are different ways to create a breakpoint in Apache NetBeans:

- By toggling a breakpoint in the gutter (the area where the line numbers are displayed) will create or delete a *Class Breakpoint, Field Breakpoint, Line Breakpoint,* or *Method Breakpoint*

- By using the menu item *New Breakpoint* (⇧-⌘-F8 on Mac or Ctrl+Shift+F8 on Windows/Linux) from the *Debug* menu in the main menu, all types of breakpoints can be created.

Creating a new breakpoint using the New Breakpoint action allows a complete configuration of a breakpoint at creation time. The first step is the selection of the debugger, which in turn changes the list of breakpoint types available. For the *Java* debugger, the breakpoint types are the following:

- **Class**. Stops the debugged process based on class states.

- **Exception**. Stops the debugged process based on exceptions thrown.

- **Field**. Stops the debugged process if a field is accessed.

- **Line**. Stops the debugged process if special line in a file is reached.

- **Method**. Stops the debugged process on method-related states.

- **Thread**. Stops the debugged process on thread-related states.

- **AWT/Swing Component**. Stops the debugged process on component-related events.

All breakpoint types allow for additional properties to be configured. They are grouped into two categories, *Conditions* and *Actions*, and may differ between breakpoint types. The New Breakpoint dialog is shown in Figure 6-20.

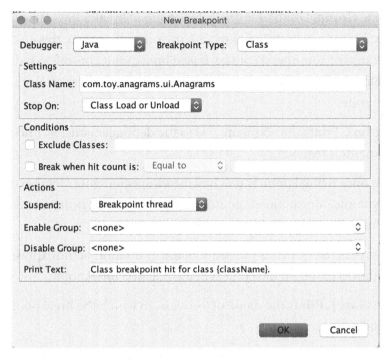

Figure 6-20. *New Breakpoint dialog*

The *Actions* properties describe what happens once a breakpoint is reached. There are four different actions associated with every breakpoint type.

- **Suspend**. Allows the selection of which threads will be suspended if the breakpoint is reached. Possible values are *Breakpoint Thread* (the thread on which the breakpoint was reached), *All threads*, or *No thread (continue)*. Selecting *No thread* will only print the text under the action *Print Text* but not stop any threads. This is helpful if only a list of values at different points is required, but no further interaction with the debugged process is needed, for example, in a multi-threaded application where stopping threads will change runtime behavior.

- **Enable Group**. Enables the selected group of breakpoints once this breakpoint is reached. Together with the next action, this enables some kind of automated context-based breakpoint control, to reduce the effort to manually enable or disable breakpoints in special areas of the code.

- **Disable Group**. Disables the selected group of breakpoints once this breakpoint is reached. Together with the previous action, this enables some kind of automated context-based breakpoint control, to reduce the effort to manually enable or disable breakpoints in special areas of the code.

- **Print Text**. Prints the configure text to the debugger console, once the breakpoint is reached.

Printing text once a breakpoint is reached uses a special syntax for dynamic information. Dynamic information is guarded by {}, while everything outside is just plain text. The following dynamic syntaxes are supported:

- {=<expression>}. Prints the result of the evaluation of the expression (see above) based on the context at the reached breakpoint;

- {className}. Prints the name of the class, in which the breakpoint was defined;

- {exceptionClass}. Prints the name of the exception class with regard to the breakpoint definition;

- {exceptionMessage}. Prints the message of the exception with regard to the breakpoint definition;

- {fieldName}. Prints the actual name of the field, in which the breakpoint was defined;

- {lineNumber}. Prints the actual line number;

- {methodName}. Prints the actual name of the method, in which the breakpoint was defined;

- {threadName}. Prints the name of the thread, on which the breakpoint was reached;

- {? threadStarted}{}{}. Prints either the text in the first or in the second group, depending on the state of threadStarted. Both groups can contain dynamic syntax elements.

Not all of those dynamic elements are available for all breakpoint types, for example, threadStarted. An example text is prefilled in the *Print Text* action text field.

The *Conditions*, describing the constraints the debugger considers for stopping at a reached breakpoint, are not the same for all breakpoint types, but most breakpoint types adhere to the following two constraints:

- **Condition**. Describes an expression (see evaluation) that must evaluate to true for the debugger to stop.

- **Break when hit count is**. Describes how often the breakpoint must be hit to make the debugger stop.

There are different comparators available for the hit count:

- **Equal to**. The hit count must be equal to the defined value for the debugger to stop.

- **Greater than**. The hit count must be greater than the defined value for the debugger to stop.

- **Multiple of**. The hit count must be a multiple of the defined value for the debugger to stop.

The full generic Conditions can be seen in Figure 6-21.

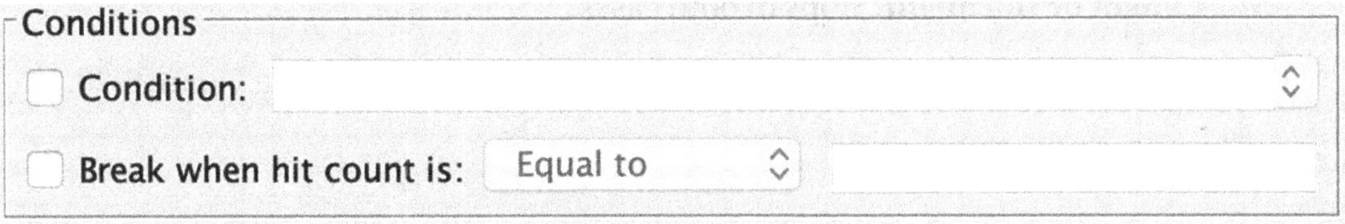

Figure 6-21. Generic Breakpoint conditions

The *Settings*, describing the setup of the breakpoint type, are different for every breakpoint type so let's go through them one by one.

Class Breakpoints

A *Class Breakpoint* is defined by a full qualified class name and the state of the class from the class loader perspective, which is observed by the debugger:

- **Class Load**. Debugger stops during class loading.

- **Class Unload**. Debugger stops during class unloading.

- **Class Load or Unload**. Debugger stops during class loading and unloading.

The *Settings* configuration of the *Class Breakpoint* can be seen in Figure 6-22.

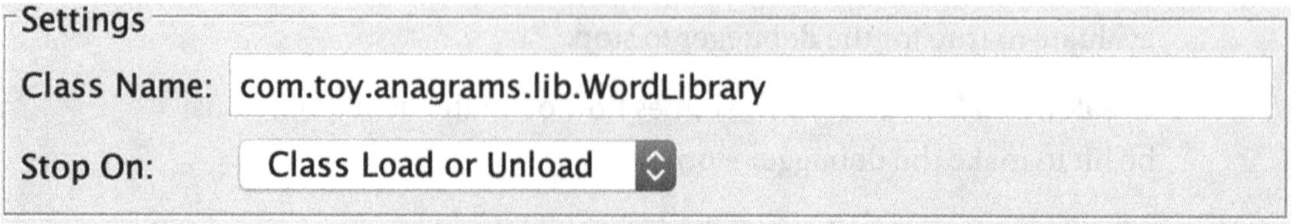

```
┌─ Settings ──────────────────────────────────────────────┐
│  Class Name:  com.toy.anagrams.lib.WordLibrary           │
│                                                          │
│  Stop On:        Class Load or Unload    ◊               │
└──────────────────────────────────────────────────────────┘
```

Figure 6-22. *Class Breakpoint settings*

Exception Breakpoints

An *Exception Breakpoint* stops in case of a thrown exception. It is defined by a full qualified exception class name and the state of the exception as observed by the debugger:

- **Caught**. Stops only if the exception is caught.

- **Uncaught**. Stops only if the exception is not caught.

- **Caught or Uncaught**. Stops in both cases.

The *Settings* configuration of the *Exception Breakpoint* can be seen in Figure 6-23.

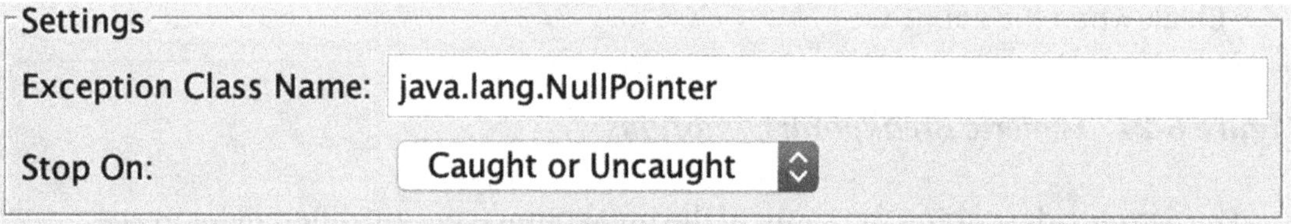

```
┌─ Settings ──────────────────────────────────────────────┐
│  Exception Class Name:  java.lang.NullPointer            │
│                                                          │
│  Stop On:              Caught or Uncaught   ◊            │
└──────────────────────────────────────────────────────────┘
```

Figure 6-23. *Exception Breakpoint settings*

Because the more interesting cases for configuring the breakpoint behavior of an *Exception Breakpoint* are not defined by the exception class, the *Conditions* of such an exception have an additional customization option:

- **Filter on Classes throwing the Exception**. Restricts the breakpoint to specific classes throwing the specified exception. Class names for *Match Classes* and *Exclude Classes* have to be specified full qualified, but an asterisk can be used at the end as a wildcard. Multiple patterns can be specified by separating these by commas.

The *Conditions* configuration of the *Thread Breakpoint* can be seen in Figure 6-24.

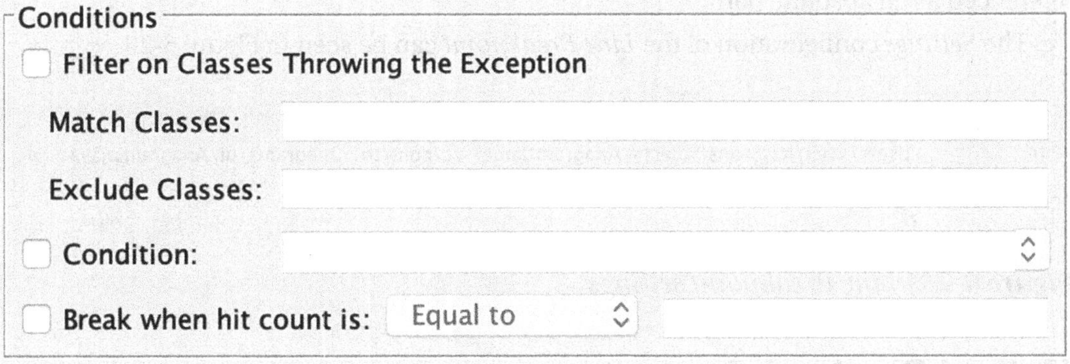

Figure 6-24. *Exception Breakpoint conditions*

Field Breakpoints

A *Field Breakpoint* stops the debugged process if a field of a defined class is accessed. It is defined by a full qualified class name and respective field name and selecting in which access cases the debugger will stop:

- **Field Access**. Stops if the field is accessed, for example, read access.

- **Field Modification**. Stops if the field is written to.

- **Field Access or Modification**. Stops if the field is accessed or written to.

The *Settings* configuration of the *Field Breakpoint* can be seen in Figure 6-25.

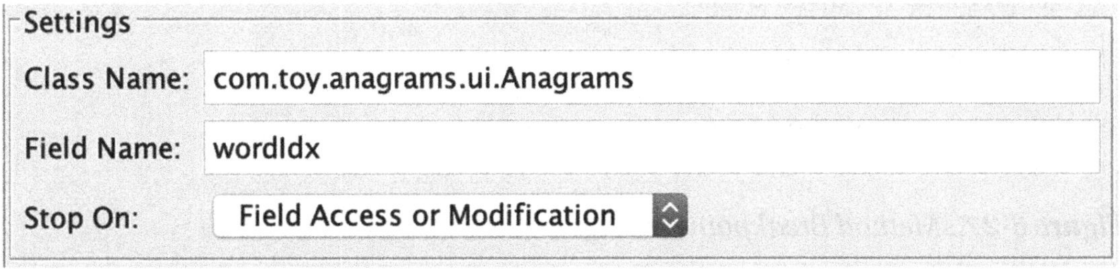

Figure 6-25. *Field Breakpoint settings*

Line Breakpoints

A *Line Breakpoint* is defined by a line in a source code file, which points to an executable line of code, that is, not a class, method, or field declaration. The source code file is referenced as an absolute path.

The *Settings* configuration of the *Line Breakpoint* can be seen in Figure 6-26.

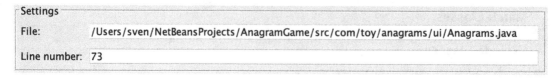

Figure 6-26. *Line Breakpoint settings*

Method Breakpoints

A *Method Breakpoint* is defined by a full qualified class name and a method specification, either a concrete method name or all methods of the defined class. In addition, it is required to specify when to stop:

- **Method Entry**. Stops before entering the method.

- **Method Exit**. Stops before exiting the method.

- **Method Entry and Exit**. Stops before entering and before exiting the method.

The *Settings* configuration of the *Method Breakpoint* can be seen in Figure 6-27.

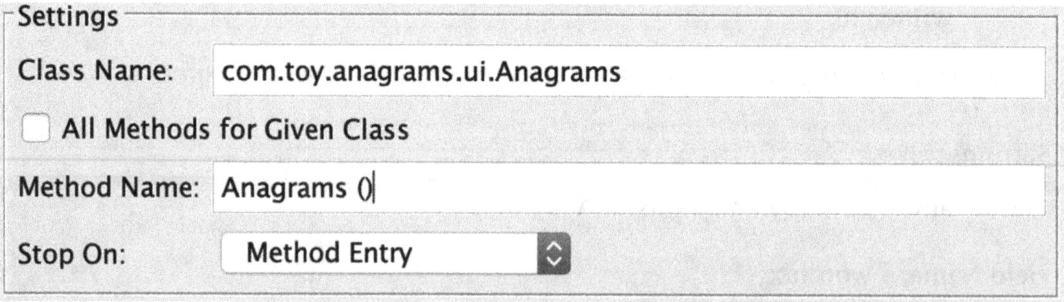

```
Settings
Class Name:     com.toy.anagrams.ui.Anagrams
☐ All Methods for Given Class
Method Name:  Anagrams ()
Stop On:        Method Entry  ◇
```

Figure 6-27. *Method Breakpoint settings*

Thread Breakpoints

Due to the nature of a *Thread Breakpoint*, there are only limited configuration options available. It can be defined when to stop:

- **Thread Start**. Stops if a new thread is started.

- **Thread Death**. Stops if a thread dies.

- **Thread Start or Death**. Stops on new thread starts and thread deaths.

The *Settings* configuration of the *Thread Breakpoint* can be seen in Figure 6-28.

```
┌─Settings──────────────────────────────────────────────────┐
│  Stop On:    Thread Start                    ⌄             │
└───────────────────────────────────────────────────────────┘
```

Figure 6-28. *Thread Breakpoint settings*

The only condition that is usable for a *Thread Breakpoint* is the hit count. If you use this option, you will only get a stopped debugger for every hit count creations and or deaths of a thread. The *Conditions* configuration of the *Thread Breakpoint* can be seen in Figure 6-29.

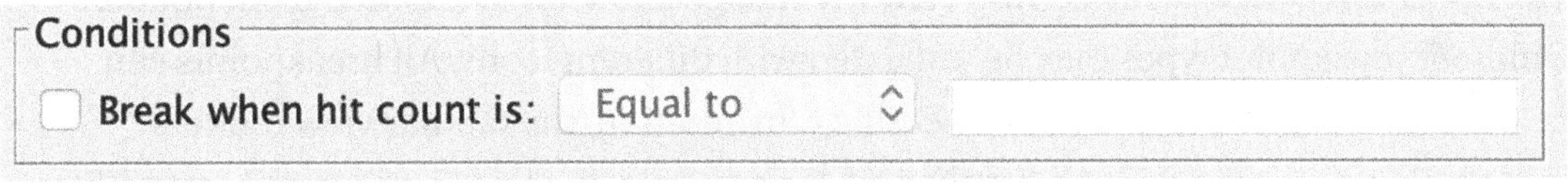

```
┌─Conditions────────────────────────────────────────────────┐
│  ☐ Break when hit count is:    Equal to    ⌄              │
└───────────────────────────────────────────────────────────┘
```

Figure 6-29. *Thread Breakpoint settings*

AWT/Swing Component Breakpoints

The *AWT/Swing Component Breakpoint* can only be defined if a snapshot of the UI has been taken (see *Visual Swing Debugging*, later in this chapter, for further details). If an editor tab is active, it is possible to select one component and create a new breakpoint. The component name cannot be manually entered, but is based on the selection in the UI snapshot. There are three possible ways to stop the debugger with regard to the component:

- **Add/remove from container**. Stops if the component is removed or added.

- **Show/hide**. Stops if the component is shown or hidden.

- **Repaint**. Stops on repainting the component.

The *Settings* configuration of the *AWT/Swing Component Breakpoint* can be seen in Figure 6-30.

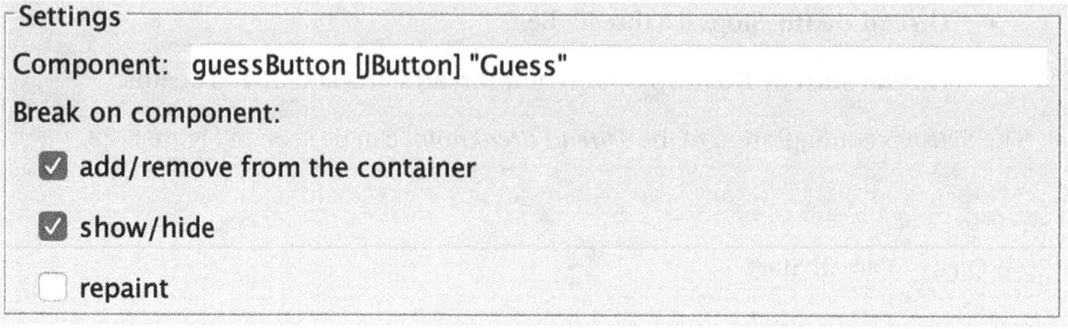

```
┌─Settings──────────────────────────────────────────────
│ Component:  guessButton [JButton] "Guess"
│ Break on component:
│   ☑ add/remove from the container
│   ☑ show/hide
│   ☐ repaint
└───────────────────────────────────────────────────────
```

Figure 6-30. *AWT/Swing Components Breakpoint settings*

All the listed breakpoints are shown in a tabular view in the *Breakpoints* view.

Breakpoints View

The *Breakpoints* view is the central view to manage and view all defined breakpoints. Different breakpoint types may be indicated with different icons. All breakpoints can be enabled or disabled by using a check box. In addition, the tabular view renders information about the defined breakpoint, for example, the line number and source file or exception class. In a column hidden by default, the actual hit count of a breakpoint can be shown. A context menu is available on every breakpoint with the following actions:

- **Go to Source**. Opens the source code associated with the breakpoint in the editor area. If no source code is available, a disassembled substitute is shown instead.

- **Enable/Disable**. Toggles the state of the breakpoint from enabled to disabled or vice versa.

- **Move Into Group**. Moves the selected breakpoint into a breakpoint group, allowing finer-grained control with regard to enabling, disabling, or deletion.

- **New Breakpoint**. Opens the dialog to create a new breakpoint.

- **Enable All**. Enables all breakpoints. Only active if at least one breakpoint can be enabled.

- **Disable All**. Disables all breakpoints. Only active if at least one breakpoint can be disabled.

- **Delete**. Deletes the breakpoint.

- **Delete All**. Deletes all breakpoints.

- **Properties**. Shows the properties of the breakpoint to allow inspection and changing of the *Settings*, *Conditions*, and *Actions*.

As shown in Figure 6-31, breakpoints that belong to a special group are shown below those groups in a tree-like manner. The context menu on a breakpoint group contains the following actions:

- **Rename Group**. Renames the breakpoint group.

- **Enable All Grouped**. Enables all breakpoints in the group.

- **Disable All Grouped**. Disables all breakpoints in the group.

- **Delete All Grouped**. Deletes all breakpoints in the group, effectively deleting the group as well.

Besides the tabular view, there is a small toolbar on the left-hand side offering three actions:

- **Create new Breakpoint**. Opens the dialog to create a new breakpoint.

- **Deactivate all breakpoints in current session**. Deactivates all breakpoints in the current debugging session.

- **Select breakpoint groups**. Shows a list of possible grouping strategies for the breakpoints in the list, based on custom groups or a selection of predefined groups.

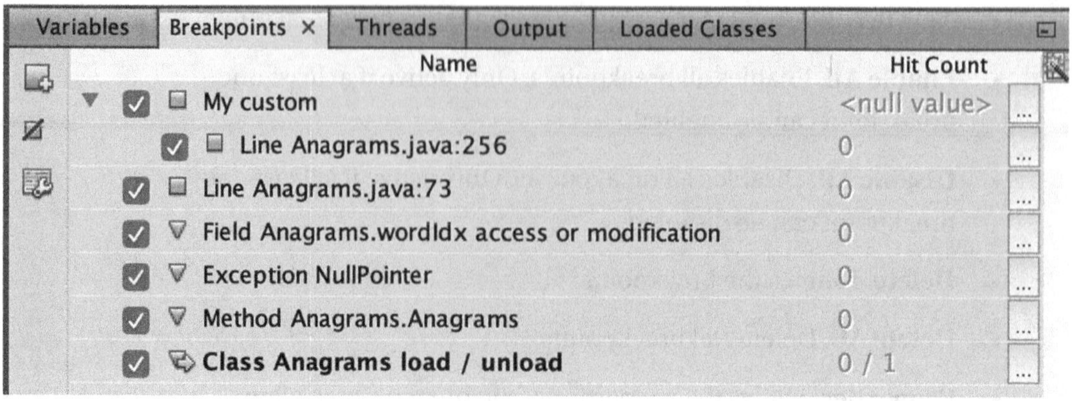

			Name	Hit Count	
▼	☑	☐ My custom		<null value>	...
	☑	☐ Line Anagrams.java:256		0	...
	☑	☐ Line Anagrams.java:73		0	...
	☑	▽ Field Anagrams.wordIdx access or modification		0	...
	☑	▽ Exception NullPointer		0	...
	☑	▽ Method Anagrams.Anagrams		0	...
	☑	⮑ Class Anagrams load / unload		0 / 1	...

Figure 6-31. *Breakpoints view*

Visual Swing Debugging

Apache NetBeans has an additional feature for supporting debugging of a Swing application. If the debugged process has a Swing UI, it is possible to snapshot the actual component hierarchy to inspect it in a visual manner. There is a special button in the debug toolbar that triggers the snapshot and opens a *Snapshot Editor* tab, which can be seen in Figure 6-32.

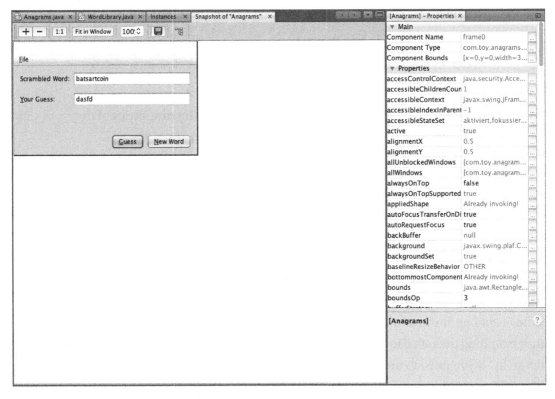

Figure 6-32. *Snapshot of Swing*

The snapshot allows you to select the different components, for example, buttons or text fields, and inspect their field attributes. If a property is writable, it is possible to change the value by entering a new value in the property editor in the *Properties* view. The context menu of the components shown in the snapshot has some very helpful actions:

- **Go To Component Declaration**. Opens the relevant source code at the line where the selected component is declared. This is not the line where the component is created, but rather the line of the field definition.

- **Go To Component Source**. Opens the source code file in an editor tab, which defines the component, for example, for JButton it opens the `javax.swing.JButton` source file (if source is available).

- **Show Listeners**. Opens a new view called *Events* view. The events view shows registered listeners, allows navigation to source code, and displays a log of events (if configured).

- **Create Fixed Watch**. Creates a fixed watch for this component.

- **Toggle Component Breakpoint**. Creates a component breakpoint based on visual selection (for details regarding breakpoints, please refer to the breakpoints section).

- **Breakpoint Properties**. Opens a dialog to show the properties of the component breakpoint and allow changes to the properties.

- **Properties**. Opens a standalone dialog showing the property sheet associated with the selected component.

The *Event* view shows additional logical information based on the selected component in the *Snapshot* or *Navigator* view. The first row identifies the selected component, followed by two groups of listeners; the first group shows all custom listeners, that is, a listener not added by the UI toolkit itself, but by user code. The second group lists all listeners added from the UI toolkit itself. The last section in the list of information is the *Event Log*. It shows a list of events issued by the component. This helps in better understanding the behavior in terms of events triggered and reactions of the component hierarchy. If you need to debug the Swing component hierarchy behavior, this type of debugging reduces the amount of setup you need to do yourself and gives you direct and simple access to the internals of Swing. An example view can be seen in Figure 6-33.

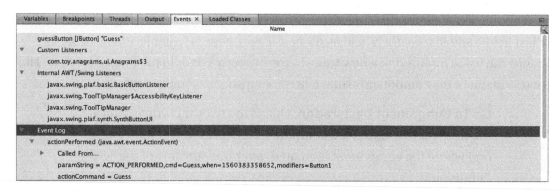

Figure 6-33. *Event view showing listeners and event log*

For the entries in the *Event Log* section to show up, it is necessary to configure some type of listener to be selected for logging. This can be done using the context menu *Setup Logging Events* of the *Event Log* item. It will open a dialog showing the possible listeners. All listeners selected will lead to entries in the *Event Log*, if events are sent to those types. The list of listeners is shown in Figure 6-34.

Figure 6-34. *Select events for logging*

The context menu item *Clear* on the *Log Event* item can be used to clear the current list of log entries.

While being in active GUI snapshot mode, the navigator displays the Swing component hierarchy, identifying each component with their respective variable name, if the name can be derived. In addition, a textual representation of the component is rendered to help identify the component in the snapshot view, for example, the text shown in a label or button. The actions that can be performed are the same as on the selected component in the UI snapshot. An example Swing hierarchy based on the Anagram Game can be seen in Figure 6-35.

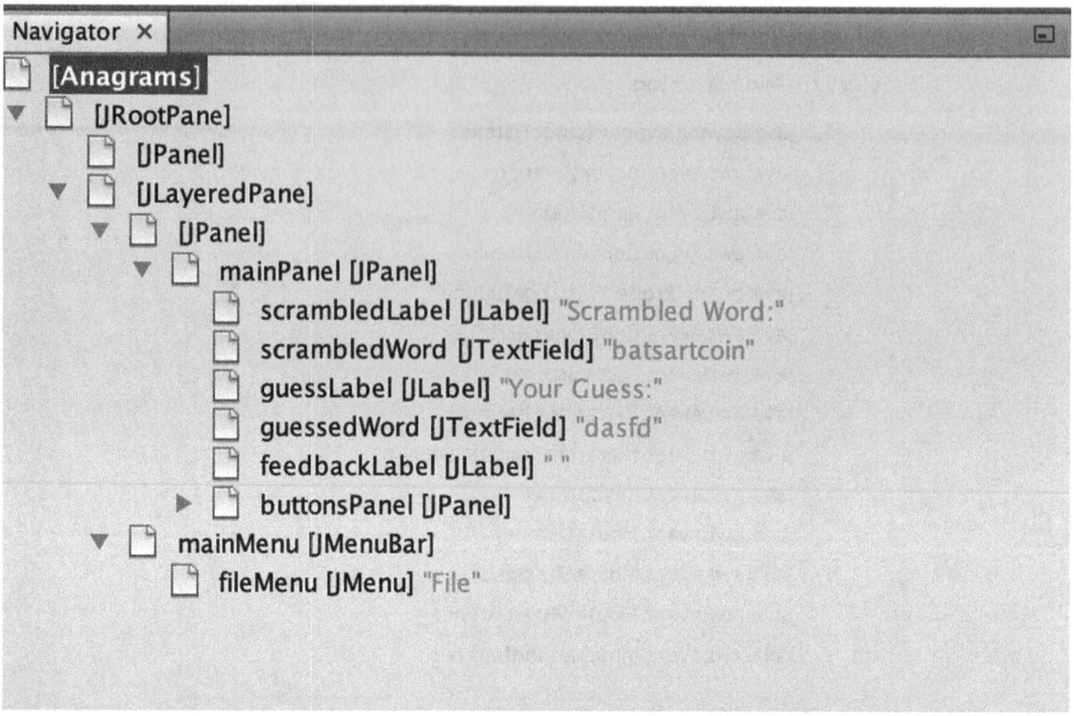

Figure 6-35. *Swing Hierarchy in Navigator view*

Selecting a component in the navigator view highlights the component in the *Snapshot* Editor tab, which helps identifying a component in the visual *Snapshot* view. The selection also changes the content of the *Properties* view to display the properties of the component selected in the *Navigator* view.

Multi-Session Debugging

The Apache NetBeans debugger supports having multiple debugging sessions running at the same time. This is very helpful if you have to debug, for example, some integration issue between the Java front end and back end, and you can simultaneously debug both processes. The debugger seamlessly integrates the multi-session capabilities into the default views and workflows. In the *Debugging* view, an additional combo box is shown, allowing you to select the debugging session the threads are shown for, as in Figure 6-36.

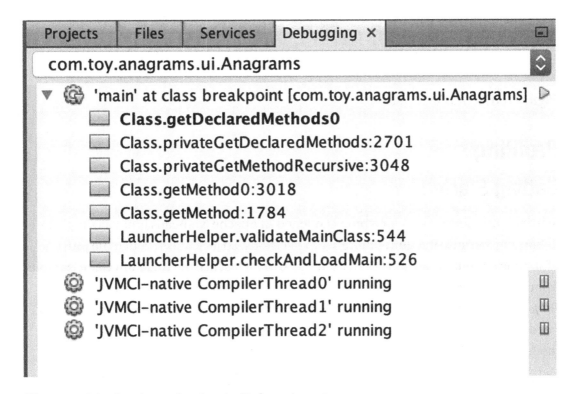

Figure 6-36. *Session selection in Debugging view*

In addition to enhancing the *Debugging* view with necessary information for the multi-session workflow, there is a dedicated *Sessions* view showing all debugging sessions, with their state, programming language, and the host they are executed on (remember debugging sessions could be running attached to a process on a remote host). There is a context menu on every session providing interaction with the sessions:

- **Make Current**. Toggle the debugger to actively debug this session.

- **Scope**. Selects if all threads or just the current thread should be debugged.

- **Language**. Selects the debugger to use for this process, in case multiples may be applicable.

- **Finish**. Finishes the debugging session.

- **Finish All**. Finishes all debugging sessions.

An example of the Sessions view showing two processes is shown in Figure 6-37.

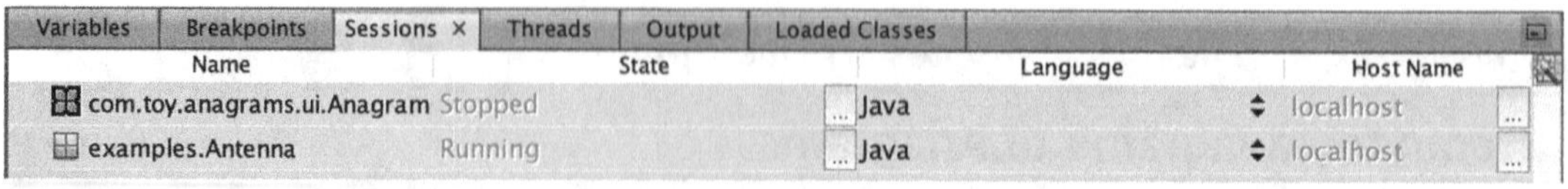

Variables	Breakpoints	Sessions ×	Threads	Output	Loaded Classes			
Name			State			Language		Host Name
com.toy.anagrams.ui.Anagram Stopped					Java			localhost
examples.Antenna		Running			Java			localhost

Figure 6-37. *Sessions view*

Profiling

Getting Started

Starting a profiling session for a project opened in Apache NetBeans is not as simple as debugging, because it requires more setup decisions. So let's walk through the process of starting a profiling session (as an example, we will just use the Anagram Game sample from Apache NetBeans). If the project is already open, select the project node in the *Projects* view and press the **Profile Project** button in the toolbar. The first step you now need to take is the configuration of your profiling session. This has to be done, because the Apache NetBeans Profiler supports multiple profiling modes:

- **Telemetry**. Monitors CPU and Memory usage, number of threads, and loaded classes.

- **Methods**. Profiles method execution times and invocation counts, including call trees.

- **Objects**. Profiles size and count of allocated objects, including allocation paths and generational count.

- **Threads**. Monitors thread states and times.

- **Locks**. Collects lock contention statistics.

- **SQL Queries**. Display executed SQL Queries, their duration, and invocation paths.

There is a more complex setup for profiling a remote VM, which requires setting up the remote JVM with a special agent.

We will now have a deeper look into all of the profiling modes, but first some basics.

Basic Profiling Actions

During profiling an application, there is a set of generic actions, which can always be triggered to support the profiling process. The actions are available at the right end of the profiling toolbar labeled with *Process*.

- **Take thread dump from profiled process**. Takes a thread dump from the profiled process and opens it in a *Thread Dump* view.

- **Take heap dump from profiled process**. Takes a heap dump from the profiled process and opens it in a *Heap Walker* view (see *Heap Walker* later in this chapter).

- **Request garbage collection in the profiled process**. Requests an explicit garbage collection to be run in the profiled process. This can be used to ensure that heap dumps are not polluted with too many objects, which are not live anymore.

Telemetry

Telemetry is a very basic profiling mode. It allows us to track the following:

- CPU load differentiated between real CPU time and time consumed by GC.

- Heap size and used heap.

- Key garbage collection parameters, for example, surviving generations (an ever-increasing number indicates either a cache or a memory leak) and GC intervals.

- Threads and loaded classes.

For each of the above bullets, there is a special graph shown in the telemetry view as seen in Figure 6-38.

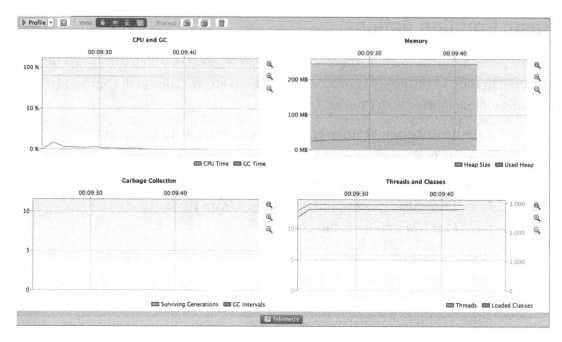

Figure 6-38. *Telemetry view*

Methods

Methods profiling or execution profiling is a tool to help understand the runtime execution performance of an application. If a request to a server takes too long, an execution profiling of the application may help to figure out the bottleneck (there are other techniques, but these can be studied in deeper detail in a performance tuning handbook).

Starting the profiling session with methods will open a view similar to the one shown in Figure 6-39.

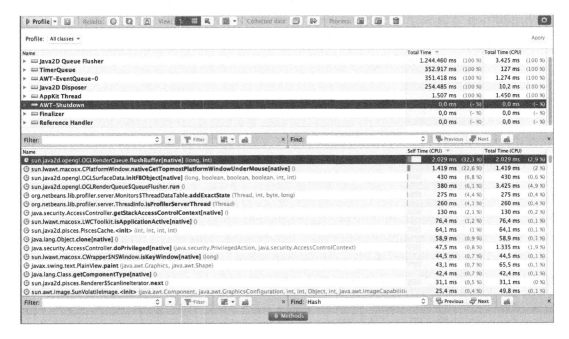

Figure 6-39. *Methods view live*

The view as shown has two parts, which are live updated. The first is a *thread view*, showing where in a special thread most of the time is consumed. The second (shown at the bottom) is a view displaying the *hot spots* of the application in terms of which methods have been executed, how often, and how long were they running on the CPU. This can give a live impression on what is going in the application. Because a lot of threads may be running and metrics for thousands of methods will be generated, both views can be filtered either by *thread name* or by *class name* for the method view. To open the filter bar at the bottom of the view, click **Filter** in the context menu of the view. The filter allows for different type of matches:

- **Contains**. Shows all classes with a fully qualified class name containing the filter string.

- **Does not contain**. Shows all classes with a fully qualified class name not containing the filter string.

- **Regular Expression**. Shows all classes with a fully qualified class name matching the filter string as a regular expression.

In addition to these filter expressions, there are predefined filters available:

- JPA

- JavaEE

- JavaEE Servers

- Java Reflection

- Java SE

Because of the overhead *Methods* profiling introduces overhead into the profiled application, it is very important to configure the methods to be profiled. This can be done using the gear icon in the upper right-hand corner. This opens up a configuration area that allows us to select which methods will be instrumented for methods profiling. The default configuration is shown in Figure 6-40.

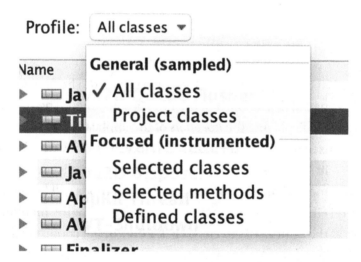

Figure 6-40. *Methods configuration*

The default configuration is just using a sampling profiling technique for methods profiling. It is less overhead compared to the instrumented profiling, but it not very exact. The configuration differentiates between different sets of classes or methods. The most important mode due to overhead is *Defined* classes. This allows for an explicit selection of which classes are of interest for the profiling session as can be seen in Figure 6-41.

Figure 6-41. *Methods profile defined classes only*

There is even the possibility to inhibit profiling of the whole tree by using the *exclude outgoing calls* option. Having set up all this and having followed the live results, you want to have a more detailed look at what is really happening. You can do this by creating a result snapshot from the toolbar, which opens a separate tab for the snapshot. The result view shown is not very different to the live view, as can be seen in Figure 6-42.

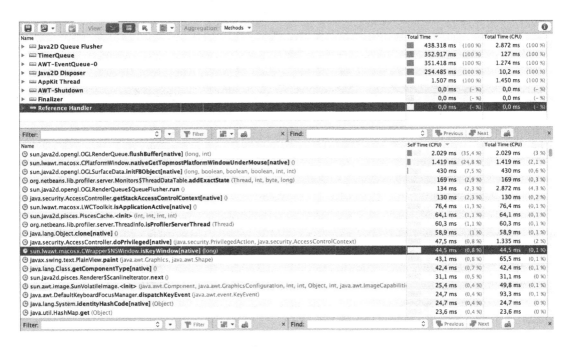

Figure 6-42. *Methods Result Snapshot*

In the live view of the *Methods* profiling, another nice feature is available. Using a button in the toolbar, you can switch the live view to display delta values, that is, all absolute values are used as the baseline and only changes compared to this baseline are displayed, so only methods executed after triggering the delta mechanism will show up with values larger than 0 in the views. This can be used to get rid of the start-up overhead in the analyzed data.

Objects

Objects profiling is a tool to help with the analysis of memory allocation and consumption. If we are looking at memory, we typically talk about the Java heap, that is, objects allocated on the heap. Starting the profiling session in the Objects profiling mode will open a live view showing a histogram of all class instances (objects). The tabular view shows the full qualified class names, the estimated live bytes consumed by this class's instances on the heap, and a count of live objects on the heap per class. The view has the same filtering options described for the *Methods* profiling. An example view is shown in Figure 6-43.

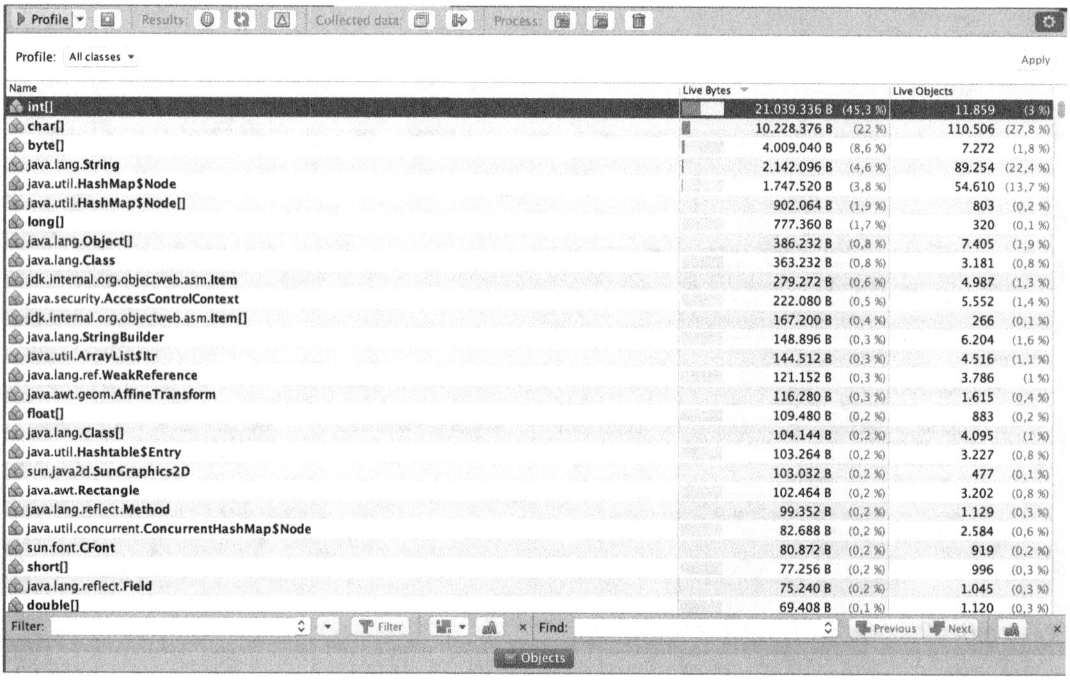

Figure 6-43. *Objects View live*

Similar to the *Methods* profiling, the *Objects* profiling can be configured with regard to which class instances shall be tracked by the profiler. It is possible to use a sampling profiling mode here as well, which just takes samples from the heap at defined intervals. However, in this mode the profiler may miss many allocations if they die fast enough, that is, allocation and garbage collection happen in between two samples. The possible configuration types that can be selected are shown in Figure 6-44.

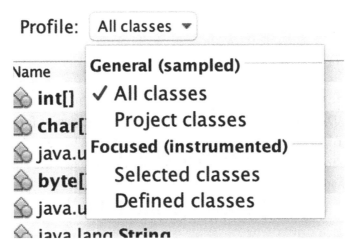

Figure 6-44. *Objects configuration*

The default configuration is to use a low overhead sampling for all classes. This may be appropriate if you do not have any clue where a memory problem is originating. Using a sampling mode only for project classes reduces the amount of tracked information and puts a focus onto your own domain code. Since this may not be enough, for example, imagine a leak caused by caching instances of core Java classes, the Apache NetBeans Profiler offers two instrumented profiling modes in addition to the sampling mode. Let's first take a look at the *Defined classes* mode. It allows us to specify a list of classes to be profiled by using fully qualified class names. If you need to profile all classes from a package or package tree, you can use an asterisk or a double asterisk as wildcards for those use cases. Once you have added what you need to the list (one pattern per line), there are two more options to pick from

- **Track only live objects**. Defines whether only live objects or also already created objects (including released ones) are profiled.

- **Limit allocations depth**. Defines the depth of the stack that is recorded for allocations. If unchecked, always the full stack is recorded, or else only the top number of stack frames are stored for anaylsis. This setting has a major impact on the overhead introduced to the target VM during profiling.

The updated configuration needs to be applied, which triggers an update to the instrumentation of the target VM. The configuration UI is shown in Figure 6-45.

Figure 6-45.   Objects defined

The other mode for defining the classes profiled for allocation is *Selected classes*. It is very similar to the *Defined classes* mode, besides the fact that classes for profiling are not defined by a pattern, but are selected from projects or jar files by selecting them explicitly using a simple UI. To start the selection process, you need to click the add button as shown in Figure 6-46.

Figure 6-46.   Objects selected

The add button opens a new dialog, allowing you to select classes from projects, which are opened in the IDE. The dialog consists of three lists (*Projects*, *Packages*, and *Classes*), which can all be filtered for faster access to the specific items. The content of the *Packages* list can be switched to contain the packages from the projects and or contain the packages from dependencies (the two toggle buttons below the list view). The *Classes* list shows the classes from the selected package. This list can also show inner classes and anonymous classes for selection (using the toggle buttons below the list view). The full UI is shown in Figure 6-47.

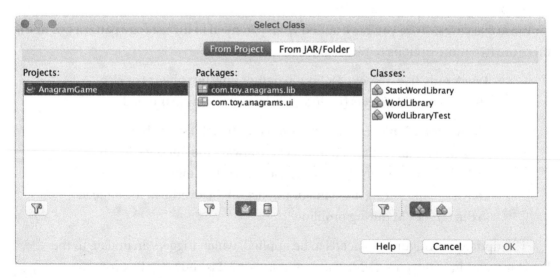

Figure 6-47.   Objects selected from projects

The dialog can be switched from the project-based selection to a jar file based selection of classes. Files/Folders to use can be added or removed using the buttons below the *Files* list, which displays the actual list of files and folders used. The *Packages* and *Classes* list work similar to the project-based selection list, as can be seen in Figure 6-48.

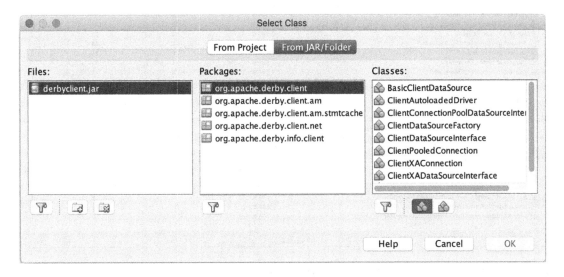

Figure 6-48. *Objects selected from jars*

Using the live results is very powerful, for example, by making use of the delta mode by using the toolbar to switch the view to *Show absolute values*. This is similar to what is available for the *Methods* profiling, but even more useful for the profiling of the heap. The values shown depict the change in memory consumption starting with the moment of toggling the view. This opens the opportunity to baseline the actual memory consumption and just follow what happens in terms of memory allocation during execution of a special part of your application code. The live result shown in Figure 6-49 depicts the additional power of an instrumented profiling session compared to the sampling mode, for example, a generational count is available on the right-hand side.

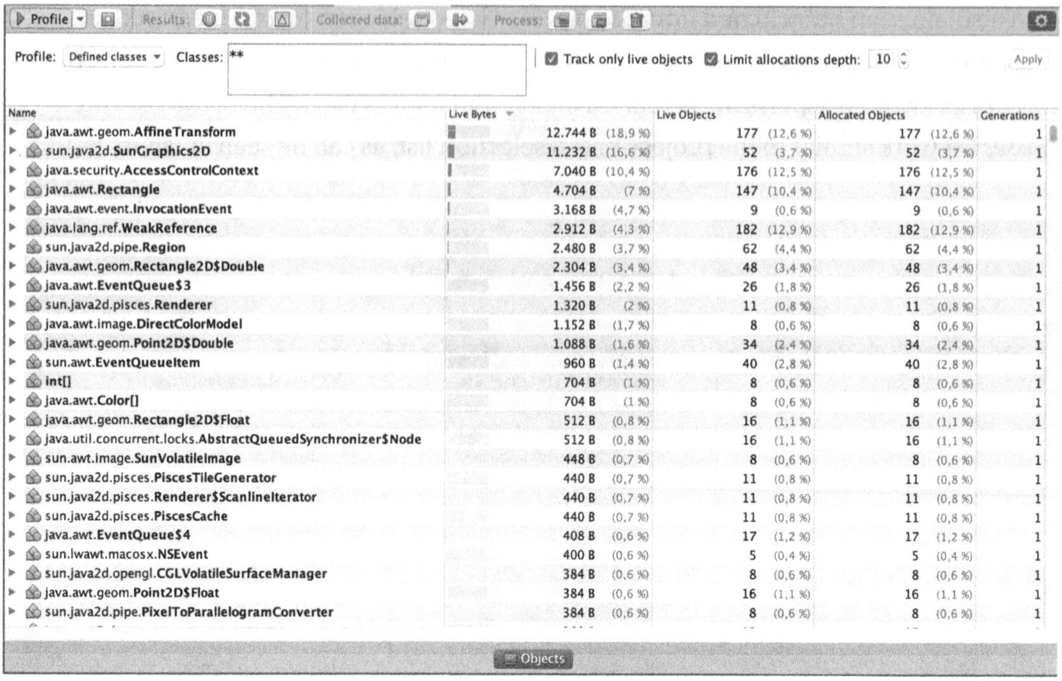

Figure 6-49. *Objects live view with instrumentation*

Below the statistics line for every class, the recorded allocation stack traces can be shown by extending the tree view using the small arrows in front of every class name. The view will show a merged reverse stack trace tree, which shows how many instances have been allocated through which code path. This is crucial information for figuring out the culprit of a memory leak. An example of such a tree is shown in Figure 6-50.

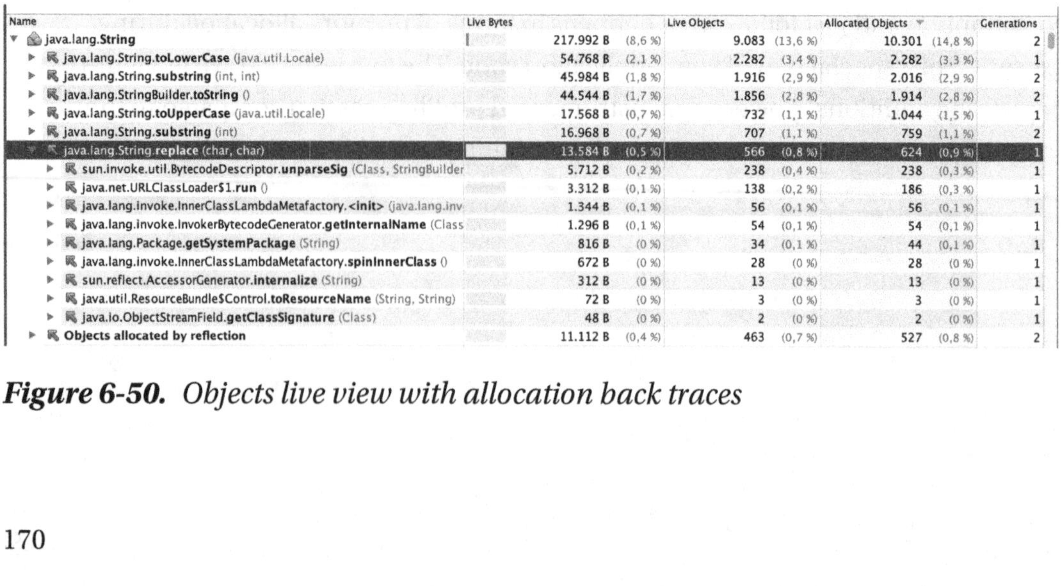

Figure 6-50. *Objects live view with allocation back traces*

Besides the live results, it is possible to create a result snapshot of the current *Objects* profiling session by using the using the toolbar action *Take snapshot of collected results.* This allows us to store the results for later consumption or comparison with other snapshots taken. An example snapshot view is shown in Figure 6-51.

Name	Live Bytes		Live Objects		Allocated Objects		Generations
▼ java.lang.String	217.992 B	(8,5 %)	9.083	(13,6 %)	10.301	(14,8 %)	2
▶ java.lang.String.toLowerCase (java.util.Locale)	54.768 B	(2,1 %)	2.282	(3,4 %)	2.282	(3,3 %)	1
▶ java.lang.String.substring (int, int)	45.984 B	(1,8 %)	1.916	(2,9 %)	2.016	(2,9 %)	2
▶ java.lang.StringBuilder.toString ()	44.544 B	(1,7 %)	1.856	(2,8 %)	1.914	(2,8 %)	2
▶ java.lang.String.toUpperCase (java.util.Locale)	17.568 B	(0,7 %)	732	(1,1 %)	1.044	(1,5 %)	1
▶ java.lang.String.substring (int)	16.968 B	(0,7 %)	707	(1,1 %)	759	(1,1 %)	2
▶ java.lang.String.replace (char, char)	13.584 B	(0,5 %)	566	(0,8 %)	624	(0,9 %)	1
▶ Objects allocated by reflection	11.112 B	(0,4 %)	463	(0,7 %)	527	(0,8 %)	2
▶ java.lang.StringBuffer.toString ()	5.064 B	(0,2 %)	211	(0,3 %)	235	(0,3 %)	1
▶ java.lang.String.concat (String)	4.128 B	(0,2 %)	172	(0,3 %)	230	(0,3 %)	1
▶ sun.net.www.ParseUtil.encodePath (String, boolean)	1.680 B	(0,1 %)	70	(0,1 %)	94	(0,1 %)	1
▶ java.util.zip.ZipCoder.toString (byte[], int)	1.440 B	(0,1 %)	60	(0,1 %)	84	(0,1 %)	1
▶ java.lang.String.valueOf (char[])	648 B	(0 %)	27	(0 %)	27	(0 %)	1
▶ sun.awt.FontConfiguration.getString (short)	360 B	(0 %)	15	(0 %)	15	(0 %)	1
▶ java.io.BufferedReader.readLine (boolean)	120 B	(0 %)	5	(0 %)	5	(0 %)	1
▶ sun.launcher.LauncherHelper.makePlatformString (boolean, byte[])	24 B	(0 %)	1	(0 %)	1	(0 %)	1
▼ java.util.HashMap$Node	175.520 B	(6,9 %)	5.485	(8,2 %)	5.485	(7,9 %)	2
▼ java.util.HashMap.newNode (int, Object, Object, java.util.HashMap.Nod	175.520 B	(6,9 %)	5.485	(8,2 %)	5.485	(7,9 %)	2
▼ java.util.HashMap.putVal (int, Object, Object, boolean, boolean)	175.520 B	(6,9 %)	5.485	(8,2 %)	5.485	(7,9 %)	2
java.util.HashMap.put (Object, Object)	175.488 B	(6,9 %)	5.484	(8,2 %)	5.484	(7,9 %)	2
▶ java.util.HashMap.putMapEntries (java.util.Map, boolean)	32 B	(0 %)	1	(0 %)	1	(0 %)	1
▶ java.security.AccessControlContext	116.440 B	(4,6 %)	2.911	(4,4 %)	2.911	(4,2 %)	2
▶ java.awt.geom.AffineTransform	112.824 B	(4,4 %)	1.567	(2,3 %)	1.567	(2,3 %)	1
▶ jdk.internal.org.objectweb.asm.Item	112.280 B	(4,4 %)	2.005	(3 %)	2.030	(2,9 %)	1
▶ sun.java2d.SunGraphics2D	99.792 B	(3,9 %)	462	(0,7 %)	462	(0,7 %)	1
▶ java.lang.ref.WeakReference	94.464 B	(3,7 %)	2.952	(4,4 %)	2.961	(4,3 %)	2
▶ java.util.Hashtable$Entry	92.256 B	(3,6 %)	2.883	(4,3 %)	2.883	(4,1 %)	2
▶ sun.font.CFont	80.872 B	(3,2 %)	919	(1,4 %)	919	(1,3 %)	1
▶ java.util.ArrayList$Itr	68.608 B	(2,7 %)	2.144	(3,2 %)	2.154	(3,1 %)	1
▶ java.awt.Rectangle	68.032 B	(2,7 %)	2.126	(3,2 %)	2.126	(3,1 %)	1
▶ java.util.concurrent.ConcurrentHashMap	64.000 B	(2,5 %)	1.000	(1,5 %)	1.000	(1,4 %)	2
▶ java.lang.reflect.Field	63.000 B	(2,5 %)	875	(1,3 %)	876	(1,3 %)	2

Figure 6-51. *Objects Snapshot Result*

Threads and Locks

Threads and *Locks* profiling gives a more in-depth view on how your application code is really executed. Both modes together, combined by using the *Enable Multiple Modes* setting in the *Profile* drop-down menu, allow for analysis, if your code is really running on the CPU or is blocked by waiting for locks or other resources, for example, synchronous I/O.

The *Threads* view shows a filterable list (see Methods section above for handling of the filter mechanism) with colored coded thread states. This allows us to see live feedback on how your application is using threads and if threads are really running or just blocked, for example, for a long time or frequently for a short time. A simple example of a live *Threads* view is shown in Figure 6-52.

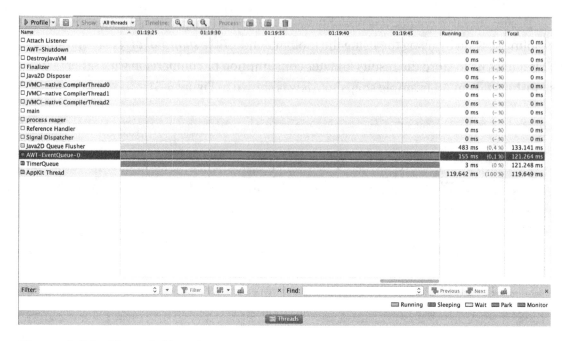

Figure 6-52. *Threads live view*

In contrast to the *Methods* and *Objects* profiling modes, the *Threads* mode does not offer a result snapshot feature. Now that you have seen threads being blocked from execution, the question is what blocks them from execution. The answer to this question can be given by activating *Locks* profiling. The *Locks* view gives a detailed view of why which thread has been blocked and for how long. A very simple example is shown in Figure 6-53.

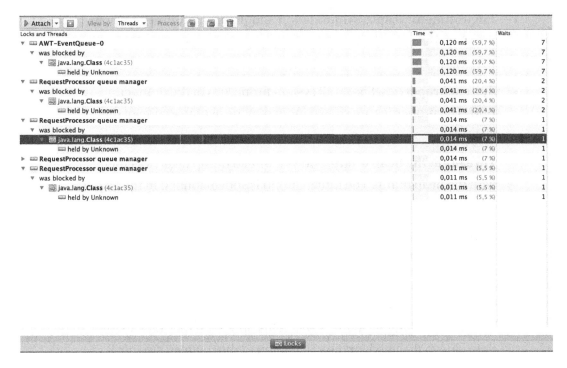

Figure 6-53. *Locks live view*

SQL Queries

Profiling SQL Queries is just an additional layer of sugar. SQL profiling analyses of your application's SQL queries collects the traces and execution times of the statements. It can also track the establishing of connections to the database, which may be useful in tuning your connection pool.

Heap Walker

The *Heap Walker* is a tool set for analyzing heap dumps taken with the OpenJDK internal heap dump mechanism (can also be triggered using some actions during profiling). It is a very thorough analysis tool with lots of capabilities for dissecting the heap dump.

First there is a *Summary* available showing relevant data concerning the heap dump in multiple categories:

- **Basic Info**. Displays basic information, for example, file size, date of dump.

- **Environment**. Displays information about the environment; where the snapshot was taken on, for example, operating system; JVM details as vendor and version.

- **System properties**. Shows all system properties of the dumped JVM. The properties are shown inlined in the actual section of the view.

- **Threads at the heap dump**. Shows a thread dump taken together with the heap dump. The thread dump is shown inlined in the actual section of the view.

- **Application windows**. Lists all top-level Swing windows, with direct access to the instance in the *Instances* view.

- **Biggest Objects**. Triggers the determination of the biggest objects on the heap, based on the retained sizes of its object tree, that is, everything belonging to the object. This operation may take some time, due to the need for the calculation of the retained size of all objects in the dump.

An example of the *Summary* view is shown in Figure 6-54.

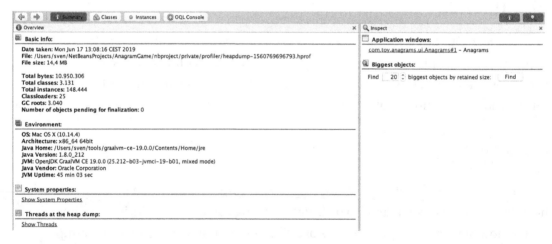

Figure 6-54. *Heap Walker Summary*

The next view is the *Classes* view. It displays the histogram of instances of classes on the heap. The tabular view can be sorted by instances, size, or name of the class. A filter at the bottom of the view allows for a faster drill down, for example, just looking for instances of your domain classes not JDK core classes. There is an initial hidden column, which would display the retained size. As already described, the computation can be a lengthy operation, so this column is hidden by default, although the information is sometimes really helpful. A simple example is shown in Figure 6-55.

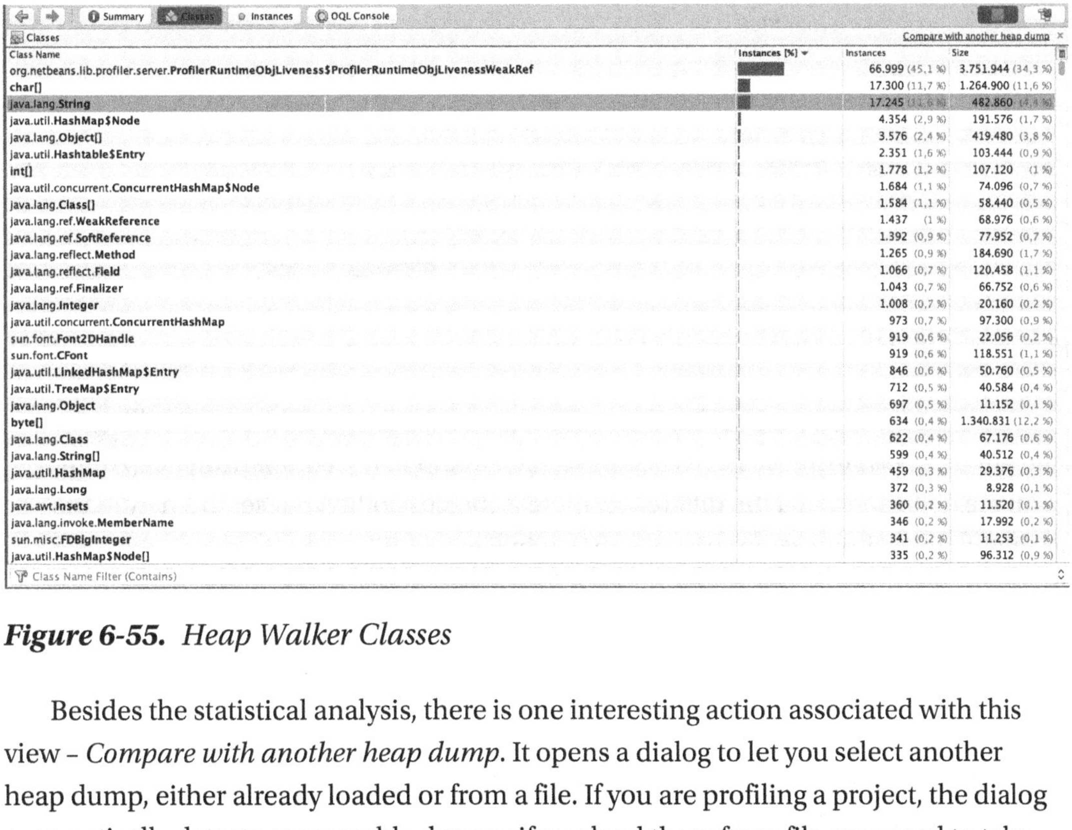

Class Name	Instances [%]	Instances	Size
org.netbeans.lib.profiler.server.ProfilerRuntimeObjLiveness$ProfilerRuntimeObjLivenessWeakRef		66.999 (45,1 %)	3.751.944 (34,3 %)
char[]		17.300 (11,7 %)	1.264.900 (11,6 %)
java.lang.String		17.245 (11,6 %)	482.860 (4,4 %)
java.util.HashMap$Node		4.354 (2,9 %)	191.576 (1,7 %)
java.lang.Object[]		3.576 (2,4 %)	419.480 (3,8 %)
java.util.Hashtable$Entry		2.351 (1,6 %)	103.444 (0,9 %)
int[]		1.778 (1,2 %)	107.120 (1 %)
java.util.concurrent.ConcurrentHashMap$Node		1.684 (1,1 %)	74.096 (0,7 %)
java.lang.Class[]		1.584 (1,1 %)	58.440 (0,5 %)
java.lang.ref.WeakReference		1.437 (1 %)	68.976 (0,6 %)
java.lang.ref.SoftReference		1.392 (0,9 %)	77.952 (0,7 %)
java.lang.reflect.Method		1.265 (0,9 %)	184.690 (1,7 %)
java.lang.reflect.Field		1.066 (0,7 %)	120.458 (1,1 %)
java.lang.ref.Finalizer		1.043 (0,7 %)	66.752 (0,6 %)
java.lang.Integer		1.008 (0,7 %)	20.160 (0,2 %)
java.util.concurrent.ConcurrentHashMap		973 (0,7 %)	97.300 (0,9 %)
sun.font.Font2DHandle		919 (0,6 %)	22.056 (0,2 %)
sun.font.CFont		919 (0,6 %)	118.551 (1,1 %)
java.util.LinkedHashMap$Entry		846 (0,6 %)	50.760 (0,5 %)
java.util.TreeMap$Entry		712 (0,5 %)	40.584 (0,4 %)
java.lang.Object		697 (0,5 %)	11.152 (0,1 %)
byte[]		634 (0,4 %)	1.340.831 (12,2 %)
java.lang.Class		622 (0,4 %)	67.176 (0,6 %)
java.lang.String[]		599 (0,4 %)	40.512 (0,4 %)
java.util.HashMap		459 (0,3 %)	29.376 (0,3 %)
java.lang.Long		372 (0,3 %)	8.928 (0,1 %)
java.awt.Insets		360 (0,2 %)	11.520 (0,1 %)
java.lang.invoke.MemberName		346 (0,2 %)	17.992 (0,2 %)
sun.misc.FDBigInteger		341 (0,2 %)	11.253 (0,1 %)
java.util.HashMap$Node[]		335 (0,2 %)	96.312 (0,9 %)

Figure 6-55. *Heap Walker Classes*

Besides the statistical analysis, there is one interesting action associated with this view - *Compare with another heap dump*. It opens a dialog to let you select another heap dump, either already loaded or from a file. If you are profiling a project, the dialog automatically detects comparable dumps; if you load them from file, you need to take care of that for yourself. The loading UI is shown in Figure 6-56.

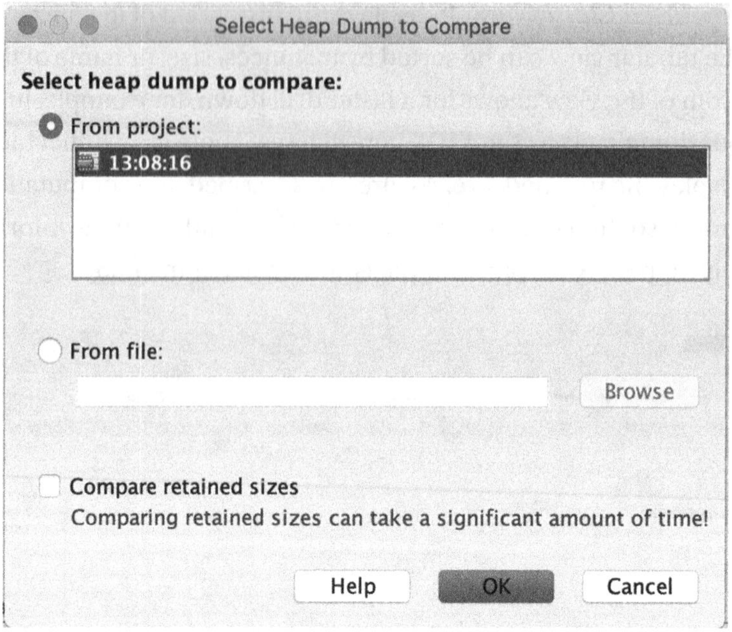

Figure 6-56. *Heap Walker Load Comparison Heap Dump*

Once the dump is loaded, the view switches to a delta comparison view telling how many more or less instances of a class have been found in the comparison heap dump. If you are done analyzing the difference, there is the possibility to reset the view to the original state. A simple comparison is shown in Figure 6-57.

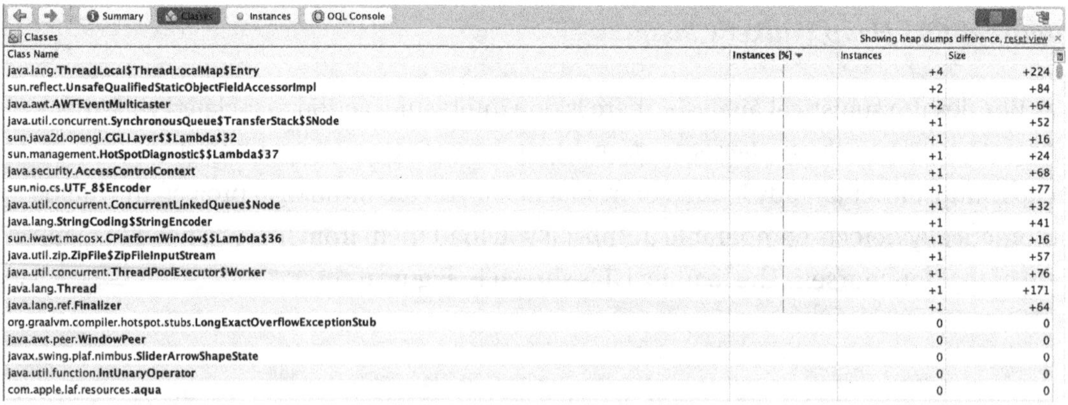

Figure 6-57. *Heap Walker Classes Comparison*

Double-clicking on a class in the *Classes* view opens the *Instances* view showing a list of all instances of this class. The view is practically identical to the *Instances* view described in the *Debugger* section. The upper-left corner shows the instances available (grouped if there are too many for a flat list), the lower-left corner shows a value representation of the object instance if possible. On the right-hand side the structure of the selected instance is shown in the *Fields* view and below this is the *References* view showing the reference chain of this instance up to the garbage collection root, which keeps the instance alive on the heap. This is critical information if a memory leak appears and it is not quite clear, why some instance will not get garbage collected, for example, some static field holding a strong reference to the instance. An example showing a profiling result in the *Instances* view can be found in Figure 6-58.

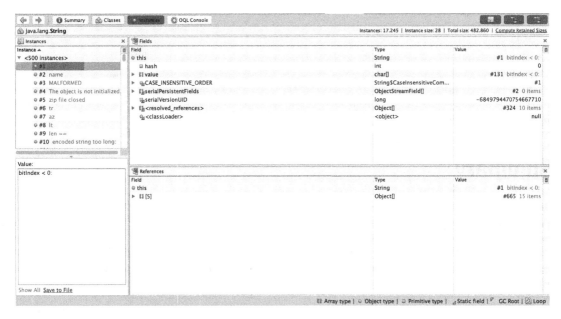

Figure 6-58. *Heap Walker Instances*

The final view is the *OQL Console*. This view allows you to do an interactive analysis using a special OQL syntax for querying the heap. There are some queries as examples already available on the lower right-hand side in the *Saved Queries* view. The *Query Editor* on the lower right offers code completion to simplify creating new queries, which can be saved for later reusage. Once you execute a query, the result will be shown in the *Query Results* view, the upper half of the *OQL Console view*. The result of a query is always a list of instances, which can be selected and analyzed in the *Instances* view. The usage of the *OQL Console* is especially interesting if there are a lot of instances of the same object and you want to figure out a subset of those, for example, all empty maps. An example session with the OQL Console is shown in Figure 6-59.

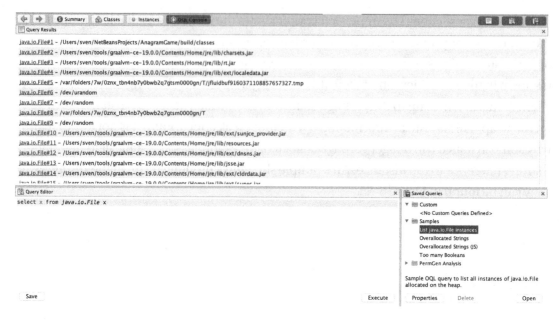

Figure 6-59. *Heap Walker OQL*

Summary

In this chapter we had a detailed look at two of the Apache NetBeans crown jewels, *Debugging* and *Profiling*.

You have learned how to use the debugger to tackle issues in your application code, debug multi-threaded applications, and interact with your application from the debugger.

In case of performance problems, we showed you how to profile your application to understand the underlying memory allocation and execution performance behavior. We introduced you to the built-in features, which help you analyze the data collected during the profiling runs.

Both of the features shown in this chapter are easy to use and should be part of your developer tool belt. Now we will move on to Part II, "Extending Apache NetBeans."

PART II

Extending Apache NetBeans

CHAPTER 7

Mastering the Core Platform

As we saw in Chapter 4, NetBeans eases the development of desktop applications written with either Swing or JavaFX. While Swing is a stable and well-entrenched library, the newer JavaFX API offers an improved rich media solution. However, both libraries lack a framework. That is, both lack an out-of-the-box solution with a window management system and true Model-View-Controller parts that sophisticated desktop applications require.

You're probably familiar with the NetBeans IDE as a development tool. However, NetBeans is also a platform for building modular applications. The NetBeans IDE is built on top of the *NetBeans Rich Client Platform* or *RCP*.

The NetBeans Rich Client Platform is a generic framework that provides the "plumbing" when developing desktop applications, such as the code for managing windows, connecting actions to menu items, and updating applications at runtime. The NetBeans Platform provides all of these out of the box on top of a reliable, flexible, and well-tested modular architecture. It is for desktop applications what the Java Enterprise Edition framework is for web applications.

This chapter is a big picture description of what the NetBeans Rich Client Platform offers to desktop application developers and an executive summary of what you can expect to learn in Part 2 of the book.

First, you will learn the ***core*** of the NetBeans Platform (or RCP) (this chapter):

- The Module system

- The File system

- Lookups

© Ioannis Kostaras, Constantin Drabo, Josh Juneau, Sven Reimers, Mario Schröder, Geertjan Wielenga 2020
I. Kostaras et al., *Pro Apache NetBeans*, https://doi.org/10.1007/978-1-4842-5370-0_7

After you have acquired a good background of the *core*, we move to the GUI part (Chapter 8), which is built on top of Swing:

- Window system

- Nodes

- Explorer Views

- Action system

We also describe two alternative technologies:

- JavaFX and the NetBeans Platform

- HTML/Java UI

We apply the above by porting a Swing application to the NetBeans Platform in Chapter 9.

Finally, we teach you some extras (Chapter 10):

- Visual Library

- Dialogs

- Wizards

- Branding, distribution, and internationalization

Chapter 11 uses the information you learned in the previous chapters to help you build a plugin for NetBeans.

Figure 7-1 shows the architecture of the NetBeans platform on which Part 2 of the book is based.

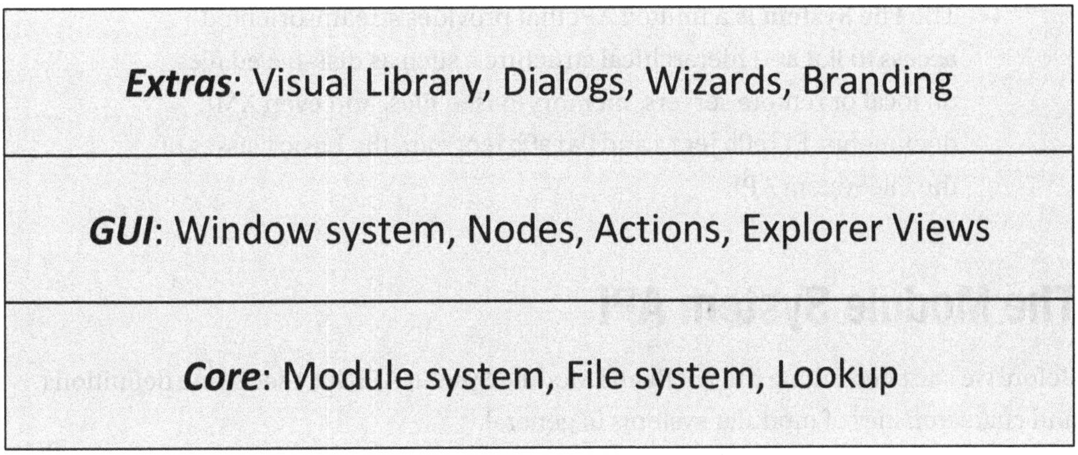

Extras: Visual Library, Dialogs, Wizards, Branding
GUI: Window system, Nodes, Actions, Explorer Views
Core: Module system, File system, Lookup

Figure 7-1. *Overview of the NetBeans Platform architecture*

This link (`https://platform.netbeans.org/screenshots.html`) provides a list of desktop applications written on top of NetBeans RCP.

The Core Platform

In this chapter we will learn the *Core* NetBeans Rich Client Platform (see Figure 7-1 in Chapter 7), which consists of the following systems (APIs):

- The **Module System**: Modularity offers a solution to "JAR hell" by letting you organize code into strictly separated and versioned modules. Only modules that have explicitly declared dependencies on each other are able to use code from each other's exposed packages. The NetBeans Module system preexisted the Java 9 module system (Jigsaw) and is based on OSGi. A comparison of the two module systems is provided.

- The **Lookup** API is a loose coupling mechanism enabling a component to place a query for a particular interface and get back pointers to all registered instances of that interface across all modules of the application. Simply put, `Lookup` is an observable `Map`, with `Class` objects as keys and instances of those `Class` objects as values, and it allows loosely coupled communication between modules.

- The **File System** is a unified API that provides stream-oriented access to flat and hierarchical structures, such as disk-based files on local or remote servers, memory-based files, and even XML documents. `FileObjects` and `DataObjects` are the basic classes of the FileSystem API.

The Module System API

Before we start describing the NetBeans Module System API, let's see some definitions and characteristics of modular systems in general.

Modularization is the act of decomposing a system into self-contained modules. *Modules* are identifiable artifacts containing code, with metadata describing the module and its relation to other modules. A *modular application*, in contrast to a *monolithic* one of tightly coupled code, in which every unit may interface directly with any other, is composed of smaller, separate chunks of code that are well isolated.

Modular systems have a number of characteristics:

- **Strong encapsulation**: A module must be able to conceal part of its code from other modules. Consequently, encapsulated code may change freely without affecting users of the module.

- **Well-defined interfaces**: Modules should expose well-defined and stable interfaces to other modules.

- **Explicit dependencies**: Dependencies must be part of the module definition, in order for modules to be self-contained. In a module graph, nodes represent modules, and edges represent dependencies between modules.

- **Versioning**: Dependencies on a specific or a minimum version of a module.

The NetBeans platform Module API is the following:

- an architectural framework,

- an execution environment that supports a module system called the *Runtime Container*.

It provides a way to divide your application into cohesive parts and helps you build loosely coupled applications that can evolve without breaking. It also lets you add/remove features during runtime(!) without breaking your application.

The *Runtime Container* consists of the minimum modules required to load and execute your application and manages all of the modules in your application.

A *module* is a collection of functionally related classes stored in a JAR file along with metadata, which provide information to the Runtime Container about the module, such as the following:

- the module's name,

- version information,

- dependencies, and

- a list of its public packages, if any.

Figure 7-2 shows an explicit dependency of *Module A* to *Module B*.

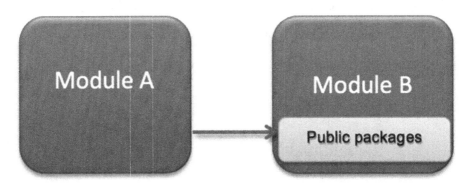

Figure 7-2. *An explicit dependency between two modules*

In order to use or access code in another module:

1. You must put *Module B* classes that identify the module's interface in a `public` package, assign a version number, and export it.

2. *Module A* must declare a dependency on a specified version of *Module B*.

Usually you put public interfaces of a module into a public package.

In other words, a module in the NetBeans Module System cannot reference classes in another module without declaring a dependency on that other module, and with that other module agreeing that the classes referenced are the ones that are the actual API of this module. This way you can design applications with high cohesion and low coupling.

All modules have a life cycle, which you can hook into via annotations. Thus, you can execute code when a module starts, shuts down, and when the window system initializes.

The *NetBeans Runtime Container* consists of the following six modules:

- *Bootstrap*: loads and executes the *Startup* module;

- *Startup*: contains the Main method of the application and initializes the module system and the virtual file system;

- *Module system*: manages modules, enforces module visibility and dependencies, and provides access to module life-cycle methods;

- *Utilities*: provides general utility classes;

- *File System*: provides a virtual file system for your application;

- *Lookup*: allows modules to communicate with each other.

Figure 7-3 shows the relationships between these modules.

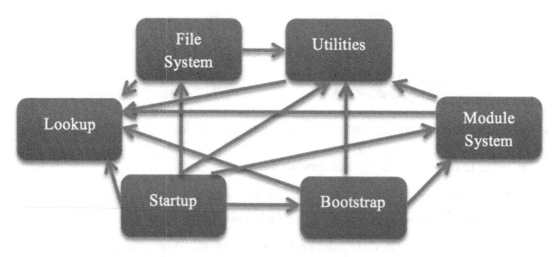

Figure 7-3. *NetBeans Platform Runtime Container*

Lookup API

NetBeans uses a component-based way of development. Modules or components developed by independent groups or individuals must be able to communicate with each other in a loosely-coupled way.

Previously we learned about how the Module System allows you to break up your application into loosely coupled parts. These modules need a loosely coupled way to communicate with each other, too. This is where the *Lookup* API fits in.

One of the biggest challenges in the history of software design is how to design *loosely-coupled* systems with *high cohesion*. "In computing and systems design a loosely coupled system is one in which each of its components has, or makes use of, little or no knowledge of the definitions of other separate components," according to Wikipedia (https://en.wikipedia.org/wiki/Loose_coupling).

Cohesion means that all code (and resources) related to a particular feature should be organized within the same module or the same set of modules. *Coupling*, on the other hand, refers to the degree to which the modules depend on each other. Modules should be independent of each other, as much as possible, enabling components to be modified or moved around without a big impact on the application. The higher the level of cohesion and the lower the level of coupling, the more sustainable and robust with respect to future modifications (less maintenance headache) the architecture is.

Let's assume that the Client and the ProviderImpl exist in two different modules (see Figure 7-4). How does the Client find the ProviderImpl (in a loosely coupled way)? Spring uses *dependency injection* or *inversion of control* via its xml files. Java 6 uses a Query-based approach, the ServiceLoader that we briefly describe later in this chapter.

NetBeans RCP introduces a new way to accomplish loose coupling, the @ServiceProvider:

```
@ServiceProvider(service = Provider.class, position=1)
public class ProviderImpl implements Provider { }
```

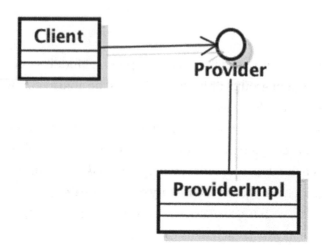

Figure 7-4. *A loosely coupled system*

The magic line is the first line that tells NetBeans that this class is an implementation of the service `Provider.class`. NetBeans creates a text file `package.Provider` inside `build/classes/META-INF/services/` folder of the module that contains the fully qualified names of the implementation classes, for example, `package.ProviderImpl`. If you have worked with `ServiceLoader`, then this is not new to you.

However, the big question has not been answered yet. How does the client find the implementation? In NetBeans this is done with the use of *lookups*! The client looks in the *default lookup* for the *interface* (not the implementation). The *default Lookup* (also known as *service registry*) is a `Lookup` that evaluates the service declarations in the `META-INF/services` folder. It is callable through the `Lookup.getDefault()` method. By asking for a service interface in this way, you receive instances of implementing classes registered in the `META-INF/services` folder.

A *lookup* is an observable map with class objects as keys and sets of instances of these class objects as values, that is,

`Lookup = Map<Class, Set<Class>>`

for example: `Map<String, Set<String>>` or `Map<Provider, Set<Provider>>`.

It was created to allow for inter-component binding and dependencies.

NetBeans provides a number of methods to access a lookup (see Listing 7-1).

Listing 7-1. Accessing the default lookup for a single implementation

```
Provider provider = Lookup.getDefault().lookup(Provider.class);
provider.aMethod();
```

or if you have more than one implementation of `Provider` (see Listing 7-2).

Listing 7-2. Accessing the default lookup for many implementations

```
Collection <? extends Provider> providers =
    Lookup.getDefault().lookupAll(Provider.class);
for (Provider provider : providers) { ... }
```

You may also request a `Lookup.Result<T>` that allows adding a `LookupListener` in order to be informed about content changes (Listing 7-3).

Listing 7-3. Adding a LookupListener

```
Lookup.Result<Provider> providers =
              Lookup.getDefault().lookupResult(Provider.class);
Collection<? extends Provider > allProviders =
                                  providers.allInstances();
providers.addLookupListener = new LookupListener(){
  @override
  public void resultChanged(LookupEvent e){
    // do something
    }}
);
```

As you can see from the above code examples, the client has no clue about which implementation it uses; it only knows the interface. Loose coupling!

Imagine the lookup as a map in memory that stores implementations of all the services of your application. You put the service implementation in the lookup when you define it with the `@ServiceProvider` annotation, and then you search for it using the above commands. Service implementations can be in different modules and in *non-*public packages.

NetBeans also allows you to order implementations by ascending `positions`, that is, instances with smaller numbers in the `position` attribute of the `@ServiceProvider` annotation are returned before instances with larger numbers.

We have seen two attributes of the @ServiceProvider annotation, service and position. There are two more, not that commonly used: path, a path in the *System FileSystem* where the provider is registered; and supersedes, a list of implementations, which this implementation supersedes.

There are other lookups in NetBeans apart from the *default lookup*, which is used to store services' implementations, and this often brings confusion. For example, each OutlineView or TopComponent associates with it a lookup to store the nodes that are selected at a specific time. You should not confuse this lookup with the default lookup. Here is a short summary of *Lookups*:

- *Global Lookup* is a singleton and works like a central registry. There are two important global lookups:

  - *Default Lookup* or *Service Registry*, which has been already described earlier, is available by Lookup.getDefault(). It is an application-wide repository for modules to discover and provide services. It is a central registry of *services* allowing you to look up the service implementation classes inside the META-INF/services folder. A client module can thus use a service without being aware of or dependent on its implementation (loose coupling between modules).

  - *Actions Global Context* available by Utilities.actionsGlobalContext() proxies the Lookup of whatever has currently the focus in the application.

- *Local Lookup:* classes may implement the Lookup.Provider interface and store objects in their own Lookup. You may think of a lookup as a "bag of objects" that an object can carry with it (Listing 7-4).

Listing 7-4. Lookup.Provider interface

```
public interface Lookup.Provider {
    Lookup getLookup();
}
```

For example, TopComponent, as we shall see in the next chapter, implements this interface (Listing 7-5).

Listing 7-5. TopComponent's Lookup

```
TopComponent tc = WindowManager.getDefault().findTopComponent("aTopComponent");
Lookup tcLookup = tc.getLookup();
```

TopComponents (are like JFrames) usually put into their Lookup whatever is selected. You can track the selection by adding a listener to the TopComponent (Listing 7-6).

Listing 7-6. Adding a LookupListener to a TopComponent

```
Lookup.result<Node> result = tcLookup.lookupResult(Node.class);
Collection<? extends Node> allNodes = result.allInstances();
result.addLookupListener(myLookupListener);
```

You may provide your own Lookup to the TopComponent, too:

```
tc.associateLookup(mylookup);
```

Creating Your Own Lookups

In addition to the built-in lookups, you can also create your own. The following subsections show the different possibilities that are available.

Empty Lookup

You may initialize a Lookup to an EMPTY Lookup:

```
Lookup emptyLookup = Lookups.EMPTY
```

Lookup Containing One Object

The most basic one is Lookups.Singleton, a Lookup that only contains one object:

```
Lookup singleObjLookup = Lookups.singleton(obj);
```

Lookup with Fixed Number of Objects

There's also an implementation for creating a lookup with more than one entry, still with fixed content:

```
Lookup fixedObjLookup = Lookups.fixed(obj1, obj2);
```

Lookup with Dynamic Content

You may also use a Lookup to dynamically add content to it. The most flexible way is to use an InstanceContent object to add and remove content:

```
InstanceContent content = new InstanceContent();
Lookup dynamicLookup = new AbstractLookup(content);
content.add(obj1);
content.add(obj2);
```

Besides its name, AbstractLookup, it is *not* an abstract class; it is a Lookup whose contents can change. Attaching a LookupListener to a Lookup.Result assigned to the Lookup lets you receive notifications of changes in the AbstractLookup.

ProxyLookup Merges Other Lookups

If you would like to query more than one Lookup at a time, you may use a ProxyLookup. The following example combines two Lookups into one:

```
Lookup compoundLookup =
    new ProxyLookup(singleObjLookup, fixedObjLookup);
```

Lookup Delegating Searches to Lookup of Some Object

A Lookup returned by a given object may change from time to time: for example, under some conditions, it may be the tool that is currently active, such as an ActionMap, etc. The created Lookup delegates to another Lookup that checks if the returned object is the same, fires change events, and updates all existing and referenced results.

```
Lookup delegating = Lookups.proxy(
    new Lookup.Provider () {
        public Lookup getLookup () {
```

```
            return lookup;
        }
    }
);
```

Exclude Classes from a Lookup

You may also filter out specific classes from a Lookup:

```
Lookup filtered =
        Lookups.exclude(originalLookup, SomeObj.class, ActionMap.class);
```

If you register your service in the layer.xml (see below), you can get a lookup for a certain folder like this:

```
Lookup lookup = Lookups.forPath("ServiceProviders");
```

We will see other lookups in the following chapters of Part II of the book.

The NetBeans Module System API versus the Java 9 Module API

Since JDK 9, project Jigsaw introduced modules in the Java language. A number of JEPs implemented the Jigsaw project:

- 200: The Modular JDK (Jigsaw/JSR 376 and JEP 261)

- 201: Modular Source Code

- 220: Modular Run-Time Images

- 238: Multi-Release JAR Files

- 260: Internal APIs Encapsulation

- 261: Module System

- 275: Modular Java Application Packaging

- 282: jlink: The Java Linker

The purpose was to make Java SE more flexible, scalable, maintainable, and secure; make it easier to construct, maintain, deploy, and upgrade applications; and enable improved performance.

Before Java 9, classes were arranged into *packages*. For example, com.company.app. MyClass is stored into the file com/company/app/MyClass.java. Packages are globally visible and open for extension. The unit of delivery is a *Java archive (jar)*. Access control is only managed at the level of classes/methods. Classes and methods can restrict access by three access modifiers as shown in Table 7-1.

Table 7-1. *Package Access Modifiers*

Access Modifier	Class	Package	Subclass	Unrestricted
Public	✓	✓	✓	✓
Protected	✓	✓	✓	
- (default or package)	✓	✓		
Private	✓			

How do you access a class from another package while preventing other classes from using it? You can only make the class public, thus exposing it to all other classes (i.e., break encapsulation). There are no explicit dependencies; explicit import statements are only at compile time; there is no way to know which other JAR files your JAR requires at runtime; the developer has to provide correct jars in the classpath during execution and in the correct order.

Maven solves compile-time dependency management by defining POM (Project Object Model) files (*Gradle* works in a similar way). *OSGi* solves runtime dependencies by requiring imported packages to be listed as metadata in JARs, which are then called *bundles.*

Once a classpath is loaded by the JVM, all classes are sequenced into a flat list, in the order defined by the classpath argument. When the JVM loads a class, it reads the classpath in fixed order to find the right one. As soon as the class is found, the search ends and the class is loaded. What happens when duplicate classes are in the classpath? Only one (the first one encountered) wins. The JVM cannot efficiently verify the completeness of the classpath upon starting. If a class cannot be found in the classpath, then you get a runtime exception. The term *"Classpath Hell"* or *"JAR Hell"* should now be clearer to you.

With project Jigsaw, Java now has its one module system. Modules can either export or strongly encapsulate packages. Modules express dependencies on other modules explicitly. Each JAR becomes a module, containing explicit references to other modules. A module has a publicly accessible part and an encapsulated part. All this information is available at compile time and runtime accidental dependencies on code from other non-referenced modules can be prevented. Optimizations can be applied by inspecting transitive dependencies.

The benefits of Java 9 module system are these:

- **Reliable configuration**: The module system checks whether a given combination of modules satisfies all dependencies before compiling or running code.

- **Strong encapsulation**: Modules explicitly express dependencies on other modules.

- **Scalable development**: Teams can work in parallel by creating explicit boundaries that are enforced by the module system.

- **Security**: No access to internal classes of the JVM (like `Unsafe`).

- **Optimization**: Optimizations can be applied by inspecting (transitive) dependencies. It also opens up the possibility to create a minimal configuration of modules for distribution.

As a consequence, JDK now consists of 19 platform modules.

As already mentioned in Chapter 3, a module has a name (e.g., `java.base`), groups related code and possibly other resources, and is described by a *module descriptor*. Like packages are defined in `package-info.java`, modules are defined in `module-info.java` (in root package). A modular jar is a jar with a `module-info.class` inside it. In Chapter 3, we also saw how NetBeans provides support for Java 9 modules.

Table 7-2 provides a comparison between the NetBeans Module API and the Java 9 modular API.

Table 7-2. *NetBeans Module API vs. Java 9 Modules Comparison*

	Java 9 modules	NetBeans Module API
Encapsulation	✓	✓
Interfaces	✓	✓
Explicit dependencies	✓	✓
Versioning	✗	✓
Cyclic dependencies*	✓	✓
Services	ServiceLoader	ServiceProvider

As already described, both modular systems provide support for encapsulation and exporting public interfaces and explicitly handle dependencies while both don't allow cyclic dependencies. Java 9 doesn't allow cyclic dependencies during compile time, but it does during runtime. The Java 9 module system doesn't support versioning, something that has been criticized by the Java community.

As already mentioned, loose coupling between modules is achieved in NetBeans RCP via the lookups and the ServiceProvider interface. Jigsaw, on the other hand, uses a Query-based approach from Java 6, the ServiceLoader (Listing 7-7).

Listing 7-7. ServiceLoader interface

```
ServiceLoader<Provider> serviceLoader =
      ServiceLoader.load(Provider.class);
for (Provider provider : serviceLoader) { return provider; }
...
ServiceLoader<Provider> serviceLoader =
    ServiceLoader.load(Provider.class).stream().filter(...);
```

However, the ServiceLoader has a number of problems:

- It isn't dynamic (you cannot install/uninstall a plugin/service at runtime).

- It does all service loading at startup (as a result it requires longer startup time and more memory usage).

- It cannot be configured; there is a standard constructor and it doesn't support factory methods.

- It is a final class with hard-coded behavior so it cannot be extended.

- It doesn't allow for ranking/ordering, that is, we cannot choose which service to load first.

Java 9 introduced a number of modifications to Java 6 `ServiceLoader`:

- No relative services; the new module-based service locator does not have relative behavior.

- Ordering of services (as they were discovered) is lost.

- All service interfaces and implementations on the module path are flattened into a single, global namespace.

- No extensibility / customizability of service loading; the service layer provider must provide a fixed mapping of available services up front.

- Multiple-site declarations; every module that uses a service must also declare that the service is being used in the module descriptor; no global layer-wide service registry.

`ServiceProvider` does not have the drawbacks of `ServiceLoader`. It is dynamic, so you can plug in/unplug modules while your application is running, it doesn't load all services at startup, and it allows you to set priorities (with the `position` attribute). It is extensible, supports listeners, understands the NetBeans platform module system, and one can create as many `Lookups` as they wish (there can be only one instance of `ServiceLoader` per classloader).

And now the big questions:

- Which module system to use?

- Can the Jigsaw module system and the NetBeans Module API work together?

As we saw, both module systems have their pros and cons. NetBeans Module System API can also work outside of NetBeans; just use the related JAR files (they can be found inside `platform/lib` folder of your NetBeans IDE installation): `boot.jar`, `core.jar`, `org-openide-filesystems.jar`, `org-openide-modules.jar`, and `org-openide-util.jar`.

Don't mix up module systems, that is, don't use both Jigsaw and NetBeans Module System in your project. It will unnecessarily complicate things, and it won't give any extra benefit to your application.

The File System API

The NetBeans Platform File System API provides an abstraction for standard files. The *File System API* handles both files and folders (you can think of them as *resources*) on the physical file system as well as on the NetBeans virtual file system (e.g., they may reside in memory, in a JAR or ZIP or XML file, or even on a remote server).

A FileSystem is a collection of FileObjects that can reside anywhere. A FileSystem is hierarchical and has a *root*. A FileObject represents either a file or a directory (folder) in the FileSystem; it must physically exist in the FileSystem (unlike Java's java.io.File) and has a *MIME type*, which determines how the file is handled. A FileObject is an implementation of the *Composite* design pattern, that is, it can contain other FileObjects (files or subdirectories). A FileObject also includes support for attributes (which are key-value pairs or type String).

You may listen for changes to a FileObject (such as file/folder creation, renaming, modification, deletion, or attribute changing) with the FileChangeListener interface. Finally, FileUtil is a utility class with many methods that manipulates FileSystems, FileObjects, and even standard java.io.File objects.

A summary of the above is depicted in Figure 7-5 in a graphical way.

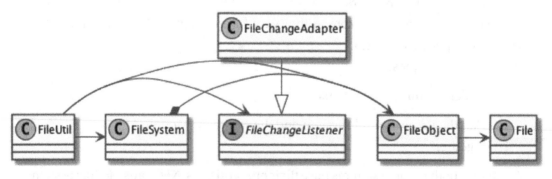

Figure 7-5. *Class diagram of the FileSystem API main classes*

Let's see some code examples (Listings 7-8 and 7-9).

Listing 7-8. FileSystem API examples

```
String aPath = ...;
File dir = new File(aPath);
FileObject myfolder = FileUtil.toFileObject(dir);
if (null == myfolder) {
   try {
      // Create folder
      myfolder = FileUtil.createFolder(dir);
   } catch (IOException ex) {
      Exceptions.printStackTrace(ex);
   }
}
if (myfolder != null) {
   // Is there a file called myfile.txt in this folder?
   FileObject myfile = myfolder.getFileObject("myfile.txt");
   if (null == myfile) {
      try {
            // Create file
            myfile = myfolder.createData("myfile.txt");
      } catch (IOException ex) {
            Exceptions.printStackTrace(ex);
      }
   }
}
if (myfile != null) {
    // write some text to myfile
    if (myfile.canWrite()) {
        try (PrintWriter output =
          new PrintWriter(myfile.getOutputStream())) {
          output.println("This is some text");
        } catch (IOException ex) {
          Exceptions.printStackTrace(ex);
        }
    }
```

```
    // read file
    if (myfile.canRead()) {
        System.out.println("MIME Type: " + myfile.getMIMEType());
        try {
            for (String line : myfile.asLines()) {
                System.out.println(line);
            }
        } catch (IOException ex) {
            Exceptions.printStackTrace(ex);
        }
    }
}
// Rename myfile.txt; requires a lock
FileLock lock = null;
try {
    lock = myfile.lock();
    // Rename will fail if the new name already exists.
    myfile.rename(lock, "mynewfile", myfile.getExt());
} catch (IOException ex) {
    Exceptions.printStackTrace(ex);
} finally {
    if (lock != null) {
        lock.releaseLock();
    }
}
try {
    // delete file; FileObject delete()  method takes care of
    // acquiring and releasing a lock. Deleting a FileObject
    // folder recursively deletes its contents.
    myfile.delete();
} catch (IOException ex) {
    Exceptions.printStackTrace(ex);
}
```

The previous example created a new folder, a new file inside it, renamed the file, and then deleted it. As already mentioned, you can attach FileChangeListeners to

`FileObjects` (either files or folders) and also attach recursive `FileChangeListeners` to folders in a directory tree. The `FileChangeListener` interface has six methods to override as shown in Listing 7-9.

Listing 7-9. FileChangeListener interface

```
private final FileChangeListener fcl = new FileChangeListener() {
    @Override
    public void fileFolderCreated(FileEvent fe) { ... }

    @Override
    public void fileDataCreated(FileEvent fe) {    ... }

    @Override
    public void fileChanged(FileEvent fe) { ... }

    @Override
    public void fileDeleted(FileEvent fe) { ... }

    @Override
    public void fileRenamed(FileRenameEvent fre) { ... }

    @Override
    public void fileAttributeChanged(FileAttributeEvent fae) { }
}
myfolder.addRecursiveListener(fcl);
```

System FileSystem or Layer.xml

A file system in the NetBeans Platform is a generic and highly abstract concept. A NetBeans Platform file system is a place where you can hierarchically store and read files, and it doesn't have to be on a physical disk. A concrete implementation of this is in the *MultiFileSystem* class, which lets you construct a single namespace that merges a set of discrete file systems called *layers* and acts as if the content of all of them live in the same namespace. For example, if two different layers contain a folder *MyFolder* with different content, listing the content of the *MultiFileSystem MyFolder* folder gives you the content of both. To deal with collisions (i.e., two files with the same name and path), *MultiFileSystem* contains a stack order of layers, meaning the one on top is used.

NetBeans' implementation of a *MultiFileSystem* is the so-called *System FileSystem*. It is used to define all of the actions, menus, menu items, icons, key bindings, toolbars, and services available in your application.

It can be viewed from the *Files* window under the build directory as classes/METAINF/generated-layer.xml. In previous versions of NetBeans, the developer had to edit a layer.xml file like the above in order to configure actions, menu and toolbar items, key bindings, service providers, etc. Nowadays, all these should be taken care by annotations, as we shall see in the next chapter. However, there are still some specialized things that you can only do by editing this file. Furthermore, the layer.xml file is the gateway to your NetBeans Platform application's complete configuration data. The *FileSystem API* handles this virtual file system in the same way (Listing 7-10).

Listing 7-10. Accessing layer.xml with the FileSystem API

```
FileObject root = FileUtil.getConfigRoot();
FileObject someFolder = FileUtil.getConfigFile("someFolder");
JToolBar tb = FileUtil.getConfigObject("/path/to/fileobject", JToolBar.class)
```

The *System FileSystem* provides another type of inter-module communication (the other is the Lookup). Using the layer.xml file, a module can register folders and files that another module can use.

The File System API vs. Java NIO

The NetBeans File System API existed before the Java NIO2, which was introduced in Java 7. Java NIO2 provides similar functionalities as the NetBeans FileSystem API. Table 7-3 is a comparison of the basic classes of the two (not a 100% match).

Table 7-3. *FileSystem API vs. Java 7 NIO2*

FileSystem API	Java 7 NIO2
org.openide.filesystems.FileSystem	java.nio.file.FileSystem
org.openide.filesystems.FileObject	java.nio.file.Path
-	java.nio.file.attribute

(continued)

Table 7-3. (*continued*)

FileSystem API	Java 7 NIO2
`org.openide.filesystems.FileUtil`	`java.nio.file.Files` `java.nio.file.FileVisitor`

`org.openide.filesystems.`
`FileChangeListener`
	`java.nio.file.WatchService`
	`java.nio.file.Watchable`
	`java.nio.file.StandardWatchEventKinds`

-	`java.nio.channels.*`

Which one to use depends on your application. If you wish to develop an application that will display the files/folders to a GUI using the NetBeans RCP, it would be better for you to use the NetBeans FileSystem API. NIO2 is a more powerful API than the FileSystem API (which was created mainly to manage `layer.xml`) however the NetBeans FileSystem API is simpler and more straightforward.

DataSystem API

The *Data System API* is an important bridge between the *FileSystem API* and the *Nodes API* (that we shall describe in the next chapter). The main classes of this API are `DataObject` and `DataNode`. The `DataObject` wraps a `FileObject`, and the `DataNode` displays it in the UI or presentation layer. All of them have a `Lookup`, which is important for accessing the capabilities associated with a file. `DataLoaders` recognize the `FileObject` type via its MIME type, and create the `DataObject` associated with it.

```
DataObject dob = DataObject.find(myfile);
```

Note that multiple `FileObjects` can be associated with a `DataObject` (e.g., a Swing Design form – a `DataObject` – uses two files – `FileObjects` - a `.java` file and a `.form` file). However, one of them is designated as the primary file:

```
FileObject fob = dob.getPrimaryFile();
```

Finally, here is how you can get access to the relevant `Node` from a `DataObject` and vice versa:

```
Node node = dob.getNodeDelegate();
DataObject mydob = ((DataNode)node).getDataObject();
```

We shall describe the Node API in the next chapter. Additionally, we will see an application of the *FileSystem* and *DataSystem* APIs in Chapter 11 where we will develop a plugin for NetBeans. There we will learn how to create a new file type and register this file type with our plugin.

An Example Application

Let's try to apply what we have learned so far by porting a Swing ToDo application to NetBeans RCP. If you wish to download the ToDo Swing application and build it yourself, please proceed; otherwise you may skip to the section of this chapter "*The Todo Swing Application*." You may also find the fixed version in the book's source code.

Build the Todo Swing Application

Download the original Swing application from here (http://netbeans.org/community/ magazine/code/nb-completeapp.zip), unzip it, and open it in NetBeans. Since this is a rather old application, you will encounter a number of problems. Press the **Resolve Problems** button to get a list of the problems. Click **Resolve...** in order for NetBeans to try to resolve them.

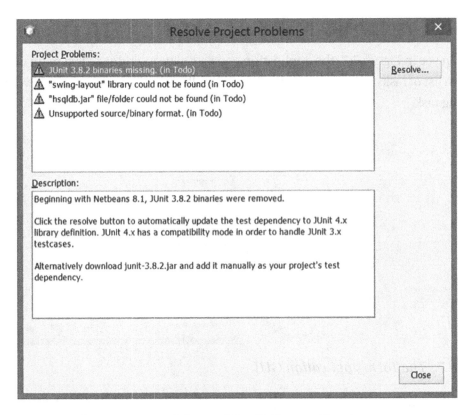

Figure 7-6. *Resolve Project Problems of the ToDo application*

NetBeans will resolve the first and the last as shown in Figure 7-6. The other two need to be resolved manually. Follow the instructions in this FAQ (`http://wiki.netbeans.org/FaqFormLayoutGenerationStyle`) to resolve the "swing-layout" library issue.

Download *hsqldb.zip* (from `http://hsqldb.org`), create a `lib` folder inside *TodoNB5,* and copy in there the `hsqldb.jar` file from `hsqldb.zip`. Right-click on *Libraries* and select **Add JAR/folder...** from the pop-up menu. Navigate to the `lib` folder and select the `hsqldb.jar` (make sure you have *relative path* selected).

You should now be able to run it. When you run it, you should see the error in the status bar: **"Cannot fetch from the database".** This is due to the version of HSQLDB. Open `TaskManager.java`, locate method `listTasksWithAlert()`, and replace `curtime()` with `CURRENT_TIMESTAMP`. Rerun the application. You should now be able to see a window with empty tasks.

The Todo Swing Application

As you can see in Figure 7-7, the application consists of two windows. The main window provides a list of tasks. The *Task Details* dialog box allows the user to create a new or edit an existing task.

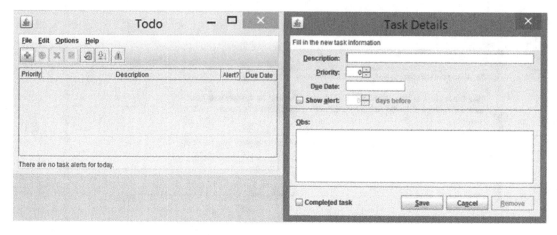

Figure 7-7. *The ToDo application GUI*

Here is a short list of requirements of the application:

- Tasks should have a priority, so users can focus first on higher-priority tasks.

- Tasks should have a due date, so users can instead focus on tasks that are closer to their deadline.

- There should be visual cues for tasks that are either late or near their deadlines.

- Tasks can be marked as completed, but this doesn't mean they have to be deleted or hidden.

There are two main windows for the Todo application: a *tasks list* and a *task-editing form*. A rough sketch for both is shown in Figure 7-8.

Figure 7-8. *Sketch of the ToDo application*

The Todo application is going to be developed in three steps:

Step 1. Build a "static" visual prototype of the user interface, using a visual GUI builder.

Step 2. Build a "dynamic" prototype of the application, coding user interface events and associated business logic, and creating customized UI components as needed.

Step 3. Code the persistence logic.

It consists of three packages: `todo.model, todo.view, todo.controller` (see Figure 7-9).

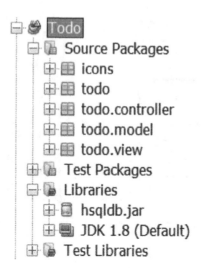

Figure 7-9. *Package structure of the ToDo application*

As shown in Figure 7-10, the Swing ToDo application follows the *Model-View-Controller* architecture.

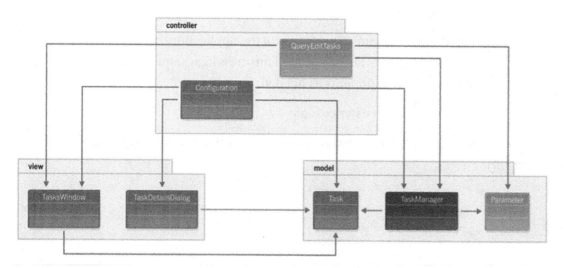

Figure 7-10. *The ToDo application architecture*

We shall create a similar architecture using the NetBeans platform module system, using modules instead of packages (see Figure 7-11).

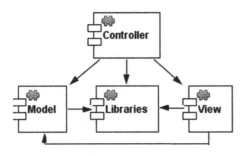

Figure 7-11. *The TodoRCP application architecture*

Let's get started. Click on the **New Project** toolbar button and select the *NetBeans Platform Application* in the *NetBeans Modules* category (see Figure 7-12). Use *"TodoRCP"* as the project name and choose a suitable project location. Then click **Finish**.

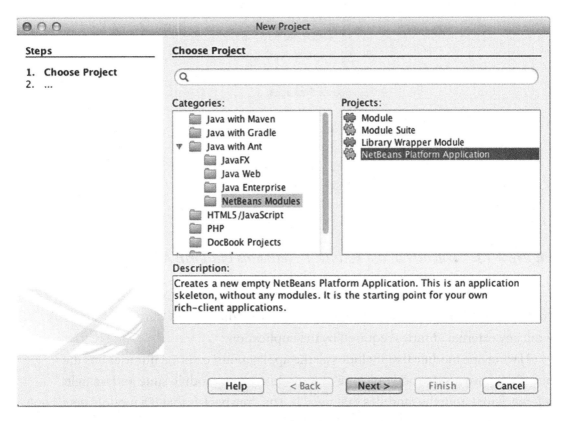

Figure 7-12. *Create a new NetBeans Platform Application project*

NetBeans creates the NetBeans Platform Application project containing an empty *Modules* folder and an *Important Files* folder. This is the container for the modules that will be created in the rest of this part of the book. We shall create the same *Model-View-Controller* structure for our *TodoRCP* application.

Right-click the *Modules* folder icon and choose **Add New**. Type *"View"* as the module name and click **Next**. Type todo.view as the *Code Base Name* and then click on **Finish**. You should see the structure shown in Figure 7-13.

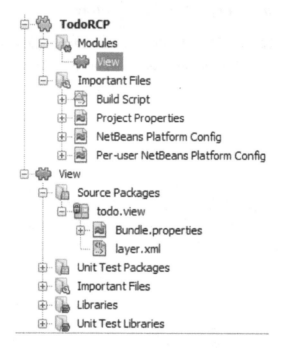

Figure 7-13. *Structure of the TodoRCP NetBeans Platform Application project*

Create the other two modules, *"Model"* (todo.model) and *"Controller"* (todo.controller), the same way. Finally, create a new module called *"Libraries"* that will wrap any external libraries required by the application.

Having one module that includes all the applications' external libraries has the benefit that we need to add only one new module to our module suite and a single reference to it from the modules that need it. The drawback is that if a module needs only one jar, it needs to reference all other jars that are wrapped inside the *Libraries* module.

We shall wrap two java libraries (a.k.a. jar files) inside this module: the hsqldb.jar that we downloaded earlier in this chapter, and the *SwingX* library that is not included any longer in the `ide/modules/ext/` folder. Download it instead from here (`https://mvnrepository.com/artifact/org.swinglabs.swingx/swingx-all`).

Let's create the module and add the external libraries that we will need for the *TodoRCP* application:

1. Right-click the *Modules* folder icon of the *TodoRCP* module suite and choose **Add New**. Type `Libraries` as the module name and click **Next**. Type `lib` as the *Code Base Name* and then **Finish**.

2. Right-click on the newly created module and select **Properties ➤ Libraries ➤ Wrapped JARs**. Click on **Add JAR** and add the `swingx-all-x.x.x.jar`. Repeat the procedure to the add `hsqldb.jar`.

3. Select the *API Versioning* category from the left panel of the opened **Project Properties ➤ Libraries** dialog box and make the following packages `public` by checking them:

   • `org.hsqldb`

   • `org.jdesktop.swingx`

4. After clicking on **OK**, clean and build the *Libraries* module.

The TodoRCP module suite should now contain four modules (see Figure 7-14).

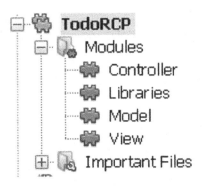

Figure 7-14. *The TodoRCP suite with all the modules*

There is a plugin to visualize the dependencies between modules. Download the *DisplayDependencies* plugin from `https://sourceforge.net/projects/netbeansmoddep/`. Click on **Tools ➤ Plugins** menu and then on the **Downloaded** tab. Click on the **Add Plugins...** button and navigate to the location that you saved the downloaded *1475781757_eu-dagnano-showdependencies.nbm* file. Click on **Install** button and follow the wizard to install the plugin. A new button with tooltip *Show Dependencies* is displayed on the toolbar. Click on a module or on the module suite and then on the **Show Dependencies** button to view a graph like the one in Figure 7-11 (without all the dependencies yet).

Copy the Task.java from the *ToDo* Swing application to the todo.model package of the *Model* module. To ease our development, we shall use a mock *TaskManager* that stores the tasks to memory instead of the database.

The *TaskManager* class is a *DAO (Data Access Object)*. Being the only DAO on the application, it contains many methods that would otherwise be in an abstract superclass. Its implementation is very simple, so there's lots of room for improvement. We can extract the following interface in *Model* module based on the persistent *TaskManager* of the original article. Copy *TaskManager* from *ToDo* application, inside the todo.model package of the *Model* module. Select the class name inside the editor and click on menu **Refactor ➤ Extract Interface**. Select only the methods shown in Figure 7-15.

Figure 7-15. *Extract Interface*

You may adapt it a bit to look like the code in Listing 7-11.

Listing 7-11. TaskManagerInterface

```
package todo.model;
import java.util.List;

public interface TaskManagerInterface {
    void addTask(Task task) throws ValidationException;
    void updateTask(final Task task) throws ValidationException;
    void removeTask(final int id);
    List<Task> listAllTasks(boolean priorityOrDate);
    List<Task> listTasksWithAlert() throws ModelException;
    void markAsCompleted(final int id, final boolean completed);
}
```

Copy ValidationException and ModelException classes from the *ToDo* application to resolve the errors, too. Click now on the bulb on the left of the TaskManagerInterface name and select **Implement Interface**. Give it the name *TaskManager* and click **OK**. NetBeans generates a skeleton implementation. Refactor-move it to a new package todo.model.impl. It is a good strategy to implement *TaskManager* as a service provider of the *TaskManagerInterface* service (Listing 7-12).

Listing 7-12. TaskManager as a service provider

```
package todo.model.impl;

import java.util.*;
import todo.model.ModelException;
import todo.model.Task;
import todo.model.TaskManagerInterface;
import todo.model.ValidationException;
import org.openide.util.lookup.ServiceProvider;

@ServiceProvider(service = TaskManagerInterface.class)
public class TaskManager implements TaskManagerInterface {

    private final List<Task> tasks = new ArrayList<>();

    public TaskManager() { // mock data
        final GregorianCalendar cal = new GregorianCalendar(TimeZone.
        getTimeZone("Europe/Athens"));
```

213

```java
        cal.set(2019, Calendar.JULY, 2, 10, 00, 00);
        tasks.add(new Task(1, "Hotel Reservation", 1, cal.getTime(), true));
        cal.set(2019, Calendar.JULY, 15, 16, 30, 00);
        tasks.add(new Task(2, "JCrete 2019", 1, cal.getTime(), true));
        cal.set(2019, Calendar.JULY, 5, 12, 45, 00);
        tasks.add(new Task(3, "Reserve time for visit", 2, cal.getTime(),
        false));
    }

    @Override
    public List<Task> listAllTasks(final boolean priorityOrDate) {
        Collections.sort(tasks, priorityOrDate ? new PriorityComparator() :
        new DueDateComparator());
        return Collections.unmodifiableList(tasks);
    }

    @Override
    public List<Task> listTasksWithAlert() throws ModelException {
        final List<Task> tasksWithAlert = new ArrayList<> (tasks.size());
        for (Task task : tasks) {
            if (task.hasAlert()) {
                tasksWithAlert.add(task);
            }
        }
        return Collections.unmodifiableList(tasksWithAlert);
    }

    @Override
    public void addTask(final Task task) throws ValidationException {
        validate(task);
        tasks.add(task);
    }

    @Override
    public void updateTask(final Task task) throws ValidationException {
        validate(task);
        Task oldTask = findTask(task.getId());
```

```java
        tasks.set(tasks.indexOf(oldTask), task);
    }

    @Override
    public void markAsCompleted(final int id, final boolean completed) {
        Task task = findTask(id);
        task.setCompleted(completed);
    }

    @Override
    public void removeTask(final int id) {
        tasks.remove(findTask(id));
    }

    private boolean isEmpty(final String str) {
        return str == null || str.trim().length() == 0;
    }

    private void validate(final Task task) throws ValidationException {
        if (isEmpty(task.getDescription())) {
            throw new ValidationException("Must provide a task description");
        }
    }

    private Task findTask(final int id) {
        for (Task task : tasks) {
            if (id == task.getId()) {
                return task;
            }
        }
        return null;
    }

    private static class PriorityComparator implements Comparator<Task> {

        @Override
        public int compare(final Task t1, final Task t2) {
            if (t1.getPriority() == t2.getPriority()) {
                return 0;
```

```
        } else if (t1.getPriority() > t2.getPriority()) {
            return 1;
        } else {
            return -1;
        }
    }
}

private static class DueDateComparator implements Comparator<Task> {

    @Override
    public int compare(final Task t1, final Task t2) {
        return t1.getDueDate().compareTo(t2.getDueDate());
    }

}
}
```

Don't hesitate to create the new *Task* constructor. To resolve the error of the *ServiceProvider*, click on the bulb and select **Search Module Dependency for ServiceProvider**. The dialog box of Figure 7-16 will be displayed, which will prompt you to select the (surprise, surprise) *Lookup API.*

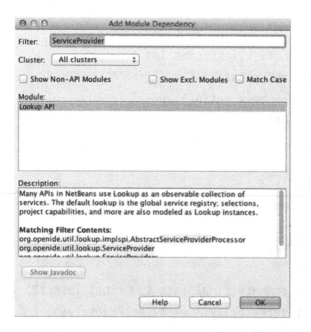

Figure 7-16. *The Add Module Dependency dialog box*

You just added a new dependency from your *Model* module to the *Lookup API* module.

Clean and build your module to resolve any errors.

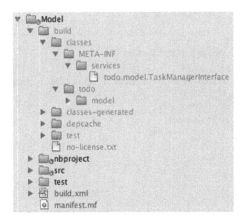

Figure 7-17. *META-INF/services folder*

In the *Files* tab, expand the *Model* module as shown in Figure 7-17 to verify that a new file `META-INF/services/todo.model.TaskManagerInterface` has been created, which contains the various implementations of the service, in our case `todo.model.impl.TaskManager`.

TaskManagerDB will be another service provider of *TaskManagerInterface*. In the next chapter, we shall see how we can use these services. Please notice that *TaskManager* or *TaskManagerDB* may exist in other modules of your application, and in non-public packages.

As an exercise, you may wish to refactor these two classes to use Java 8 syntax and libraries, for example, the new `java.time.*` classes and/or lambdas/streams.

Finally, we need to expose the `todo.model` package to other modules so that when other modules add dependencies to the *Model* module, they can access the classes inside this public package. Right-click on the *Model* module, select **Properties | API Versioning**, and check the `todo.model` package from the *Public Packages* section to make it public (see Figure 7-18). Clean and build the *Model* module.

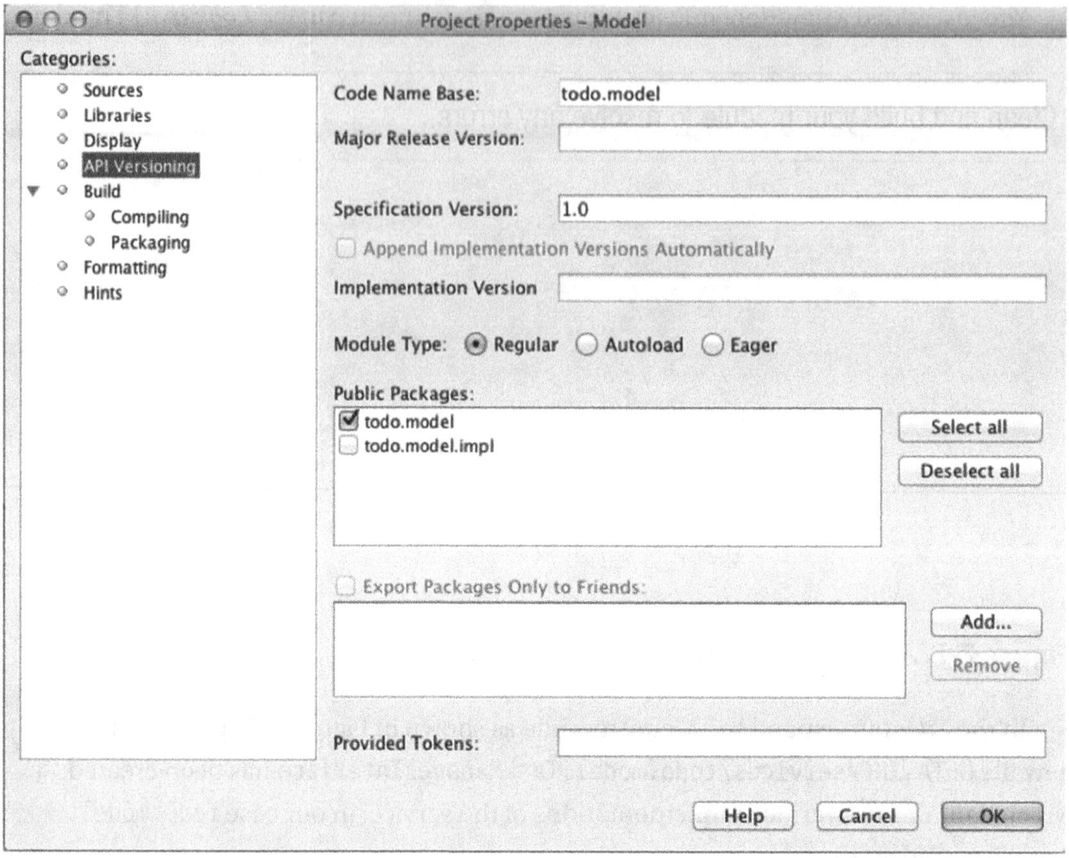

Figure 7-18. *Make a package public to other modules*

In the next chapter we shall see how to add dependencies between modules.

For an overview of the NetBeans platform modules, right-click on the *TodoRCP* module suite, select **Properties,** and click on the **Libraries** category. Expand the *platform* node to view a list of all platform modules included or not to your application.

Before we close this chapter, we shall take a brief look at the *System FileSystem* or layer.xml we described earlier.

To generate the layer.xml file, select the *View* module, right-click and select **New ➤ Other** from the context menu, then the **Module Development** category and the **XML Layer** file type. Follow the wizard and you will see a new layer.xml file created in the module's *Source Package*. In the *Projects* window, expand it,[1] and you will see `<this layer>` and `<this layer in context>` (see Figure 7-19). Entry `<this layer>` refers to configuration information in this module, and entry `<this layer in context>` refers to the entire application (in other words, it combines all `layer.xml` file contents of all the modules of the application, that is, it is the *System FileSystem*). You will notice that `layer.xml` for our module is empty and only contains `<filesystem/>`. The `layer.xml` file consists of four main tags: `<filesystem>`, `<folder>`, `<file>`, and `<attr>`.

One can access/create objects in the `layer.xml` using the *FileSystem API* that was described earlier in this chapter.

We shall learn how we can customize our application by editing this file in the next chapter.[2]

Figure 7-19. *layer.xml file*

---

[1]It exists in two places: inside the root package in the *Source Packages* and inside the *Important Files*.

[2]Be aware of a bug that was introduced in NetBeans 11.2 (see `https://issues.apache.org/jira/browse/NETBEANS-3290`), when you compile a NetBeans module project with a layer.xml and how to fix it.

219

Summary

In this chapter we learned the core of the NetBeans platform: the *Module System API*, the *Lookup API*, and the *FileSystem API*. The module system API allows you to create loosely coupled designed code that explicitly exposes the interfaces and the dependencies between the modules. Loosely coupled communication between the modules is achieved through the Lookup API. Finally, the FileSystem API provides another way to look at the file system, giving you extra capabilities. We explored the classes `FileSystem`, `FileObject`, `FileUtil`, `FileChangeListener`, and `DataObject`. Finally, we started applying what we have learned by porting a Swing application to NetBeans RCP.

CHAPTER 8

Mastering the User Interface

In this chapter we will look at the *GUI* components of the NetBeans Rich Client Platform:

- The **Window System**: is for your application what the Window Manager is for an operating system. A window system allows organizing the windows of your application workspace (by dragging, undocking, selecting, minimizing, or even grouping windows). It also has a persistence mechanism to save the state of the windows in order to be available in the same location and size on application restart. It also allows you to assign roles to different window configurations.

- The **Action System**: built on top of Swing `ActionListener` interface and `Action` class, allows you to concentrate on your business logic without worrying about presentation and enablement of the actions. Context-sensitive actions and capabilities allow you to create loosely coupled, modular applications.

- The **Node System**: Nodes are a data wrapper that allows data to be visualized in a number of Explorer Views and Property Sheets.

- The **Explorer Views and Property Sheets**: are the actual UI components, built on top of Swing UI components –the render nodes. You may choose from a number of UI components to display trees, tables, lists, images, etc. We shall also see alternatives like how to integrate JavaFX to the Window system as well as using the new HTML/JAVA UI instead of the Explorer Views and Property Sheets.

© Ioannis Kostaras, Constantin Drabo, Josh Juneau, Sven Reimers, Mario Schröder, Geertjan Wielenga 2020
I. Kostaras et al., *Pro Apache NetBeans*, https://doi.org/10.1007/978-1-4842-5370-0_8

Window System

In Chapter 2 we saw that NetBeans IDE supports a number of windows that shape the layout. The IDE's windowing system enables you to arrange any window the way you like by dragging and dropping it to the appropriate position (see Figure 2-1). You can also minimize, maximize, float, or dock a window.

The NetBeans IDE is a very good example of what the NetBeans Window System API can offer: pluggable multiple windows that can be arranged logically in a container, window state (open/closed, selected/unselected, activated/deactivated), etc.

Neither Swing nor JavaFX offers a framework with window management features. Developers can, of course, build a window management system themselves, but it takes a tremendous effort to create such a system. The NetBeans Platform Window System provides this functionality in the form of annotations.

Benefits and Features

One of the benefits of the NetBeans RCP Window System API is that application code is completely independent of how its components are rendered onscreen.

A *Window System*:

- includes a *window manager* that responds to user actions such as dragging, undocking, selecting, grouping, resizing, or minimizing windows to manage work space;

- includes a *persistence mechanism* that "remembers" the layout so that users aren't required to reconfigure the application on each restart;

- provides a way to specify an application's window layout and a way to group windows that have a common behavior;

- provides *roles* (or perspectives) based on which you can configure the application's layout (e.g. 'admin' role, 'user' role, etc.)

The NetBeans Platform Window System includes a window manager that keeps track of an application's windows, modes, window groups, and roles allowing developers to focus on building their business logic instead of reinventing the wheel. You can configure it by clicking on **Tools ➤ Options** (or **NetBeans ➤ Preferences** on MacOS) ➤ **Appearance** (see Figure 8-1).

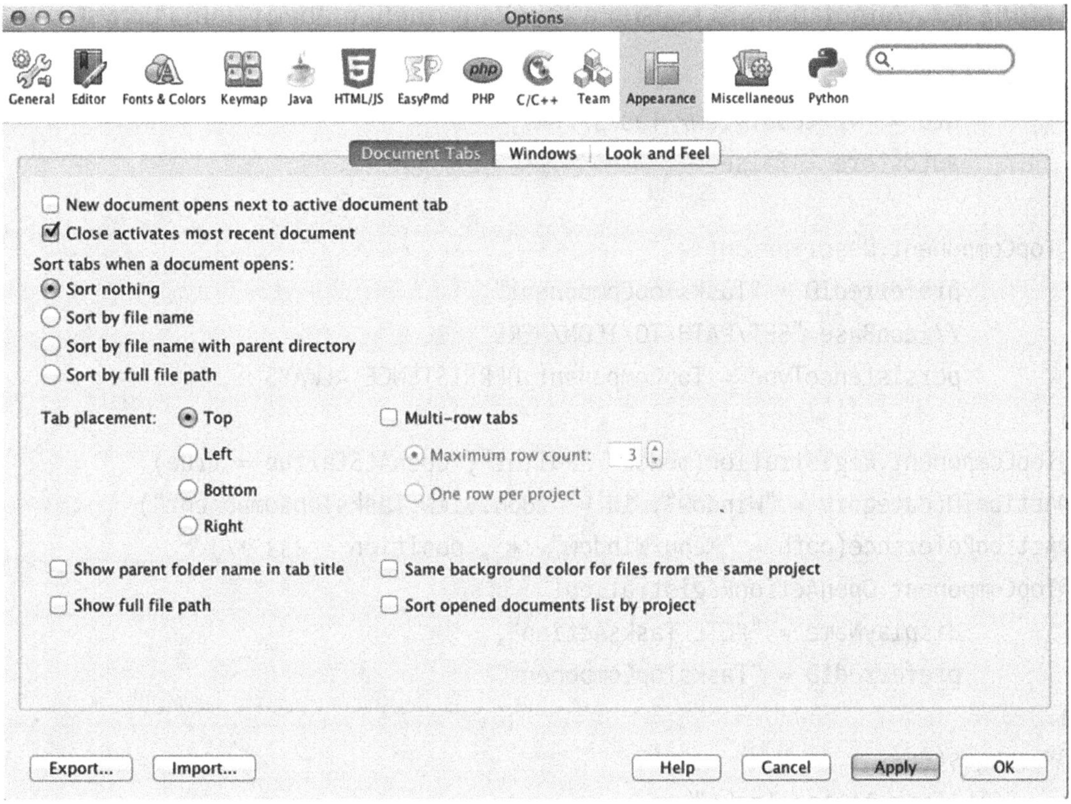

Figure 8-1. *Configure Appearance*

While creating the main window of a Swing application, you need to create a `JFrame`. To take advantage of the NetBeans Platform Window System, one needs to create a `TopComponent`. `TopComponent`, in turn, extends `JComponent` (a Swing-based container). With `TopComponent`, all application windows automatically integrate into the window system, that is, they are managed by the NetBeans Platform Window Manager and support a rich set of window operations. *Documents* are `TopComponents` in the editor mode.

As shown in Listing 8-1, these annotations allow the `TopComponent` to be registered with the Window System. The appearance and configuration of the `TopComponent` is also done via these annotations.

Listing 8-1. Annotations to register a TopComponent to the System FileSystem

```
@ConvertAsProperties(
        dtd = "-//todo.view//Tasks//EN",
        autostore = false
)
@TopComponent.Description(
        preferredID = "TasksTopComponent",
        //iconBase="SET/PATH/TO/ICON/HERE",
        persistenceType = TopComponent.PERSISTENCE_ALWAYS
)
@TopComponent.Registration(mode = "editor", openAtStartup = true)
@ActionID(category = "Window", id = "todo.view.TasksTopComponent")
@ActionReference(path = "Menu/Window" /* , position = 333 */)
@TopComponent.OpenActionRegistration(
        displayName = "#CTL_TasksAction",
        preferredID = "TasksTopComponent"
)
@Messages({
    "CTL_TasksAction=Tasks",
    "CTL_TasksTopComponent=Tasks Window",
    "HINT_TasksTopComponent=This is a Tasks window"
})
public final class TasksTopComponent extends TopComponent {
//...
```

@TopComponent.Description contains three attributes:

- iconBase (defines an optional path to an 16x16 pixels image to be displayed in the tab of the TopComponent)

- preferredID (unique name or identity of the TopComponent)

- persistenceType (can be PERSISTENCE_ALWAYS, PERSISTENCE_NEVER, or PERSISTENCE_ONLY_OPENED); whether to store or not the state of the TopComponent when the application closes. This is done by overriding writeProperties() and readProperties() methods.

@TopComponent.Registration defines the *mode*, that is, the position where the TopComponent is to be displayed in the window layout (see Figure 8-2). Optional element position specifies the relative position of a window within a mode. That is, if more than one TopComponent opens in the same mode, a lower position value places the window on the left.

@ActionID defines an action that will open the TopComponent when it is closed. @ActionReference defines the path in the *System FileSystem* (layer.xml) where the menu is to be defined (in this case, it will be an action under the **Window** menu). The position attribute defines the position of it in the menu (lower number means higher in the menu). You can also specify menu item separators with optional elements separatorBefore and separatorAfter. @TopComponent.OpenActionRegistration, finally, does exactly this: creates the *Open Action* to open the window.

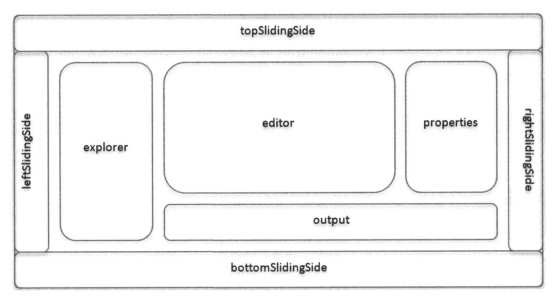

Figure 8-2. *Window modes*

The following methods control the life cycle of a TopComponent: open(), close(), requestVisible(), requestActive(), while the following are notification methods when the TopComponent's state has changed: componentOpened(), componentClosed(), componentShowing(), componentActivated(), componentDeactivated(), componentHidden().

Lookup

TopComponent implements the Lookup.Provider interface, so it has its own Lookup. Normally, it proxies the Lookups of whatever Nodes are currently selected. The Lookup of a TopComponent is defined in its constructor via its associateLookup() method, for example (see Listing 8-2).

Listing 8-2. Create a Lookup for the TopComponent

```
public final class TasksTopComponent extends TopComponent {
    private InstanceContent ic = new InstanceContent();
    public TasksTopComponent() {
        //...
        associateLookup(new AbstractLookup(ic));
    }
}
```

In Listing 8-2, we used a dynamic lookup, as explained in the previous chapter, but depending on what you need, you might use a static lookup (e.g., a singleton lookup). Whatever you add in the InstanceContent is being proxied to the *Global Lookup*, a.k.a. Utilities.actionsGlobalContext(), whenever the TasksTopComponent receives the focus.

Nodes

You are probably aware of the MVC (or Model-View-Controller) design pattern, where the View doesn't communicate directly with the Model but only via the Controller. This has the advantage that you can use the same data displayed by different views without strongly coupling the views to the model.

Swing has tried to implement this pattern by providing model classes for each of the presentation classes. For example, JList is backed up by ListModel, JTree by TreeModel, and JTable by TableModel, etc. If you wish to display the same data by a JTree and a JTable, you must create two different view models, that is, a TreeModel and a TableModel to present the same data in order to be rendered correctly by the respective views, which is not very convenient.

NetBeans RCP solves this problem by providing the Node class. A Node is the visual representation of a particular piece of data — a Task, for example. Nodes are a presentation layer between data and the UI classes. When you select a row on a table, you are actually selecting a Node instance. Rather than subclassing a different model class for each GUI component, as is done for Swing, simply subclass the Node class and seamlessly display the data across multiple different GUI components simultaneously.

A Node contains what is common data representation, like a display name, an icon, actions on the node, children nodes (for tree-like structures), and even properties (to be displayed in the Properties Sheet). Nodes also implement the Lookup.Provider interface; hence they can enable/disable actions based on the instances they add in their lookup (called historically *cookies*).

The *Node API* provides several nodes that are shown in Figure 8-3, each one with a different purpose.

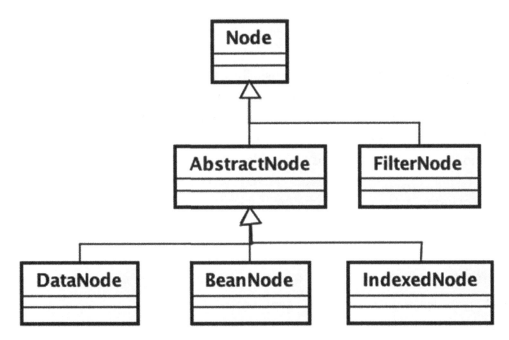

Figure 8-3. *Node class hierarchy*

Node is an abstract class, while AbstractNode is not! BeanNode uses reflection to retrieve the properties of a JavaBean and expose them as Node properties to be displayed in a Properties sheet. It also retrieves the name and the icon if these are available in its BeanInfo. Use a DataNode if you wish to display files. IndexedNode allows reordering

227

of its children. Finally, `FilterNode` is a decorator for another node, and as its name suggests, it can filter specific nodes by applying a filter.

Listing 8-3 shows an example implementation of a `BeanNode`.

Listing 8-3. A BeanNode implementation

```
package todo.view;

import java.beans.IntrospectionException;
import org.openide.nodes.BeanNode;
import todo.model.Task;

class TaskNode extends BeanNode<Task> {

    public TaskNode(Task bean) throws IntrospectionException {
        super(bean);
    }
}
```

Listing 8-3 creates a single Node that usually plays the role of a root node. Nodes usually contain child nodes, in a number of levels deep that could be infinite. If you need to display them in a tree, then you can create any number of subnodes; in a table though, only a flat list of subnodes (or leaf nodes) is needed.

Subnodes are represented by `org.openide.nodes.Children` object that creates child Nodes on demand. `Children` nodes are created by a `ChildFactory`, as shown in the example of Listing 8-4.

Listing 8-4. A ChildFactory implementation

```
package todo.view;

import java.beans.IntrospectionException;
import java.util.List;
import org.openide.nodes.ChildFactory;
import org.openide.nodes.Node;
import org.openide.util.Exceptions;
import org.openide.util.Lookup;
import todo.model.Task;
import todo.model.TaskManagerInterface;
```

```
class TaskChildFactory extends ChildFactory<Task> {

    @Override
    protected boolean createKeys(final List<Task> toPopulate) {
        final TaskManagerInterface taskManager =
          Lookup.getDefault().lookup(TaskManagerInterface.class);
        toPopulate.addAll(taskManager.listAllTasks(true));
        return true;
    }

    @Override
    protected Node createNodeForKey(final Task key) {
        TaskNode taskNode = null;
        try {
            taskNode = new TaskNode(key);
        } catch (IntrospectionException ex) {
            Exceptions.printStackTrace(ex);
        }
        return taskNode;
    }
}
```

When TaskChildFactory is initialized, the createKeys() method is automatically called. Once true is returned in createKeys(), the method createNodeForKey() is automatically called. As the API mentions, return true if the list of keys has been completely populated, false if the list has only been partially populated; and this method should be called again to batch more keys (which is most of the times unnecessary, so always return true).

A typical use of the above factory is:

```
Children tasks = Children.create(new TaskChildFactory(), true);
```

true here means that the ChildFactory will create the list of keys in a background thread, which happens, for example, when the user tries to expand a Node.

Lookup

As already mentioned, Nodes implement the Lookup.Provider interface. How can one add something to a Node's lookup? Listing 8-5 shows how to add a Task object to the TaskNode's lookup.

Listing 8-5. Add a Task to the TaskNode's lookup

```java
class TaskNode extends BeanNode<Task> {

    public TaskNode(Task bean) throws IntrospectionException {
        super(bean, Children.LEAF, Lookups.singleton(bean));
    }
}
```

The singleton lookup contains only one object, which in this case is the task associated to the node. Now, as we shall see, when you select one or more nodes, the conditionally enabled actions that listen for Tasks in the global lookup are enabled accordingly. How this is done is explained in the next section.

Actions

A user can right-click on a node to display a pop-up menu with a number of menu items or actions to perform on the node. You can override these actions by overriding the respective method of the Node class as shown in Listing 8-6.

Listing 8-6. Actions on a Node

```java
@Override
public Action[] getActions(boolean context) {
    List<? extends Action> taskActions = Utilities.
    actionsForPath("Actions/Task");
    return taskActions.toArray(new Action[taskActions.size()]);
}

@Override
public Action getPreferredAction() {
    return Actions.forID("Task","todo.controller.EditTaskAction");
}
```

Similarly, the getPreferredAction() provides a single Action that is invoked when the user double-clicks on a Node. It is a good practice to define your actions in the *System FileSystem* so that other classes or modules can reuse them.

Explorer Views

We saw previously how the *Nodes API* provides a universal way of representing data to the UI. But what UIs does NetBeans Platform provide?

The *Explorer & Property Sheet API* consists of a set of GUI components, known as explorer views or explorers, which render Nodes. You can display the nodes to more than one explorer view or you can easily swap between them without any change to the nodes: true MVC. Compare this to the amount of rewriting you would need in Swing to change code that uses a JTree to use a JTable or vice versa.

Table 8-1 shows the correspondence of the Explorer views to Swing UI classes.

Table 8-1. *Explorer Views and Swing Classes*

Explorer View	Swing
BeanTreeView	JTree
OutlineView	JTable/JTree
ListView	JList
PropertySheetView	JList
IconView	-
ChoiceView	JComboBox

Listing 8-7 provides an example of an OutlineView that can be added in the constructor of a TopComponent.

Listing 8-7. An OutlineView implementation

```
OutlineView ov = (OutlineView)outlineView;

//Set the columns of the outline view,
//using the name of the property
//followed by the text to be displayed in the column header
```

```
ov.setPropertyColumns(
      "priority", "Priority",
      "description", "Task",
      "alert", "Alert",
      "dueDate", "Due Date");
add(ov);
```

priority, description, alert, and duedate are attributes of the Task JavaBean. OutlineView is a special tree/table view that displays tree nodes, and table rows as properties. In the next chapter, we shall see how to use and customize an OutlineView to display a table of tasks.

All the explorer views are managed by an ExplorerManager, which controls and maintains the selection of the nodes in the view. Explorer views automatically find their ExplorerManager when they are added to a java.awt.Container such as a TopComponent. When they are added to a container, the explorer views search through their parent containers until they find the first that implements ExplorerManager. Provider. The explorer view then starts using the ExplorerManager returned by that component's getExplorerManager() method. The ExplorerManager maintains knowledge about the shared state of the Nodes, and notifies any PropertyChangeListeners when the selected Nodes change.

In Listing 8-8 we have modified our TasksTopComponent to implement ExplorerManager.Provider interface. The OutlineView will find the ExplorerManager defined in the constructor of the TasksTopComponent, will call getExplorerManager(), and then display the root Node from the ExplorerManager.

Listing 8-8. Implementation of ExplorerManager in the TopComponent

```
public final class TasksTopComponent extends TopComponent
implements ExplorerManager.Provider {
    private final ExplorerManager em = new ExplorerManager();

    public TasksTopComponent() {
    ...

      em.setRootContext(new AbstractNode(Children.create(new
      TaskChildFactory(), true))); // asynchronously
    }
    ...
```

```
@Override
public ExplorerManager getExplorerManager() {
    return em;
}
```

You can easily add other explorer views in the same TopComponent, and they all share the same ExplorerManager, and thus nodes. Not only will the same data be displayed in all explorer views, but when an item is selected in one of them, it will automatically be selected in the other, too.

So, if you want to map all of these to the MVC design pattern we referred to in the beginning of this chapter, you need to remember the following:

- Nodes represent the *Model*; they are wrappers of the actual model data.

- Explorer Views represent the *View.*

- ExplorerManager represents the *Controller.*

Lookup

In Listing 8-8 we saw how we can add something to a Node's lookup. ExplorerManagers maintain the selected nodes in views. What we didn't explain is how to make the selected Node(s) available to the *Global Lookup*, so that other objects such as Actions and other TopComponents can use them.

This is done with the help of ExplorerUtils class, which lets you define a special Lookup via its createLookup() method, representing the selected Node(s). Then, simply add this lookup to the TopComponent's lookup via the TopComponent.associateLookup() method, which must be called in the constructor of the TopComponent (see Listing 8-9).

Listing 8-9. Make selected nodes available to the Global Lookup

```
associateLookup (ExplorerUtils.createLookup (em, getActionMap()));
```

Thanks to the statement in Listing 8-9, the Lookup of the TopComponent will automatically proxy the Lookup(s) of the selected Node(s) in the explorer view components. When the TopComponent is selected, its Lookup is exposed via Utilities. actionsGlobalContext().

When the user selects a TaskNode in the OutlineView, the TasksTopComponent that contains the OutlineView will automatically proxy the Lookup of the TaskNode. The TasksTopComponent will be activated, and as a consequence the Global Lookup, Utilities.actionsGlobalContext(), will proxy the Lookup of the TasksTopComponent. Any component in the application that listens to the Global Lookup will be notified that a new Task object is available (e.g., an action will become enabled).

The action map is a map of actions that can be used in the TopComponent's views. In Listing 8-10, we enhance it with the *Cut, Copy, Paste,* and *Delete* actions.

Listing 8-10. Add actions to the ActionMap of the TopComponent

```
ActionMap map = this.getActionMap();
map.put(DefaultEditorKit.cutAction, ExplorerUtils.actionCut(em));
map.put(DefaultEditorKit.copyAction, ExplorerUtils.actionCopy(em));
map.put(DefaultEditorKit.pasteAction, ExplorerUtils.actionPaste(em));
map.put("delete", ExplorerUtils.actionDelete(em, true)); // true displays
                                                          a confirmation
                                                          dialog prior to
                                                          the deletion

associateLookup (ExplorerUtils.createLookup (em, map));
```

We shall talk more about Actions later in this chapter.

Properties

The *Properties* window (**Window ➤ IDE Tools ➤ Properties**) listens to the global Lookup, Utilities.actionsGlobalContext(), for the presence of Nodes, and displays its properties. In other words, the properties of the selected node are displayed in the *Properties* window.

All the properties of a BeanNode are displayed in the *Properties* window by default. If you need to customize them, either do it in the BeanInfo.java of the JavaBean, or convert your Node to extend AbstractNode instead, and override the method shown in Listing 8-11.

Listing 8-11.   Create a PropertySheet for your nodes

```
@Override
protected Sheet createSheet() {
    Sheet sheet = super.createSheet();
    Sheet.Set basicSet = Sheet.createPropertiesSet();
    basicSet.setName("Basic");
    basicSet.setDisplayName("Basic");
    try {
        Property daysBeforeProperty =
            new PropertySupport.Reflection<Integer>(
                task, Integer.class, "Days Before");
        basicSet.put(daysBeforeProperty);
        Property completedProperty =
            new PropertySupport.Reflection<Boolean>(
                task, Boolean.class, "Completed");
        basicSet.put(completedProperty);
    } catch (NoSuchMethodException ex) {
        Exceptions.printStackTrace(ex);
    }
    sheet.put(basicSet);
    return sheet;
}
```

`PropertySupport.Reflection` is used to define a `Property` object. Other subclasses are `PropertySupport.ReadOnly`, `PropertySupport.ReadWrite`, and `PropertySupport.WriteOnly`.

JavaFX and the NetBeans Platform

The Explorer Views API is based on Swing. However, there is a way to use JavaFX components instead. JavaFX is the successor of Swing and allows you to build advanced graphical applications. In this chapter we will see how to integrate JavaFX with the NetBeans Platform.

Keep in mind that JavaFX is fully integrated in JDK 8–10 but not from JDK 11 onward, where you can download it independently from `https://gluonhq.com/products/javafx/`.

The secret to integrate JavaFX with the NetBeans Platform is JFXPanel. Simply add a JFXPanel to a TopComponent, and you can work with JavaFX as you would in a standalone JavaFX application. When the first JFXPanel object is created, it implicitly initializes the JavaFX runtime (the *JavaFX Application Thread*). When the final JFXPanel is destroyed, the JavaFX runtime exits. If you set Platform.setExplicitExit(false), the JavaFX Application Thread does *not* exit after the last JavaFX content window closes. This setting is necessary to close and then reopen JavaFX enabled windows.

You also need to wrap the code that creates the JavaFX content in a runnable and invoke it with Platform.runLater(() -> createScene());. TopComponent code executes on the *Swing EDT*, whereas JavaFX code that creates and manipulates the scene graph must run on the *JavaFX Application Thread*.

JFXPanel is a Swing JComponent specifically implemented to embed JavaFX content in a Swing application. JFXPanel starts up the JavaFX runtime and transparently forwards all input (mouse, key) and focus events to the JavaFX runtime. JFXPanel allows both Swing and JavaFX to run concurrently. To manipulate the Swing UI from JavaFX, you wrap the code in a Runnable and use the following:

```
SwingUtilities.invokeLater(() -> {
// Change Swing UI
});
```

Conversely, to manipulate the JavaFX UI from Swing, wrap the code in a Runnable and call:

```
Platform.runLater(() -> {
// Change JavaFX UI
});
```

In the next chapter we shall see how to transform the ToDo Swing application to a NetBeans RCP application, where the view is rendered by JavaFX.

HTML/Java API

So far in this chapter we have learned how to create TopComponent objects, Explorer Views, Properties Sheets, etc., to build the UI of our application. In the previous section we saw how we can use JavaFX instead of these to build our UI. In this section we shall see how we can render our UI using HTML 5 and JavaScript.

The HTML/Java UI API, donated to Apache NetBeans from the architect of NetBeans, *Jaroslav Tulach*, allows us to write true cross-platform UIs using Java as the back end and HTML 5 and JavaScript in the front end. In other words, you can write true *Write Once Run Everywhere* code. It is based on *DukeScript* (`https//www.dukescript.com`), a new technology for creating cross-platform desktop, mobile, and web applications. It allows you to write your logic in Java and render the result to a number of clients, which can be web browser, portable devices, etc. As of version 1.5.1, HTML/JAVA UI has been donated to Apache Foundation (`http://apache.org/`), and the code is now hosted in the incubator repository (`http://github.com/apache/incubator-netbeans-html4j`) along other Apache incubating projects.

HTML/Java UI API claims to have a clean separation of design and development using the *Model-View-ViewModel (MVVM)* design pattern. It achieves this by using *Knockout.js* (`http://knockoutjs.com/`) for binding the rendered HTML to the model. It lets you create a direct connection between the underlying data and its presentation (automatic dependency tracking).

Knockout.js (KO) uses the *Model-View-ViewModel (MVVM)* (`https://en.wikipedia.org/wiki/Model%E2%80%93view%E2%80%93viewmodel`) design pattern, which is a variant of the classic *Model-View-Controller (MVC)* (`https://en.wikipedia.org/wiki/Model%E2%80%93view%E2%80%93controller`) design pattern. As in the MVC, the *Model* is the stored data, and *View* is a visual representation of the data (e.g., in HTML5). But for the connection between the two, MVVM uses a *ViewModel* instead of a *Controller*. This is the model used by the View. It represents the state of the View. It is the unsaved data the user works with. As an example, imagine an application that opens a dialog box or form for the user to modify some data. If the user decides to press on **Cancel,** then the ViewModel automatically restores the data from the ViewModel. In the MVC, we work directly with the Model, so the modifications made by the user cannot be undone if s/he decides to press on **Cancel**, unless we keep a copy of the model data elsewhere.

In KO, the *ViewModel* is a JavaScript representation of the model data, along with associated functions for manipulating the data. Knockout.js creates a direct connection between the *ViewModel* and the *View*, which is how it can detect changes to the underlying data and automatically update the relevant aspects of the user interface.

Knockout.js uses *observables* to track a ViewModel's properties; they observe their changes and automatically update the relevant parts of the view. To connect a user interface component in the view to a particular observable, you have to bind an HTML element to it. After binding an element to an observable, Knockout.js is ready to display changes to the *ViewModel* automatically. Knockout.js includes several built-in bindings that determine how the observable appears in the user interface.

While Knockout.js uses JavaScript as the back end, HTML/Java UI uses pure Java. In other words, HTML/Java UI is a technology that allows you to render Java directly to HTML 5.

Listing 8-12 shows how the binding is achieved between the HTML and the Java code. Here the *value* the user enters in an HTML text field is bound to the property text of the class Task. In HTML/Java UI, the ViewModel is defined by annotations (@Model, @Property) in order to reduce the amount of typing for the developer.

Listing 8-12. Data-binding between the HTML and the Java implementation

Tasks.html
```
<input data-bind="value: text"></input>
```

TasksCntrl.java
```
@Model(className = "Task", targetId = "", properties = {
    @Property(name = "text", type = String.class)
})
```

In Listing 8-12 we define our ViewModel class Task that contains one property named text of type String. This property is bound to the input field of the HTML code.

We can actually try the code using the *Development Environment for Web* or *DEW* (http://dew.apidesign.org/dew/). *DEW* is a development environment for the Java programming language that runs entirely in a browser (using the *Bck2Brwsr* VM developed by NetBeans' architect Jaroslav Tulach). DEW is your ultimate fiddle (*https://jsfiddle.net/*) environment that gives you an easy way to fork existing snippets and show your own creativity by saving your own code snippets as Github Gists (http://wiki.apidesign.org/wiki/Gist).

Figure 8-4 shows another example. This time the property say, defined in the ViewModel class Hello, is bound to the H1 heading of the HTML code. When you press **Run**, you should see the Hello World! message displayed as heading 1 at the bottom of the DEW page. You may modify the above message and run it again to see the result at the output. You may save it as gist, too (you need a valid GitHub account). As an exercise, modify the example code in the DEW with the code of Listing 8-12.

Figure 8-4. *Development Environment for the Web (DEW)*

In Figure 8-4 you also notice that the model is defined as part of a controller class, HelloViaKO. Inside the main() method, you see the call to the applyBindings() method, which is actually the method that applies the bindings between the view model and the HTML code. This is done in a static method or a static block.

Bindings. data-bind can take values as shown in the below examples:

data-bind=

- "click: addNew"

- "event: {mouseover: enable, mouseout: disable"}

- "submit: validate"

- "enable: play"

- "disable: stop"

- "value: name"

- "textInput: description"

- "hasFocus: isSelected"

- "checked: completed"

- "options: ides, selectedOptions: chosenIdes"

239

- "template: templateName"

- "foreach: sortedAndFilteredTasks"

In Listing 8-13 we see a more realistic example of a view model that demonstrates the use of ObservableArrays (array = true).

Listing 8-13. Use of ObservableArrays

```
@Model(className = "TasksWindow", targetId = "", properties = {
    @Property(name = "tasks", type = Task.class, array = true)
})
public final class TasksWindowCntrl {

    @Model(className = "Task", targetId = "", properties = {
        @Property(name = "id", type = int.class),
        @Property(name = "description", type = String.class),
        @Property(name = "priority", type = int.class),
        @Property(name = "dueDate", type = String.class),
        @Property(name = "alert", type = boolean.class),
        @Property(name = "daysBefore", type = int.class),
        @Property(name = "obs", type = String.class),
        @Property(name = "completed", type = boolean.class)
    })
    public static class TaskModel {
        //...
    }
}
```

TasksWindow contains a property tasks of type Task, which has an attribute array = true making it an observable array. *Observable arrays* let Knockout.js track lists of items. Knockout.js automatically updates any associated HTML elements whenever items are added to or removed from an observable array.

Listing 8-14 shows an example binding.

Listing 8-14. Example binding of an observable array

```
<div data-bind="foreach: tasks" >
...
</div>
```

Computed properties are observable properties derived from other properties. This also means that whenever one of the Properties is depending on changes, the ComputedProperty changes as well. Computed properties are used wherever we wish to return a new value based on other properties (see Listing 8-15).

Listing 8-15. Example binding of a computed property

```
@ComputedProperty
public static int numberOfTasksWithAlert(List<Task> tasks) {
    return listTasksWithAlert(tasks).size();
}

<label data-bind="text: numberOfTasksWithAlert"/></label>
```

Functions perform actions but do not return a value (void) (see Listing 8-16).

Listing 8-16. Example binding of a function

```
@Function
public static void removeTask(Tasks tasks, Task data) {
    tasks.getTasks().remove(data);
}

<button type="button" data-bind="click: $parent.removeTask">
</button>
```

Knockout.js defines a number of binding contexts (https://knockoutjs.com/documentation/binding-context.html).

A *binding context* is an object that holds data that you can reference from your bindings. While applying bindings, Knockout automatically creates and manages a hierarchy of binding contexts. The *root* level of the hierarchy refers to the ViewModel that called applyBindings() method.

The following binding contexts are defined:

- $root: refers to the top-level ViewModel.

- $data: refers to the ViewModel object of the current context (can be omitted).

- $parent: refers to the parent ViewModel object (useful for nested loops).

- $index: contains the current item's index in the array.

In Listing 8-16 we call $parent because we are inside a loop iterating over Tasks (see Listings 8-13 and 8-14), and we refer to a function defined in the parent model.

HTML/Java UI also supports *Knockout templates* (http://knockoutjs.com/documentation/template-binding.html%23note-2-using-the-foreach-option-with-a-named-template).

The template binding has a name parameter. Knockout will look for a script tag with the same id as specified by the templateName computed property (see Listing 8-17).

Listing 8-17. Example of a template binding

```
@ComputedProperty
static String templateName() {
    return "window";
}
```

```
<div data-bind="template: templateName"></div>
<script type="text/html" id="window">
```

HTML/Java UI gives the capability to display a modal HTML dialog. Listing 8-18 shows an example of displaying an alerts dialog, using @HTMLDialog annotation (https://bits.netbeans.org/10.0/javadoc/).

Listing 8-18. Display a modal HTML dialog

```
@HTMLDialog(url = "TasksWindow.html")
static void showAlertsDialog(String t) {
    new ShowAlertsDialog(t).applyBindings();
}
```

```java
@Model(className = "ShowAlertsDialog", targetId = "", properties = {
    @Property(name = "text", type = String.class)})
static final class ShowAlertsDialogCntrl {

    @ComputedProperty
    static String templateName() {
        return "showAlertsDialog";
    }
}

<script type="text/html" id="showAlertsDialog">
    <div><label data-bind="text: text"></label></div>
</script>
```

With HTML/Java UI, you may also call JavaScript from your Java code
(use @JavaScriptResource (http://137.254.56.27/html4j/1.0/net/java/
html/js/JavaScriptResource.html) and the @JavaScriptBody annotation
(http://137.254.56.27/html4j/1.0/net/java/html/js/JavaScriptBody.html) to
provide a type-safe way to call its JavaScript functions from Java.

Finally, HTML/Java UI has also good relations with REST and JSON:

- @OnReceive: is used to establish a REST endpoint, for example.

  @OnReceive(method = "DELETE", url = "{url}/{id}", onError =
  "cannotConnect")

  "{url}/{id}" is a URL pattern and its two parameters are set
  dynamically.

This section was a small introduction to the HTML/Java UI API. We shall see an
application of it in the next chapter.

Action System

If you have ever developed a standalone Java application in Swing, you will have
most probably encountered the problem of having the same action as a button in a
toolbar, a menu item, and/or maybe a pop-up menu item. You may, of course, create
a JButton and a JMenuItem and/or a JPopupMenu and use the same code in their
actionPerformed() methods, but I guess that you have heard about the *DRY* principle

(*Don't Repeat Yourself*), haven't you? A better way would be to put all the logic in a `javax.swing.AbstracAction` instance, and pass it in the `JButton`'s and `JMenuItem`'s constructors.

A display name or tooltip, an icon, and an optional shortcut key identify an action. Actions have also state (pressed/not pressed). In Swing, you need to configure your `JButtons`, `JMenuItems`, and `JPopupMenus` with icons, tooltips, etc.

The NetBeans' Platform *Action System* relieves you from all this hassle; it provides a configurable UI that allows you to concentrate only on your business logic and also provides ways to dynamically enable and disable actions and customize behavior based on selection context. Separating the presentation of an `Action` from its implementation is a good design decision, and NetBeans achieves this by using *annotations* for the presentation and a Swing `ActionListener` interface for the implementation, which is done once.

Annotations are used to register an action in the menu or a toolbar and to specify the action's display name, icon, and shortcut key sequence. The only thing that the developer needs to complete is the `ActionListener`'s implementation `actionPerformed()` method, that is, the business logic of the action. Using an `ActionListener` simplifies the process of porting Java Swing applications to the NetBeans Platform, too. Additionally, the **New Action** wizard makes the life of the developer easier by allowing you to configure the various annotations in the wizard. The wizard does the following:

- Registers an Action in `layer.xml` (under folder `Actions`)

- Creates resource bundle entries (e.g. `CTL_MyAction`)

- Registers Icons

- Registers key bindings

- Creates default implementation

Actions are registered in a central registry (`layer.xml`). Only one instance is generated. They can be reused in different contexts (e.g., Menu bar and Toolbar). They can be accessed from different modules. Because all actions are registered in the same way, users can configure menus and toolbars as we saw in the previous chapter.

An example `Action` generated by the **New Action** wizard is shown in Listing 8-19.

Listing 8-19. An example Action generated by the New Action wizard

```
@ActionID(
        category = "Edit",
        id = "todo.controller.edit.AddTaskAction"
)
@ActionRegistration(
        iconBase = "todo/controller/edit/add_obj.gif",
        displayName = "#CTL_AddTaskAction"
)
@ActionReferences({
    @ActionReference(path = "Menu/Edit", position = 10),
    @ActionReference(path = "Toolbars/Edit", position = 10),
    @ActionReference(path = "Shortcuts", name = "INSERT")
})
@Messages("CTL_AddTaskAction=Add Task...")
public final class AddTaskAction implements ActionListener {

    @Override
    public void actionPerformed(ActionEvent e) {
        // TODO implement action body
    }
}
```

An `Action` is assigned a *category* and an *ID* via `@ActionID`. Visual attributes such as a *display name* or an *icon* are assigned via `@ActionRegistration`. You may also define a key with a value to delegate its `actionPerformed()` to any other `Action` that needs to integrate with it. Default icons are 16x16 pixels and you may provide 24x24 pixels, too (for toolbars with small or large icons). The actual component (`JMenuItem`, `JButton` etc.) that will be created for the `Action` is assigned via `@ActionReference`. Valid attributes are the `path` to a folder in the `layer.xml`, the position (i.e., the relative order to other items), and `separatorBefore` or `separatorAfter`. Finally, localizable texts are set via `@NbBundle.Messages`.

Shortcuts are defined as shown in Table 8-2 (for platform compatibility).

Table 8-2. *Shortcut Keys You Can Use in*
Actions to Be Compatible with Any Platform

PC	Mac	Shortcut Key
Alt-	Ctrl-	O-
Ctrl-	Command(⌘)-	D-
Shift-	Shift-	S-

Two categories of actions are supported:

- *Always-enabled actions.* These actions don't depend on the availability of objects, data, or files for their execution or on user-selected item(s) in any of the application's windows. **File ➤ Open** or **Edit ➤ AddTask** are examples of always-enabled actions.

- *Conditionally enabled actions.* The actions depend on the availability of objects, data, or files for their execution or on user-selected item(s) in any of the application's windows. You need to provide what is called a *Cookie class*, which when found on a TopComponent's or Node's Lookup, enables the action. Then that Lookup is proxied by the currently selected window, which is proxied by Utilities. actionsGlobalContext() (which is the equivalent of Lookup. getDefault()). **Edit ➤ DeleteTask** action is an example of a conditionally enabled action that is enabled when one or more tasks are selected in the tasks table. *Context-aware* actions fall under this category and they are enabled when their context is in the Lookup of a selected entity (e.g., a Node or a TopComponent).

Callback actions are global actions with different behaviors depending on which component has the focus registered with a key. In TopComponents callback actions are added in the TopComponent's ActionMap. An ActionMap provides a mapping between a key String and an Action object. You can use the TopComponent's ActionMap to enable NetBeans Platform actions (such as **Cut**, **Copy**, **Paste**) for your TopComponent.

For example, you may add the cut-to-clipboard to the ActionMap of any JComponent, together with the Action that should be performed like in Listing 8-20.

Listing 8-20. Add an action to the ActionMap of a JComponent

```
final ActionMap actionMap = getActionMap();
actionMap.put("copy-to-clipboard", new AbstractAction() {
        @Override
        public void actionPerformed(ActionEvent actionEvent) {
                //do something
        }
});
```

An example of a conditionally enabled action is shown in Listing 8-21.

Listing 8-21. An example of a conditionally enabled action

```
@ActionID(
        category = "Edit",
        id = "todo.controller.edit.EditTaskAction"
)
@ActionRegistration(
        iconBase = "todo/controller/edit/configs.gif",
        displayName = "#CTL_EditTaskAction"
)
@ActionReferences({
    @ActionReference(path = "Menu/Edit", position = 20),
    @ActionReference(path = "Toolbars/Edit", position = 20),
    @ActionReference(path = "Shortcuts", name = "O-ENTER")
})
@Messages("CTL_EditTaskAction=Edit Task...")
public final class EditTaskAction implements ActionListener {

    private final Task context;

    public EditTaskAction(Task context) {
        this.context = context;
    }
```

```
    @Override
    public void actionPerformed(ActionEvent ev) {
        // TODO use context
    }
}
```

When a task is selected, the action is enabled.

Another example is shown in Listing 8-22. In this case, when one or more tasks are selected on the TopComponent that has the focus (i.e., found in the Utilities. actionsGlobalContext() lookup), the action is enabled.

Listing 8-22. An example of a conditionally enabled action that is enabled on multi-selection

```
@ActionID(
        category = "Edit",
        id = "todo.controller.edit.MarkAsCompletedTaskAction"
)
@ActionRegistration(
        iconBase = "todo/controller/edit/complete_tsk.gif",
        displayName = "#CTL_MarkAsCompletedTaskAction"
)
@ActionReferences({
    @ActionReference(path = "Menu/Edit", position = 40, separatorBefore = 35),
    @ActionReference(path = "Toolbars/Edit", position = 40),
    @ActionReference(path = "Shortcuts", name = "D-SPACE")
})
@Messages("CTL_MarkAsCompletedTaskAction=Mark as completed")
public final class MarkAsCompletedTaskAction implements ActionListener {

    private final List<Task> context;

    public MarkAsCompletedTaskAction(List<Task> context) {
        this.context = context;
    }
```

```
@Override
public void actionPerformed(ActionEvent ev) {
    for (Task task : context) {
        // TODO use task
    }
}
}
```

While one can transform the `Action` to anything that accepts an `Action`, for example, `JButton`, `JToggleButton` etc., this doesn't guarantee that the NetBeans toolbar will render it correctly. For example, the state of a `JToggleButton` (pressed/unpressed) is not shown. NetBeans Platform offers some alternatives. For example, for non-context actions, one can use the deprecated `org.openide.util.actions.BooleanStateAction`.

Since this class implements an `ActionListener` interface, we don't need to include it in the declaration (see Listing 8-23). The `@ActionRegistration(lazy=true)` is important, and it denotes whether a factory should be used or not. It's selected by default, so you need to set it to be unselected in the `initialize()` method.

Listing 8-23. An example of BooleanStateAction

```
@ActionID(
        category = "Options",
        id = "todo.controller.options.ShowCompletedTasksAction"
)@ActionRegistration(
        iconBase = "todo/controller/options/showtsk_tsk.gif",
        displayName = "#CTL_ShowCompletedTasksAction",
        lazy = true
)
@ActionReferences({
    @ActionReference(path = "Menu/Options", position = 10),
    @ActionReference(path = "Toolbars/Options", position = 10),
    @ActionReference(path = "Shortcuts", name = "F10")
})
```

```
@Messages("CTL_ShowCompletedTasksAction=Show completed tasks")
public final class ShowCompletedTasksAction extends BooleanStateAction {

    @Override
    protected void initialize() {
        super.initialize();
        setBooleanState(false);
    }

    @Override
    public String getName() {
        return Bundle.CTL_ShowCompletedTasksAction();
    }

    @Override
    public HelpCtx getHelpCtx() {
        return HelpCtx.DEFAULT_HELP;
    }
    @Override
    public void actionPerformed(ActionEvent e) {
        super.actionPerformed(e);
        //...
    }
}
```

An overview of the various actions that NetBeans Platform provides is shown in Figure 8-5. BooleanStateAction and *Callback* actions have been already described earlier in this chapter.

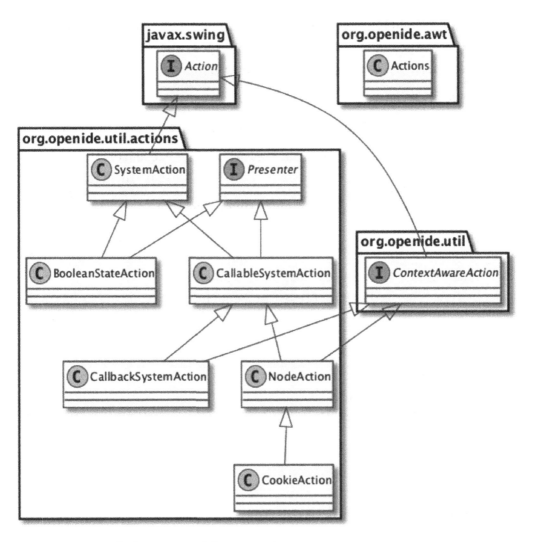

Figure 8-5. *Provided Actions of the Action's API*

Check also `org.openide.awt.DropDownButtonFactory`. This factory class allows you to create buttons with a small arrow icon that shows a pop-up menu when clicked.

If you like the ribbon toolbar introduced in MS-Office 2007, then the good news is that you can use a similar toolbar to your NetBeans RCP applications! This tutorial (`https://platform.netbeans.org/tutorials/nbm-ribbonbar.html`) explains how.

We already show in Listings 8-19, 8-21, and 8-22 how to use Presenters with the @ActionReference annotation. The display of an Action can be further customized by using Presenters. In CallableSystemAction one can override:

- public JMenu getMenuPresenter() // Presenter.Menu interface

- public JMenu getPopupPresenter() // Presenter.Popup interface

- public Component getToolbarPresenter() // Presenter.
                                          Toolbar interface

Listing 8-24 shows an example of creating submenus.

Listing 8-24. How to create submenus

```
public final class MyAction extends AbstractAction
                  implements Presenter.Menu {

 @Override
 public JMenuItem getMenuPresenter() {
   JMenu m = new JMenu();
   m.setIcon(this.getIcon());
   m.add(new JMenuItem(this));
   return m;
 }

 @Override
 public void actionPerformed(ActionEvent e) {
  // ...
 }
}
```

In Listings 8-22 and 8-23, we saw how NetBeans Platform can support context-sensitive actions. For more fine-grained support, one can use a CookieAction, which implements the ContextAwareAction interface. A CookieAction is activated when a selected node implements a certain marker interface (Cookie). It then gets one or more selected Nodes in its performAction() method to perform the action upon them. Its mode() method allows to choose among one (as in Listing 8-21) or more cookies (i.e., selected objects) (as in Listing 8-22). Listing 8-25 shows an example of a CookieAction.

Listing 8-25. An example of a CookieAction

```
protected int mode() {
    return CookieAction.MODE_EXACTLY_ONE;
    // MODE_ALL, MODE_ANY, MODE_ONE, MODE_SOME
}
```

The `Actions` class provides helper methods for menu and toolbar presenters. It provides a number of static helper methods to, for example, create an *always-enabled* action (`Actions.alwaysEnabled(...)`), a `ContextAwareAction` (`Actions.callback(...)`), various `connect()` methods that allow you to attach menu items, check boxes, etc. to actions or to locate a specific action programmatically (`forID(String category, String id)`).

Summary

In this chapter we learned the User Interface components that the NetBeans Platform offers: the *Window System API*, the *Nodes API,* and the *Explorer & Properties Sheet API*. The window system API releases you of all the hassle of having to take care of window layout and windows actions by providing you all the functionality you need out of the box. The *Nodes* and the *Explorer & Properties Sheet* APIs offer you a truly MVC design of powerful UI components to build your application. The *Nodes* API allows you to create a representation of your data once to be rendered by any number of Explorer Views. Finally, the *Actions API*, built on top of the `ActionListener` interface, and with the power of *Lookups*, lets you concentrate on your business logic without needing to worry about presentation and enablement.

In the next chapter, we shall see how to apply all these by implementing our *TodoRCP* application.

CHAPTER 9

Porting an Application to the NetBeans Platform

Let's see how we can apply what we learned in the previous chapter. In this chapter we shall continue porting the Swing *ToDo* application that we started in Chapter 7, to NetBeans RCP.

In Chapter 7 we modularized our application and ported the *Model* part (using a mock `TaskManager` class that stores the tasks in memory instead of a persistent storage). In this chapter we shall port the *Controller* and the *View* parts.

Our *ToDo* application consists of two windows as shown in Figure 8-7.

As we already mentioned in Chapter 6, we shall develop our application in three parts:

1. Build a "static" visual prototype of the user interface.

2. Build a "dynamic" prototype of the application, coding user interface events and associated business logic, and creating customized UI components as needed.

3. Code the persistence logic.

Step 1 – Build the "Static" Prototype

To create the main window, instead of creating a `JFrame Form` as is done in the Swing application, we will create its equivalent in NetBeans platform, as we learned in the previous chapter, a `TopComponent`.

© Ioannis Kostaras, Constantin Drabo, Josh Juneau, Sven Reimers, Mario Schröder, Geertjan Wielenga 2020
I. Kostaras et al., *Pro Apache NetBeans*, https://doi.org/10.1007/978-1-4842-5370-0_9

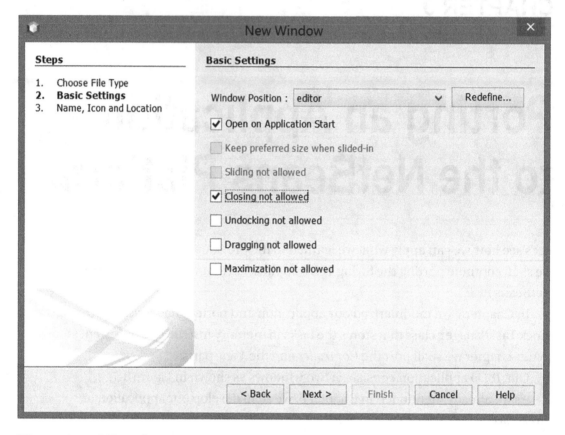

Figure 9-1. *Wizard to create a new TopComponent, Step 2*

Right-click on the *View* module and select **New ➤ Window** (see Figure 9-1).

The wizard asks you for the window position. NetBeans IDE has various positions as shown in Figure 8-2. Make the selections shown in Figure 9-1 and press **Next**.

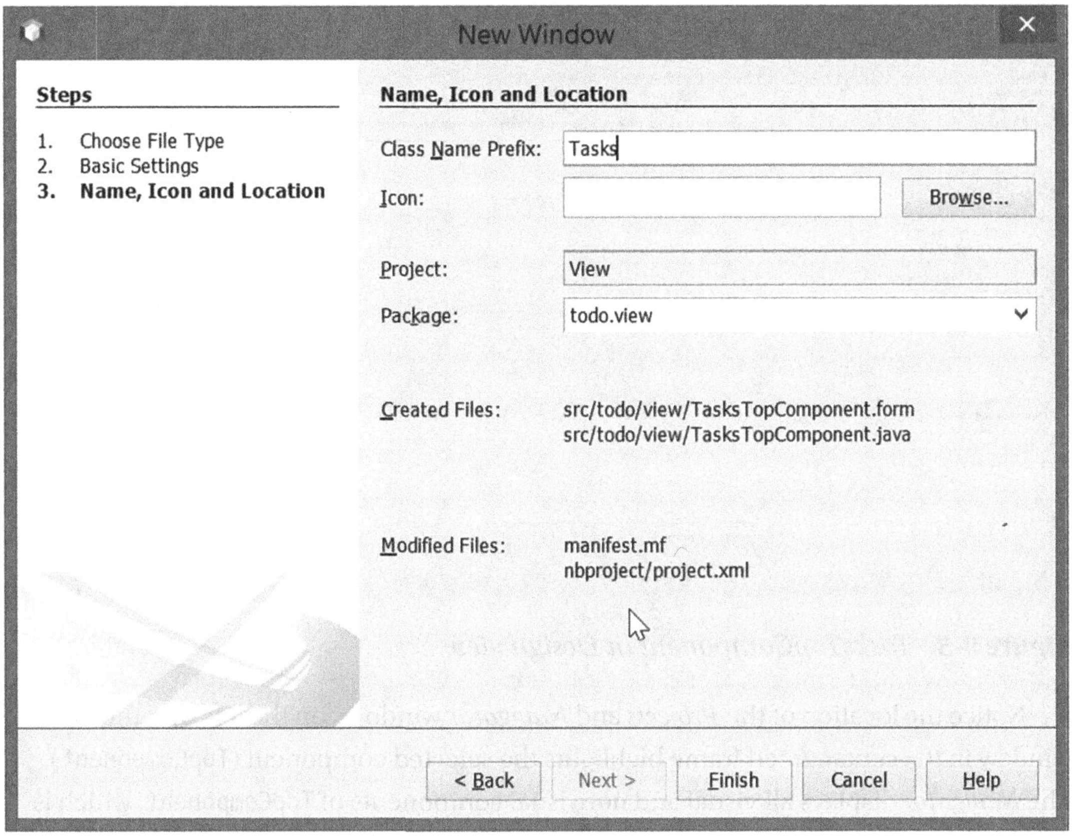

Figure 9-2. *Wizard to create a new TopComponent, Step 3*

The *Class Name Prefix* is the name of the Frame or Panel that will be created along with some other help files. Provide the name "*Tasks*" (instead of "*TasksWindow*" in the Swing application), as shown in Figure 9-2, and press **Finish**.

Two files are created, TasksTopComponent.java and TasksTopComponent.form, and the form has been opened in *Design mode* in the editor along with the *Palette* (Figure 9-3).

If you can see the TasksTopComponent.form file in the *Projects* tab and NetBeans complains that it cannot recognize the file when you open it, you need to activate *Java SE* plugin from **Tools ➤ Plugins ➤ Installed**.

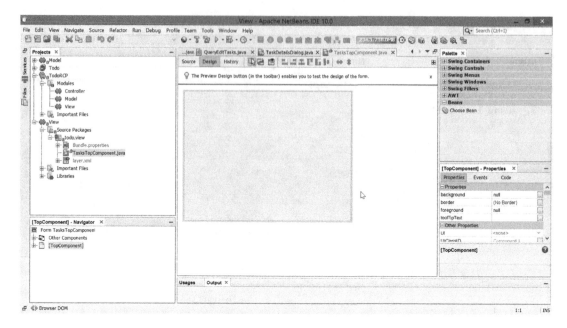

Figure 9-3. *TasksTopComponent in Design view*

Notice the location of the *Projects* and *Navigator* windows on the left, and the *Editor* window in the center. A red frame highlights the selected component (TopComponent). The *Navigator* displays all visual and nonvisual components of TopComponent, which is handy when you need to change the properties of a component that's hidden by another or that's too small to be selected in the drawing area.

To the right is the *Palette* window, which by default shows the standard Swing components (you can also add third-party JavaBeans). Also, to the right is the *Properties* window. Properties are categorized to ease access to the ones most commonly used, and changed properties have their names highlighted in bold.

To change the visual layout of the IDE, you can drag each window to another corner of the main window or even leave some windows floating around by right-clicking their tab and selecting **Float**.

Click on the **Source** button to view the annotations of Listing 8-1 and compare it with the dialog boxes of Figures 9-1 and 9-2. Notice that mode = "editor" (if not, here's your chance to change it) and openAtStartup = true (again, if not, here's your chance to change it).

The NetBeans IDE visual editor allows developers to truly develop applications visually. Just right-click inside TopComponent and select the **Set Layout** menu item. You see that the default choice isn't a traditional Swing/AWT layout manager; it's something named *Free Design*. This means you're using the Matisse Visual GUI builder. Matisse configures TopComponent to use the GroupLayout layout manager developed in the SwingLabs java.net project, which is included as a standard layout manager in Java SE 6.

As shown in Figure 7-7 in Chapter 7, the task list consists of a menu bar, a toolbar, a table, and a status bar. Apart from the table, which in NetBeans RCP is called OutlineView, the platform handles all the rest. To add an OutlineView, you need to add a dependency to the *Explorer & Property Sheet API*. Right-click the *Libraries* folder of the *View* module and select **Add Module Dependency**, select **Explorer & Property Sheet API**, and click **OK**. Right-click TopComponent in the Design view and change its layout to **BorderLayout**.

Drag a *Scroll Pane* from the *Palette window* and drop it in the center of TasksTopComponent. Right-click JScrollPane in the *Navigator* window (look at the left bottom) and change its variable name to outlineView. In the *Properties* window, click **Code**, and then click the small button **[...]** of the *Custom Creation Code* property, add new OutlineView(), and click the **OK** button. Switch to the Source view in the *Editor window*, right-click, and select **Fix Imports** to fix the errors.

When you run the application, you will see something similar to Figure 9-4.

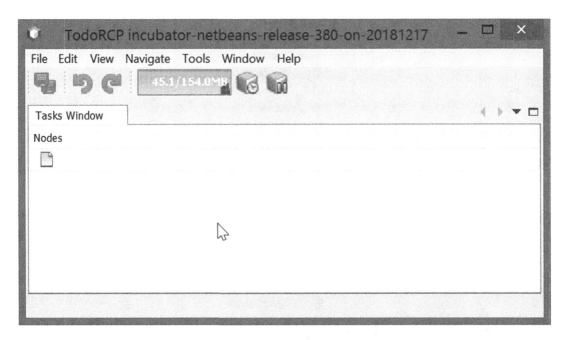

Figure 9-4. *First execution of the TodoRCP application*

Look at how many things you get out of the box with NetBeans RCP, which in a normal Swing application you would have to develop yourself: a menu bar and a toolbar (which need customization), a status bar, and a strange tree-table component—and all of these with just one line of code.

Let's start by customizing the menu. As already explained in the previous chapters, a central registry holds information about every module of the NetBeans RCP ToDo application. You can find the menu bar in this central registry if you click **Important Files** ➤ **XML Layer** ➤ **<this layer in context>** ➤ **Menu Bar** (see Figure 9-5).

In Figure 7-7, we see that we need only *File*, *Edit*, and *Options* menus. So, keep *File* and *Edit*, rename *Tools* to *Options* (by selecting it, right-clicking, and selecting **Rename**), and remove the rest, as well as the content actions (by selecting them, right-clicking, and selecting **Delete**). Clean and build *View* module and execute the application again.[1] The result should look something like Figure 9-6.

You may need to restart NetBeans after you rename *Tools* to *Options*.

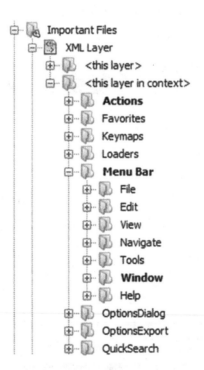

Figure 9-5. *Layer XML – central registry*

---

[1]If your build fails, then check of a bug that was introduced in NetBeans 11.2 (see https:// issues.apache.org/jira/browse/NETBEANS-3290), when you compile a NetBeans module project with a layer.xml and how to fix it.

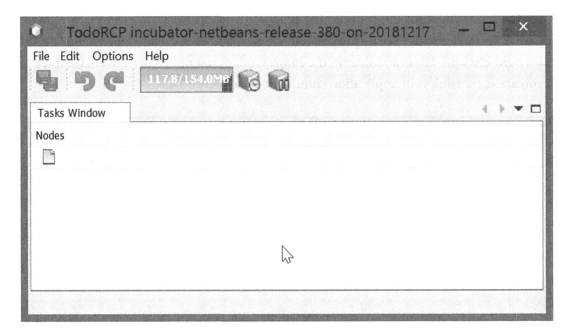

Figure 9-6. *TodoRCP application with customized menu bar*

Let's build our table with some demo data. Click on **Source**, and at the end of the TasksTopComponent's constructor, add the lines of code shown in Listing 9-1.

Listing 9-1. Creating the OutlineView

```
OutlineView ov = (OutlineView)outlineView;

//Set the columns of the outline view,
//using the name of the property
//followed by the text to be displayed in the column header
ov.setPropertyColumns(
      "priority", "Priority",
      "description", "Task",
      "alert", "Alert",
      "dueDate", "Due Date");

//Hide the root node, since we only care about the children:
ov.getOutline().setRootVisible(false);
TableColumnModel columnModel = ov.getOutline().getColumnModel();
ETableColumn column = (ETableColumn) columnModel.getColumn(0);
((ETableColumnModel) columnModel).setColumnHidden(column, true);
```

To be able to compile the code, you need to add one more dependency to the *ETable and Outline* module (and **Fix Imports**). You remember how to do this, right? Here's a hint: right-click the *Libraries* folder in the *Projects* tab or refer to Figure 7-16 in Chapter 7. If you are successful, your application should look like Figure 9-7.

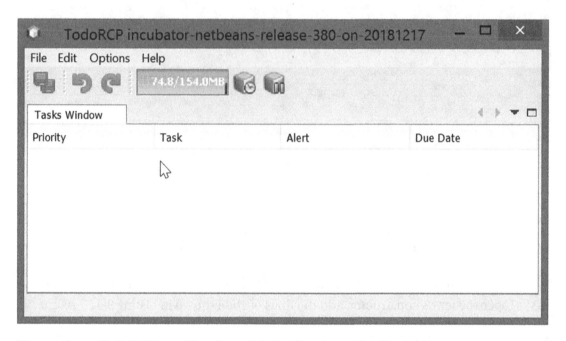

Figure 9-7. *TodoRCP application with OutlineViews' columns*

Let's create the status bar next. To display a `StatusBar` in NetBeans, a class must implement the `StatusLineElementProvider` interface and declare it as a service. Right-click the `todo.view` package and select **New ➤ Java Class**. Name it `StatusBar` and click **Finish**. Then copy the code shown in Listing 9-2 and paste it in (you may need to format the code; right-click inside the editor and select **Format** from the pop-up menu).

Listing 9-2. The StatusBar as a Service Provider implementation

```
package todo.view;

import java.awt.Component;
import javax.swing.JLabel;
import org.openide.awt.StatusLineElementProvider;
import org.openide.util.lookup.ServiceProvider;
```

```
/**
 * The application's status bar.
 */
@ServiceProvider(service=StatusLineElementProvider.class, position=1)
public class StatusBar implements StatusLineElementProvider {

    @Override
    public Component getStatusLineElement() {
        return new JLabel("There are no task alerts for today.");
    }
}
```

ServiceProviders and Lookups revisited. The StatusLineElementProvider interface is flexible; you can return any component you want – a JLabel, JButton, JPanel, and so on. But of course, the magic thing is the first line, which declares the StatusBar class as a service provider of StatusLineElementProvider.class. As you should already know by now, this line adds your class to the application's *default lookup*, which NetBeans then searches for StatusLineElementProvider.class, and then it adds all the providers it finds to the status bar.

Next, let's create the toolbars. A toolbar contains actions, so you'll create the actions and insert them into the appropriate toolbars in the central registry. You'll need the icons from the original ToDo application. Repeat the steps that you performed above for the *Menu Bar* in the central registry for the *Toolbars*. Leave only two entries: *Edit, Options* (by renaming some and deleting the rest).

The actions are controllers. Open the *Controller* module and create the Java packages todo.controller.file, todo.controller.edit, and todo.controller.options. Right-click the todo.controller.edit package and select **New Action**. Create the *Add Task* action, which is always enabled, and click **Next**.

Then select a category for the action. The categories represent semantic groupings of the actions. You can select a preexisting category or create a new one. In our case, select the preexisting *Edit* category. In addition, assign your action to the *Edit* menu bar and the *Edit* toolbar, and set the position where the action will be displayed. Drop-down menus show you possible locations for display. *"HERE"* identifies the location where the display of your action will be inserted. Don't forget to add a keyboard shortcut (*Insert*, as in the old to-do application). See Figure 9-8.

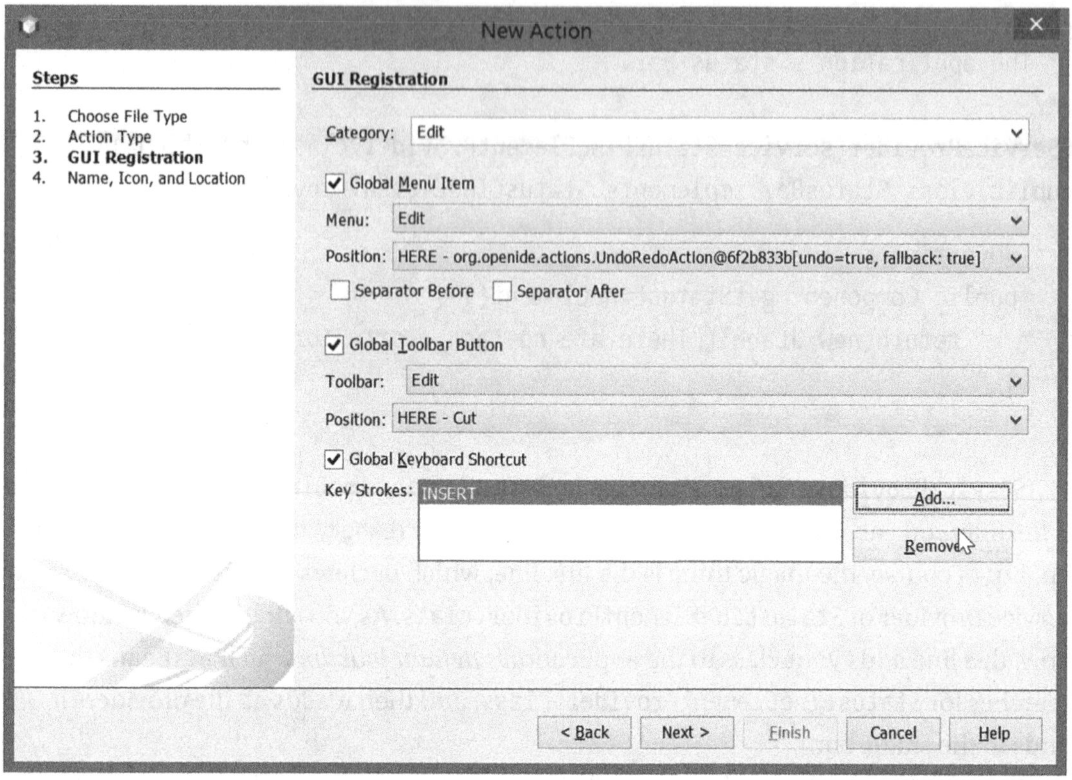

Figure 9-8. *New Action wizard, Step 3*

Name the class as shown in Figure 9-9, and don't forget to add an icon (browse to the icons folder of the original ToDo application or use your own icons if you prefer).

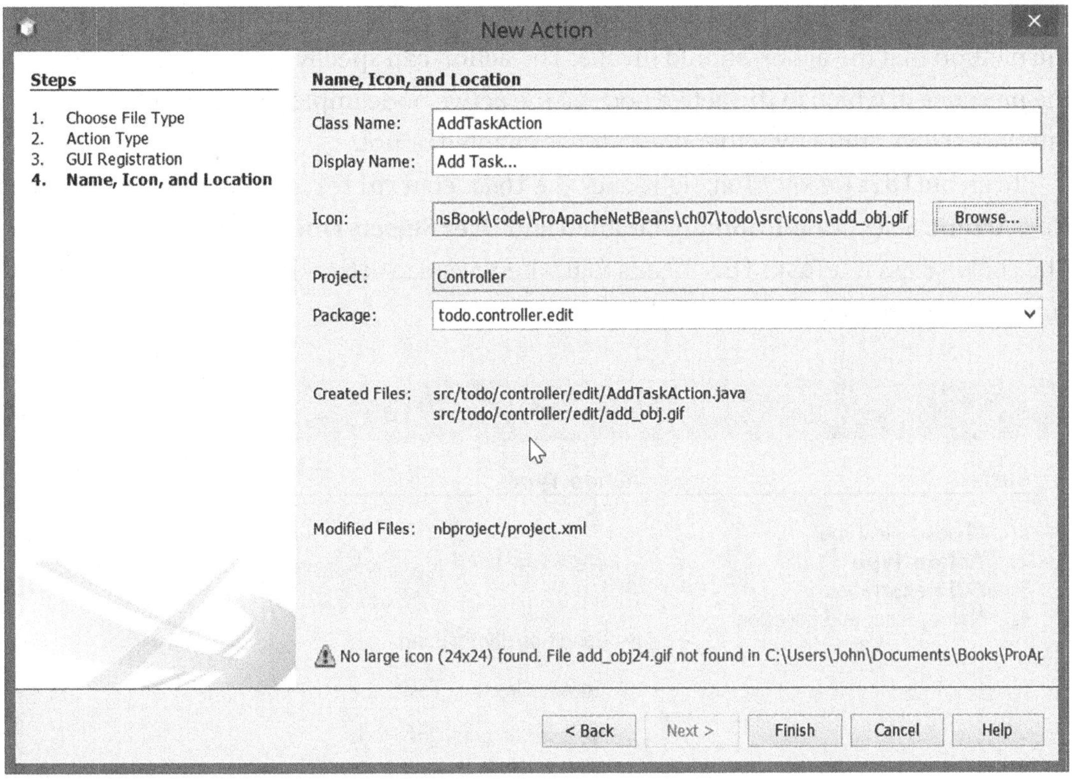

Figure 9-9. *New Action wizard, Step 4*

Click **Finish**.

The AddTaskAction class is created (see Listing 8-19 in Chapter 8). Look how the input from the wizard is translated into Java annotations in NetBeans RCP. In versions prior to NetBeans IDE 7.0, this information was added directly in layer.xml. As a reminder, we added the layer.xml to our module in Chapter 7. Modify the position to be 10 in both cases to avoid mix-ups with the next actions you create. Add 10 to the position of every new action—that is, for EditTaskAction set the position to 20, for DeleteTaskAction set it to 30, and so on. Leave the action body empty for the moment.

By executing the old ToDo application, you might have noticed that while the **Add Task** action is always enabled, the other task actions are enabled only when you select one or more tasks from the table—in other words, they are *context* actions. You can accomplish the same functionality by using a *conditionally enabled* action. These actions operate on *nodes*. A node is the visual representation of a particular piece of data—a task, in our example. When you select a row from the table, you are actually selecting a task node. Context sensitivity is constructed from interfaces, which are called

265

cookies. The node, which the action is to operate on, implements an interface specifying the method that the action should invoke. The action can specify a set of cookies, the presence of which in the active node (if the active node implements one of these interfaces) determines whether the action is enabled or not.

To create `EditTaskAction`, right-click the `todo.controller.edit` package and select **New Action**. Select **Conditionally Enabled** and **User Selects One Node** (see Figure 9-10). The cookie class is a `Task`. This means that whenever a task (row) is selected in the `OutlineView`, this action is enabled.

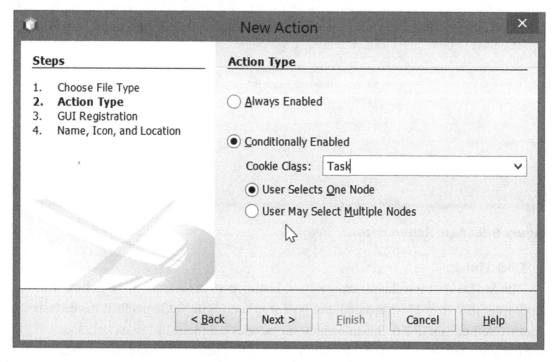

Figure 9-10. *Conditionally enabled action*

Click **Next** and complete the rest of the steps as you did for `AddTaskAction`. If you completed the wizard correctly, you should see the output shown in Listing 8-21 in Chapter 8. The compiler complains because it can't find a `Task` class. Add a dependency between the *Controller* and the *Model* modules. You do this by right-clicking *Libraries* under the *Controller* module and selecting the **Add Module Dependency** action. Check **Show Non-API Modules** and search for *Model* and click **OK**. Now you may fix imports and have `todo.model.Task` added as an import to `EditTaskAction`.

Repeat these steps to create the rest of the actions, trying to make the TodoRCP application as similar as possible to the Swing ToDo application. That means that EditTaskAction, DeleteTaskAction, and MarkAsCompletedTaskAction are conditionally enabled while the rest are always enabled. DeleteTaskAction and MarkAsCompletedTaskAction should be conditionally enabled, and you may select multiple nodes since they can be applied to many tasks at once (see Listing 8-22 in Chapter 8).

Also, make sure that you use the *Options* toolbar and menu (see Figure 9-11) for the actions that belong to them, that is, **Show completed tasks**, **Sort by priority**, **Sort by due date**, and **Show Alerts**.

The static visual prototype should look similar to Figure 9-12. If the order of the toolbars isn't correct, you can modify it either by right-clicking *XML Layer* and selecting **Open** or by right-clicking the *Toolbars* node and selecting **Go to Declaration.** The layer.xml file opens, and you can locate the toolbars and change their Position attribute (a smaller value means that the toolbar is displayed first).

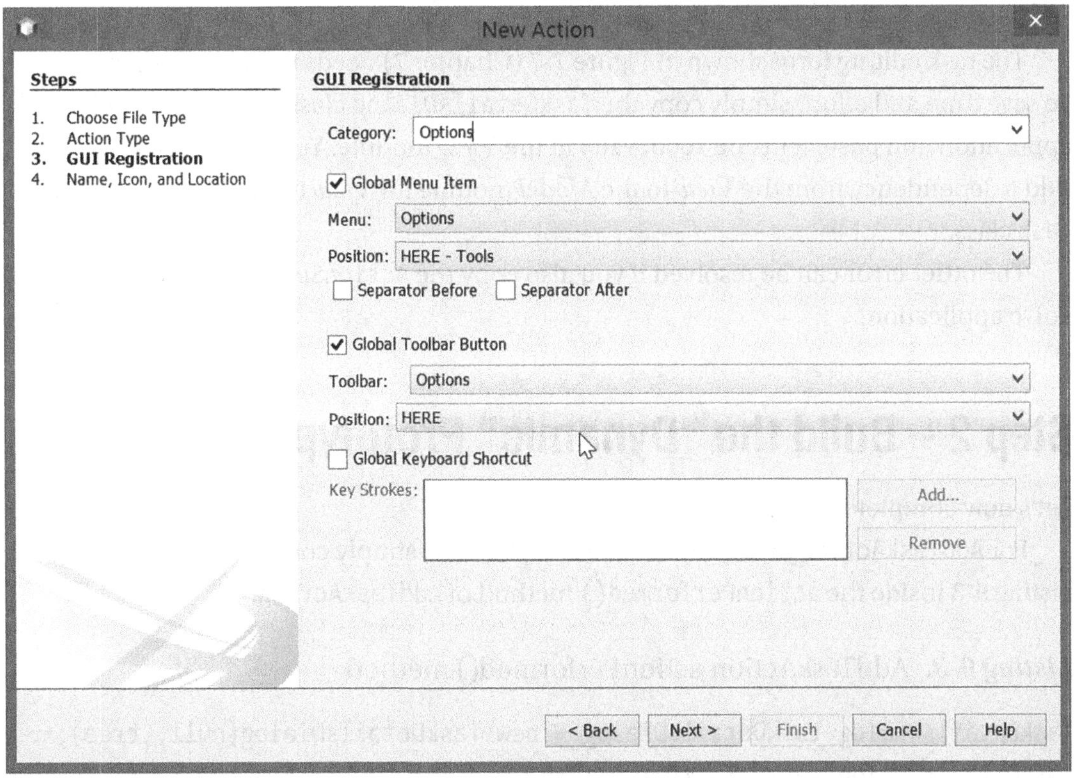

Figure 9-11. *New Action wizard*

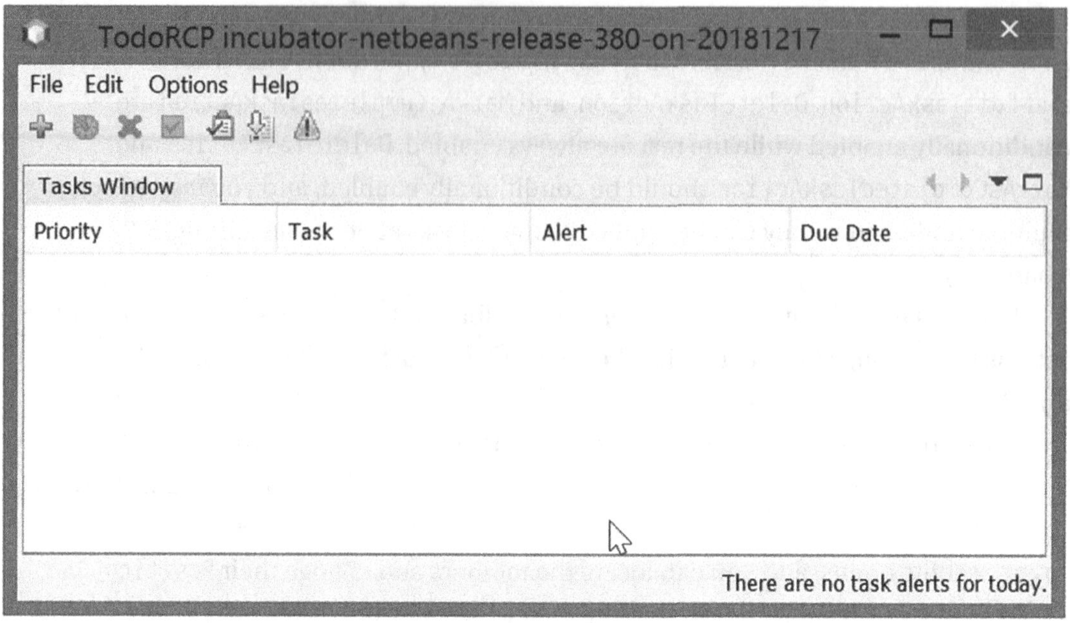

Figure 9-12. *Static prototype TodoRCP application*

The task editing form shown in Figure 7-7 (Chapter 7) needs to be created, too. To save time and effort, simply copy the TaskDetailsDialog class from the old ToDo application and paste it inside todo.view in the *View* module. You'll notice some errors. Add a dependency from the *View* to the *Model* module for *View* to be able to access the Task class.

The other error can be resolved if you also copy the ActionSupport class from the old ToDo application.

Step 2 – Build the "Dynamic" Prototype

Let's now complete our actions.

For AddTaskAction to display TaskDetailsDialog, simply copy the code of Listing 9-3 inside the actionPerformed() method of AddTaskAction:

Listing 9-3. AddTaskAction actionPerformed() method

```
TaskDetailsDialog taskDetailsDialog = new TaskDetailsDialog(null, true);
taskDetailsDialog.setNewTask(true);
taskDetailsDialog.setTask(new Task());
```

```
//        taskDetailsDialog.addActionListener(this);
taskDetailsDialog.setVisible(true);
```

You need to add a dependency from *Controller* to *View* in order to be able to fix imports for TasksDetailsDialog, making todo.view package public first.

EditTaskAction is also easy to write (see Listing 9-4).

Listing 9-4. EditTaskAction

```
public final class EditTaskAction implements ActionListener {

    private final Task context;

    public EditTaskAction(Task context) {
        this.context = context;
    }

    public void actionPerformed(ActionEvent ev) {
        TaskDetailsDialog taskDetailsDialog =
                                    new TaskDetailsDialog(null, true);
        taskDetailsDialog.setNewTask(false);
        taskDetailsDialog.setTask(context);
//        taskDetailsDialog.addActionListener(this);
        taskDetailsDialog.setVisible(true);
    }
}
```

Let's see how we can display some mock data to the OutlineView. As we learned in the previous chapter, we need to wrap the data to nodes, that is, wrap our model (Task) to a Node, and more specifically, to a BeanNode, which uses reflection to retrieve the attributes of the *Value Objects* (Task in our case). Create the class of Listing 8-3 of Chapter 8 inside the *View* module (and add a dependency on the *Node API*).

To display tasks in OutlineView, you need a flat list of nodes. A flat list of nodes is a root node that provides leaf nodes only; that is, one-level-deep children only. Factories are used to create children (see Listing 8-4 in Chapter 8).

OutlineView is populated with mock data, as shown in the method createKeys() in Listing 8-4 (Chapter 8). Look how TaskChildFactory uses the default lookup in order to retrieve the TaskManager implementation to retrieve all the tasks. Loose-coupling!

Finally, `TasksTopComponent` needs to be modified, as shown in Listing 8-8 (Chapter 8).

`ExplorerManager`, which is the controller of the explorer views, needs a root node element. Pass it an `AbstractNode`; its `Children` are derived from the `TaskChildFactory`.

With many fewer lines of code than in the original Swing ToDo application, you now have a running prototype with populated data. Build and run it to see a view similar to that shown in Figure 9-13.

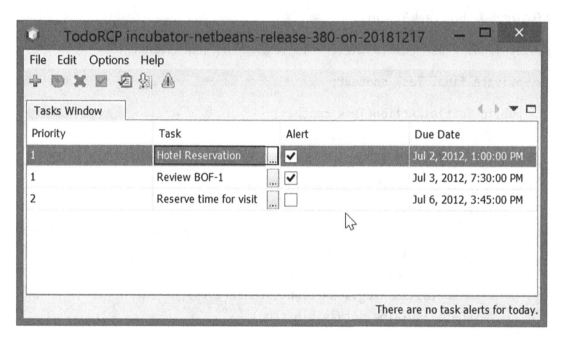

Figure 9-13. *TodoRCP with sample data*

However, when you select one or more rows, the conditionally enabled actions aren't enabled accordingly. To fix this, you need to add the `Task` object to the `TaskNode`'s lookup, and then you need to set the `TopComponent`'s lookup to be that of its nodes. To do that, modify `TaskNode` as shown in Listing 8-5 (Chapter 8), which adds the task to the node's lookup.

The singleton lookup contains only one object, which in this case is your task. Set the `TopComponent`'s lookup to be that of the node's by adding the code of Listing 8-9 (Chapter 8) after the line where you set the root context for the `ExplorerManager`.

Handling Events

Now that you have a display of tasks ready, it's time to add some event handling. In the original ToDo application, it was useful to separate GUI events into two mutually exclusive categories:

- *Internal events*, which affect just the view itself

- *External events*, which cause model methods to execute

Internal events include selection changes and clicks on **Cancel** buttons. In the original ToDo application, these were handled by the view classes themselves and were not exposed as part of the view classes' public interfaces. For example, the selection of a task should enable the **Edit task** menu item and the **Remove task** menu item, and the corresponding toolbar buttons. Such events are now handled by conditionally enabled actions with cookies inside the *Controller* module, not in the *View* package anymore.

View classes should *not* handle the category of events that the author of the original ToDo application calls "external." These events should instead be forwarded to controller classes, which usually implement the workflow logic for a specific use case or a related set of use cases.

The original ToDo application includes the `todo.view.ActionSupport` class, which simply keeps a list of `ActionListeners` and forwards `ActionEvents` to them. But `ActionSupport` is itself an `ActionListener`. This is done to avoid having lots of event-related methods, such as `addNewTaskListener()`, `removeNewTaskListener()`, `addEditTaskListener()`, `removeEditTaskListener()`, and so on. Instead, view classes generate only an `ActionEvent`. The `ActionSupport` classes capture `ActionEvents` from the view components and forward them to the controller, which registers itself as a view `ActionListener`.

All these classes aren't needed in the *TodoRCP* application because the NetBeans RCP framework takes care of all this. What you need to do is simply complete the `actionPerformed()` methods of your actions. So, your job is to transfer the logic from `QueryEditTasks` to your actions. Listing 9-5 shows how they map.

Listing 9-5. MarkAsCompletedTaskAction and DeleteTaskAction

```java
public final class MarkAsCompletedTaskAction implements ActionListener {
    private final List<Task> context;
    private final TaskManagerInterface taskManager;

    public MarkAsCompletedTaskAction(List<Task> context) {
        this.context = context;
        this.taskManager =
            Lookup.getDefault().lookup(TaskManagerInterface.class);
    }

    @Override
    public void actionPerformed(ActionEvent ev) {
        for (Task task : context) {
            task.setCompleted(true);
        }
    }
}
public final class DeleteTaskAction implements ActionListener {

    private final List<Task> context;
    private final TaskManagerInterface taskManager;

    public DeleteTaskAction(List<Task> context) {
        this.context = context;
        this.taskManager =
            Lookup.getDefault().lookup(TaskManagerInterface.class);
    }

    public void actionPerformed(ActionEvent ev) {
        for (Task task : context) {
            int response = JOptionPane.showConfirmDialog(null,
                    "Are you sure you want to remove task\n["
                    + task.getDescription() + "] ?",
                    "Remove Task",
                    JOptionPane.YES_NO_OPTION);
```

```
        if (response == JOptionPane.YES_OPTION) {
            taskManager.removeTask(task.getId());
        }
    }
  }
}
```

ActionSupport, which you copied from the original ToDo application to eliminate
the errors of TaskDetailsDialog, isn't needed anymore, so remove it from the *View*
module and tackle the errors. Initially, remove all statements from TaskDetailsDialog
that refer to ActionSupport. Add a reference to TaskManager, as shown in Listing 9-6.

Listing 9-6. TaskDetailsDialog

```
private final TaskManagerInterface taskManager;

public TaskDetailsDialog(java.awt.Frame parent, boolean modal) {
    super(parent, modal);
    initComponents();
    setLocationRelativeTo(parent);
    taskManager =
        Lookup.getDefault().lookup(TaskManagerInterface.class);
}
```

Then add actions to the **Remove** and **Save** buttons, as shown in Listing 9-7.

Listing 9-7. Remove and Save actions in TaskDetailsDialog

```
private void removeActionPerformed(java.awt.event.ActionEvent evt) {
  taskManager.removeTask(getTask().getId());
}

private void saveActionPerformed(java.awt.event.ActionEvent evt) {
  try {
    if (isNewTask()) {
      taskManager.addTask(getTask());
    } else {
      taskManager.updateTask(getTask());
    }
```

```
    } catch (ValidationException ex) {
        Exceptions.printStackTrace(ex);
    }
    cancel.doClick();
}
```

Go to Design view, select a button, right-click on it, and select **Events ➤ Action ➤ actionPerformed**. This will create the respective method in the source code.

You can add an in-place editor for dates (see Figure 9-14) by following the "NetBeans Property Editor Tutorial" and, most specifically, the section "Creating a Custom Inplace Editor" (`http://platform.netbeans.org/tutorials/nbm-property-editors.html#inplace-editor`).

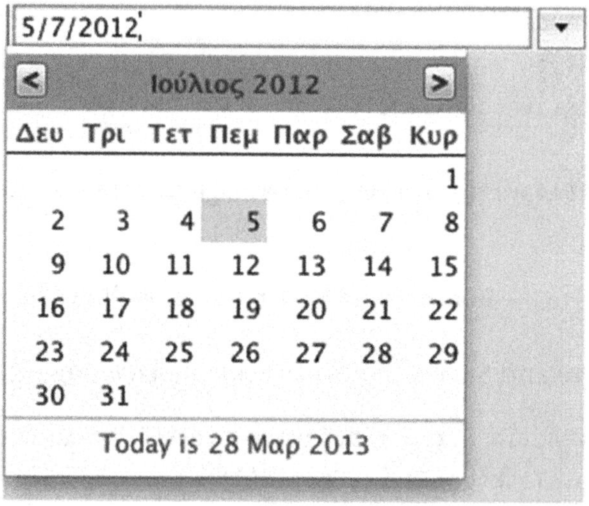

Figure 9-14. In-place editor to display a calendar

Use the date picker component of the *SwingX* library, which we have wrapped in the *Libraries* module in Chapter 7. Add a dependency to the *Libraries* module in the *View* module. Now you're ready to make use of the date picker, which involves implementing a couple of NetBeans IDE–specific interfaces:

- **ExPropertyEditor**: A property editor interface through which the property sheet can pass an "environment" object (**PropertyEnv**) that gives the editor access to the **Property** object it is editing and more.

- **InplaceEditor.Factory**: An interface for objects that own an **InplaceEditor**.

- **InplaceEditor**: An interface that allows a custom component to be provided for display in the property sheet.

The implementation details are found in the source code of this book.

Sorting behavior is delivered out of the box in **OutlineViews** just by clicking the specific header/field. Clicking once sorts the column in ascending order, clicking once more sorts in descending order, and clicking once more leaves the order as it was originally. However, if you want to implement **SortByDateAction** and **SortByPriorityAction** to see how sorting can be done programmatically, create a new **Utilities** class inside **todo.view**, and then copy the code from Listing 9-8 and paste into to the **Utilities** class.

Listing 9-8. Utilities.sortBy() method

```
/**
 * Sort the outline view {@code ov} on the given {@code field}.
 * @param ov outline view to sort
 * @param field to sort upon
 * @param ascending if {@code true} then the list is sorted in ascending
   order,
 * if {@code false} in descending order.
 */
public static void sortBy(final OutlineView ov, final String field, final
boolean ascending) {
  ETableColumnModel columnModel = (ETableColumnModel) ov.getOutline().
  getColumnModel();
  int columnCount = columnModel.getColumnCount();
  columnModel.clearSortedColumns();
```

```
  for (int i = 0; i < columnCount; i++) {
    ETableColumn column = (ETableColumn)columnModel.getColumn(i);
    if (column.getHeaderValue().equals(field)) {
      columnModel.setColumnSorted(column, ascending, 1);
    }
  }
  TableModel model = ov.getOutline().getModel();
  ov.getOutline().tableChanged(new TableModelEvent(model, 0, model.
  getRowCount()));
}
```

Since the Utilities class contains only static utility methods, make it final and add an empty private constructor to it to avoid initialization. Add the missing dependency to the *ETable and Outline* module. Add the method shown in Listing 9-9 to TasksTopComponent.

Listing 9-9. Sort the OutlineView

```
public void sortBy(final String field, final boolean ascending) {
    Utilities.sortBy((OutlineView)outlineView, field, ascending);
}
```

This step is to avoid adding a dependency to the *Explorer & Property Sheet API* in the *Controller* module because to call the original method in the Utilities class, you need to add a reference to OutlineView, which is contained in the *Explorer & Property Sheet API* in your *Controller* module. This workaround saves us this dependency, as shown in Listing 9-10.

Listing 9-10. SortByPriorityAction class

```
public final class SortByPriorityAction implements ActionListener {

    public void actionPerformed(ActionEvent e) {
        TasksTopComponent tasksTopComponent = (TasksTopComponent)
        WindowManager.getDefault().findTopComponent("TasksTopComponent");
        tasksTopComponent.sortBy("Priority", true);
    }
}
```

```
public final class SortByDateAction implements ActionListener {

    public void actionPerformed(ActionEvent e) {
        TasksTopComponent tasksTopComponent = (TasksTopComponent)
        WindowManager.getDefault().findTopComponent("TasksTopComponent");
        tasksTopComponent.sortBy("Due Date", true);
    }
}
```

You need to add a dependency on the *Explorer & Property Sheet API* and on the *Utilities API* modules for the errors to go away.

ShowAlertsAction displays a warning (see Figure 9-15) for each task that hasAlert()==true. The implementation can be found in the source code of the book.

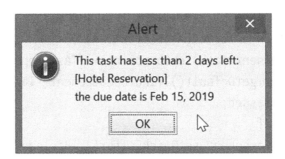

Figure 9-15. Alert information dialog box

Regarding filtering, you can right-click a row in the OutlineView and select **Show only rows where** and then select a criterion to filter. Remove the filter by following the same procedure and selecting **No filter**. However, ShowCompletedTasksAction can't be displayed by these out-of-the-box filters.

The Outline class provides a method setQuickFilter(int col, Object filterObject), and filterObject can either be a value that matches one of the values of the column or a QuickFilter object (see Listing 9-11).

Listing 9-11. QuickFilter interface

```
public interface QuickFilter {

    /** If the object is accepted its row is displayed by the table. */
    public boolean accept(Object aValue);
}
```

In this case, the accepted value is simply true, which means that you should just accept those rows that contain the value true. Listing 9-12 shows how this action can be implemented:

Listing 9-12. ShowCompletedAction class

```
public final class ShowCompletedTasksAction extends JToggleButton
implements ActionListener {
    private boolean pressed;

    @Override
    public void actionPerformed(ActionEvent e) {
        TasksTopComponent tasksTopComponent = (TasksTopComponent)
        WindowManager.getDefault().findTopComponent("TasksTopComponent");
        pressed = !pressed;
        if (pressed) {
            tasksTopComponent.setQuickFilter(3, Boolean.TRUE);
        } else {
            tasksTopComponent.unsetQuickFilter();
        }
    }
}
```

where 3 refers to the third column of the OutlineView. The only caveat is that the NetBeans toolbar doesn't display its state (pressed/unpressed). To make it behave as it should, we need to make it extend org.openide.util.actions.BooleanStateAction as described in the previous chapter (see Listing 8-23). The actionPerformed() method is the same as in Listing 9-12.

However, if you run the application and try to add a new task by using the *Task Details* dialog box, your new task never appears in the OutlineView because OutlineView is never notified of changes to the model. To fix this, first, modify TaskManagerInterface by adding two more methods to it:

```
void addPropertyChangeListener(PropertyChangeListener listener);
void removePropertyChangeListener(PropertyChangeListener listener);
```

Implement these methods in TaskManager, as shown in the source code provided with the book.

Finally, TaskChildFactory needs to be notified (see Listing 9-13), too.

Listing 9-13. TaskChildFactory class

```java
public class TaskChildFactory extends ChildFactory<Task> {

    private TaskManagerInterface taskManager;
    private final transient PropertyChangeListener pcl = new
    PropertyChangeListener() {

        @Override
        public void propertyChange(final PropertyChangeEvent evt) {
            refresh(true);
        }
    };

    public TaskChildFactory() {
        taskManager = Lookup.getDefault().lookup(TaskManagerInterface.class);
        taskManager.addPropertyChangeListener(pcl);
    }

    @Override
    protected boolean createKeys(final List<Task> toPopulate) {
        taskManager = Lookup.getDefault().lookup(TaskManagerInterface.class);
        toPopulate.addAll(taskManager.listAllTasks(true));
        return true;
    }
//...
}
```

These changes should allow the OutlineView to be updated accordingly. However, you'll notice one more problem. When you edit a task, it isn't updated until you click another cell. To cope with this problem, you need to make some more changes. The first change is to your Task class (make it an observable to notify listeners of changes to its fields); second, add a firePropertyChange() to all setter methods that affect the outline view. An example is shown in Listing 9-14, but you need to do the same thing for the other setters, too.

Listing 9-14. Make Task an observable

```
public class Task implements Serializable {

    ...

    private PropertyChangeSupport pcs = null;

    /** @return a thread-safe PropertyChangeSupport */
    private PropertyChangeSupport getPropertyChangeSupport() {
     if (pcs == null) {
       pcs = new PropertyChangeSupport(this);
     }
     return pcs;
    }

     public void addPropertyChangeListener(final PropertyChangeListener
     listener) {
        getPropertyChangeSupport().addPropertyChangeListener(listener);
    }

     public void removePropertyChangeListener(final PropertyChangeListener
     listener) {
        getPropertyChangeSupport().removePropertyChangeListener(listener);
    }

    ...
    public void setDueDate(Date dueDate) {
        Date oldValue = this.dueDate;
        this.dueDate = dueDate;
```

```
    getPropertyChangeSupport().firePropertyChange("DUE DATE CHANGED",
    oldValue, dueDate);
  }
  ...
}
```

Then, TaskNode must be notified of any changes (see Listing 9-15).

Listing 9-15. TaskNode change notification

```
public class TaskNode extends BeanNode<Task> {

    private final transient PropertyChangeListener pcl = new
    PropertyChangeListener() {

        @Override
        public void propertyChange(final PropertyChangeEvent evt) {
            firePropertySetsChange(null, getPropertySets());
        }
    };

    public TaskNode(Task bean) throws IntrospectionException {
        super(bean, Children.LEAF, Lookups.singleton(bean));
        bean.addPropertyChangeListener(pcl);
    }
}
```

Now that you have fully functional view and model classes, you can replace the mock implementations of the model classes by real logic using persistent storage. In large application projects, you could have a team working on the UI – building the two prototypes in sequence as you did – and another team working on business and persistence logic, preferably using test-driven development (TDD). They can work in parallel and join up at the end, putting together functional view and controller implementations with functional model implementations.

Most of the work in this Step 2 was just coding. NetBeans IDE provides nice code editors and a good debugger that provide the usual benefits: code completion, Javadoc integration, and refactoring support. But NetBeans IDE can go beyond: it's easy to build in new plugin modules to package your project coding standards, such as project templates, controller class templates, and so on.

In the source code of this book you will find a `TaskManagerDB`, which is another implementation of `TaskManagerInterface` that persists the tasks to an HSQLDB database. The implementation of the last two actions, **New Task List** and **Open Task List,** under **File** menu should be straightforward.

JavaFX and the NetBeans Platform

In this section we shall learn how to integrate the NetBeans Platform with JavaFX. JavaFX is included in JDK in versions 8–10. From version 11 onward, it is developed separately and can be downloaded from Gluon's website (`https://gluonhq.com/products/javafx/`).

Gluon's *SceneBuilder* (`https://gluonhq.com/products/scene-builder/`) is also useful if you wish to develop the GUI of your JavaFX application. To integrate *SceneBuilder* with NetBeans, follow these steps:

1. In NetBeans, navigate to **Tools ➤ Options ➤ Java ➤ JavaFX** (Windows/Linux) or to **NetBeans ➤ Preferences ➤ Java ➤ JavaFX** (MacOSX) and click **Activate** if JavaFX support is not yet activated.

2. After activation is finished, set the *Scene Builder Home* to be the Gluon directory (on Mac this should typically be `/Applications/ SceneBuilder`). Some Windows installers install *SceneBuilder* without asking you for a directory. *SceneBuilder* is installed by default in `C:\Program Files\SceneBuilder` or in `C:\ Users\<YourUser>\AppData\Local\SceneBuilder` in previous versions.

3. Click on **OK** and you are ready to start.

Note!   If NetBeans complains with the message "Selected location ... does not represent a valid Java FX Scene Builder installation," then do the following workaround.

–   Navigate to the directory where *SceneBuilder* was installed.

–   Enter app folder.

–   Make a duplicate of `SceneBuilder.cfg` to `SceneBuilder.properties` in the same folder.

Apache NetBeans provides two ways to develop a JavaFX application, using *Ant* or using *Maven*. If you wish to use Java 11 and JavaFX 11, the wizard that uses Ant doesn't work as of this writing with Apache NetBeans 11. Watch this video (`https://www.youtube.com/watch?v=l9aoicDiQ_A`) to see how to develop a JavaFX 11 application using Ant.

Developing a JavaFX version of the *ToDo* Swing application is outside the scope of this chapter. In the source code of the book you will find *TodoFX,* which is a standalone JavaFX 10 application. Figure 9-16 shows the structure of the source code. `todofx.model` package contains a copy of the model and one can use either the store-in-memory `TaskManager` or the persistent `TaskManagerDB` class. FXML was used for the two windows of the application (`TaskMain.fxml` and `TaskDetailsDialog.fxml`) using *SceneBuilder.* The `Stage`, `Scenes`, etc., are created in the `Main` class.

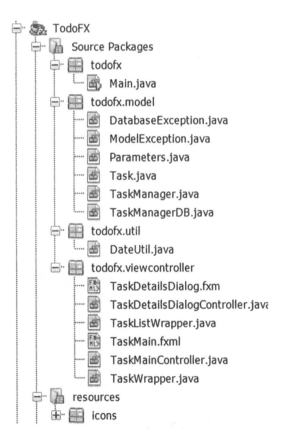

Figure 9-16. *TodoFX application source code structure*

To build a NetBeans RCP application that uses JavaFX as it's GUI, follow these steps:

1. Create a new **NetBeans Platform Application**, as we learned in
    Chapter 7, and name it *TodoFXRCP*.

2. Create two modules, *Model* (todo.model) and *ViewController*
    (todo.viewcontroller) as we learned in Chapter 7.

3. Copy the contents of *Model* module of the *TodoRCP* application
    we developed in the beginning of this chapter to the *Model*
    module of *TodoFXRCP* (see Figure 9-17).

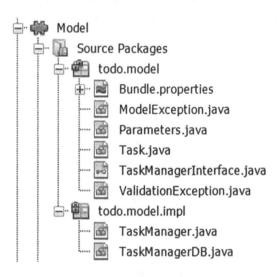

Figure 9-17. *TodoFXRCP application Model module*

4. Add a new TopComponent to the *View* module; name it
    TasksTopComponent, as we did for the *TodoRCP* application.

5. Copy the files TaskMain.fxml, TaskMainController.java,
    TaskDetailsDialog.fxml, TaskDetailsDialogController.
    java, TaskWrapper.java, and TaskListWrapper.java from the
    TodoFX application inside todo.viewcontroller of *TodoFXRCP*.
    Add the necessary modules (as well as a dependency to *Model*
    module). Make sure to update fx:controller inside *FXMLs* to
    point to the correct controller, for example fx:controller="todo.
    viewcontroller.TaskMainController". Some more
    modifications are needed, for example, to retrieve TaskManager
    from the default lookup instead of using its singleton method.

If you want to use a JDK version that doesn't have JavaFX integrated, like, for example, JDK 7 or 11, then you need to create a library wrapper to contain jfxrt.jar. As we did for the TodoRCP application, create a new module called *Libraries* (lib) and wrap hsqldb.jar and jfxrt.jar (for JavaFX 11 you need to add javafx.base.jar, javafx.control.jar and javafx.fxml.jar at minimum). Don't forget to make the needed packages public in the *API Versioning* category of the module and make a dependency from *ViewController* to the *Libraries* module.

6. In design view, change the layout of the TasksTopComponent to BorderLayout. Then, add the code in Listing 9-16 (additions shown in bold).

Listing 9-16. TasksTopComponent with JavaFX support

```
public final class TasksTopComponent extends TopComponent {

    private static JFXPanel fxPanel;

    public TasksTopComponent() {
        initComponents();
        setName(Bundle.CTL_TasksTopComponent());
        setToolTipText(Bundle.HINT_TasksTopComponent());
        putClientProperty(TopComponent.PROP_CLOSING_DISABLED, Boolean.TRUE);
        init();
    }

    private void init() {
        fxPanel = new JFXPanel();
        add(fxPanel, BorderLayout.CENTER);
        Platform.setImplicitExit(false);
        Platform.runLater(() -> createScene());
    }
```

```java
private void createScene() {
    try {
        Parent root = FXMLLoader.load(getClass().getResource("TaskMain.
        fxml"));
        Scene scene = new Scene(root, Color.LIGHTBLUE);
        fxPanel.setScene(scene);
    } catch (IOException ex) {
        Exceptions.printStackTrace(ex);
    }
}
```

Or if you need a reference to the controller:

```java
private TaskMainController mainController;

private void createScene() {
    try {
        URL location = getClass().getResource("TaskMain.fxml");
        FXMLLoader fxmlLoader = new FXMLLoader();
        fxmlLoader.setLocation(location);
        fxmlLoader.setBuilderFactory(
                new JavaFXBuilderFactory());
        Parent root = fxmlLoader.load(location.openStream());
        Scene scene = new Scene(root, Color.LIGHTBLUE);
        fxPanel.setScene(scene);
        mainController =
                (TaskMainController) fxmlLoader.getController();
    } catch (IOException ex) {
        Exceptions.printStackTrace(ex);
    }
}
```

The magic of integrating JavaFX to NetBeans platform is provided by JFXPanel.
When the first JFXPanel object is created, it initializes the JavaFX runtime (the *JavaFX Application Thread*). When the final JFXPanel is destroyed, the JavaFX runtime exits; this is why we set Platform.setExplicitExit(false). This setting is necessary to close and then reopen JavaFX-enabled windows.

Don't forget to "Give back to Caesar what is Caesar's and to God what is God's." In other words, use `Platform.runLater(() -> {...});` to execute JavaFX code in the *JavaFX Application Thread*, and `SwingUtilities.invokeLater(() -> { ...});` to execute Swing code in the EDT thread.

The code in `createScene()` is analogous to the code in a JavaFX application's `start()` method. Copy the method `showTaskDetailsDialog()` from `Main` class of *TodoFX*, to `TasksTopComponent`, too (see Listing 9-17).

Listing 9-17. showTaskDetailsDialog() method

```
public boolean showTaskDetailsDialog(TaskWrapper task) {
    try {
        // Load the fxml file and create a new stage for the popup dialog.
        FXMLLoader loader = new FXMLLoader();
        loader.setLocation(
        TasksTopComponent.class.getResource("TaskDetailsDialog.fxml"));
//...
```

With only few modifications *TodoFXRCP* is ready to be executed. Note that we didn't modify the FXML files (apart from setting the correct path to their controller).

As a final step, get rid of the *Toolbars* and *Menu Bar* from `layer.xml`, and follow the advice provided here (`https://blogs.oracle.com/geertjan/farewell-to-space-consuming-weird-tabs-part-2`) and here (`https://blogs.oracle.com/geertjan/farewell-to-space-consuming-weird-tabs`) in order to get rid of the tab from the `TopComponent`.

To get rid of the status bar, follow this FAQ (`http://wiki.netbeans.org/DevFaqRemoveStatusBar`).

The result is shown in Figure 9-18.

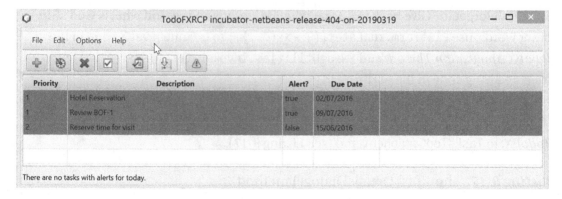

Figure 9-18. TodoFXRCP application

HTML/Java UI API

In the previous sections, we saw how to port the *ToDo* Swing Application UI to the *Window* and *Explorer and Properties System* APIs of the NetBeans Rich Client Platform and to JavaFX. In this section we shall see how to port the UI to the new HTML/Java UI API.

1. Create a new NetBeans Platform Application named as
   TodoHTMLJava.

2. Create a new module in the application (Name: View, Code Name
   Base: todo.view).

3. Create a new Portable HTML UI. Open the module (if not already
   open), right-click on *todo.view* package, and select **New ➤
   Other...** from the pop-up menu (see Figure 9-19). Click **Next**.

4. Provide Tasks as *Class Name Prefix,* provide an icon for the button
   that will be created and click **Finish**.

5. The generated file structure is shown in Figure 9-20.

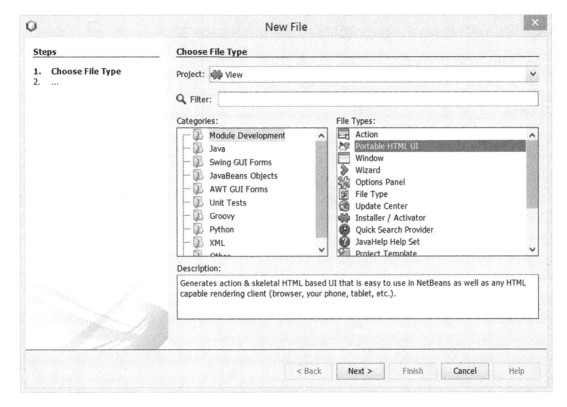

Figure 9-19. Create new Portable HTML UI wizard

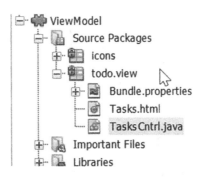

Figure 9-20. File structure of the View module

Right-click on the *View* module and select **Run**. You should see a window similar to the one shown in Figure 9-21. Click on the button with the icon you chose in order to see the *TasksWindow* tab appearing. Press the **Ask!** Button to display the dialog box.

An HTML UI running inside a NetBeans RCP!

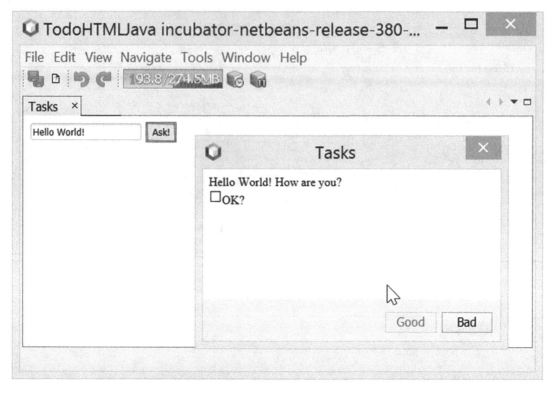

Figure 9-21. *The running sample application*

The code consists of only two files:

- `TasksWindow.html,` which builds the UI of the application and contains bindings for the Java class.

- `TasksWindowCntrl.java,` which contains the controller and model (more specifically the *ViewModel* and the *Model*) of the application.

Listing 9-18. `TasksWindow.html`

```html
<div data-bind="template: templateName"></div>

<!-- UI of the main window -->
<script type="text/html" id="window">
    <input data-bind="value: text"></input>
    <button data-bind="click: showDialog, enable: text">Ask!</button>
</script>

<!-- UI of the dialog -->
```

```html
<script type="text/html" id="dialog">
    <div><span data-bind="text: text"></span> How are you?</div>
    <!-- you need to check the checkbox to enabled the OK button -->
    <input type="checkbox" data-bind="checked: ok">OK?<br>
    <!-- next button is enabled when the checkbox is checked -->
    <button id='OK' hidden data-bind="enable: ok">Good</button>
    <button id='BAD' hidden>Bad</button>
</script>
```

The two windows are defined inside <script> tags. data-binds (if you are familiar with Knockout JS) bind the UI elements with the back end, the TasksWindowCntrl.java. The first line of Listing 9-18 tells the UI to search for a method called templateName() in the Java file. In Listing 9-19 you see that the defined templateName() returns the string "window" that must match the id in <script type="text/html" id="window"> in the *html* file.

Listing 9-19. TasksWindowCntrl class with the @Model definition

```java
@Model(className = "TasksWindow", targetId = "", properties = {
    @Property(name = "text", type = String.class)
})
public final class TasksWindowCntrl {
...
    @ComputedProperty
    static String templateName() {
        return "window";
    }

@ActionID(
        category = "Tools",
        id = "todo.view.TasksWindow"
)
@ActionReferences({
```

```
    @ActionReference(path = "Menu/Tools"),
    @ActionReference(path = "Toolbars/File"),})
@NbBundle.Messages("CTL_Tasks=Open HTML Hello World!")
@OpenHTMLRegistration(
        url = "TasksWindow.html",
        displayName = "#CTL_Tasks",
        iconBase = "todo/controller/resources/icons/taskmrk_tsk.gif"
)
public static Tasks onPageLoad() {
    return new TasksWindow("Hello World!").applyBindings();
}
```

The class `TasksWindowCntrl` defines an action on the toolbar and on the *Tools* menu. This returns a new instance of the generated class `TasksWindow`. `TasksWindow` class is defined by the `@Model` annotation. As you can see in Listing 9-20, it defines a property with name "text" of type `String`, which is bound to `<input data-bind="value: text"></input>`. So, the text that is passed to the constructor of `TasksWindow` ("Hello World!") is displayed on that text field.

Listing 9-20. Property to HTML binding

```
"Hello World!" → @Property(name = "text", type = String.class) → <input
data-bind="value: text"></input>
```

The necessary model classes are generated from annotations, thus saving you time from typing them.

We already saw the `@Model` annotation in the previous chapter, which defines a class that represents some kind of model and `@Property`, which represents an attribute of this class. We also saw an example of the `@ComputedProperty` annotation.

The `@Function` annotation responds to an action from the UI. For example, the following function is being called when the user clicks on the **Ask!** button (`<button data-bind="click: showDialog, enable: text">Ask!</button>`) (see Listing 9-21).

Listing 9-21. A @Function example

```
@Function
 static void showDialog(TasksWindow model) {
    String reply = Pages.showTasksWindowDialog(model.getText());
    if ("OK".equals(reply)) {
        model.setText("Happy World!");
    } else {
        model.setText("Sad World!");
    }
 }
```

Finally, the @HTMLDialog annotation is used to display a dialog box (see Figure 9-21 and Listing 9-22).

Listing 9-22. @HTMLDialog to display a dialog box

```
@HTMLDialog(url = "TasksWindow.html")
static void showTasksWindowDialog (String t) {
    new TasksWindowDialog (t, false).applyBindings();
}
```

TodoHTMLJava

Let's see how can we rebuild our *ToDo* application UI using this API. Since the UI is HTML with some Knockout bindings, we may use any CSS library to create our UI.

With the help of Bootstrap CSS (https://getbootstrap.com/), we built our UI as shown in Figures 9-22 and 9-23.

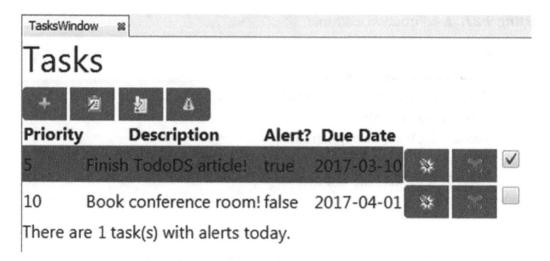

Figure 9-22. The TasksWindow of the TodoHTMLJava application

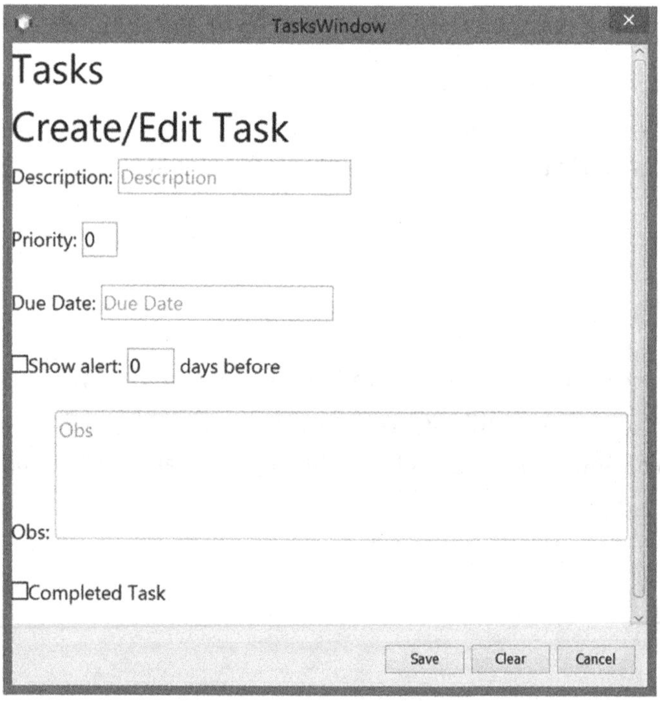

Figure 9-23. The Create/Edit task dialog box of the TodoHTMLJava application

We need to define each window inside a `<script>` tag, for example.

```
<script type="text/html" id="tasksWindow">
```

We define three windows with ids `tasksWindow` (for the main tasks window), `editor` (to edit a task), and `showAlertsDialog` (for the dialog box shown in Figure 9-24 when the user clicks on the respective button).

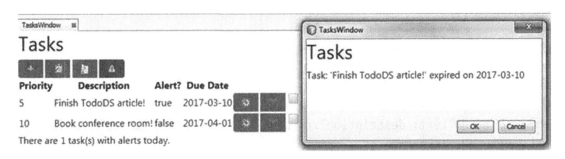

Figure 9-24. *The Alerts dialog box of the TodoHTMLJava application*

Next, we need to define our *ViewModels* and apply the bindings. In Listing 9-23 we define the `TasksWindow` view model, which contains only one property of type `array`, an array of `Tasks`.

Listing 9-23. TaskWindow ViewModel

```
@Model(className = "TasksWindow", targetId = "", properties = {
    @Property(name = "tasks", type = Task.class, array = true)
})
public final class TasksWindowCntrl {
...
    @Model(className = "Task", targetId = "", properties = {
        @Property(name = "id", type = int.class),
        @Property(name = "description", type = String.class),
        @Property(name = "priority", type = int.class),
        @Property(name = "dueDate", type = String.class),
        @Property(name = "alert", type = boolean.class),
        @Property(name = "daysBefore", type = int.class),
        @Property(name = "obs", type = String.class),
        @Property(name = "completed", type = boolean.class)
    })
```

```
    public static class TaskModel {
...
    }
...
}
```

Task view model is defined in its own (nested) class. You can now apply the bindings (see Listing 9-24).

Listing 9-24. Bindings with the view model

```
<tr>
<td data-bind="text: priority"></td>
<td data-bind="text: description"></td>
<td data-bind="text: alert"></td>
<td data-bind="text: dueDate"></td>
...
</tr>
```

Buttons are usually bound to @Functions:

Listing 9-25. Button bindings to @Functions

```
<button type="button" class="btn btn-secondary"
 data-bind="click: showAlerts">
    <img src="resources/icons/warning.gif" alt="Show Alerts..." title="Show
    Alerts..."/>
</button>

@Function
static void showAlerts(TasksWindow model) {
    String reply = Pages.showAlertsDialog(getExpiredTasks(model.
    getTasks()));
}

@HTMLDialog(url = "TasksWindow.html")
static void showAlertsDialog(String t) {
    new ShowAlertsDialog(t).applyBindings();
}
```

```
@Model(className = "ShowAlertsDialog", targetId = "", properties = {
  @Property(name = "text", type = String.class)})
static final class ShowAlertsDialogCntrl {
  @ComputedProperty
  static String templateName() {
    return "showAlertsDialog";
  }
}
```

Listing 9-25 doesn't only show how the button is bound to the showAlerts() function, but also how it calls showAlertsDialog() to display a dialog box (@HTMLDialog) with a properly prepared HTML text passed as a String to its text property, prepared by the getExpiredTasks() private method.

The source code can be found in the repository of this book.

You may find these relevant articles, *TodoKO* (http://wiki.netbeans.org/TodoKO) and *TodoDS* (http://wiki.netbeans.org/TodoDS) useful. The API is here (http://137.254.56.27/html+java/1.6/index.html). The *HTML UI API* is available here (https://bits.netbeans.org/10.0/javadoc/).

Summary

In this chapter we applied what we learned in the previous chapter, by developing *TodoRCP, TodoFXRCP,* and *TodoHTMLJava* module suite applications. They all use the same model while the *View* is implemented by using *Explorer & Properties Sheets, JavaFX* and *HTML/Java UI* respectively.

In the next chapter, we will see some extra APIs that you may find useful while developing your Rich Client Platform applications.

CHAPTER 10

Learning the Extras of the Platform

In this chapter we will learn some extra features provided by the NetBeans RCP that might be useful to your applications:

- the **Dialogs** API including the **Wizard** API

- the **Visual Library** and the **Palette**

- the **Status Bar** and **Notifications**

- How to use the **progress bar**

- **QuickSearch** and the **Output** window

- How to define and persist the settings of your application in the **Options** window

- How to brand and distribute your application

Let's get started.

Dialogs API

The *Dialogs API* is similar to `javax.swing.JOptionPane` and lets you create and display dialogs and wizards in an easy way. One can display predefined dialogs, custom dialogs, and multi-step wizards.

Displaying a dialog requires two steps: creating a `NotifyDescriptor` to configure the dialog, and a `DialogDisplayer` to display it. Before you use it, add a dependency to the *Dialogs API* module.

© Ioannis Kostaras, Constantin Drabo, Josh Juneau, Sven Reimers, Mario Schröder, Geertjan Wielenga 2020
I. Kostaras et al., *Pro Apache NetBeans*, https://doi.org/10.1007/978-1-4842-5370-0_10

Predefined Dialogs

NetBeans includes various predefined dialogs for common use cases such as displaying messages to users. Listing 10-1 invokes a dialog that displays a message along with an **OK** button.

Listing 10-1. Display a message dialog using the Dialogs API

```
NotifyDescriptor d = new NotifyDescriptor.Message("Message");
DialogDisplayer.getDefault().notify(d);
```

The result is shown in Figure 10-1. The commands from Listing 10-1 are equivalent to JOptionPane.showMessageDialog(...).

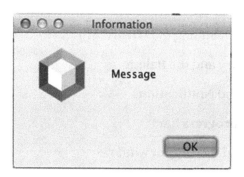

Figure 10-1. *Simple information message dialog*

Listing 10-2, on the other hand, displays the confirmation dialog shown in Figure 10-2.

Listing 10-2. Display a confirmation dialog using the Dialogs API

```
NotifyDescriptor d = new NotifyDescriptor.Confirmation(
      "Message", "Title");
Object retVal = DialogDisplayer.getDefault().notify(d);
if (retVal == NotifyDescriptor.YES_OPTION) {
    // do something
}
```

These commands are equivalent to JOptionPane.showConfirmDialog(...).

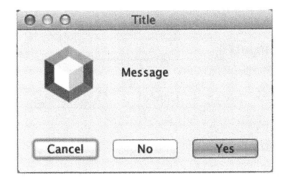

Figure 10-2. *Confirmation dialog*

You can compare retVal to the following constant values of NotifyDescriptor:

- OK_OPTION: The **OK** button was clicked.

- YES_OPTION: The **Yes** button was clicked.

- NO_OPTION: The **No** button was clicked.

- CANCEL_OPTION: The **Cancel** button was clicked.

- CLOSED_OPTION: The dialog was closed without any button having been pressed.

Listing 10-3 displays the input dialog of Figure 10-3.

Listing 10-3. Display an input dialog using the Dialogs API

```
NotifyDescriptor d = new NotifyDescriptor.InputLine(
     "Input:", "Title");
Object retVal = DialogDisplayer.getDefault().notify(d);
if (retVal == NotifyDescriptor.OK_OPTION) {
   String text =
            ((NotifyDescriptor.InputLine) d).getInputText();
}
```

These commands are equivalent to JOptionPane.showInputDialog(...).

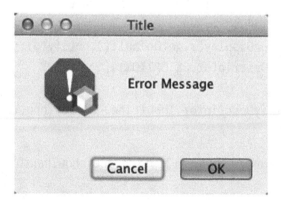

Figure 10-3. *Input dialog*

One can also use the NotifyDescriptor class to define the properties of a standard dialog as shown in Listing 10-4.

Listing 10-4. Display an error dialog using the Dialogs API

```
NotifyDescriptor d = new NotifyDescriptor(
    "Message", // message
    "Title", // title
    NotifyDescriptor. DEFAULT_OPTION, // option type
    NotifyDescriptor.ERROR_MESSAGE, // message type
    null, // custom buttons (as Object[])
    null); // default value
DialogDisplayer.getDefault().notify(d);
```

The result is shown in Figure 10-4. These commands are equivalent to JOptionPane. showOptionDialog(...).

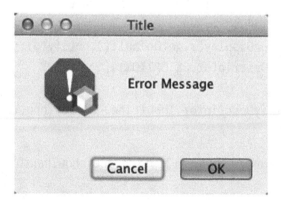

Figure 10-4. *Error message dialog*

Option type (3rd parameter) can take one of the following values:

- `NotifyDescriptor.DEFAULT_OPTION`

- `NotifyDescriptor.OK_CANCEL_OPTION`

- `NotifyDescriptor.YES_NO_OPTION`

- `NotifyDescriptor.YES_NO_CANCEL_OPTION`

Message type (4th parameter) can take one of the following values, which you may also pass as the 2nd parameter to `NotifyDescriptor.Message()` described in Listing 10-1:

- `NotifyDescriptor.PLAIN_MESSAGE`

- `NotifyDescriptor.INFORMATION_MESSAGE`

- `NotifyDescriptor.QUESTION_MESSAGE`

- `NotifyDescriptor.WARNING_MESSAGE`

- `NotifyDescriptor.ERROR_MESSAGE`

The 5th parameter can be used to pass in an `Object` array to add custom buttons to the dialog. Arrays of type `String`, `Component`, or `Icon` can be used. Listing 10-5 provides an example.

Listing 10-5. Display a dialog with custom buttons using the Dialogs API

```
String[] buttons = new String[3];
buttons[0] = "Play";
buttons[1] = "Pause";
buttons[2] = "Stop";
NotifyDescriptor d = new NotifyDescriptor(
    "Message", // message
    "Title", // title
    NotifyDescriptor.DEFAULT_OPTION, // option type
    NotifyDescriptor.PLAIN_MESSAGE, // message type
    buttons, // custom buttons (as Object[])
    "Play"); // default value
DialogDisplayer.getDefault().notify(d);
```

The resulting dialog is shown in Figure 10-5.

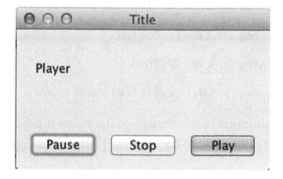

Figure 10-5. *Dialog with custom buttons*

As an exercise, replace JOptionPane instances with the *Dialogs API* in the *TodoRCP* application of the previous chapter.

Custom Dialogs

One can also create custom dialogs via the DialogDescriptor class that extends NotifyDescriptor. An example is shown in Listing 10-6, which displays a custom Login dialog (designed in LoginPanel JPanel class).

Listing 10-6. Display a custom dialog using the Dialogs API

```
DialogDescriptor d = new DialogDescriptor(
     new LoginPanel(), // Component
     "Login",          // title
     true,             // modality
     null);            // ActionListener
DialogDisplayer.getDefault().createDialog(d).setVisible(true);
```

In short, you can pass any kind of java.awt.Component as the first parameter. As an example, let's extend our *TodoRCP* application by providing a *Login* dialog asking for credentials when the application starts, at which point the application should be blocked until the user has been authenticated.

Securing Access

We don't want anybody to be able to access our tasks. We need to secure them by asking for credentials to access our *TodoRCP* application. Here are the steps to follow in order to display a Login dialog on application start-up:

1. Create a new module, as explained in Chapter 7, making sure to add it to the *TodoRCP* module suite. Name the module *Login* and give it the *Code Base Name* todo.login.

2. Open the *Login* module, if not already open; right-click on the todo.login package; select **New ➤ Other** from the pop-up menu to display the *New File* dialog; select the category *Swing GUI Forms*; and select the *JPanel Form* file type. Click **Next**.

3. In Step 2, enter LoginPanel in the *Class Name* field and click **Finish**.

4. Create the login form shown in Figure 10-6 using:

   - A label for Username: lblUsername

   - A label for Password: lblPassword

   - A label for the error message displayed on the bottom (shown as a red rectangle in Figure 10-6 but will be invisible on your form): lblInfo

   - A text field for Username: txtUsername

   - A password field for Password: txtPassword

Figure 10-6. *LoginPanel*

5.   Switch to *Source* view in the editor window, and add the following
     methods in Listing 10-7 at the end of the LoginPanel class

Listing 10-7. Access methods of the LoginPanel

```
public String getUserName() {
    return txtUsername.getText();
}

public char[] getPassword() {
    return txtPassword.getPassword();
}

public void setInfo(String info) {
    lblInfo.setText(info);
}
```

6.   Create a new module installer by right-clicking on the todo.login
     package and selecting **New ➤ Other**, then *Module Development*
     category followed by *Installer / Activator* as the file type. Then
     complete the code as shown in Listing 10-8. Notice that apart from
     createDialog(), that DialogDisplayer also offers both notify()
     and notifyLater(). The latter allows displaying the Dialog
     immediately after the initialization phase, which is directly after
     the splash screen.

Listing 10-8. The Module Installer class allows the login dialog to be displayed
on application start-up

```
public class Installer extends ModuleInstall {

    private LoginPanel loginPanel = new LoginPanel();
    private DialogDescriptor d = null;

    @Override
    public void restored() {
        d = new DialogDescriptor(loginPanel, "Login", true, this);
        d.setClosingOptions(new Object[]{}); // not closeable
        DialogDisplayer.getDefault().notifyLater(d);
    }
```

DialogDescriptor expects an ActionListener as the constructor's fourth parameter. Listing 10-9 shows an example of what such an ActionListener would look like.

Listing 10-9. Module Installer actionPerformed() method implementation

```
public class Installer extends ModuleInstall implements ActionListener {
//...
@Override
    public void actionPerformed(ActionEvent e) {
        if (e.getSource() == DialogDescriptor.CANCEL_OPTION) {
            LifecycleManager.getDefault().exit();
        } else if (!validate(loginPanel.getUserName(), loginPanel.
        getPassword())) {
            loginPanel.setInfo("Wrong Username or Password");
        } else {
            d.setClosingOptions(null);// can close
        }
    }
}
```

The validate(String username, char[] password) method checks in the database whether the provided credentials are valid. You may find its implementation in the source code of the book.

If you play with the login dialog a bit, you will notice that you can close the login window overriding authentication by clicking on the **X** close button of the window. We can fix that by adding the code shown in Listing 10-10 to the constructor of the LoginPanel.

Listing 10-10. Disallow closing the dialog from the X close button

```
// if someone simply closes the dialog using the X close button
d.addPropertyChangeListener(new PropertyChangeListener() {
    @Override
    public void propertyChange(PropertyChangeEvent e) {
        if (e.getPropertyName().equals(DialogDescriptor.PROP_VALUE)
            && e.getNewValue() == DialogDescriptor.CLOSED_OPTION) {
                LifecycleManager.getDefault().exit();
```

```
        }
    }
});
```

Another way is to create a Java class that implements Runnable and annotate it with @OnStart (which also requires a dependency to the *Module System API*). Listing 10-11 is left as an exercise to the user.

Listing 10-11. A module installer using the @OnStart annotation

```
@OnStart
public class LoginInstaller implements Runnable, ActionListener {
    private final LoginPanel loginPanel = new LoginPanel();
    private DialogDescriptor d = null;

    @Override
    public void run() {
        // same as restored() method (Listing 10-8)
    }
    // code from Listings 10-9, 10-10 goes here
}
```

Wizards

You have already encountered how to use the NetBeans wizards (or multi-pane dialogs) by creating a new *File* or *Project* from the **File** menu of the IDE. The good news is that you can create your own wizards for your projects by using the *Dialogs API*. Additionally, NetBeans provides a wizard for creating wizards. To use it, right-click on your module, choose **New ➤ Other**, then choose *Module Development* category followed by *Wizard* file type, and click **Next**.

In the second step of the wizard (see Figure 10-7), you have a number of choices. The registration types **New File with Swing UI**, **New File with HTML/Java UI** and **New File with HTML/JS UI** will register a *file type* in the **New File** or **New Project** dialog box of the application under a *category* of your choice. The *Custom* registration type won't, needing to be called programmatically from somewhere in your code, typically from an Action.

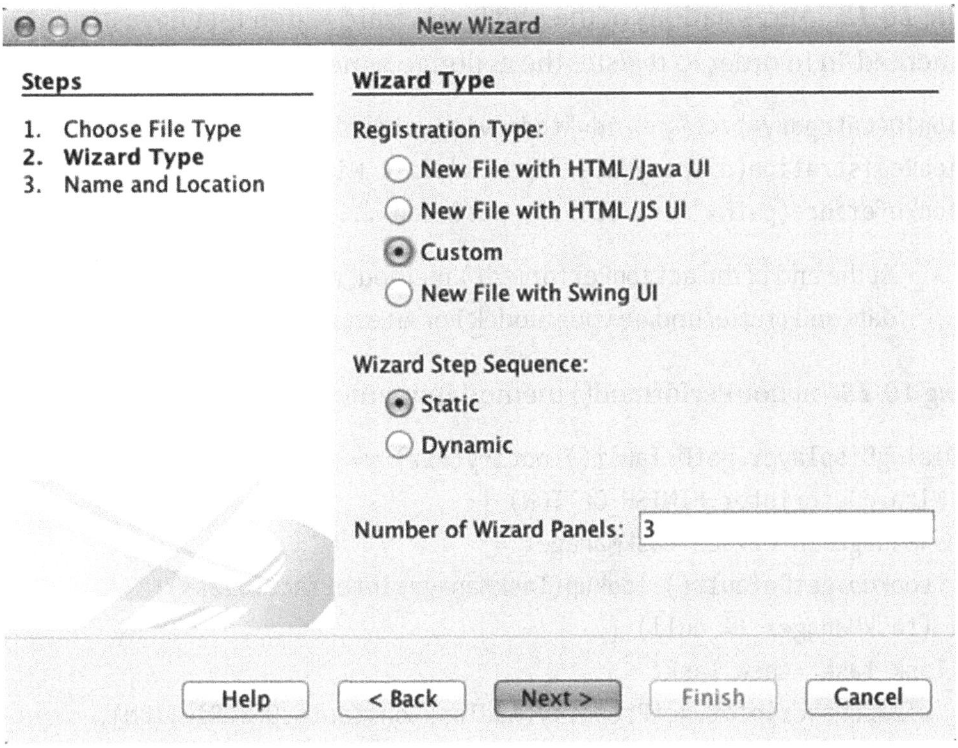

Figure 10-7. *New Wizard wizard*

For custom wizards, you can choose if the wizard should pass through a sequence of separate steps in a linear fashion that are fixed and don't change (*Static*), or *dynamically* based on the choices made by the user (i.e., the user will be able to skip some steps). The first option creates code that lets the user pass through the sequence of panels forward and backward without branching off or skipping panels. The second creates code that, by default, gives you full control over the order of the panels and allows a dynamic ordering of the panels to be created.

Static Wizards

Let's create a custom static wizard first with three panels. Clicking **Next** in the *Wizard Type* dialog brings you to the *Name and Location* dialog. Set the *Class Name Prefix* to AddTask in Step 2 and click **Finish**. You end up with the following files:

- AddTaskWizardAction: the action to invoke the wizard. You need to comment-in the annotations on top in order to register the action to a menu or a toolbar. Listing 10-12 shows these annotations.

309

Listing 10-12. Annontations of the AddTaskWizardAction that have been commented-in in order to register the action to a menu or toolbar

```
@ActionID(category="...",   id="todo.view.wizard.AddTaskWizardAction")
@ActionRegistration(displayName="Open AddTask Wizard")
@ActionReference(path="Menu/Tools", position=...)
```

- At the end of the `actionPerformed()` method, you need to gather all data and create/update your model. For an example, see Listing 10-13.

Listing 10-13. actionPerformed() method implementation

```
if (DialogDisplayer.getDefault().notify(wiz) ==
    WizardDescriptor.FINISH_OPTION) {
  TaskManagerInterface taskManager =
    Lookup.getDefault().lookup(TaskManagerInterface.class);
  if (taskManager != null) {
    Task task = new Task(
    wizardDescriptor.getProperty(AddTaskConstants.DESCRIPTION),
    ...);
    taskManager.addTask(task);
  }
}
```

- `AddTaskWizardPanel1`, `AddTaskWizardPanel2`, `AddTaskWizardPanel3`: `WizardDescriptor.Panel` classes are responsible for controlling each step. They check the validity of entered values (via method `isValid()`), support context sensitive help (by returning a help context via the `getHelp()` method), and initialize the visual panels by reading settings (`readSettings()` method) as well as storing settings (`storeSettings()` to be read the next time the user visits this panel or by the other panels). Usually you define an interface with some constant property names to be used by these methods as keys to save the properties. If a wizard panel's valid status depends on user input, the wizard panel must implement `addChangeListener()` and `removeChangeListener()` and fire state change events to its `ChangeListeners`.

- AddTaskVisualPanel1, AddTaskVisualPanel2, AddTaskVisualPanel3: JPanels for the visual representation of each step.

You may also use the *Simple Validation API* (ide/modules/ext/ ValidationAPI.jar) for your validations. You need to wrap it to a module (e.g., in the *Libraries* module of the *TodoRCP* application) and make org. netbeans.validation.api public. You may also add ValidationPanel to the palette to use it to your panels (with the help of the *Palette Manager*). The API provides a number of useful validators: REQUIRE_NON_EMPTY_STRING, NO_WHITESPACE, REQUIRE_VALID_INTEGER, REQUIRE_NON_NEGATIVE_ NUMBER, numberRange(minValue, maxValue), EMAIL_ADDRESS, FILE_MUST_EXIST, URL_MUST_BE_VALID, REQUIRE_JAVA_IDENTIFIER, REQUIRE_VALID_FILENAME. You may create your own, too, if you are not satisfied with them. Once you have dropped a ValidationPanel to your JPanels, you can validate the input there (and *not* in the WizardDescriptor. Panel) by calling group = validationPanel1.getValidationGroup() and then group.add()adding one or more of the validators above.

Dynamic Wizards

In the case of a dynamic wizard, an AddTaskWizardIterator (of type WizardDescriptor. Iterator) is created instead of an AddTaskWizardAction (Listing 10-14).

Listing 10-14. A dynamic wizard

```
public final class AddTaskWizardIterator implements WizardDescriptor.
Iterator<WizardDescriptor> {
    // Example of invoking this wizard:
    // @ActionID(category="...", id="...")
    // @ActionRegistration(displayName="...")
    // @ActionReference(path="Menu/...")
    // public static ActionListener run() {
    //    return new ActionListener() {
    //       @Override public void actionPerformed(ActionEvent e) {
```

The navigation is done with the help of the following methods (Listing 10-15) that update the index accordingly: current(), hasNext(), hasPrevious(), nextPanel(), previousPanel(). The **New File with Swing UI** option registers the wizard to a file type, as explained earlier.

Listing 10-15. Registration of the dynamic wizard to a file type

```
@TemplateRegistration(
    folder = "Other",
    displayName = "#AddTaskWizardIterator_displayName",
    iconBase = "todo/view/wizard/file/addtsk_tsk.gif",
    description = "addTask.html")
@Messages("AddTaskWizardIterator_displayName=Create New Task")
public final class AddTaskWizardIterator implements WizardDescriptor.Instan
tiatingIterator<WizardDescriptor> {
```

During execution, an entry to execute the above wizard can be found in the **File ➤ New** dialog wizard inside category *Other*. To register the dynamic wizard that you created earlier to a category of the **File ➤ Project** dialog wizard, enter, for example, folder = "Projects/Other".

Instead of InstantiatingIterator, the AddTaskWizardIterator may also extend AsynchronousInstantiatingIterator (the instantiate() method is invoked outside the *EDT*), BackgroundInstantiatingIterator (the wizard closes and the instantiate() method is invoked in a background thread), or ProgressInstantiatingIterator (the instantiate() method is invoked outside the *EDT* and it is called with a ProgressHandle to display its progress in a progress bar, which is described later in this chapter).

WizardPanel, instead of WizardDescriptor.Panel, may also extend WizardDescriptor.ValidatingPanel (for additional validation when the **Next** or **Finish** button is clicked), WizardDescriptor.AsynchronousValidatingPanel (for asynchronous validation), WizardDescriptor.ExtendedAsynchronousValidatingPanel (prefer this to AsynchronousValidatingPanel), or WizardDescriptor.FinishablePanel (when **Finish** button needs to be dynamically enabled; this allows the user to click the **Finish** button before the final step, because for example s/he accepts the default values of the following steps).

Other Properties of Wizards

When using the custom wizard, you can use some properties of `WizardDescriptor`:

- `PROP_AUTO_WIZARD_STYLE`: set to `true` to enable using the other properties.

- `PROP_CONTENT_BACK_COLOR`: set background color of left pane.

- `PROP_CONTENT_DATA`: sets the array of content items.

- `PROP_CONTENT_DISPLAYED`: set to `true` for displaying the left pane.

- `PROP_CONTENT_FOREGROUND_COLOR`: set foreground color of left pane.

- `PROP_CONTENT_NUMBERED`: set to `true` for displaying numbers in the left pane.

- `PROP_CONTENT_SELECTED_INDEX`: represents index of left pane that will be highlighted.

- `PROP_ERROR_MESSAGE`: error message displayed at bottom of the wizard. The wizard's **Next** button is disabled when there are errors.

- `PROP_IMAGE`: set the image to be displayed in the left pane.

- `PROP_IMAGE_ALIGNMENT`: set the image's alignment.

Finally, regarding the other two options displayed in Figure 10-7, consult the documentation at `http://wiki.netbeans.org/HtmlUIForTemplates`.

As an exercise, build a custom static wizard for the `AddTask` action. The wizard will contain three steps, and the first panel will ask for the *description* and the *priority* of a task (description is mandatory); the second panel the *due date*, the *alert*, and the *days before*; and the third panel the *observations* and whether the task is *completed* or not. Try also to create the same wizard for the *TodoFXRCP* application. Hint! Use `JFXPanels` in place of `JPanels`.

As another exercise, use the **New File with HTML/Java UI** wizard to create a wizard to add a new task for the *TodoHTMLJava* application.

Miscellaneous

Here we describe some APIs of the NetBeans Platform that you may find useful in your projects.

Status Bar

In Listing 9-2 of the previous chapter, we saw how to display messages in the status bar by registering to the StatusLineElementProvider service provider interface. If you want to display simple text, use the command of Listing 10-16.

Listing 10-16. Display a message in the status bar

```
StatusDisplayer.getDefault().setStatusText("Status message").
```

Notifications

The NetBeans Platform provides a mechanism to display balloon-shaped pop-ups in the far right of the status bar. Use NotificationDisplayer for that purpose, which requires a dependency to the *UI Utilities* module. Listing 10-17 provides the various possibilities to customize the balloon.

Listing 10-17. Display a ballon-shaped pop-up in the status bar

```
NotificationDisplayer.getDefault().notify(String title, Icon icon, String
detailsText, ActionListener detailsAction);

NotificationDisplayer.getDefault().notify(String title, Icon icon, String
detailsText, ActionListener detailsAction, Priority priority);

NotificationDisplayer.getDefault().notify(String title, Icon icon,
JComponent balloonDetails, JComponent popupDetails, Priority priority);

NotificationDisplayer.getDefault().notify();
```

You can also include an icon in the balloon. An example adding an alert ⚠ icon is shown in Listing 10-18.

Listing 10-18. Display a ballon-shaped pop-up with an icon in the status bar

```
NotificationDisplayer.getDefault().notify(
    "Alert1",
    ImageUtilities.loadImageIcon("todo/view/illegal.png", false),
    "Alert Details1",
    null);
```

As an exercise, modify *TodoRCP* to display the alerts at start-up as notifications instead of JOptionPane messages (see Figure 10-8).

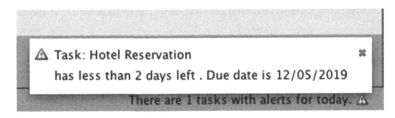

Figure 10-8. *Notifications*

If ActionListener is not null, then a hyperlink is displayed that, when clicked, executes the action. Priority can be: HIGH, NORMAL, LOW, or SILENT.

ImageUtilities

org.openide.util.ImageUtilities is a utility class providing static methods for manipulation and conversion of images and icons. Results are cached. Useful methods include loadImage(), loadImageIcon(), icon2Image(), image2Icon, mergeImages(), etc. We saw an example in Listing 10-18.

Quick Search

Typically, in the top right of the toolbar a search field is displayed (see Figure 10-9). A QuickSearch box searches for keywords you type in its text box.

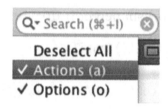

Figure 10-9. *Quick Search in the toolbar*

If the search field is not shown automatically, then you need to include the XML tags shown in Listing 10-19 in `layer.xml`:

Listing 10-19. XML tags in layer.xml to display the quick search field in the toolbar

```
<folder name="Toolbars">
    <folder name="QuickSearch">
        <file name="org-netbeans-modules-quicksearch-QuickSearchAction.shadow">
        <attr name="originalFile"
stringvalue="Actions/Edit/org-netbeans-modules-quicksearch-
QuickSearchAction.instance"/>
        </file>
    </folder>
</folder>
```

You can choose to display the quick search in the menu bar instead of in the toolbar. When doing that, it is good practice to include a spacer, which ensures that the search field will be right aligned in the menu bar. You can do these things by adding the code from Listing 10-20 to your `layer.xml` file.

Listing 10-20. Display the quick search in the menu bar instead of the toolbar

```
<folder name="Menu">
    <file name="Spacer.instance">
        <attr name="instanceCreate"
methodvalue="javax.swing.Box.createHorizontalGlue"/>
        <attr name="position" intvalue="9005"/>
    </file>
```

```
<file name="org-netbeans-modules-quicksearch-QuickSearchAction.shadow">
    <attr name="originalFile"
stringvalue="Actions/Edit/org-netbeans-modules-quicksearch-
QuickSearchAction.instance"/>
    <attr name="position" intvalue="9010"/>
  </file>
</folder>
```

To display the quick search on the menu on Mac OSX, you will need to exclude the
Apple Application Menu module from the platform cluster (right-click on the *TodoRCP*
module suite and select **Properties**, then the *Libraries* category as shown in Figure 10-10)
in order not to use the Apple menu bar instead.

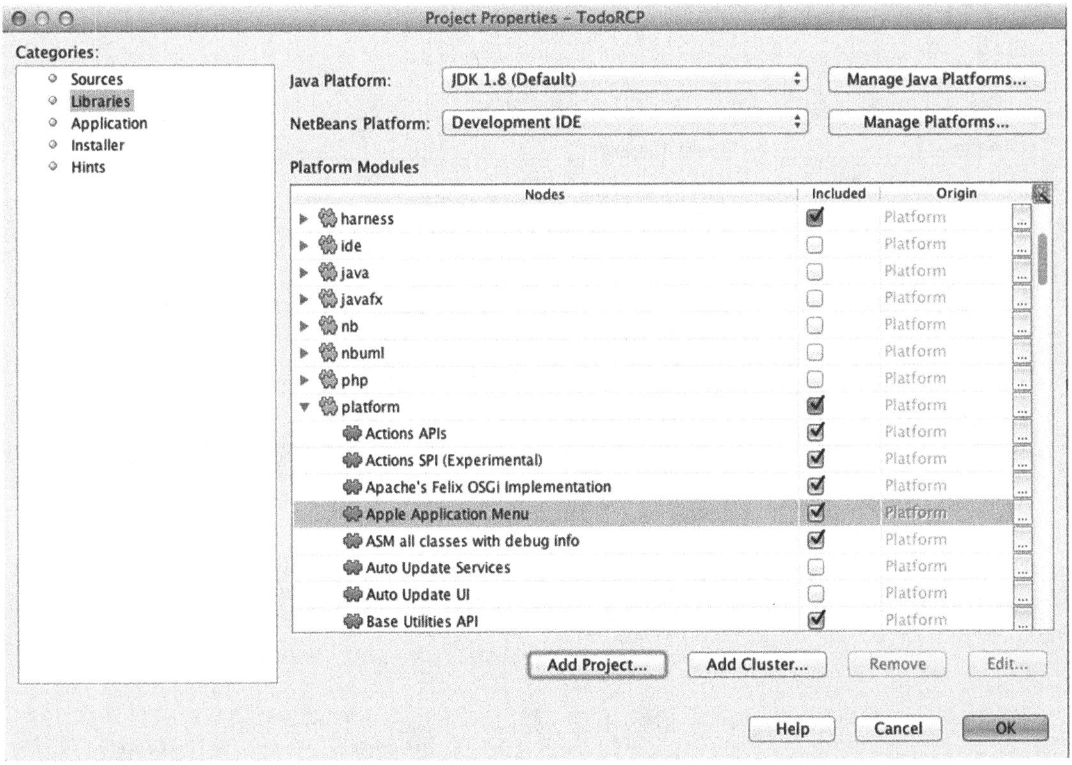

Figure 10-10. *Remove Apple Application Menu module from platform cluster*

If you need to add the quicksearch filter tool to your own panel/toolbar, then follow the tricks found here: http://layerxml.wordpress.com/2011/02/16/place-the-quicksearch-component-anywhere-you-like/, and also at https://blogs.oracle.com/geertjan/place-the-quicksearch-component-anywhere-you-like-part-2.

You can search for actions, but how can you search for tasks? The answer is by following these steps:

1. Right-click on the *View* module and select **New ➤ Other**.

2. In the *New File* dialog, choose **Module Development ➤ Quick Search Provider** (see Figure 10-11) and click **Next**.

3. In the Quick Search Provider panel, set the provider class name, etc. (see Figure 10-12).

4. Click on **Finish**.

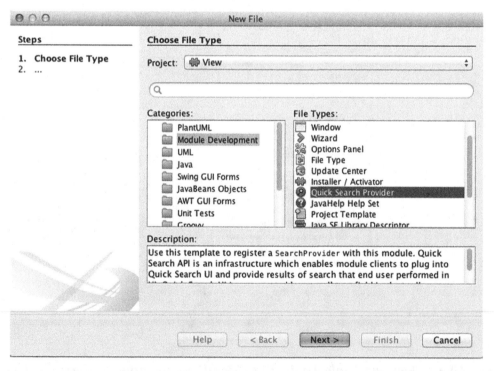

Figure 10-11. *New Quick Search Provider wizard (step 1)*

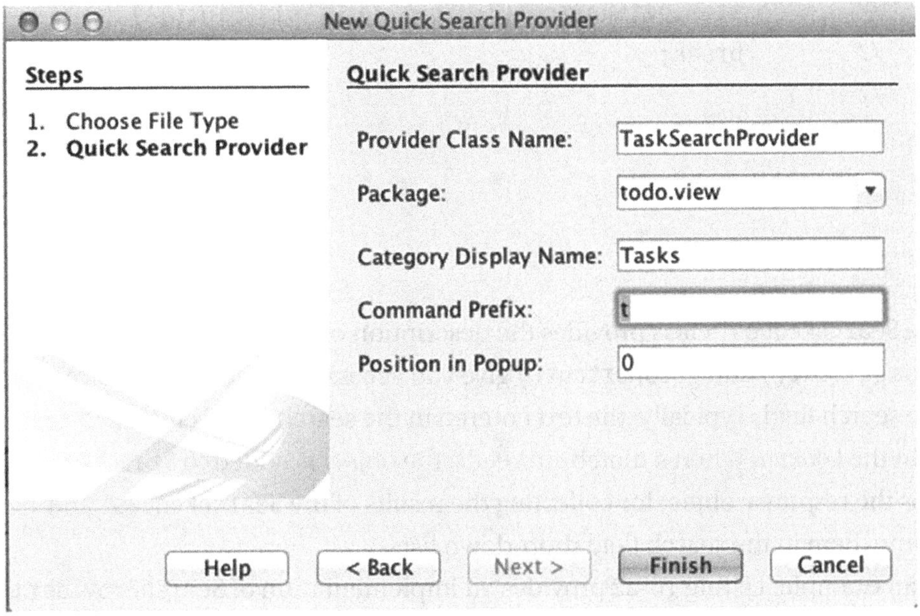

Figure 10-12. *New Quick Search Provider wizard (step 2)*

The wizard will create the stub shown in Listing 10-21.

Listing 10-21. TaskSearchProvider generated by the Quick Search Provider wizard

```
package todo.view;

import org.netbeans.spi.quicksearch.SearchProvider;
import org.netbeans.spi.quicksearch.SearchRequest;
import org.netbeans.spi.quicksearch.SearchResponse;

public class TaskSearchProvider implements SearchProvider {
    @Override
    public void evaluate(SearchRequest request, SearchResponse response) {
        //sample code
        //for (SearchedItem item : getAllItemsToSearchIn()) {
        //    if (isConditionSatisfied(item, request)) {
        //        if (!response.addResult(item.getRunnable(), item.
                getDisplayName(),
```

```
//          item.getShortcut(), item.getDisplayHint()))) {
//          break;
//      }
//      }
//}
    }
}
```

The SearchRequest class provides the description of the quick search request. The methods getText() and getShortcut() give you access to the text and shortcut typed into the search field. Typically, the text entered in the search field is matched against an object in the Lookup. When a match succeeds, the object is added to SearchResponse, which is the response object for collecting the results of the SearchRequest and displaying them in the search field drop-down list.

As an example, Listing 10-22 provides an implementation of SearchProvider that finds all Nodes in TasksTopComponent, then searches through their Lookups for Task objects.

Listing 10-22. Example implementation of SearchProvider

```java
@Override
public void evaluate(final SearchRequest request, final SearchResponse
 response) {
    SwingUtilities.invokeLater(new Runnable() {
        @Override
        public void run() {
            TopComponent tc = WindowManager.getDefault().findTopComponent("
            TasksTopComponent");
            final ExplorerManager em = ((ExplorerManager.Provider) tc).
            getExplorerManager();
            Node root = em.getRootContext();
            for (final Node node : root.getChildren().getNodes()) {
                Task task = node.getLookup().lookup(Task.class);
                if (accept(task, request)) {
                    response.addResult(new Runnable() {
                        @Override
                        public void run() {
```

```
                           try {
                               em.setSelectedNodes(new Node[]{node});
                           } catch (PropertyVetoException ex) {
                               Exceptions.printStackTrace(ex);
                           }
                       }
                   }, task.getDescription());
               }
           }
       }
    });
}

private boolean accept(Task task, SearchRequest request) {
    return task != null && task.getDescription().contains(request.
    getText());
}
```

The wizard also creates the code shown in Listing 10-23, placing that code into
`layer.xml`.

Listing 10-23. QuickSearch folder generated in layer.xml from the Quick Search
Provider wizard

```
<folder name="QuickSearch">
    <folder name="Tasks">
        <attr name="command" stringvalue="t"/>
        <attr name="position" intvalue="0"/>
        <file name="todo-view-TaskSearchProvider.instance">
            <attr name="displayName" bundlevalue="todo.view.Bundle
            #QuickSearch/Tasks/todo-view-TaskSearchProvider.instance"/>
        </file>
    </folder>
</folder>
```

QuickSearch is not to be confused with *QuickFilter*. Check
ShowCompletedTasksAction implementation in the source code bundle to
see how to filter the OutlineView (see also *https://jnkjava.wordpress.
com/2014/02/26/recipe-9-how-to-filter-an-outlineview/*). You
may also add your own custom quick filter in order to filter the OutlineView
by following the instructions described in this blog (https://jnkjava.
wordpress.com/2015/02/01/recipe-14-how-to-add-a-quick-
filter/).

Output Window

The *Output window* is a display area, usually at the bottom of the NetBeans IDE window,
for showing messages to the user (see Figure 10-13). Messages from multiple sources can
be displayed in different tabs simultaneously.

To use the *Output window* in your application, add a dependency to *I/O API and SPI*
module. An example use case is shown in Listing 10-24.

Listing 10-24. Output window code example

```
InputOutput io = IOProvider.getDefault().getIO("Hello World!", true);
io.show();   // display Output window if it is not open
try (OutputWriter writer = io.getOut()) {
    writer.println("This is a message.");
}
```

Passing true as the second parameter to IOProvider.getDefault().getIO()
ensures that a new tab is created in the *Output window* for each call. Pass false to write
the output to the same tab. InputOutput.show() ensures that the *Output window* opens,
if it is closed.

Figure 10-13. *Output window*

Settings

NetBeans IDE provides the *Options* window (menu **Tools ➤ Options** or **NetBeans ➤ Preferences** on MacOS) that allows the user to customize it (see Figure 10-14).

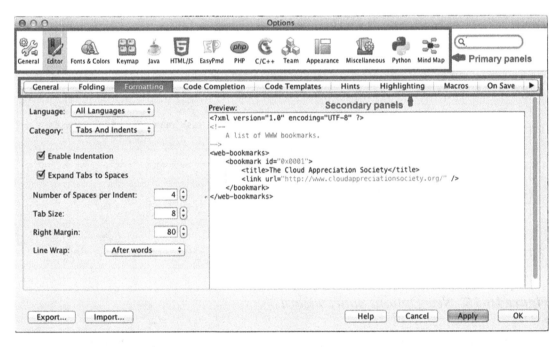

Figure 10-14. *Options window*

As you can see in Figure 10-14, there are *Primary panels* (for example *General, Miscellaneous*) and *Secondary panels* (for example *Formatting, Hints,* etc.). The Primary Panels can be used to configure the most important groupings of settings in an application. Secondary Panels can be used for less important settings needed for configuring the application. You can also export and import your settings with the two respective buttons in the bottom left of the *Options* window.

The Apache NetBeans Platform *Options Dialog API and SPI* allow modules to customize the Options window. To use this API, right-click on your module, and select **New ➤ Other**. Select the *Module Development* category and the *Options Panel* file type. In the next step, choose among Primary and Secondary panel (see Figure 10-15). The keywords enable the user to quickly open the *Options* window from the *Quick Search field* as we learned previously.

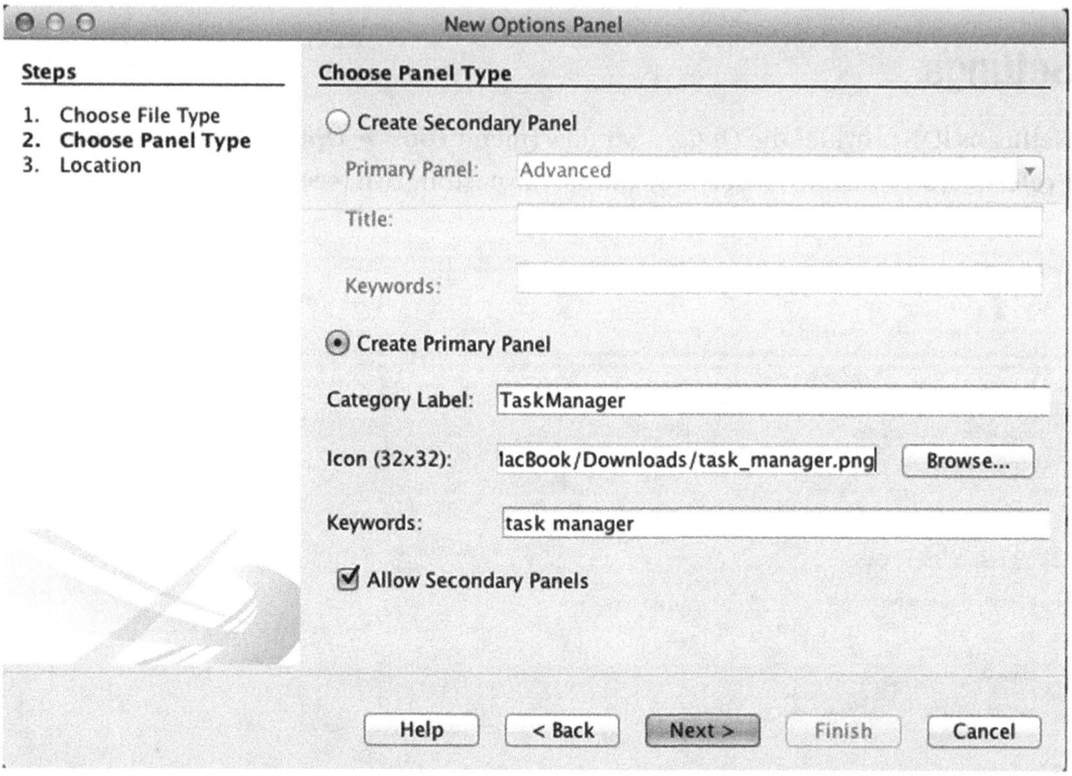

Figure 10-15. *New Options panel wizard*

The wizard will create a `package-info.java` file with the contents shown in Listing 10-25 for a primary panel.

Listing 10-25. package-info.java contents

```
@OptionsPanelController.ContainerRegistration(
    id = "TaskManager",
    categoryName = "#OptionsCategory_Name_TaskManager",
    iconBase = "todo/view/task_manager.png",
```

```
  keywords = "#OptionsCategory_Keywords_TaskManager",
  keywordsCategory = "TaskManager")
@NbBundle.Messages(
  value = {"OptionsCategory_Name_TaskManager=TaskManager",
  "OptionsCategory_Keywords_TaskManager=task manager"})

package todo.view;

import org.netbeans.spi.options.OptionsPanelController;
import org.openide.util.NbBundle;
```

For a secondary panel, the wizard will create a `Controller` class annotated as shown in Listing 10-26 as well as a `JPanel` for you.

Listing 10-26. The TasksOptionsPanelController for the secondary panel

```
@OptionsPanelController.SubRegistration(
        location = "TaskManager",
        displayName = "#AdvancedOption_DisplayName_Tasks",
        keywords = "#AdvancedOption_Keywords_Tasks",
        keywordsCategory = "TaskManager/Tasks"
)
@org.openide.util.NbBundle.Messages(
{"AdvancedOption_DisplayName_Tasks=Tasks", "AdvancedOption_Keywords_
Tasks=task"})
public final class TasksOptionsPanelController extends
OptionsPanelController {
...
```

Whatever you set in this panel is persisted (stored) into the NetBeans Platform user directory with the help of `org.openide.util.NbPreferences` class to be available the next time you open the application.

You can easily locate the NetBeans Platform user directory by displaying the *About* dialog box from **Help ➤ About** or **NetBeans ➤ About NetBeans** (in MacOS) and verifying the *User Directory* entry (see Figure 10-16).

Figure 10-16.   *About NetBeans dialog box*

Progress

More often than not, when dealing with large amounts of data, the calculation and display of them may take some noticeable time to the user. For example, retrieving data from a filesystem or database can take several seconds on a good day. As a good *User Experience* rule, the user should be given some visual feedback of the progress that a long task takes.

For example, expanding a Node that creates child elements synchronously in the *Event Dispatch Thread (EDT)* will freeze the UI. During this time, no UI updates are performed and user gestures are ignored, making the UI unusable for the duration of the process. That is the reason why creating the child elements is done in a different thread. Meanwhile, you should inform the user that child elements are being created and are about to be displayed. During this time, normally a wait cursor and a status message are shown.

In Chapter 8 we saw how ChildFactory class offers support for creating child elements asynchronously (by passing true as the second parameter of the Children. create() method).

By default, the NetBeans Platform status bar has an integrated progress bar. When you are working with long-running tasks, you can plug into the progress bar to let the user visualize progress, either of a single task or multiple tasks.

To plug into the progress bar, you need to add a dependency to the *Progress API*. The ProgressHandleFactory creates ProgressHandle objects, which display progress and, optionally, enables the user to cancel the progress display. Progress can be displayed with a definite or an indefinite runtime.

For example, the code snippet of Listing 10-27 could be used inside the createKeys() method of TaskChildFactory to display the progress of loading and displaying a large number of tasks in the OutineView of the *TodoRCP* application.

Listing 10-27. Example to display the progress of loading a large number of tasks

```
ProgressHandle handle = ProgressHandleFactory.creatHandle("Tasks progress");
handle.start(100);    // 100 percentiles, i.e. 0-100
...
handle.progress(25);
...
handle.progress(50);
...
handle.progress(75);
...
handle.finish();
```

To handle a long task that spans many modules, use the ProgressContributor as described in the API (http://bits.netbeans.org/dev/javadoc/org-netbeans-api-progress/index.html).

Visual Library

The *Visual Library* is used to display selectable, movable, and changeable graphic components (called *widgets*) on a *Scene*. The Visual Library is based on Java2D and uses a lightweight window system so that it can be used with Swing, JavaFX, etc.

The Visual Library is normally used in combination with the *Component Palette*, which allows for dragging and dropping items onto components (like *Scenes*). To open your appetite, you may start your adventure by exploring the Visual Library examples (`https://platform.netbeans.org/graph/examples.html`) to see the capabilities of the library as well as take a look at some tutorials and real applications that actually use it (`https://platform.netbeans.org/graph/`).

Before you can use the Visual Library in your projects, you need to add the *Visual Library API* from the *platform* cluster, which is not added by default. You do this by right-clicking on your Module suite and selecting **Properties** as described and illustrated earlier in Figure 10-10.

The main classes of the Visual Library are described in the subsections to follow.

Widgets

Widgets are lightweight graphical components that can be used to draw graphs. As shown in Figure 10-17, `Widget` follows the *Composite design pattern* (widgets contain widgets), and the various widgets are organized into a tree hierarchy.

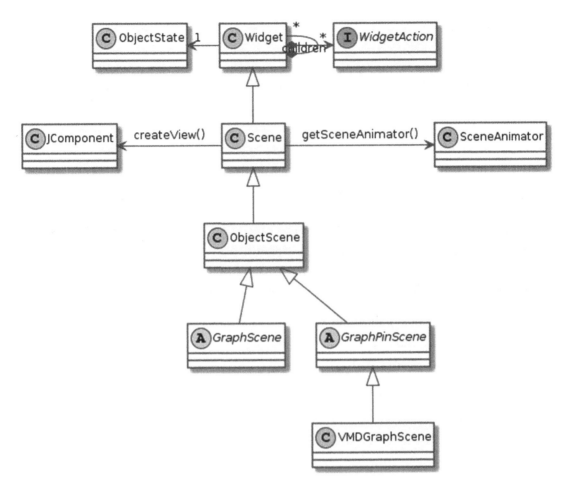

Figure 10-17. *Visual Library class diagram*

A variety of Widget implementations are provided by the Visual Library (see Figure 10-18), each incorporating predefined behavior consisting of customizable actions, borders, and layouts. Together, Widgets are arranged and displayed in a Scene, of which there are various implementations, too (see Figure 10-17).

Widgets have efficient validation and repaint mechanisms. A widget (as shown in Figure 10-17) has also a *state,* and that state can take on one of several values: *selected, highlighted* (also called *secondary selection*), *object-hovered, widget-hovered, widget-aimed.*

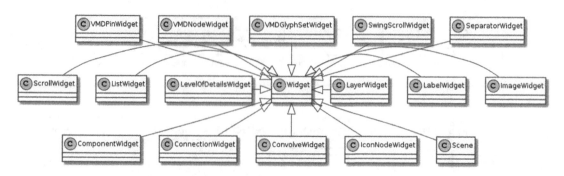

Figure 10-18. *Widget implementations*

Finally, Widget has a Lookup, which can be used to add objects to it. Listing 10-28 provides an example of using a Lookup in a Widget.

Listing 10-28. A Widget with a Lookup to store model objects

```
class MyWidget extends LabelWidget {
    private Lookup lookup;
    private InstanceContent ic;

    public MyWidget(Scene scene) {
        super(scene);
        ic = new InstanceContent();
    }

    @Override
    public Lookup getLookup() {
        if (lookup == null) {
            lookup = new AbstractLookup(ic);
        }
        return lookup;
    }
}
```

This Lookup is usually proxied by the TopComponent that contains the visual components, which is in turn proxied by Utilities.actionsGlobalContext(), as we have learned in the previous chapters.

Scene

The Scene (see Figures 10-17 and 10-18) is a kind of Widget, too. It is a top-level Widget (the *root* element of the hierarchical tree structure) that contains other Widgets. It is usually displayed in a Swing component like, for example, a JScrollPane. There are various types of Scenes as one can see in Figure 10-17. For example, ObjectScene maps a Widget to a data object. GraphScene, GraphPinScene and VMDGraphScene (*VMD* stands for *Visual Mobile Designer*) are used to simplify creating graphs.

To create a Scene and add Widgets to it, you typically follow the steps shown in Listing 10-29.

Listing 10-29. Steps to create a Scene

```
public class TaskViewerTopComponent extends TopComponent {
    public TaskViewerTopComponent() {
        setLayout(new BorderLayout());
        Scene scene = new Scene();
        LayerWidget mainLayer = new LayerWidget(scene);
        LabelWidget labelWidget =
            new LabelWidget(scene, "ATask");
        mainLayer.addChild(labelWidget);
        scene.addChild(mainLayer);
        add(new JScrollPane(scene.createView()), BorderLayout.CENTER);
    }
}
```

With createView() or createSatelliteView() methods, you create a JComponent that can be embedded in any Swing container. Similarly, with getSceneAnimator() method, you can create a SceneAnimator (which contains a few built-in animations). LayerWidget acts like a JGlassPane and it is typically used as a container for other widgets.

ConnectionWidget

The ConnectionWidget represents a connection between two locations. The locations are resolved by Anchors (see Figure 10-19). The path of the connection is specified by *control points*, which are resolved by Routers (see Figure 10-20).

A number of anchor types are supported (created by AnchorFactory): center, circular, directional, fixed, or rectangular. Routers (created by RouterFactory) can be orthogonal, direct, or free (DirectRouter is used by default).

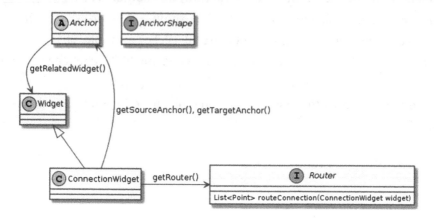

Figure 10-19. *ConnectionWidget*

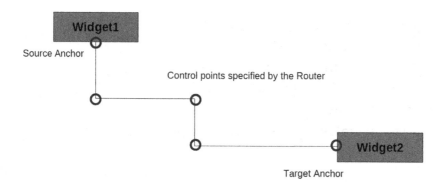

Figure 10-20. *ConnectionWidget example with control points*

Borders

Each Widget has a border, which by default is an empty border, provided by the EmptyBorder class. Borders implement the Border interface. Examples of borders are LineBorder, BevelBorder, DashedBorder, ImageBorder, ResizeBorder. Switching to a different border is done via Widget.setBorder() as shown in Listing 10-30. Borders are created via BorderFactory.

Listing 10-30. Define a Border for a Widget

```
widget.setBorder(BorderFactory.createLineBorder(2,Color.BLUE));
```

Layouts

A widget can be a container for additional widgets and also has a layout defined and managed by a `LayoutManager`. The following layout variants are provided:

`AbsoluteLayout, FlowLayout, CardLayout, OverlayLayout`. Listing 10-31 shows how to assign a layout to a widget using the `LayoutFactory`.

Listing 10-31. Define a layout for a Widget

```
layerWidget.setLayout(LayoutFactory.createVerticalFlowLayout());
```

WidgetAction

The behavior of a `Widget` is described by its *Actions*, which are defined by the `WidgetAction` interface (see Figure 10-21). This interface defines methods called by corresponding events, such as the click of a mouse on the Widget to which the Action is assigned. The Visual Library provides predefined Actions, which can also be customized, for standard functionality, such as moving and editing of Widgets. Examples of Actions include `MoveAction, HoverAction, ZoomAction, PanAction`.

Actions do not need to be defined and instantiated. Instead, they are assigned to a `Widget` by the `ActionFactory` class. To create actions for widgets, use `ActionFactory` and add them to the widgets with method `addAction()` (see Listing 10-32). Some `ActionFactory` methods require a provider (such as the `EditAction`). Other actions have default providers (such as the `MoveAction`). If you wish to deviate from the default behavior, though, use another provider.

Available providers: `AcceptProvider, ConnectProvider, ContiguousSelectProvider, CycleFocusProvider, EditProvider, HoverProvider, InplaceEditorProvider, MoveControlPointProvider, MoveProvider, PopupMenuProvider, ReconnectProvider, RectangularSelectProvider, ResizeProvider, SelectProvider, TwoStateHoverProvider`.

Actions are chained. `WidgetAction.Chain` class represents a chain of widget actions; it receives user events and forwards them to the related Actions. When you call `getActions()` on a `Widget`, you actually get the `Chain`. Of course, order of actions is important.

Listing 10-32. Add an action to a Widget

```
labelWidget.getActions().addAction(
    ActionFactory.createMoveAction());
```

Actions can also be grouped together. This can be done by calling `Scene.setActiveTool()` method and then using `getActions("activeTool")` instead of `getActions()`.

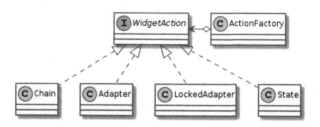

Figure 10-21. *Widget actions*

Palette

You usually use the Visual Library in combination with the `Palette` to drag `Widgets` from the `Palette` to a `Scene`. The `Palette` is a `TopComponent` containing items that can be dragged and dropped onto a component of your choice within any other `TopComponent`.

The `TopComponent` publishes a `PaletteController` in its `Lookup`, together with Actions that hook into the right-click pop-up menus on categories and items in the Palette. The `Palette` opens together with the `TopComponent`, if a `PaletteController` is found in the `Lookup` of the `TopComponent`. The `PaletteFactory.createPalette()` method returns an implementation of the `PaletteController` and associates it with the `TopComponent` by putting it into its `Lookup` (see Listing 10-33).

Listing 10-33. Associate the Palette with the TopComponent's Lookup

```
associateLookup(Lookups.singleton(
    PaletteFactory.createPalette(...)));
```

By default, when an item is dragged from a Palette, it cannot be dropped. You must explicitly define a component as a *drop target*; otherwise it cannot be a recipient of a Palette's *drop event*. If you wish to combine the Palette with the Visual Library, then the drop target is a Scene.

The code example of Listing 10-34 shows how whenever a drop occurs on the Scene, a new LabelWidget is created. One can configure the Palette by right-clicking on it and selecting the **Palette Manager** action from the pop-up menu.

Listing 10-34. Create a new LabelWidget when drag&drop on a Scene

```
scene.getActions().addAction(
    ActionFactory.createAcceptAction(
        new AcceptProvider() {
            @Override
            public ConnectorState isAcceptable(
                Widget widget, Point point, Transferable t) {
                return ConnectorState.ACCEPT;
            }
            @Override
            public void accept(Widget widget, Point point, Transferable t) {
                Node node = NodeTransfer.node(t, NodeTransfer.DND_COPY_OR_
                MOVE);
                LabelWidget labelWidget =
                    new LabelWidget(scene, node.getDisplayName());
                labelWidget.getActions().addAction(
                                    ActionFactory.createMoveAction());
                labelWidget.setPreferredLocation(point);
                layerWidget.addChild(labelWidget);
            }
        }
    )
);
```

As an exercise, add a new module (Visual, todo.visual) to *TodoRCP* that allows the user to drop the Tasks stored in the application from the Palette on a Scene. The user should also be able to connect tasks in order to show dependencies among them.

Branding, Distribution, and Internationalization

What remains to be done is to replace the splash screen and the *About* box, and you're almost ready to distribute your application. The following are a few of the things you can do to brand and distribute your application:

1. Right-click your project and select **Branding**. Here you can select a splash screen and the icon to display when the application is minimized as well as the title to show in the application's title bar. You can also control the windows behavior of your application (for example, you may disable floating) and finally internationalize the application, that is, change the UI in your preferred language (*Internationalization Resource Bundles* tab) by translating the resource bundles to that language.

2. Right-click your project and select **Properties**. In the *Application* category, you can change the application's name. In the *Libraries* category, you can choose which clusters and modules to include to improve performance.

3. To create a distributable *.zip* or *installer* of your application, right-click your project, select **Properties**, and then the *Installer* category. Check the platform(s) that you wish to create installer(s) for (such as Windows, Mac OSX, Solaris, and Linux), and click **OK**. You may also provide a license. Right-click the project again, and select **Package as** and select one of the available options, such as *Installers* or *Zip distribution*.

If everything ran smoothly, you created a new `dist` folder inside your project's folder, which contains the deployed application. Unzip it, if needed, navigate inside (for example, `dist/todorcp/bin`) and execute the executable file (depending on your platform, which could be, for example, `todorcp.exe` or something similar).

You can also allow online updates of your applications' modules via the *Update center*, the same way that you download plugins, in order for example to provide bug fixes or new features. To provide this capability for your application, follow these steps:

1. Enable the *Auto Update Services* and *Auto Update UI* modules in the *platform* cluster (see Figure 10-10). After clean and build, verify that you have a **Tools ➤ Plugins** menu item that opens the *Plugin Manager*.

2. Right-click on the project, and select **Package as ➤ NBMs**. An .nbm (or *NetBeans Module*) file is created for each module in the build/updates/ directory. The *Update Center descriptor* (updates.xml) is also created. You need to publish these files to a web server.

3. In the *Plugin Manager* window, click on **Settings** tab, then click **Add** and enter the URL to the *Update Center descriptor* (updates. xml).

4. Here (https://www.codenameone.com/blog/netbeans-plugin-update-center.html) is an example.

Summary

Table 10-1 shows a grouping of modules that provide functionality from the Apache NetBeans Platform. The table is a summary of the provided functionality by that platform. You may use most of the jar files mentioned in the table outside the NetBeans IDE, that is, using another IDE or a text editor to develop an application based on Apache NetBeans RCP.

In the next chapter you will apply what you have learned so far in order to create a plugin for NetBeans.

Table 10-1. *Apache NetBeans Platform Modules Overview*

Modules grouping	Provided functionality
Core	

`boot.jar`
`core.jar`
`org-openide-filesystems.jar`
`org-openide-modules.jar`
`org-openide-util-lookup.jar`
`org-openide-util.jar`
	Provide the runtime container.

`org-netbeans-modules-masterfs.jar`	Provides the central registry file system functionality (a.k.a. layer).
UI	

`org-netbeans-core.jar`
`org-netbeans-core-execution.jar`
`org-netbeans-core-ui.jar`
`org-netbeans-core-windows.jar`
	Provide the basic UI components.

`org-netbeans-windows.jar`	Provides the API for processing the window system.
`org-openide-actions.jar`	Provides a number of configurable system actions (for example "Cut," "Copy," "Paste").

`org-openide-nodes.jar`
`org-openide-explorer.jar`
`org-netbeans-swing-outline.jar`
	Provide the APIs for *Nodes* and *Explorer views*, that is, the UI part of the platform.

`org-netbeans-core-multiview.jar`	Provides the MultiView window.

`org-netbeans-swing-plaf.jar`
`org-netbeans-swing-tabcontrol`
`org-jdesktop-layout.jar`
	Provides the look and feel and the display of tabs and a wrapper for the Swing Layout Extensions library.

(*continued*)

Table 10-1. (*continued*)

Modules grouping	Provided functionality
Extras	
`org-openide-awt.jar`	Provides many helper classes for displaying UI elements (for example notifications, see Figure 10-8).
`org-openide-dialogs.jar`	Provides an API for displaying standard and customized dialogs and wizards (see beginning of this chapter).
`org-netbeans-api-visual.jar`	Provides the widget and graph library API for modeling and displaying visual representations of data.
`org-netbeans-spi-quicksearch.jar`	Provides the API for integrating items into the *Quick Search* field (see Figure 10-9).
`org-netbeans-modules-options-api.jar`	Provides the *Options* window API (see Figure 10-14).
`org-netbeans-modules-settings.jar`	Provides an API for saving module-specific settings in a user-defined format.
`org-netbeans-api-progress.jar` `org-openide-execution.jar` `org-netbeans-modules-progress-ui.jar`	Provides support for asynchronous long-running tasks and integration for long-running tasks with the NetBeans Platform's progress bar.
`org-netbeans-core-output2.jar` `org-openide-io.jar`	Provides the Output window (see Figure 10-13).

(*continued*)

Table 10-1. (*continued*)

Modules grouping	Provided functionality
`org-netbeans-modules-autoupdate-services.jar` `org-netbeans-modules-autoupdate-ui.jar`	Provides the update center and plugins functionality.
`org-netbeans-modules-favorites.jar`	Provides the *Favorites* window functionality (menu **Window ➤ Favorites**).
`org-openide-loaders.jar`	Provides an API to work with file types.
`org-netbeans-modules-mimelookup.jar` `org-netbeans-modules-editor-mimelookup.jar`	Provides an API for discovery and creation of settings specific to file types.
`org-netbeans-modules-javahelp.jar`	Provides the *JavaHelp* runtime library that enables JavaHelp sets from different modules to be merged into a single help set.
`org-netbeans-modules-queries.jar`	Provides an API for getting information about files and an SPI for creating your own queries.
`org-netbeans-modules-sendopts.jar`	Provides an API and SPI for registering your own handlers for accessing the command line.
`org-openide-text.jar`	Provides an extension to the `javax.swing.text` API.

CHAPTER 11

Writing a Plugin for NetBeans

Apache NetBeans is a modular IDE, and therefore, it is very extensible. Not only is it easy to extend the IDE, but it is also very easy to develop entire desktop rich applications utilizing the NetBeans Platform. In this chapter, we will discuss how to build modules a.k.a. "Plugins" so that the IDE can be extended to encompass new functionality. For instance, new programming languages are being created all the time, and it is easy to extend Apache NetBeans to support new languages by developing a new plugin.

Modules are typically added to the IDE as plugins. In Apache NetBeans, the Plugins menu allows one to manage the modules that are available, installed, or downloaded to the machine, such that they can be loaded or unloaded to affect the way that Apache NetBeans appears or functions. There is an online portal (`https://netbeans.apache.org/plugins/index.html`) containing plugins that have been developed by the community. One can visit the portal to search available plugins for download. If you develop a plugin, you can make it available on the plugin portal for all to use.

In this chapter we will walk through a tutorial about creating a plugin for NetBeans. We will focus on a blockchain use case. See the source code repository of the book as a reference.

Purpose of the Plugin

We are going to create a NetBeans plugin for a blockchain implementation. Apart from support to set up a new blockchain project from scratch, you will also learn how to create features to support a new language:

- recognize the model file
- syntax highlighting

341

© Ioannis Kostaras, Constantin Drabo, Josh Juneau, Sven Reimers, Mario Schröder, Geertjan Wielenga 2020
I. Kostaras et al., *Pro Apache NetBeans*, https://doi.org/10.1007/978-1-4842-5370-0_11

- error detection

- code completion

- navigation view of the model file

You will also see how to sign and share the plugin with other users of NetBeans.

Introduction to Blockchain

A blockchain is a decentralized peer-to-peer network. Each participant of this network has a copy of a shared ledger, where data can only be appended by digitally signed transactions. The blockchain guarantees the immutability of the ledger.

A block contains an amount of transactions and some metadata. The transactions and the block are unique, identified by a hash. The block also contains a hash of the chronological previous block. The first block in the chain, which has no predecessor, is called Genesis-Block. Together those blocks build the chain. Figure 11-1 shows two blocks with their hashes and the hash of the previous block.

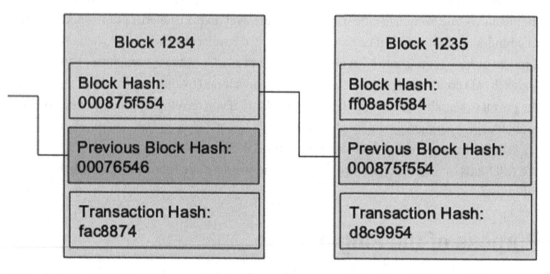

Figure 11-1. *How blocks are connected in the blockchain*

A blockchain can be distinguished between *public* and *private*. A typical example of a public blockchain is *Ethereum*. A public blockchain has built in mechanisms, *Proof of Work* or *Proof of Stake*, to prevent fraudulent actions. An example of a private blockchain is *Hyperledger*. This open source project is an effort to advance blockchain technologies, hosted by the Linux Foundation. The term private means that the access to the network is restricted. Every node has to authenticate itself, so there is no need to have the abovementioned mechanisms against fraudulent attacks and the sensitive information stays within the network. Check out the website `www.hyperledger.org` if you would like to dive deeper into Hyperledger.

When the authors started to write this book, the recommended way to set up a new *Hyperledger* project was to use the *Composer:* `https://hyperledger.github.io/composer/latest/`. A Hyperledger project contains a model file, which is written in the *Hyperledger Composer Language*. Those files end with a `cto` suffix, and we will refer to them as cto files in this chapter. The language defines resources, which are used in the business network:

- **asset:** represents a valuable object, for instance, a house;

- **participant:** stands for the parties involved in the business;

- **transaction:** submitted by a participant, it is a state change that affects the asset;

- **enum:** a collection of values as you know it from Java;

- **event:** can be emitted from transaction functions, and applications can subscribe to events.

The language has a collection of primitive types for field declaration in the resources:

- `Boolean`: a Boolean value, either true or false;

- `String`: an UTF8 encoded string;

- `Integer`: 32-bit signed number;

- `Long`: 64-bit signed number;

- `Double`: double precision 64-bit numeric value;

- `DateTime`: an ISO-8601 compatible time instance, with optional time zone and UTC offset.

The Hyperledger Composer Language does not define the rules for a transaction; this logic is part of another file, written in JavaScript.

Preparation for Hyperledger

To work with Hyperledger properly, we need to install some tools. Please ensure that your machine fulfills the prerequisites, described on `https://hyperledger.github.io/composer/latest/installing/installing-prereqs.html`.

The part for installing VSCode can be skipped, since we are developing our own editor.

When finished with those steps, please install the Hyperledger Composer Command Line Tool globally, the application generator, and Yeoman:

```
npm install -g composer-cli@0.20
npm install -g generator-hyperledger-composer@0.20
npm install -g yo
```

You should also install the Hyperledger Composer Playground, which provides a user interface for the configuration, deployment, and testing of a business network.

```
npm install -g composer-playground@0.20
```

Hyperledger Fabric is the runtime for the business networks. There are scripts to install this runtime. Download into a directory of your choice:

```
mkdir ~/fabric-dev-servers && cd ~/fabric-dev-servers
curl -O https://raw.githubusercontent.com/hyperledger/composer-tools/master/packages/fabric-dev-servers/fabric-dev-servers.tar.gz
tar -xvf fabric-dev-servers.tar.gz
```

Execute the following commands:

```
export FABRIC_VERSION=hlfv12
./downloadFabric.sh
```

You have finished preparing your environment to work with Hyperledger.

For more details, consult the installation instructions:

`https://hyperledger.github.io/composer/latest/installing/development-tools.html`.

Let's create a new skeleton business network with Yeoman in the console. This business network will be used during the development of the plugin.

```
yo hyperledger-composer:businessnetwork
? Business network name: ledger
? Description: sample
? Author name: admin
? Author email: admin@web.org
? License: Apache-2.0
? Namespace: org.example.biznet
? Do you want to generate an empty template network? No: generate a
populated sample network
   create package.json
   create README.md
   create models/org.example.biznet.cto
   create permissions.acl
   create .eslintrc.yml
   create features/sample.feature
   create features/support/index.js
   create test/logic.js
   create lib/logic.js
```

Create a New Module

Under the hood we are using Maven as a build tool. Start a new Module with: "File" ➤ "New Project" ➤ "Java with Maven" ➤ "NetBeans Module". Figure 11-2 shows NetBeans' project wizard.

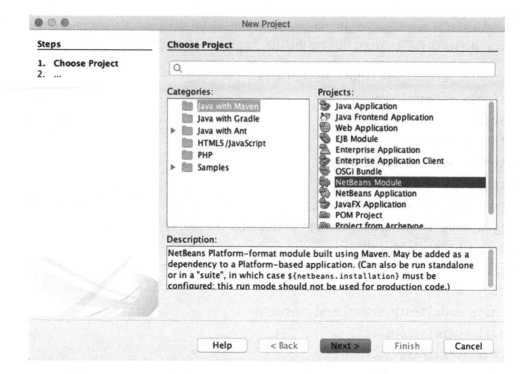

Figure 11-2. *Wizard to create a new NetBeans module with Maven*

Next, give your project a meaningful name like 'ledger' and then select your target platform, you can start with RELEASE82. Click on Finish to complete the action.

We will add test dependencies. Select the project node 'Test Dependencies', right-click, and choose 'Add Dependency'. This will bring up the dialog, shown in Figure 11-3.

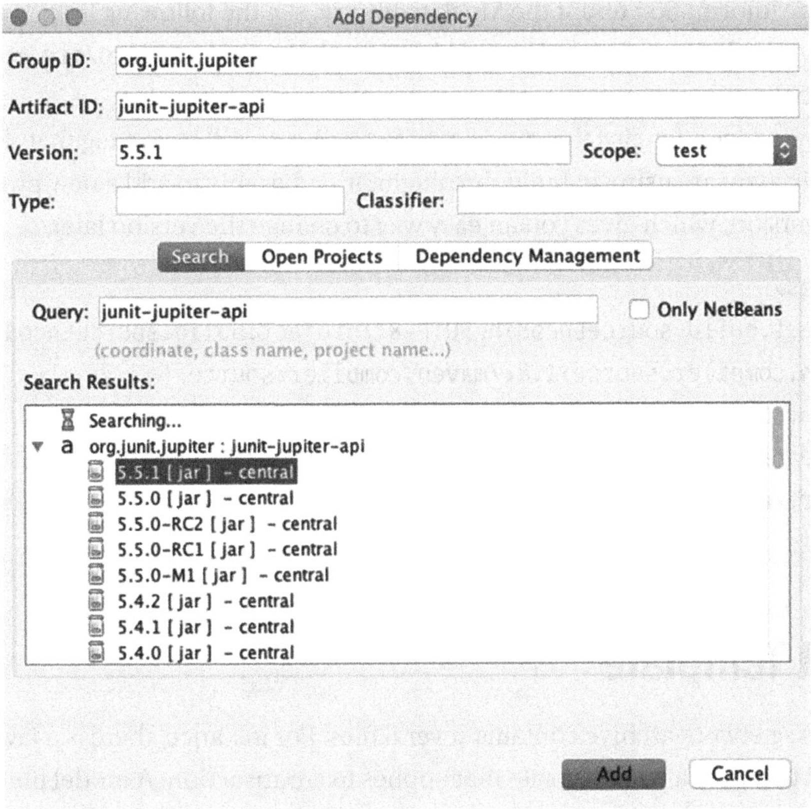

Figure 11-3. *Dialog to add dependencies*

Change the scope to test, untick 'Only NetBeans', and use the query field for the following dependencies:

- `org.junit.jupiter:junit-jupiter-api:5.5.1`

- `org.junit.jupiter:junit-jupiter-engine:5.5.1`

- `org.hamcrest:hamcrest-core:2.1`

- `org.mockito:mockito-junit-jupiter:2.28.2`

To enable an incubating feature in Mockito, which creates mocks for final classes, add a new file `src/test/resources/mockito-extensions/org.mockito.plugins.MockMaker` with a single line:

```
mock-maker-inline
```

For more information about the Mockito library, see the following link: http://static.javadoc.io/org.mockito/mockito-core/2.24.0/org/mockito/ Mockito.html.

All Maven dependencies that are related to NetBeans will have a tag that shows the version which you are using to build the plugin. It's advisable to add a new property that holds this version, which gives you an easy way to change the version later.

```
<properties>
    <project.build.sourceEncoding>UTF-8</project.build.sourceEncoding>
    <maven.compiler.source>1.8</maven.compiler.source>
    <maven.compiler.target>1.8</maven.compiler.target>
    <netbeans.version>RELEASE82</netbeans.version>
    <antlr.version>4.7.1</antlr.version>
</properties>
```

Project Template

The business network archive contains several files. For instance, there is a JavaScript file that is used to define a business rule that applies to a transaction. A model file defines the basic concept involved in the business. To avoid creating each one of those files manually for a new project, we are going to create a new project type, which will appear in the wizard for projects.

We start with a new Node.js Application, which will serve as the source folder for our template. So again, start the wizard and create a new project as shown in Figure 11-4.

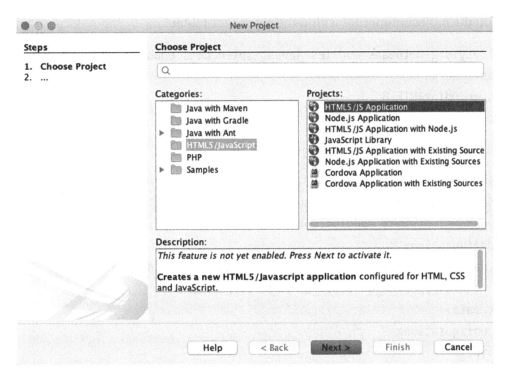

Figure 11-4. *Wizard with Node.js Application*

Remove the directory private under nbproject, as well as the main.js. Copy the source files from the business network, which we created in the previous section, into the src directory of this project.

To have support for publishing the business network from NetBeans, edit the script section of the package.json in the IDE:

```
"scripts": {
  "publish": "mkdirp ./dist && composer archive create --sourceType dir
  --sourceName . -a ./dist/ledger.bna",
  "pretest": "npm run lint",
  "lint": "eslint .",
  "test": "nyc mocha -t 0 test/*.js && cucumber-js"
}
```

Switch to the Files window in the IDE, and create a new .gitignore file with this content:

```
dist/
node_modules/
```

Edit the project.properties within the nbproject folder.

```
auxiliary.org-netbeans-modules-javascript-nodejs.enabled=true
run.as=node.js
files.encoding=UTF-8
source.folder=
```

Change the name-tag in the project.xml file:

```xml
<?xml version="1.0" encoding="UTF-8"?>
<project xmlns="http://www.netbeans.org/ns/project/1">
  <type>org.netbeans.modules.web.clientproject</type>
  <configuration>
    <data xmlns="http://www.netbeans.org/ns/clientside-project/1">
      <name>Hyperledger Business Network</name>
    </data>
  </configuration>
</project>
```

The folder for the zip file should look like this directory structure:

```
.
├── README.md
├── nbproject
│   ├── project.properties
│   └── project.xml
├── features
│   ├── sample.feature
│   └── support
│   └── index.js
├── lib
│   └── logic.js
├── models
│   └── org.example.biznet.cto
├── package.json
├── permissions.acl
└── test
    └── logic.js
```

Let's build a template, which is based on this project. Select the project in NetBeans'
Projects window, and right-click. Then create a new project template: "New File" ➤
"Module Development" ➤ "Project Template." See Figure 11-5.

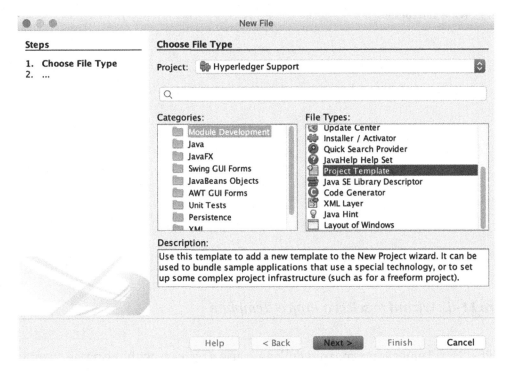

Figure 11-5. *Wizard to create a Project Template*

Select the previously created Node.js project (Figure 11-6).

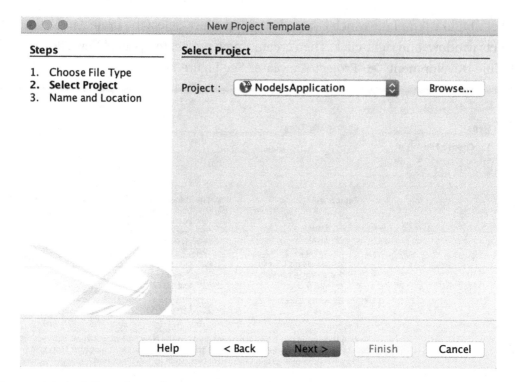

Figure 11-6. *Wizard to select a Project Template*

Click "Next," enter some meaningful name, use a package with the name "template,"
and click Finish. See Figure 11-7.

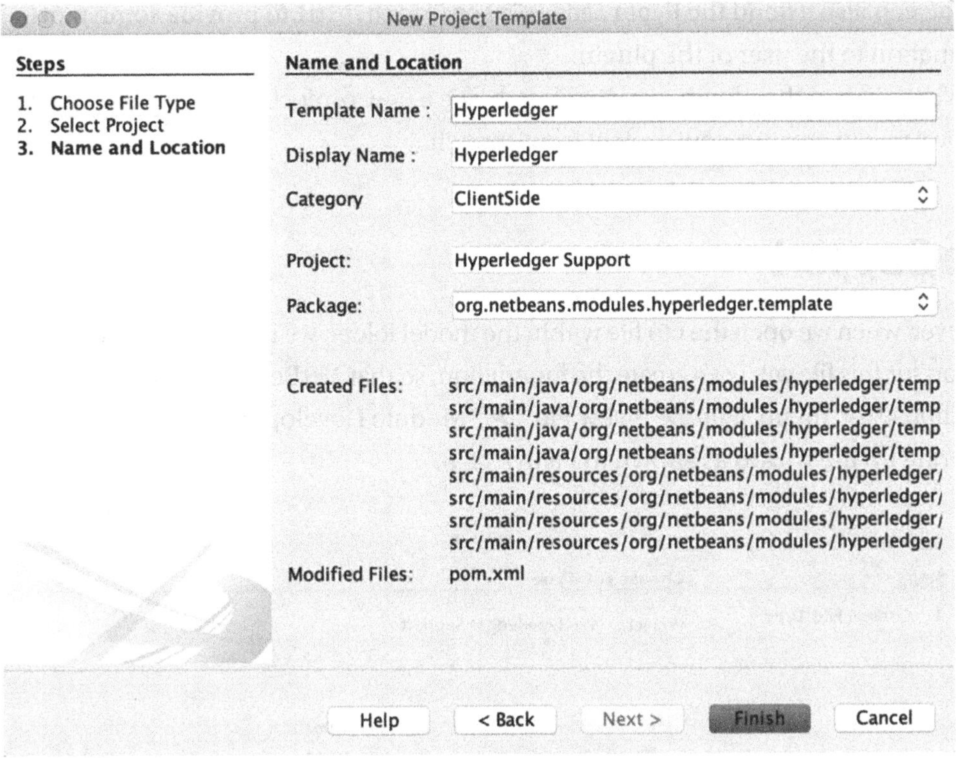

Figure 11-7. *Wizard to set name and location of the Project Template*

This process will add some dependencies to the pom.xml, create several new classes, some resources, and also a zip file with the content from the other Node.js project.

The starting point for the project template is the annotation TemplateRegistration for the HyperledgerWizardIterator. Let's change the icon there.

```
...
@TemplateRegistration(folder = "Project/ClientSide",
    displayName = "#Hyperledger_displayName",
    description = "HyperledgerDescription.html",
    iconBase = "org/netbeans/modules/hyperledger/template/blockchain.png",
    content = "HyperledgerProject.zip")
@Messages("Hyperledger_displayName=Hyperledger")
public class HyperledgerWizardIterator implements
WizardDescriptor./*Progress*/InstantiatingIterator {
...
```

You can also extend the `HyperledgerDescription.html` to provide some more information to the user of the plugin.

When we run the plugin, we can already see a new project template for Hyperledger. It allows you to create a new project from scratch.

File Support

However, when we open the cto file within the model folder, we realize that there is no support for this file yet. Let's create the foundation, so that NetBeans recognizes this file type.

Choose the menu "File" ➤ "New File" ➤ "Module Development" ➤ "File Type." This will bring up the wizard as shown in Figure 11-8.

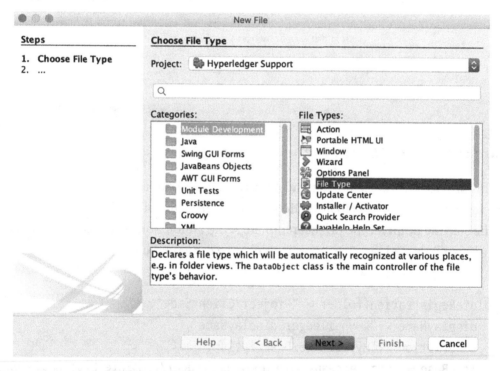

Figure 11-8. *Wizard for new file type*

It will create support for our new file type. Figure 11-9 shows the next step of the wizard. Define the MIME type and file extension and click "Next" to continue. Figure 11-10 shows the last step. There we enter "Cto" for the class name prefix, and select an icon and package. Please make sure to deselect the check box "Use Multiview." Then click on "Finish."

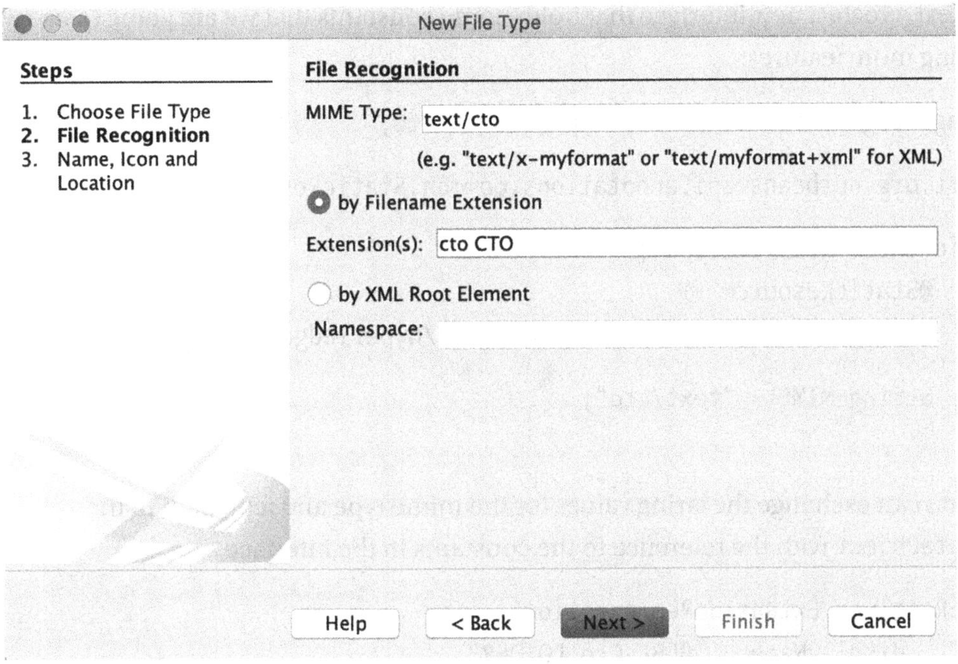

Figure 11-9. *Step 2 to edit File Recognition*

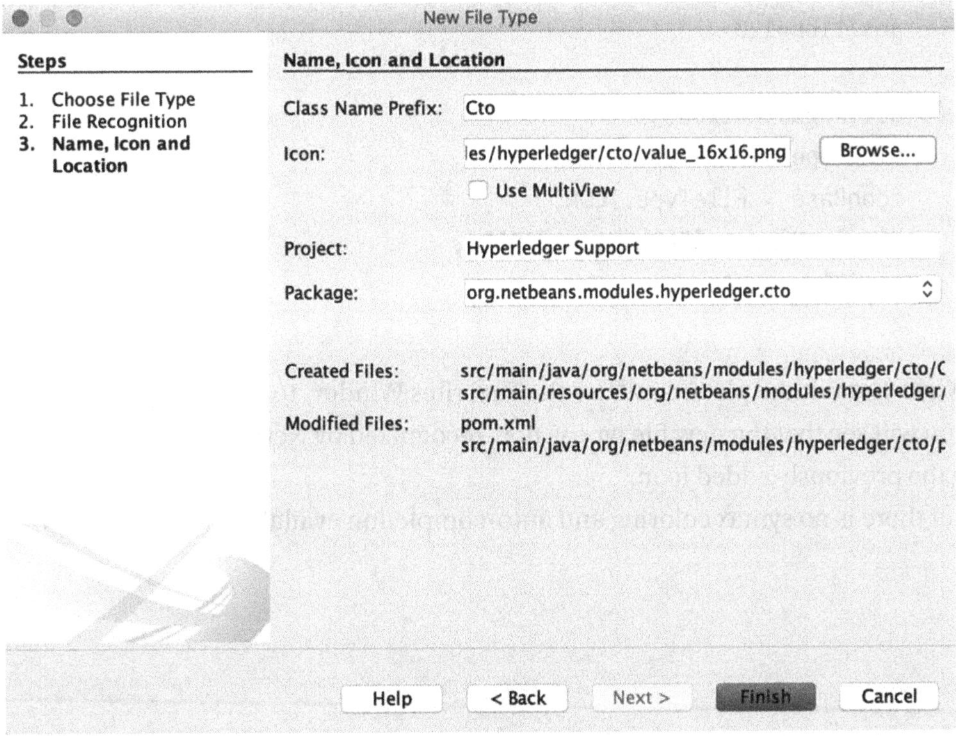

Figure 11-10. *Step 3 for Name, Icon, and Location*

Next, create a new interface that holds some constants that we are going to use while creating more features.

```
package org.netbeans.modules.hyperledger.cto;

import org.netbeans.api.annotations.common.StaticResource;

public interface FileType {
    @StaticResource
    String ICON = "org/netbeans/modules/hyperledger/cto/value_16x16.png";

    String MIME = "text/cto";
}
```

You can exchange the string values for the mime type and icon path in the CtoDataObject with the reference to the constants in the interface.

```
@MIMEResolver.ExtensionRegistration(
        displayName = "#LBL_Cto_LOADER",
        mimeType = FileType.MIME,
        extension = {"cto", "CTO"},
        position=120
)
@DataObject.Registration(
        mimeType = FileType.MIME,
        iconBase = FileType.ICON,
        displayName = "#LBL_Cto_LOADER",
        position = 300
)
```

When you run the plugin and use the Favorites Window to open the previous created file, you will see that the new file type is now recognized by NetBeans, and it is indicated using the previously added icon.

But there is no syntax coloring and auto-completion available. So let's work on that.

Syntax Highlighting

The language support contains a lexer and a parser. The lexer takes the source and converts it into tokens. The parser creates a syntax tree based on those tokens. There are several tools available to create a lexer/parser, but in this tutorial, we will use ANTLR. There is plenty of documentation available about ANTLR, so it should be relatively easy to get yourself on track when you write new grammar.

For this highlighting, we use the lexer only. So, we need the lexer grammar file. This file contains the tokens that are specific for the language. You can copy the file CtoLexer.g4 from the ANTLR grammar repository: https://github.com/antlr/grammars-v4/tree/master/cto.

It's advisable to place the file in a subdirectory of the resource folder in you project, for example, org.netbeans.modules.hyperledger.cto.grammar.

We also need to adapt the Maven pom.xml. Add the ANTLR plugin to the build section, and the ANTLR runtime and NetBeans' Lexer API to the dependency section. The version of the plugin should match the version of the ANTLR dependency. The following snippet shows the ANTLR plugin and runtime dependencies in the pom.xml.

```
...
<build>
  <plugins>
    <plugin>
      <groupId>org.antlr</groupId>
      <artifactId>antlr4-maven-plugin</artifactId>
      <version>${antlr.version}</version>
      <executions>
        <execution>
          <id>antlr</id>
          <goals>
            <goal>antlr4</goal>
          </goals>
        </execution>
      </executions>
    </plugin>
  </plugins>
</build>
```

```
...
<dependency>
  <groupId>org.antlr</groupId>
  <artifactId>antlr4-runtime</artifactId>
  <version>${antlr.version}</version>
</dependency>
<dependency>
  <groupId>org.netbeans.api</groupId>
  <artifactId>org-netbeans-modules-lexer</artifactId>
  <version>${netbeans.version}</version>
</dependency>
...
```

After a successful build, we will have a CtoLexer.java in target/generated-sources.

Next, we need to set up a service that provides the language. Therefore, we will create a new class CtoLanguageProvider, which extends the LanguageProvider from NetBeans:

```
...
@ServiceProvider(service=LanguageProvider.class)
public class CtoLanguageProvider extends LanguageProvider{

    private final Supplier<Language<?>> supplier = () -> new
    CtoLanguageHierarchy().language();

    @Override
    public Language<?> findLanguage(String mime) {
        return (FileType.MIME.equals(mime)) ? supplier.get() : null;
    }

    @Override
    public LanguageEmbedding<?> findLanguageEmbedding(Token<?> token,
    LanguagePath lp, InputAttributes ia) {
        return null;
    }
}
```

The class `CtoLanguageHierarchy` is a definition of the cto language. The method `createTokenIds` will return all tokens, based on the ANTLR grammar file. It also provides an implementation of the `Lexer` interface, which is a mapping for characters, read from an input to the cto tokens.

```
...
public class CtoLanguageHierarchy extends LanguageHierarchy<CtoTokenId> {

    private final List<CtoTokenId> tokens;
    private final Map<Integer, CtoTokenId> idToToken;

    public CtoLanguageHierarchy() {
        tokens = TokenTaxonomy.getDefault().allTokens();
        idToToken = TokenTaxonomy.getDefault().getIdTokenMap();
    }

    @Override
    protected Collection<CtoTokenId> createTokenIds() {
        return tokens;
    }

    @Override
    protected Lexer<CtoTokenId> createLexer(LexerRestartInfo<CtoTokenId> info) {
        return new CtoEditorLexer(info, idToToken);
    }

    @Override
    protected String mimeType() {
        return FileType.MIME;
    }
}
```

The `TokenTaxonomy` provides a classification for the tokens, so that we can later on choose a different styling for a group of tokens.

```java
public enum TokenTaxonomy {

    INSTANCE;

    private final List<CtoTokenId> tokens;

    private TokenTaxonomy() {
        tokens = new ArrayList<>();

        int max = CtoLexer.VOCABULARY.getMaxTokenType() + 1;
        for (int i = 1; i < max; i++) {
            CtoTokenId token = new CtoTokenId(NameMapping.map(i),
            getCategory(i), i);
            tokens.add(token);
        }
    }

    private String getCategory(int token) {
        Function<Integer, Category> mapping = t -> {
            if (t < CtoLexer.BOOLEAN) {
                return Category.KEYWORD;
            } else if (t < CtoLexer.LPAREN) {
                return Category.TYPE;
            } else if (t < CtoLexer.REF) {
                return Category.SEPARATOR;
            } else if (t < CtoLexer.DECIMAL_LITERAL) {
                return Category.FIELD;
            } else if (t < CtoLexer.WS || t == CtoLexer.CHAR_LITERAL || t
            == CtoLexer.STRING_LITERAL) {
                return Category.VALUE;
            } else if (t == CtoLexer.COMMENT || t == CtoLexer.LINE_COMMENT) {
                return Category.COMMENT;
            }
            return Category.TEXT;
        };

        return mapping.apply(token).name();
    }
```

```java
    public List<CtoTokenId> allTokens() {
        return tokens;
    }

    public List<CtoTokenId> tokens(Category category) {
        return tokens.stream().filter(t -> category.name().equals(t.
        primaryCategory())).collect(toList());
    }

    public Map<Integer, CtoTokenId> getIdTokenMap() {
        return tokens.stream().collect(toMap(CtoTokenId::ordinal, t -> t));
    }
}
```

The category itself is just another enum used for the grouping:

```java
public enum Category {
    KEYWORD, TYPE, FIELD, SEPARATOR, VALUE, COMMENT, TEXT;
}
```

The NameMapping interface uses a static method to map an int to a String, using the CtoLexer.VOCABULARY under the hood. The vocabulary contains some characters that we want to avoid later on; therefore, the method map removes unwanted characters from the string.

```java
public interface NameMapping {

    public static String map(int type) {
        String name = CtoLexer.VOCABULARY.getDisplayName(tokenType);
        return name.replaceAll("^\\'|\\'$", "");
    }
}
```

The class CtoTokenId is a very simple implementation of the interface org. netbeans.api.lexer.TokenId from NetBeans' Lexer API.

```java
public class CtoTokenId implements TokenId{

    private final String name;
    private final String primaryCategory;
    private final int id;
```

361

```
public CtoTokenId(String name, String primaryCategory, int id) {
    this.name = name;
    this.primaryCategory = primaryCategory;
    this.id = id;
}

@Override
public String name() {
    return name;
}

@Override
public int ordinal() {
    return id;
}

@Override
public String primaryCategory() {
    return primaryCategory;
}
}
```

The class CtoEditorLexer is the connection between the Lexer API and ANTLR.
It converts an ANTLR token to the CtoTokenId. As you can see, the mapping from an id
to a token is passed to the constructor. We will provide a second constructor that is used
for test purposes. This way we can easily use a mock to supply a token during testing.

```
public final class CtoEditorLexer implements Lexer<CtoTokenId> {

    private final LexerRestartInfo<CtoTokenId> info;
    private final Map<Integer, CtoTokenId> idToToken;

    private final Function<CtoTokenId, Token<CtoTokenId>> tokenFactory;
    private final Supplier<org.antlr.v4.runtime.Token> tokenSupplier;

    public CtoEditorLexer(LexerRestartInfo<CtoTokenId> info, Map<Integer,
    CtoTokenId> idToToken) {
        this(info, idToToken, new TokenSupplier(info.input()));
    }
```

```java
CtoEditorLexer(LexerRestartInfo<CtoTokenId> info, Map<Integer,
CtoTokenId> idToToken,
        Supplier<org.antlr.v4.runtime.Token> tokenSupplier) {
    this.info = info;
    this.idToToken = idToToken;
    this.tokenSupplier = tokenSupplier;
    this.tokenFactory = id -> info.tokenFactory().createToken(id);
}

@Override
public Token<CtoTokenId> nextToken() {
    Token<CtoTokenId> createdToken = null;
    org.antlr.v4.runtime.Token token = tokenSupplier.get();

    int type = token.getType();
    if (type != -1) {
        createdToken = createToken(type);
    } else if (info.input().readLength() > 0) {
        createdToken = createToken(CtoLexer.WS);
    }

    return createdToken;
}

private Token<CtoTokenId> createToken(int type) {
    Function<Integer, CtoTokenId> mapping = idToToken::get;
    return mapping.andThen(tokenFactory).apply(type);
}

@Override
public Object state() {
    return null;
}

@Override
public void release() {
    //nothing todo
}
```

```
private static class TokenSupplier implements Supplier<org.antlr.
v4.runtime.Token> {

    private final CtoLexer lexer;

    TokenSupplier(LexerInput input) {
        CharStream stream = new LexerCharStream(input);
        lexer = new CtoLexer(stream);
    }

    @Override
    public org.antlr.v4.runtime.Token get() {
        return lexer.nextToken();
    }
}
}
```

We need a way to feed the platform's input into the CtoLexer, which was generated by ANTLR. This lexer accepts an interface of org.antlr.v4.runtime.CharStream, so let's implement it. The following source is based on the org.antlr.v4.runtime. ANTLRInputStream.

```
final class LexerCharStream implements CharStream {

    private final static String NAME = "CtoChar";

    private final LexerInput input;
    private final Deque<Integer> markers = new ArrayDeque<>();

    public LexerCharStream(LexerInput input) {
        this.input = input;
    }

    @Override
    public String getText(Interval interval) {
        Objects.requireNonNull(interval, "Interval may not be null");
        if (interval.a < 0 || interval.b < interval.a - 1) {
            throw new IllegalArgumentException("Invalid interval!");
        }
        return input.readText(interval.a, interval.b).toString();
    }
```

```java
@Override
public void consume() {
    read();
}

@Override
public int LA(int ahead) {
    if (ahead == 0) {
        return 0;
    }

    int c = 0;
    for (int j = 0; j < ahead; j++) {
        c = read();
    }
    backup(ahead);

    return c;
}

@Override
public int mark() {
    markers.push(index());
    return markers.size() - 1;
}

@Override
public void release(int marker) {
    if(markers.size() < marker) {
        return;
    }

    //remove all markers from the given one
    for(int i = marker; i < markers.size(); i++) {
        markers.remove(i);
    }
}
```

```java
@Override
public int index() {
    return input.readLengthEOF();
}

@Override
public void seek(int index) {
    int len = index();
    if (index < len) {
        //seek backward
        backup(len - index);
    } else {
        // seek forward
        while (len < index) {
            consume();
        }
    }
}

@Override
public int size() {
    return -1; //unknown
}

@Override
public String getSourceName() {
    return NAME;
}

private int read() {
    int result = input.read();
    if (result == LexerInput.EOF) {
        result = CharStream.EOF;
    }

    return result;
}
```

```
    private void backup(int count) {
        input.backup(count);
    }
}
```

Let's create our first unit test with JUnit 5. Select the enum TokenTaxonomy in the Projects window, right-click, and choose "Tools" ➤ "Create/Update Tests". Figure 11-11 shows the dialog to create or update a test.

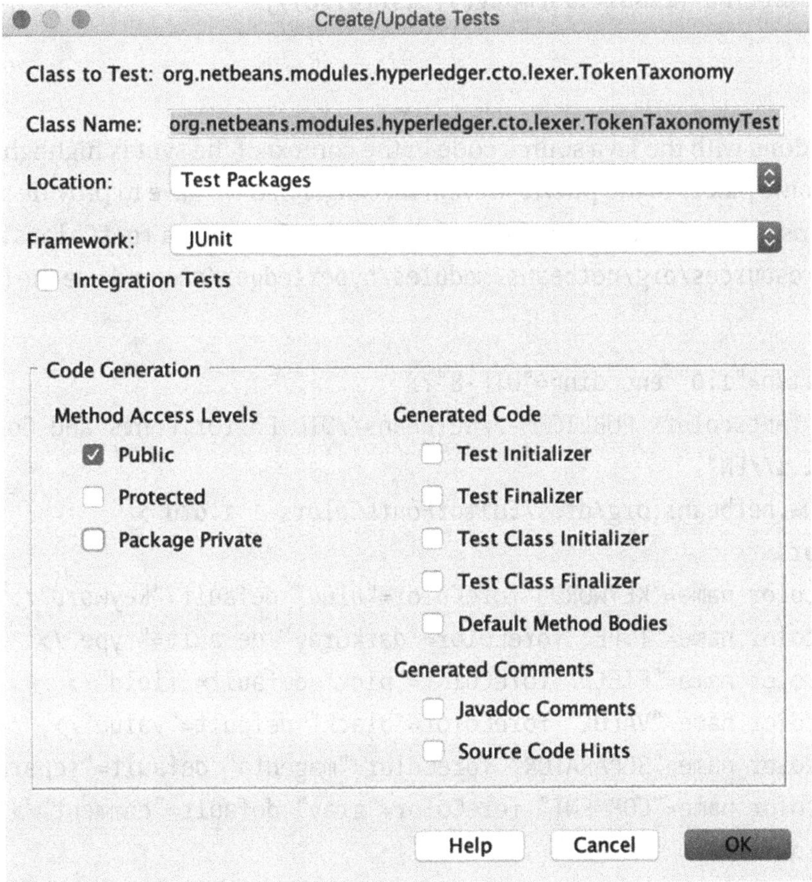

Figure 11-11. *Dialog for tests*

367

Implement the test as follows:

```
public class TokenTaxonomyTest {

    @Test
    @DisplayName("It should return a list of keyword tokens.")
    public void tokens_Keywords() {
        List<CtoTokenId> result = TokenTaxonomy.INSTANCE.tokens(Category.
        KEYWORD);
        assertThat(result.isEmpty(), is(false));
    }
}
```

We are done with the Java source code in the context of the syntax highlighting. However, some pieces of the puzzle are still missing. First, we have to provide an xml file that maps a value of the enum Category to a color. So create a fontColors.xml in src/main/resources/org/netbeans/modules/hyperledger/cto and use the following content:

```
<?xml version="1.0" encoding="UTF-8"?>
<!DOCTYPE fontscolors PUBLIC "-//NetBeans//DTD Editor Fonts and Colors
settings 1.1//EN"
"http://www.netbeans.org/dtds/EditorFontsColors-1_1.dtd">
<fontscolors>
    <fontcolor name="KEYWORD" foreColor="blue" default="keyword"/>
    <fontcolor name="TYPE" foreColor="darkGray" default="type"/>
    <fontcolor name="FIELD" foreColor="pink" default="field"/>
    <fontcolor name="VALUE" foreColor="black" default="value"/>
    <fontcolor name="SEPARATOR" foreColor="magenta" default="separator"/>
    <fontcolor name="COMMENT" foreColor="gray" default="comment"/>
</fontscolors>
```

Provide a translation for those values in the bundle file of this module in src/main/resources/org/netbeans/modules/hyperledger/Bundle.properties:

```
KEYWORD=Keyword
TYPE=Primitive Type
FIELD=Field
```

```
COMMENT=Comment
SEPARATOR=Separator
VALUE=Value
```

We need to register this mapping and provide a preview for the Options Dialog, so that the user can have a quick preview of the colors when he is changing them. This is done in the NetBeans layer system. Please add a layer.xml file in the same directory as the Bundle.properties with the following content:

```xml
<?xml version="1.0" encoding="UTF-8"?>
<!DOCTYPE filesystem PUBLIC "-//NetBeans//DTD Filesystem 1.2//EN"
"http://www.netbeans.org/dtds/filesystem-1_2.dtd">
<filesystem>
    <folder name="Editors">
        <folder name="text">
            <folder name="cto">
                <attr name="SystemFileSystem.localizingBundle"
                stringvalue="org.netbeans.modules.hyperledger.Bundle"/>
                <folder name="FontsColors">
                    <folder name="NetBeans">
                        <folder name="Defaults">
                            <file name="coloring.xml" url="cto/fontColors.
                            xml">
                                <attr name="SystemFileSystem.
                                localizingBundle" stringvalue="org.
                                netbeans.modules.hyperledger.Bundle"/>
                            </file>
                        </folder>
                    </folder>
                </folder>
            </folder>
        </folder>
    </folder>
```

```
    <folder name="OptionsDialog">
        <folder name="PreviewExamples">
            <folder name="text">
                <file name="cto" url="cto/ColorPreview.cto"/>
            </folder>
        </folder>
    </folder>
</filesystem>
```

Expand the node Important Files in the Project View and register the layer.xml file in the Module Manifest (manifest.mf). See Figure 11-12.

Figure 11-12. *Project View with extended node for Important Files*

The content of the manifest.mf file:

```
Manifest-Version: 1.0
OpenIDE-Module: org.netbeans.modules.hyperledger
OpenIDE-Module-Localizing-Bundle: org/netbeans/modules/hyperledger/Bundle.
properties
OpenIDE-Module-Layer: org/netbeans/modules/hyperledger/layer.xml
```

As you can see, we also registered a sample cto file in the layer.xml for the color preview. Therefore, let's add this file in the directory src/main/resources/org/netbeans/modules/hyperledger/cto.

```
/*
 * model file sample
 */
namespace org.basic.sample

import foo.bar

// asset
@foo("arg", 2)
```

```
abstract asset SampleAsset identified by assetId{
  o String assetId
  o Integer [] cols
  --> SampleParticipant owner
}
```

When we run the plugin, we will have a syntax highlighting in the editor (see Figure 11-13) as well a way to change the colors in the Option Dialog (see Figure 11-14).

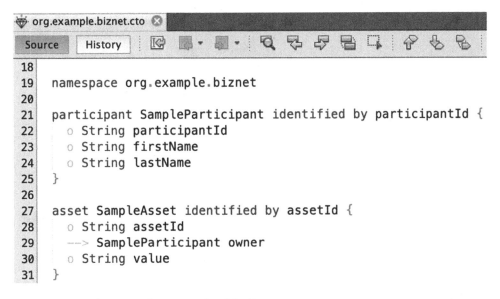

Figure 11-13. *Editor with syntax highlighting*

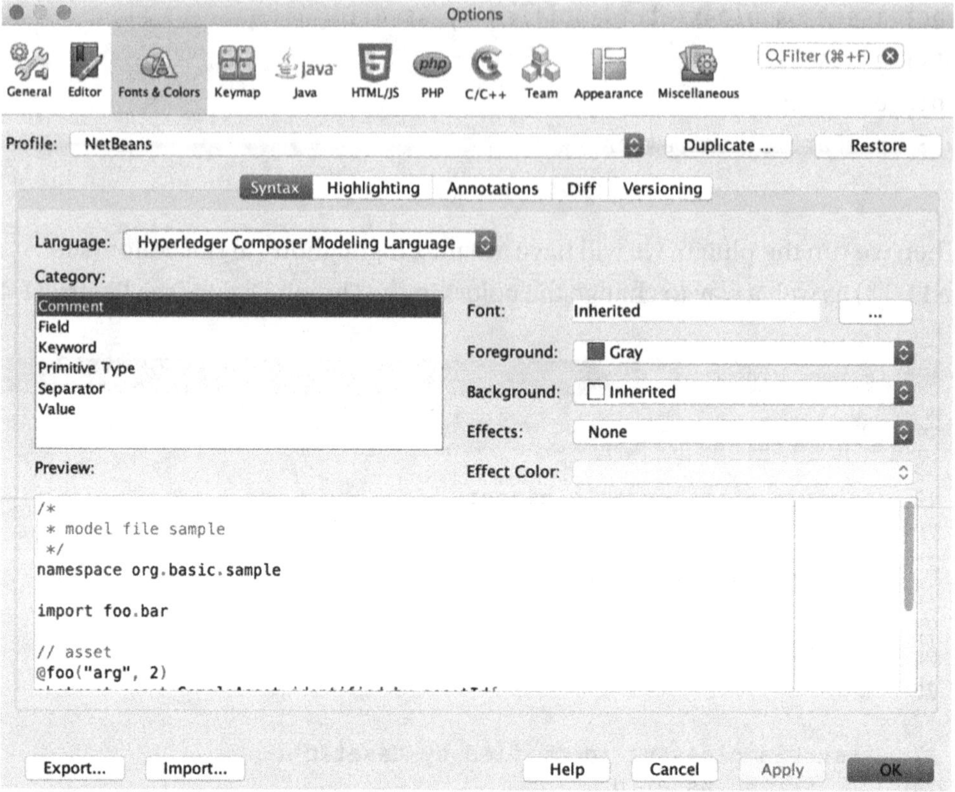

Figure 11-14. *Option dialog with color preview*

Error Hints

The syntax highlighting gives us a little clue if the typed word is a keyword or not. However, it doesn't tell us what should be actually typed when there is a syntax error. Here we can make use of the NetBeans error hints and the parser, generated by ANTLR. The parser allows us to attach an implementation of a listener, which collects all the syntax errors. Those syntax errors can be used for the error hints.

First, we add some new dependencies to the pom.xml file:

```
<dependency>
  <groupId>org.netbeans.api</groupId>
  <artifactId>org-netbeans-modules-parsing-api</artifactId>
  <version>${netbeans.version}</version>
</dependency>
```

```
<dependency>
  <groupId>org.netbeans.api</groupId>
  <artifactId>org-netbeans-spi-editor-hints</artifactId>
  <version>${netbeans.version}</version>
</dependency>
```

The Parsing API will act as a proxy for the ANTLR parser and process the parser result.

We need to define a new grammar file in the same directory where grammar for the lexer is. It is called `CtoParser.g4`. It contains rules to recognize resources in the cto file. The following snippet shows the beginning of this file with the entry point `modelUnit`. For the complete content, see the file in the source repository at GitHub: `https://github.com/antlr/grammars-v4/blob/master/cto/CtoLexer.g4`.

```
parser grammar CtoParser;

options { tokenVocab=CtoLexer; }

modelUnit
        : namespaceDeclaration importDeclaration* typeDeclaration* EOF;
```

The Maven plugin will generate the `CtoParser.java` file. It is visible in the Project View under Generated Sources.

Next, we have to create a bunch of new classes. Let's start with a new class that creates the parser. Notice the `MimeRegistration` annotation. This registers our factory to the mime lookup of NetBeans.

```
@MimeRegistration(mimeType = FileType.MIME, service = ParserFactory.class)
public class CtoParserFactory extends ParserFactory {

    @Override
    public Parser createParser(Collection<Snapshot> coll) {
        return new CtoProxyParser(ParserProvider.INSTANCE);
    }
}
```

The ParserProvider implements the Function interface and creates a new CtoParser for a given text.

```
public enum ParserProvider implements Function<String, CtoParser> {

    INSTANCE;

    @Override
    public CtoParser apply(String text) {
        CharStream input = CharStreams.fromString(text);
        Lexer lexer = new CtoLexer(input);
        TokenStream tokenStream = new CommonTokenStream(lexer);
        return new CtoParser(tokenStream);
    }
}
```

The class CtoProxyParser is a proxy for the ANTLR CtoParser. It parses a snapshot of the editor content and provides the parser result; in this case it contains a list of syntax errors.

```
public class CtoProxyParser extends Parser {

    private final Function<String, CtoParser> parserProvider;

    private CtoParserResult parserResult;

    public CtoProxyParser(Function<String, CtoParser> parserProvider) {
        this.parserProvider = parserProvider;
    }

    @Override
    public void parse(Snapshot snapshot, Task task, SourceModificationEvent
    sme) throws ParseException {

        String text = snapshot.getText().toString();
        CtoParser ctoParser = parserProvider.apply(text);
        ErrorParserListener errorListener = new ErrorParserListener();
        ctoParser.addErrorListener(errorListener);
```

```
    //do the parsing
    ctoParser.modelUnit();

    List<SyntaxError> errors = errorListener.getSyntaxErrors();
    parserResult = new CtoParserResult(snapshot, errors);
}

@Override
public Result getResult(Task task) throws ParseException {
    return parserResult;
}

@Override
public void addChangeListener(ChangeListener cl) {
}

@Override
public void removeChangeListener(ChangeListener cl) {
}

public static class CtoParserResult extends Parser.Result {

    private boolean valid = true;
    private final List<SyntaxError> errors;

    public CtoParserResult(Snapshot snapshot, List<SyntaxError> errors) {
        super(snapshot);
        this.errors = errors;
    }
    public List<SyntaxError> getErrors() {
        return errors;
    }

    @Override
    protected void invalidate() {
        valid = false;
    }
```

```java
        public boolean isValid() {
            return valid;
        }
    }
}
```

The SyntaxError class is very simple. It holds the message and corresponding line.

```java
public final class SyntaxError {

    private final String message;
    private final int line;

    public SyntaxError(String message, int line) {
        this.message = message;
        this.line = line;
    }

    public String getMessage() {
        return message;
    }

    public int getLine() {
        return line;
    }
}
```

Whereas the ErrorParserListener collects all syntax errors.

```java
public class ErrorParserListener extends BaseErrorListener{

    private final List<SyntaxError> syntaxErrors = new ArrayList<>();

    public List<SyntaxError> getSyntaxErrors() {
        return syntaxErrors;
    }

    @Override
    public void syntaxError(Recognizer<?, ?> recognizer, Object
    offendingSymbol, int line, int charPositionInLine, String msg,
    RecognitionException e) {
```

```
        syntaxErrors.add(new SyntaxError(msg, line));
    }
}
```

So when we have all the syntax errors, what are we going to do with them? We need to tell the editor to mark those lines. Let's do that in a task with low priority. NetBeans provides the org.netbeans.modules.parsing.spi.ParserResultTask that processes our result when the parser is finished. The NotificationResultTask uses the syntax errors from the parser and supplies them to the HintsController, which shows the error hints in the editor.

```
public class NotificationResultTask extends ParserResultTask {

    private static final String LAYER = "cto";

    @Override
    public void run(Parser.Result result, SchedulerEvent se) {
        CtoProxyParser.CtoParserResult ctoResult = (CtoProxyParser.
        CtoParserResult) result;

        if (ctoResult.isValid()) {

            Document document = result.getSnapshot().getSource().
            getDocument(false);
            List<SyntaxError> errors = ctoResult.getErrors();
            List<ErrorDescription> descriptions = errors.stream().map(e
                -> ErrorDescriptionFactory.createErrorDescription(
                        Severity.ERROR,
                        e.getMessage(),
                        document,
                        e.getLine())).collect(toList());
            setErrors(document, descriptions);
        }
    }

    void setErrors(Document document, List<ErrorDescription> descriptions) {
        HintsController.setErrors(document, LAYER, descriptions);
    }
```

```java
    @Override
    public int getPriority() {
        return 100; //the lower, the higher the priority
    }

    @Override
    public Class<? extends Scheduler> getSchedulerClass() {
        return Scheduler.EDITOR_SENSITIVE_TASK_SCHEDULER;
    }

    @Override
    public void cancel() {
    }
}
```

The call to the HintsController is placed in an extra method, because this way we can verify it with a spy in the unit test. So let's create a new test for this class:

```java
@ExtendWith(MockitoExtension.class)
public class NotificationResultTaskTest {

    @Mock
    private Snapshot snapshot;

    @Mock
    private Source source;

    @Mock
    private Document document;

    @Spy
    private NotificationResultTask classUnderTest;

    @Test
    @DisplayName("It should set errors in the HintsController")
    public void run() {
        given(snapshot.getSource()).willReturn(source);
        given(source.getDocument(false)).willReturn(document);
```

```
        List<CtoResource> res = singletonList(new CtoResource("foo", 0, 0));
        List<SyntaxError> errs = singletonList(new SyntaxError("bar", 0));
        CtoParserResult ctoResult = new CtoParserResult(snapshot, res, errs);
        classUnderTest.run(ctoResult, null);

        verify(classUnderTest).setErrors(eq(document), any(List.class));
    }
}
```

Last, we have to write a class that creates the above result task.

```
@MimeRegistration(mimeType = FileType.MIME, service = TaskFactory.class)
public class NotificationResultTaskFactory extends TaskFactory{

    @Override
    public Collection<? extends SchedulerTask> create(Snapshot snpsht) {
        return singletonList(new NotificationResultTask());
    }
}
```

Run the plugin, open the cto file, and the editor will mark erroneous lines as shown in Figure 11-15.

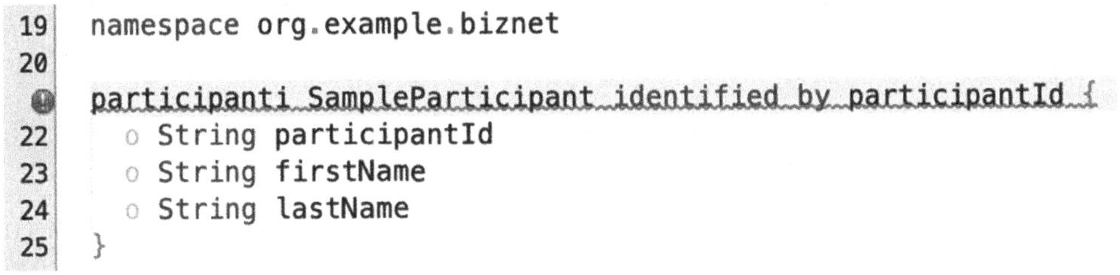

```
19   namespace org.example.biznet
20
 ⊙   participanti SampleParticipant identified by participantId {
22     ○ String participantId
23     ○ String firstName
24     ○ String lastName
25   }
```

Figure 11-15.   *Editor with error hint*

Code Completion

In this part we are going to add the code completion for the cto file. First, we need to add the following dependency to the Maven pom.xml file:

```
<dependency>
  <groupId>org.netbeans.api</groupId>
  <artifactId>org-netbeans-modules-editor-completion</artifactId>
  <version>${netbeans.version}</version>
</dependency>
```

The starting point is the interface CompletionProvider. We will provide our own implementation.

```
@MimeRegistration(mimeType = FileType.MIME, service = CompletionProvider.
class)
public class CtoCompletionProvider implements CompletionProvider{

  @Override
  public CompletionTask createTask(int type, JTextComponent jtc) {
    if(type == CompletionProvider.COMPLETION_QUERY_TYPE) {
        return new AsyncCompletionTask(new CtoCompletionQuery(), jtc);
    }
    return null;
  }

  @Override
  public int getAutoQueryTypes(JTextComponent jtc, String string) {
    return 0;
  }
}
```

If the query type is a completion query, then a new task is returned. This allows us to execute our query asynchronously.

For the method getAutoQueryTypes, we will return 0. That means the code completion will pop up only when the user presses the right keys.

The actual work is done in the CtoCompletionQuery. This class adds the items to the suggestions and also filters while the user types. Our class extends from AsyncCompletionQuery. So we need to implement the query method where we add the items. We will use the keywords and primitive types as suggestions. Some items of the keyword category will have an icon to indicate that those types are essential for the business network definition.

```
final class CtoCompletionQuery extends AsyncCompletionQuery {

  private static final String ICON_PATH = "org/netbeans/modules/
  hyperledger/cto/%s";

  private final CompletionFilter completionFilter;

  CtoCompletionQuery() {
    this(new CompletionFilter.FilterImpl());
  }

  CtoCompletionQuery(CompletionFilter completionFilter) {
    this.completionFilter = completionFilter;
  }

  @Override
  protected void query(CompletionResultSet crs, Document document, int
  offset) {
    CompletionFilter.FilterResult filterResult = completionFilter.
    filter(document, offset);
    crs.addAllItems(getKeywordItems(filterResult));
    crs.addAllItems(getPrimitiveTypeItems(filterResult));
    crs.finish();
  }

  private List<? extends AbstractCompletionItem>getKeywordItems(Completion
  Filter.FilterResult                 filterResult) {
  Function<CtoTokenId, KeywordCompletionItem> mapping = token -> {
    Optional<String> iconPath = iconPath(token.ordinal());
     return new KeywordCompletionItem(iconPath, token.name(), filterResult.
     location);
    };

    return map(filterResult.filter, Category.KEYWORD, mapping);
  }
```

```java
  private List<? extends AbstractCompletionItem> getPrimitiveTypeItems(Comp
  letionFilter.FilterResult filterResult) {
    Function<CtoTokenId, PrimitiveTypeCompletionItem> mapping = token -> {
      return new PrimitiveTypeCompletionItem(token.name(), filterResult.
      location);
    };

    return map(filterResult.filter, Category.TYPE, mapping);
  }

  private List<? extends AbstractCompletionItem> map(Optional<String>
  filter, Category category, Function<CtoTokenId, ? extends
  AbstractCompletionItem> mapping) {
    Stream<CtoTokenId> tokens = TokenTaxonomy.INSTANCE.tokens(category).
    stream();

    String name = filter.orElse("");
    if(!name.isEmpty()){
      tokens = tokens.filter(t -> t.name().startsWith(name));
    }

    return tokens.map(mapping::apply).collect(toList());
}

private Optional<String> iconPath(int type) {
  switch (type) {
    case CtoLexer.ASSET:
      return of(format(ICON_PATH, "asset.png"));
    case CtoLexer.PARTICIPANT:
      return of(format(ICON_PATH, "participant.png"));
    case CtoLexer.TRANSACTION:
      return of(format(ICON_PATH, "transaction.png"));
     default:
      return empty();
   }
  }
}
```

There is a filter for the completion items. It returns an optional typed string from the document, as well as the location where to insert the value for the item, which was selected from the pop-up menu. Create a new interface with the following content:

```
interface CompletionFilter {

    char SPC = ' ';

    static class FilterResult {
        Optional<String> filter = empty();
        Pair<Integer, Integer> location;
    }

    FilterResult filter(Document document, int offset);

    static class FilterImpl implements CompletionFilter {

        @Override
        public FilterResult filter(Document document, int offset) {
            String filter = null;
            int startOffset = offset - 1;

            try {
                StyledDocument styledDocument = (StyledDocument) document;
                int lineStartOffset = firstRowNotWhitespace(styledDocument,
                offset);
                char[] line = styledDocument.getText(lineStartOffset,
                offset - lineStartOffset).toCharArray();
                int whiteOffset = indexOfWhitespace(line);

                filter = new String(line, whiteOffset + 1, line.length -
                whiteOffset - 1);
                startOffset = (whiteOffset > 0 ) ? lineStartOffset +
                whiteOffset + 1 : lineStartOffset;
            } catch (BadLocationException ex) {
                Exceptions.printStackTrace(ex);
            }
```

```java
            FilterResult result = new FilterResult();
            result.filter = Optional.ofNullable(filter);
            result.location = Pair.of(startOffset, offset);
            return result;
        }

        private int firstRowNotWhitespace(StyledDocument doc, int offset)
                throws BadLocationException {
            Element paragraph = doc.getParagraphElement(offset);
            int start = paragraph.getStartOffset();
            int end = paragraph.getEndOffset();
            while (start + 1 < end) {
                if (doc.getText(start, 1).charAt(0) != SPC) {
                    break;
                }
                start++;
            }
            return start;
        }
        private int indexOfWhitespace(char[] line) {
            for(int i = line.length - 1; i > -1; i--) {
                if (Character.isWhitespace(line[i])) {
                    return i;
                }
            }
            return -1;
        }
    }
}
```

We distinguish between a completion item for primitives and other keywords. You have already seen the available primitive types in the introduction to Hyperledger.

```
public class PrimitiveTypeCompletionItem extends AbstractCompletionItem{

    public PrimitiveTypeCompletionItem(String name, Pair<Integer, Integer>
    location) {
        super(name, location);
    }

    @Override
    public int getSortPriority() {
        //higher value means that items will appear at the end of the popup
        return 200;
    }

    @Override
    protected ImageIcon getIcon() {
        return null;
    }
}
```

Some keyword items have an icon, which shows that they are essential for the definition of the model. If they do have an icon, then their sort priority is higher, and they will end up at the head of the suggested collection.

```
@NbBundle.Messages({
    "asset=Asset is an class definition that represent something valuable
    which is exchanged within the network.",
    "participant=Participant is a member of the network that may hold the
    asset.",
    "transaction=Transaction is the process when an assets changes the
    owner, e.g. from one participant to another."
})
public class KeywordCompletionItem extends AbstractCompletionItem {

    private final ImageIcon icon;

    public KeywordCompletionItem(Optional<String> iconPath, String name,
    Pair<Integer, Integer> location) {
        super(name, location);
```

```
        icon = iconPath.map(path -> new ImageIcon(ImageUtilities.
        loadImage(path))).orElse(null);
    }

    @Override
    public int getSortPriority() {
        return (icon != null) ? 50 : 100;
    }

    @Override
    protected ImageIcon getIcon() {
        return icon;
    }
}
```

Both item types extend the `AbstractCompletionItem`, which provides a basic implementation of the interface `org.netbeans.spi.editor.completion.CompletionItem`.

```
@NbBundle.Messages({
  "docUrl=https://hyperledger.github.io/composer/latest/reference/
  cto_language.html"
})
public abstract class AbstractCompletionItem implements CompletionItem {

    private static final String TEMPLATE = "%s ";
    private static final Color SELECTED_COLOR = Color.decode("0x0000B2");

    private final String name;
    private final int startOffset;
    private final int endOffset;

    public AbstractCompletionItem(String name, Pair<Integer, Integer>
    location) {
        this.name = name;
        this.startOffset = location.first();
        this.endOffset = location.second();
    }
```

```java
@Override
public void defaultAction(JTextComponent jtc) {
    try {
        Document doc = jtc.getDocument();
        doc.remove(startOffset, endOffset - startOffset);
        doc.insertString(startOffset, format(TEMPLATE, name), null);
        Completion.get().hideAll();
    } catch (BadLocationException ex) {
        Exceptions.printStackTrace(ex);
    }
}

@Override
public void processKeyEvent(KeyEvent ke) {
}

@Override
public int getPreferredWidth(Graphics graphics, Font font) {
    return CompletionUtilities.getPreferredWidth(name, null, graphics,
    font);
}

@Override
public void render(Graphics grphcs, Font font, Color frontCol, Color
backCol, int width, int height, boolean selected) {
    CompletionUtilities.renderHtml(getIcon(), name, null, grphcs, font,
            (selected ? Color.white : SELECTED_COLOR), width, height,
            selected);
}
@Override
public CompletionTask createDocumentationTask() {
    Optional<String> opt = getMessage(name);
    return opt.map(msg -> new AsyncCompletionTask(new
    AsyncCompletionQuery() {
```

```java
        @Override
        protected void query(CompletionResultSet completionResultSet,
        Document document, int i) {
            completionResultSet.setDocumentation(new Documentation(msg,
            getDocumentationURL()));
            completionResultSet.finish();
        }
    })).orElse(null);
}

@Override
public CompletionTask createToolTipTask() {
    return null;
}

@Override
public boolean instantSubstitution(JTextComponent jtc) {
    return false;
}

@Override
public CharSequence getSortText() {
    return name;
}

@Override
public CharSequence getInsertPrefix() {
    return name;
}

private URL getDocumentationURL() {
    String docUrl = getMessage("docUrl").orElse("");
    try {
        return new URL(docUrl);
    } catch (MalformedURLException ex) {
        return null;
    }
}
```

```java
    private Optional<String> getMessage(String key) {
        try {
            return of(NbBundle.getMessage(AbstractCompletionItem.class, key));
        } catch (MissingResourceException e) {
            return empty();
        }
    }

    protected abstract ImageIcon getIcon();

    static class Documentation implements CompletionDocumentation {

        private final String message;
        private final URL docUrl;

        public Documentation(String message, URL docUrl) {
            this.message = message;
            this.docUrl = docUrl;
        }

        @Override
        public String getText() {
            return message;
        }

        @Override
        public URL getURL() {
            return docUrl;
        }

        @Override
        public CompletionDocumentation resolveLink(String string) {
            return null;
        }

        @Override
        public Action getGotoSourceAction() {
            return null;
        }
    }
}
```

It's time to run the plugin. If you invoke the code completion in the editor, NetBeans will suggest a term to complete your input, as shown in Figure 11-16.

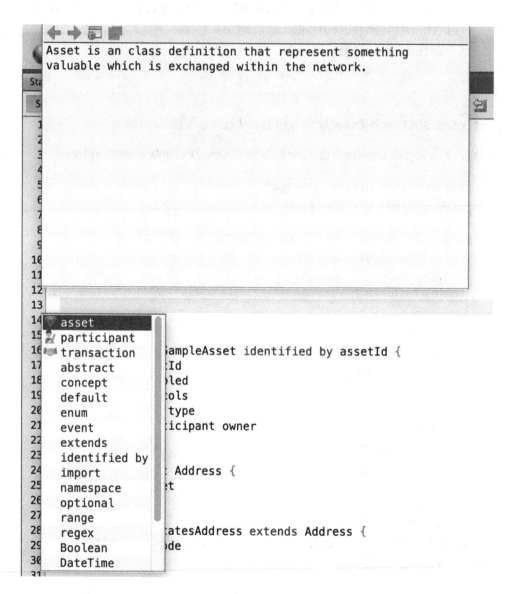

Figure 11-16. *Editor with auto suggestions*

Navigator Panel

The navigator panel gives the user a quick overview of the content in the editor window, that is, a bird's eye-view. A typical example is the navigator for a Java source file. Let's create such a view for the cto file.

First, we need to add two new Maven dependencies to the pom.xml.

```
<dependency>
    <groupId>org.netbeans.api</groupId>
    <artifactId>org-netbeans-spi-navigator</artifactId>
    <version>${netbeans.version}</version>
</dependency>
<dependency>
    <groupId>org.netbeans.api</groupId>
    <artifactId>org-openide-explorer</artifactId>
<version>${netbeans.version}</version>
</dependency>
```

Let's define a model class that represents a resource from the cto file. It has the name, the type, and an offset for its occurrence:

```
public class CtoResource {

    private final String name;
    private final int type;
    private final int offset;

    public CtoResource(String name, int type, int offset) {
        this.name = name;
        this.type = type;
        this.offset = offset;
    }

    public String getName() {
        return name;
    }

    public int getType() {
        return type;
    }
```

```java
    public int getOffset() {
        return offset;
    }
}
```

The starting point for the navigator is to implement the interface org.netbeans.spi.navigator.NavigatorPanel and register it with the annotation NavigatorPanel.Registration.

```java
@NbBundle.Messages({
    "CTO_NAV_NAME=Composer Model",
    "CTO_NAV_HINT=Overview of the resource definitions of the file."
})
@NavigatorPanel.Registration(mimeType = FileType.MIME, position = 500,
displayName = "#CTO_NAV_NAME")
public class CtoNavigatorPanel implements NavigatorPanel {

  private static final RequestProcessor RP = new  RequestProcessor
  (CtoNavigatorPanel.class.getName(), 1);

  private final JComponent view = new MembersView();
  private Optional<RootNode> rootNode = empty();
  private Lookup.Result<DataObject> selection;

  private final LookupListener selectionListener = ev -> {
    RP.post(() -> {
        rootNode.ifPresent(n -> {
          n.getFactory().cleanup();
          rootNode = empty();
        });

        if (selection != null) {
          display(selection.allInstances());
        }
    });
  };
```

```java
@Override
public String getDisplayName() {
  return CTO_NAV_NAME();
}

@Override
public String getDisplayHint() {
  return CTO_NAV_HINT();
}

@Override
public JComponent getComponent() {
  return view;
}

@Override
public void panelActivated(Lookup lkp) {
  selection = lkp.lookupResult(DataObject.class);
  selection.addLookupListener(selectionListener);
  selectionListener.resultChanged(null);
}

@Override
public void panelDeactivated() {
  selectionListener.resultChanged(null);
  selection.removeLookupListener(selectionListener);
  selection = null;
}

@Override
public Lookup getLookup() {
  return view.getLookup();
}

private void display(Collection<? extends DataObject> selectedFiles) {
  if (selectedFiles.size() == 1) {
    DataObject dataObject = selectedFiles.iterator().next();
    RootNode node = new RootNode(dataObject);
    node.getFactory().register();
```

```
      rootNode = of(node);
      view.getExplorerManager().setRootContext(node);
    } else {
      view.getExplorerManager().setRootContext(Node.EMPTY);
    }
  }
}
```

The class MembersView is a Swing component that contains the org.openide.
explorer.view.BeanTreeView from the Explorer API and connects it with the org.
openide.explorer.ExplorerManager and org.openide.util.Lookup.

```
final class MembersView extends JPanel implements ExplorerManager.Provider,
Lookup.Provider {

  private final ExplorerManager manager;
  private final Lookup lookup;
  private final BeanTreeView view;

  MembersView() {
    this.manager = new ExplorerManager();
    this.lookup = ExplorerUtils.createLookup(manager, new ActionMap());
    view = new BeanTreeView();

    view.setSelectionMode(ListSelectionModel.SINGLE_SELECTION);
    setLayout(new BorderLayout());
    add(view, BorderLayout.CENTER);
  }

  @Override
  public ExplorerManager getExplorerManager() {
    return manager;
  }

  @Override
  public Lookup getLookup() {
    return lookup;
  }
```

```
  @Override
  public boolean requestFocusInWindow() {
    return view.requestFocusInWindow();
  }
}
```

The optional root node in the class `CtoNavigatorPanel` is the parent of the resources from the cto file. When the node is created, it takes the name from the file itself, but it will be updated with the namespace after parsing the content.

```
final class RootNode extends DataNode {

  private final MembersFactory factory;

  RootNode(DataObject obj) {
    super(obj, Children.LEAF);
    factory = new MembersFactory(this);

    setIconBaseWithExtension(FileType.ICON);
    setChildren(Children.create(factory, true));
  }

  MembersFactory getFactory() {
    return factory;
  }
}
```

The class `ChildNode` is the visualization of a resource from the cto file. The class also provides an action that allows the user to navigate to the source in the editor. For this feature we use the `NbDocument` utility class:

```
public final class ChildNode extends AbstractNode{

    @StaticResource
    private static final String ICON = "org/netbeans/modules/hyperledger/
    cto/blue.png";
    private static final String MEMBER = "%s : %s";
    private static final RequestProcessor RP = new RequestProcessor();
```

```
    private final DataObject dataObject;
    private final CtoResource resource;
    private final Action openAction = new AbstractAction() {

        @Override
        public void actionPerformed(ActionEvent event) {
            RP.post(() -> {
                NbDocument.openDocument(dataObject, resource.getOffset(),
                        Line.ShowOpenType.OPEN, Line.ShowVisibilityType.
                        FOCUS);
            });
        }
    };

    public ChildNode(DataObject dataObject, CtoResource resource) {
        super(Children.LEAF);
        this.dataObject = dataObject;
        this.resource = resource;
        setIconBaseWithExtension(ICON);

        String type = NameMapping.map(resource.getType());
        setDisplayName(format(MEMBER, resource.getName(), type));
    }

    @Override
    public Action getPreferredAction() {
        return openAction;
    }
}
```

The construction of the children is delegated to a factory that extends org.openide. nodes.ChildFactory. The children will be created with the help of the CtoParser. Please create a new class with the following content:

```
final class MembersFactory extends ChildFactory<CtoResource> {

    private Collection<CtoResource> resources = new ArrayList<>();

    private final DataNode root;
```

```java
private final FileChangeAdapter adapter = new FileChangeAdapter() {
    @Override
    public void fileChanged(FileEvent fe) {
        refresh(false);
    }
};

MembersFactory(DataNode root) {
    this.root = root;
}

private FileObject getPrimaryFile() {
    return getDataObject().getPrimaryFile();
}

private DataObject getDataObject() {
    return root.getDataObject();
}

@Override
protected Node createNodeForKey(CtoResource resource) {
    if (CtoLexer.NAMESPACE == resource.getType()) {
        updateRootName(resource.getName());
        return null;
    } else {
        return new ChildNode(getDataObject(), resource);
    }
}

@Override
protected boolean createKeys(List<CtoResource> toPopulate) {
    ParserListener listener = new ParserListener();

    try {
        String text = getPrimaryFile().asText();
        CtoParser parser = ParserProvider.INSTANCE.apply(text);
        parser.addParseListener(listener);
        parser.modelUnit();
```

```
        } catch (IOException ex) {
            Exceptions.printStackTrace(ex);
        }

        resources = listener.getResources();
        resources.forEach(toPopulate::add);
        return true;
    }

    private void updateRootName(String rootName) {
        String oldName = root.getDisplayName();
        if (!rootName.equals(oldName)) {
            root.setDisplayName(rootName);
        }
    }

    void register() {
        getPrimaryFile().addFileChangeListener(adapter);
    }

    void cleanup() {
        getPrimaryFile().removeFileChangeListener(adapter);
    }
}
```

The ParserListener can be attached to the parser. It is listening to events that occur when the parser enters or exits a rule, which were previously defined in the grammar file. The listener will collect the name and type of the rule, which we want to display in the navigator.

```
public final class ParserListener extends CtoParserBaseListener {

    private final List<CtoResource> resources = new ArrayList<>();

    public List<CtoResource> getResources() {
        return resources;
    }
```

```
private void addNode(TerminalNode node, int type, int offset) {
    if (node != null && !(node instanceof ErrorNode)) {
        addNode(node.getText(), type, offset);
    }
}

private void addNode(String text, int type, int offset) {
    resources.add(new CtoResource(text, type, offset));
}

private int getStart(ParserRuleContext ctx) {
    return ctx.getStart().getStartIndex();
}

@Override
public void exitNamespaceDeclaration(CtoParser.
NamespaceDeclarationContext ctx) {
    CtoParser.QualifiedNameContext qualCtx = ctx.qualifiedName();
    if (qualCtx != null) {
        List<TerminalNode> identifiers = qualCtx.IDENTIFIER();
        String name = identifiers.stream().map(TerminalNode::getText).
        collect(Collectors.joining("."));
        addNode(name, CtoLexer.NAMESPACE, getStart(ctx));
    }
}

@Override
public void exitAssetDeclaration(CtoParser.AssetDeclarationContext ctx) {
    addNode(ctx.IDENTIFIER(), CtoLexer.ASSET, getStart(ctx));
}

@Override
public void exitParticipantDeclaration(CtoParser.
   ParticipantDeclarationContext ctx) {
    addNode(ctx.IDENTIFIER(), CtoLexer.PARTICIPANT, getStart(ctx));
}
```

```
@Override
public void exitTransactionDeclaration(CtoParser.
TransactionDeclarationContext ctx) {
    addNode(ctx.IDENTIFIER(), CtoLexer.TRANSACTION, getStart(ctx));
}

@Override
public void exitEventDeclaration(CtoParser.EventDeclarationContext ctx) {
    addNode(ctx.IDENTIFIER(), CtoLexer.EVENT, getStart(ctx));
}

@Override
public void exitEnumDeclaration(CtoParser.EnumDeclarationContext ctx) {
    addNode(ctx.IDENTIFIER(), CtoLexer.ENUM, getStart(ctx));
}

@Override
public void exitConceptDeclaration(CtoParser.ConceptDeclarationContext
ctx) {
    addNode(ctx.IDENTIFIER(0), CtoLexer.CONCEPT, getStart(ctx));
}
}
```

When we open the model file now, the navigator window (Figure 11-17) will display an overview of the resources from the file.

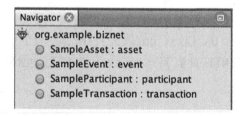

Figure 11-17. *Navigator displays resources from the file*

But if you change one of these names in the editor, you will notice that it has no immediate effect on the navigator. Only after saving the file is the content of the navigator updated. We need to listen to the changes in the editor and fire an event that forces the navigator to update the nodes. One way is to look for the currently opened editor and attach a document listener there. But that means a lot of boilerplate code. However, we already created a way to process the text from the editor in the syntax highlighting section. Let's extend it for the result from the parser listener, and then deliver it to the factory for the nodes in the navigator window.

First, open the class CtoProxyParser and add the resources to the parser result:

```
public static class CtoParserResult extends Parser.Result {

        private boolean valid = true;
        private final List<CtoResource> resources;
        private final List<SyntaxError> errors;

        public CtoParserResult(Snapshot snapshot, List<CtoResource>
        resources, List<SyntaxError> errors) {
            super(snapshot);
            this.resources = resources;
            this.errors = errors;
        }

        public List<CtoResource> getResources() {
            if (!valid) {
                return emptyList();
            }
            return resources;
        }
}
```

Extend the parse method of the CtoProxyParser, by using the parser listener and pass the result from the listener to the class that we updated:

```
@Override
public void parse(Snapshot snapshot, Task task, SourceModificationEvent
sme) throws ParseException {

    String text = snapshot.getText().toString();
    CtoParser ctoParser = parserProvider.apply(text);

    ParserListener listener = new ParserListener();
    ErrorParserListener errorListener = new ErrorParserListener();
    ctoParser.addParseListener(listener);
```

```
        ctoParser.addErrorListener(errorListener);
        //do the parsing
        ctoParser.modelUnit();

        List<CtoResource> resources = listener.getResources();
        List<SyntaxError> errors = errorListener.getSyntaxErrors();

        parserResult = new CtoParserResult(snapshot, resources, errors);
    }
```

We need a solution to send those resources to the nodes factory. Let's use NetBeans Lookup for this purpose. Therefore, create a new enum that implements a Lookup. Provider. It is advisable to place the enum in a file LookupContext.java within a completely new package, since it will act as a broker between unrelated classes or packages.

```
public enum LookupContext implements Lookup.Provider{
    INSTANCE;

    private final InstanceContent content;
    private final Lookup lookup;

    private LookupContext() {
        this.content = new InstanceContent();
        this.lookup = new AbstractLookup(content);
    }

    @Override
    public Lookup getLookup() {
        return lookup;
    }

    public void add(Object inst) {
        content.add(inst);
    }

    public void remove(Object inst) {
        content.remove(inst);
    }
}
```

We will use this `LookupContext` in `NotificationResultTask.java`, which was created for the error hints. Add the following lines to the run method of the class:

```
@Override
public void run(Parser.Result result, SchedulerEvent se) {
        CtoProxyParser.CtoParserResult ctoResult = (CtoProxyParser.
        CtoParserResult) result;

    if (ctoResult.isValid()) {
        LookupContext.INSTANCE.add(ctoResult.getResources());
...
```

Let's consume the resources in `MembersFactory.java`. Note that only the required changes within the class are shown:

```
final class MembersFactory extends ChildFactory<CtoResource> implements
LookupListener {
    private final LookupContext lookupContext = LookupContext.INSTANCE;

    private boolean fromFile = true;

    private Lookup.Result<List> selection;

    private final FileChangeAdapter adapter = new FileChangeAdapter() {
        @Override
        public void fileChanged(FileEvent fe) {
            fromFile = true;
            refresh(false);
        }
    };

    @Override
    protected boolean createKeys(List<CtoResource> toPopulate) {
        if(fromFile) {
            resources = parseFile();
            fromFile = false;
        }

        resources.forEach(toPopulate::add);
        return true;
    }
```

```java
    private List<CtoResource> parseFile() {
        ParserListener listener = new ParserListener();
        try {
            String text = getPrimaryFile().asText();
            CtoParser parser = ParserProvider.INSTANCE.apply(text);
            parser.addParseListener(listener);
            parser.modelUnit();
        } catch (IOException ex) {
            Exceptions.printStackTrace(ex);
        }
        return listener.getResources();
    };

    void register() {
        getPrimaryFile().addFileChangeListener(adapter);
        selection = lookupContext.getLookup().lookupResult(List.class);
        selection.addLookupListener(this);
    }

    void cleanup() {
        getPrimaryFile().removeFileChangeListener(adapter);
        selection.removeLookupListener(this);
    }

    @Override
    public void resultChanged(LookupEvent ev) {
        if (selection != null) {
            //consume and remove
            Collection<? extends List> results = selection.allInstances();
            if (!results.isEmpty()) {
                members = results.iterator().next();
                lookupContext.remove(members);
                refresh(false);
            }
        }
    }
}
```

Run the plugin, and you will see the effect in the navigator, while you change the name of the asset in the editor.

Signing and Sharing a Plugin

Once a plugin has been created, it can be shared with the community through the Apache NetBeans Plugin Portal. Plugins that are made available via the Plugin Portal can be installed by anyone in the community. The Plugin Portal is available online using a web browser in the URL http://netbeans-vm.apache.org/pluginportal/,[1] and it is also accessible within the Apache NetBeans IDE by choosing "Tools" ➤ "Plugins."

In order to share the plugin, it must be signed with a certificate, either self-signed or verified by a certificate authority. The signing process is much the same as with any Java JAR archive that is going to be distributed. There are a couple of different ways to sign a JAR or NBM file, those being manual or by integrating the signing process into a build. In this section, we will cover incorporating the process into the Maven build.

Signing the Project

It is possible to sign an ANT- or Maven-based project for distribution using the Java keytool utility to create a keystore and then updating the build file to incorporate the keystore into the build. In this example, the Maven-based POM file for the project will be updated to include a generated keystore. To begin, generate a keystore by opening a command line or terminal and traversing inside of the project directory. Once in the directory, issue the keytool command to generate the keystore.

```
cd ../path-to-project
keytool -genkey -storepass your-password -alias your-project-alias
-keystore nbproject/private/keystore
```

Note   Be sure to set the keystore and key password to the same value. Ensure that the nbproject/private directory is not distributed along with the archive or committed to a version control system.

---

[1]Previous URL was http://plugins.netbeans.org/

Once the keystore has been generated and saved into a directory such as nbproject/ private, the project POM file can be updated to include the nbm-maven-plugin configuration that will be required to sign the NBM file when generated. Simply add the following configuration to the nbm-maven-plugin plugin section.

```
<plugin>
  <groupId>org.codehaus.mojo</groupId>
  <artifactId>nbm-maven-plugin</artifactId>
  <version>3.14.1</version>
  <extensions>true</extensions>
  <configuration>
    <useOSGiDependencies>false</useOSGiDependencies>
    <codeNameBase>org.netbeans.modules.hyperledger</codeNameBase>
    <Author>Your Name</author>
    <homePageUrl>https://github.com/mario-s/nb-hyperledger</homePageUrl>
    <keystore>nbproject/private/keystore</keystore>
    <keystorealias>your-project-alias</keystorealias>
    <licenseName>Creative Commons BY 3.0</licenseName>
    <licenseFile>https://creativecommons.org/licenses/by/3.0/</licenseFile>
  </configuration>
</plugin>
```

Create the NBM

If you have a single plugin to package for distribution, the easiest way to create a binary file is to generate an NBM. There are a few ways to create a signed NBM. To begin, if you are not planning to sign the NBM so that it can be included in the plugin center, simply generate the NBM via Apache NetBeans. To do so, use the following procedure within Apache NetBeans:

- Right-click on the Hyperledger Support project and choose "Create NBM" (Figure 11-18). The IDE will compile and package the project into a distributable binary NBM file. The file will appear within the project "build" directory once generated.

Figure 11-18. *Create NBM File for Plugin Distribution*

To generate a signed NBM, the Maven build can be completed via the command line or terminal by traversing inside of the project directory and issuing the following command:

```
mvn clean package nbm:nbm -Dkeystorepass=your-password
```

Once the NBM has been signed and packaged, it is ready to be loaded into the plugin portal. Use the following steps to upload the plugin to the portal.

1. Upload the plugin to Maven Central using the notes provided by Sonatype (`https://central.sonatype.org/pages/ossrh-guide.html`).

2. Create Google account if you do not already have one.

3. Visit the Apache NetBeans Plugin Portal (`http://netbeans-vm.apache.org/pluginportal/`) and use the **sign-in** button in the upper corner to authenticate.

407

4. Click the "**Add Plugin**" button within the main menu.

5. Provide the pertinent information (`groupId` and `artifactId` values) for your plugin and click "**Add Plugin**" button. The two values are contained in `maven-metadata.xml` file. All other information should be added in automatically. It is a good practice to add a homepage and thumbnail for your plugin. Select "**Save Plugin**".

6. Select the appropriate Apache NetBeans version for your plugin by choosing an appropriate version within the "My Plugins" page, which will open the "Version Management" page.

7. Select the appropriate compatible Apache NetBeans version, provide optional release information, and choose "**Save Plugin Version**".

8. If you believe the plugin meets quality standards for the Plugin Portal (see wiki: `https://cwiki.apache.org/confluence/ display/NETBEANS/Quality+criteria+for+Plugin+Portal+ Update+Center`), you can select to have your plugin verified and approved for publication by choosing the "**Request Verification**" button.

Summary

In this chapter we walked through several guides about how to create a NetBeans plugin with Maven for a new language. You have seen how easy it is to create a template for a new project, how to recognize a new file type, and achieve syntax highlighting and error hint with the help of ANTLR. We also touched on the code completion and navigator window. NetBeans' lookup API was used for communication between packages. In the end, you have seen the necessary steps to sign and publish the plugin.

In the next chapter you will see why NetBeans was shifted under the umbrella of the Apache Software Foundation and how you can contribute to the project.

PART III

Participating in Apache NetBeans

CHAPTER 12

The Apache NetBeans Process

What makes the Apache Software Foundation ("Apache" for short) special and well suited to NetBeans is its governance model. Often the question is asked, "Since NetBeans is and always has been free and open source, does it need Apache at all?" That is the question we are going to address in this chapter.

By the end of this chapter, we hope you understand the background of the transition of NetBeans to Apache, the benefits of that transition, and especially how you can get involved in contributing to the project yourself.

Of Pubs and Legends

Legend has it that NetBeans found its origin in the pubs and drinking houses of Prague. In many senses, this is true. A group of students from the technical university of Prague developed a tool to support the development of Java, which was new and toolless at the time, in 1996. According to the same legend, not much was developed, though a lot was consumed; and though the plans for the tool were well described, they were only implemented after the students graduated and realized that they had a good idea whose time had come.

The curious name "NetBeans" can also be understood in that light, that is, two of the hot topics of that time were "JavaBeans" and "Network," and combining those two terms into one was as logical as current names such as "Facebook" and "Netflix." Not long thereafter, Sun Microsystems ("Sun" for short) acquired NetBeans when James Gosling, the founder of Java, and Jonathan Schwartz, who led the tooling division at Sun, saw

© Ioannis Kostaras, Constantin Drabo, Josh Juneau, Sven Reimers, Mario Schröder, Geertjan Wielenga 2020
I. Kostaras et al., *Pro Apache NetBeans*, https://doi.org/10.1007/978-1-4842-5370-0_12

it demonstrated at a conference, and recognized in it the basis of an environment that could enable new developers to quickly and comprehensively start their journey into the Java landscape.

Positioning it as a tool for onboarding new Java developers and enabling professional developers to be productive, Sun open sourced NetBeans and work was started to modularize it. According to yet another legend, the developers of NetBeans were, in any case, primarily interested in creating a modular framework and then created the NetBeans integrated development environment (IDE) on top of their modular framework purely as a means to prove the framework. In this way, the development environment was an afterthought, with the underlying NetBeans Platform (which you learned about in Part II) being the core domain of interest to its developers.

Modular Transition to Apache

Whatever the case, its modularity has turned out to be one of its key strengths, in particular, in relation to the transition to Apache.

After Oracle's acquisition of Sun in 2010, NetBeans had a number of interesting new use cases in its newly adopted company. It became the basis of Oracle's JDeveloper and several of its features were reused there, such as the window system, the GUI Builder, and the Profiler. In Oracle Labs, it became a central piece of the tooling around the new polyglot GraalVM. However, partly as a result of continuing requests from the community to be more directly involved in the development of NetBeans, partly as a result of reprioritization, and partly in an aim to share the cost of ownership, Oracle decided to donate NetBeans to Apache, in October 2016.

Very explicitly, Oracle stated that it wanted to continue to invest resources in NetBeans and that its decision to donate it to Apache did not mean in any sense that it was abandoning it. In fact, as evidence of its stated direction, a team of developers in Oracle, within the Java organization, continues to work to this day on NetBeans, specifically focused on providing Java editor enhancements related to new language features in the Java Development Kit (JDK) and Java language.

Moreover, a team within Oracle has been working from the start of the transition and meeting on a weekly basis to discuss the current state of the transition of code to Apache, assign tasks, report on progress, and so on.

Of Purgatory and Incubation

The Apache Incubator ("the Incubator" or "incubation phase" for short) is comparable to some kind of "purgatory," the Roman Catholic concept of an intermediate stage between earth and heaven where purification takes place. Or it is an "interregnum," where the old has not yet died and the new is still to be born.

To clear away one point of confusion right at the outset, releases done during the incubation phase are in no way "Beta" releases. The Incubator exists to enable an aspiring Apache project's community to figure out how to fully comply with Apache's requirements, while enabling it to learn about Apache's specific form of open governance.

Mentors are assigned by Apache to guide and assist an aspiring Apache community and to make sure the project doesn't slip off the rails or do things that do not comply with The Apache Way, a well-established set of principles according to which an Apache project is governed and by means of which source code is released.

The details of The Apache Way can be found online (`apache.org/theapacheway`), and it would be repetitive to go through each and every aspect of it here. However, it is sufficient to say that how a community works together and the licensing of the code released under the Apache banner are both clearly specified at `apache.org`, providing the basis of Apache's strong and reliable brand throughout the industry. Each project under the Apache banner can be assumed to conform to its principles, meaning that new communities aspiring to become Apache projects have a set of principles and concepts to have under its belt.

Before an aspiring Apache project can leave the Incubator and become an official Apache Project, known as a "top-level project," it needs to jump through a number of hoops that entail proving that it understands The Apache Way and is able to act as an official Apache project. A key milestone in the incubation process is a release; in fact, at least one release must be completed in the Incubator before a community is able to attempt to become a top-level project, thus leaving the Incubator.

The Apache NetBeans community achieved three releases in the Incubator and below we describe what happened in each release, in terms of the source code released, the features provided, and the progress of the project within the Incubator.

Before going further, it is important to note that Apache releases source code, not features, not installers, not executables, and not binaries, which typically are created by other organizations, such as *OpenBeans* (see `openbeans.org`), in the same way as Ubuntu packages Debian. For that reason, the focus of each release strictly from

Apache's point of view, is source code only. From Apache's point of view, whether a release provides new features or not or whether it provides a convenience binary, as an optional way of helping a user of the source code, such as an installer or not is not relevant since it is only focused on source code, thus enabling upstream organizations, such as the aforementioned *OpenBeans*, to provide business models, as needed, based on binaries and installers and other more user-friendly conveniences.

Another quick point to make is that it was decided to continue the release numbering seamlessly, that is, not to start with Apache NetBeans 1.0, but with the major release number following the last Oracle NetBeans release number, that is, starting from 8.2 onward, which means the first Apache NetBeans release number was set at "9.0."

Apache NetBeans (Incubating) 9.0

The focus of the first release in the incubator was to simply go through an Apache release process, which in itself is a strictly structured procedure, while also actually releasing a significant part of the NetBeans source code, under the banner of the Apache Incubator, which had been contributed at that stage by Oracle to Apache.

The basis of NetBeans is the underlying application framework, within the "platform" cluster of modules, and it would have made sense to purely focus on releasing that cluster as the first release Apache release of NetBeans. However, the idea was also to include some functionality that would actually be useful for a user of Apache NetBeans, that is, not purely a developer making use of the NetBeans Platform as the basis of their software.

For that reason, in addition to the "platform" cluster, the "ide" and "java" clusters were focused on for the first Apache NetBeans release, too. In that way, a Java developer would be able to use Apache NetBeans 9.0 even while all the remaining parts of it were still in the process of being readied for inclusion in subsequent releases. The key point here is that for source code to be released from Apache, it needs to be relicensed to Apache and, since some parts of NetBeans don't meet Apache's licensing requirements, parts of it need to be removed or rewritten, rather than being released. If we waited until everything has been donated and everything has been readied for release by Apache, the first release would take years to be ready, while the modular approach, as can be seen in this scenario, enables specific parts of Apache NetBeans to be released in an incremental process.

However, in another twist, the first Apache NetBeans release, focused (as stated above) on the source code related to Java development features, didn't simply provide the precise Java features that the last Oracle release of NetBeans provided. That's because since the release of NetBeans IDE 8.2, JDK 9 had been released, and developers in Oracle, prior to the donation of NetBeans to Apache, had created several features in NetBeans specifically to support new JDK 9 features. The main feature of JDK 9 was the introduction of the new Jigsaw module system, primarily created to enable the JDK itself to be modularized. However, any Java application can make use of that same module system and in Apache NetBeans 9.0, the features created by Oracle developers for NetBeans to support the JDK 9 Jigsaw module system were also released, in particular a new project type to help NetBeans users get started with Jigsaw, as well as support for the related "module-info.java" Jigsaw registration file.

JDK 9 also introduced a REPL (read-eval-print loop), named JShell, as well as a packaging tool, named JLink. For both of these new JDK features, Apache NetBeans 9.0 provided out-of-the box integration and support.

At the outset, the plan for Apache NetBeans was for it to be focused on JDK 9. However, since there were delays in handing over NetBeans from Oracle to Apache, JDK 9 had already been released. In fact, JDK 10 had already been released. For that reason, Apache NetBeans 9.0 was focused on supporting JDK 10, both in terms of being able to run on it as well as in relation to its enhancements. Fortunately, for these purposes, purely from a Java developer point of view, that is, in terms of the code that a developer writes, JDK 10 introduced only the "var" keyword, in other words, "local variable type inference." To let NetBeans users benefit from that, the Java editor was enhanced to enable switching between Java types and the "var" keyword, as well as inspections and analyzers to enable switching to be done across files, packages, and projects.

Apache NetBeans 9.0 was released on July 29, 2018, which was less than two years after Oracle's announcement of the donation of NetBeans to Apache. Under the circumstances, given the complexity of the auditing process on Oracle's end together with Apache's licensing requirements, together with the fact that everyone working on NetBeans in Apache is a volunteer, that worked out well. In fact, the two years of this initial phase gave everyone time to settle in to the new phase of the NetBeans project, get to know each other, and understand what working under the Apache banner means on a day-to-day basis.

Apache NetBeans (Incubating) 10.0

With the release of Apache NetBeans 9.0, one of the first questions asked was, "Hey, what about PHP and JavaScript? Has Apache dropped those features from NetBeans?" One of the most frustrating, but understandable, aspects is that users of an open source project tend to not follow it as closely as its developers do. A gnashing of teeth ensued, as many users of NetBeans appeared out of the woodwork to complain that apparently Apache NetBeans would henceforth only care about Java developers and not about developers of the other technologies and languages it had supported in the past.

Of course, as already explained in some detail, we were focused on releasing different pieces of NetBeans over different releases, since not everything constituting NetBeans had been received from Oracle yet and not everything had yet been relicensed to Apache.

The focus of Apache NetBeans 10.0, released on December 27, 2018, was to make the PHP features available, which also meant making the HTML5/JavaScript features available, since the former depends on the latter. Not only was the code donated by Oracle relating to these features released, since in addition, in the interim, a number of additional features, in particular new support for PHP 7.4, the latest PHP release at the time was provided for the first time, too.

In addition, the 10.0 release focused on JDK 11, in particular, aside from being able to run on JDK 11, the new support for "var" in lambda expressions. Aside from other fixes and enhancements, support for JUnit 5 was introduced in Apache NetBeans 10.0, in particular, for Apache Maven-based projects.

Apache NetBeans (Incubating) 11.0

Apache NetBeans 11.0, released on April 4, 2019, was the third major release in the Incubator.

Over the years, there had been discussion in the NetBeans community about how best to express the fact that Apache Maven and Gradle are more modern choices to be aware of than Apache Ant, complicated by the point that at the same time, one would not want to imply that there's anything wrong with using Apache Ant.

As a result, in Apache NetBeans 11.0, the "New Project wizard," that is, the entry point for NetBeans users, was redesigned. The Java wizards were moved to a subfolder named "Java with Ant," while two new categories were added: "Java with Maven" and "Java with Gradle." The hope is that this will make it easier for new users to choose a starting point of their liking for their projects, while at the same time highlighting the fact that Maven and Gradle should be given preference over Ant.

Also, initial support for Gradle was introduced for the first time. Features for integrating NetBeans with Gradle has been an open request for many users for many years. To Oracle, this was never a high priority, though an external plugin providing Gradle integration was developed and proved popular. From Oracle's perspective, this was a good-enough solution, since no resources in terms of developer time needed to be invested by Oracle, while users needing that integration had access to it via the external plugin. Of course, though, direct out-of-the box integration with external technologies, such as Gradle, is always preferable. With NetBeans being in Apache, and priorities no longer being determined by Oracle, direct integration with Gradle, out of the box, became something that was only blocked to the extent that one or more contributors would be able to provide it. That happened, with success, during the Apache NetBeans 11.0 release cycle.

Aside from these concerns, a key focus of Apache NetBeans 11.0 was the next stage of integration of code donated by Oracle to Apache, which was the cluster of features relating to enterprise Java, that is, Java/Jakarta EE. We had been busy in the months leading up to the release of Apache NetBeans 11.0 in reviewing the licenses of the "enterprise" cluster, which came from the second donation of NetBeans by Oracle to Apache, which ended in time for the release, enabling these features to be incorporated in it. As a result, users of NetBeans can, from this release onward, without needing to install plugins, create, edit, build, and deploy Java EE applications with Ant or Maven, with Gradle support scheduled for the next release.

However, explicit support of Java EE 8, for example, specific templates or mentions of the specification number in user interface elements in NetBeans, was not part of Apache NetBeans 11.0. At the same time, though, note that Java EE 8 only runs on JDK 8, and not on later releases, and so for those doing development with JavaEE 8 it is best to run NetBeans itself on JDK 8, anyway.

Finally, in the same way that Apache NetBeans 9.0 provided support for JDK 9 and 10, and Apache NetBeans 10.0 provided support for JDK 11, Apache NetBeans 11.0 did the same for JDK 12. The Apache NetBeans 11.0 release was tested on JDK 12, while new editor hints and features were provided to support developers making use of the syntax-level features in JDK 12.

Graduation to Top-Level Apache Project

All good things come to an end, and so did the time that was spent by NetBeans in the Incubator. For some time already, the helpful mentors assigned to us had been suggesting it was time for us to leave. What that means is that NetBeans would no longer be in the Incubator, meaning that it would be an official Apache project. The Incubator can be kind of confusing to outsiders, that is, some tend to wonder about the state of the code coming out of the Incubator; for example, "is this Beta quality," "can we rely on NetBeans while it is in the Incubator," and so on, were questions typically asked.

Also, the release process outside the Incubator is faster than within it, since Incubator releases go through two phases of release voting – first the community votes on whether a repository is ready for release, after which the members of the Incubator vote. If the latter fails, fixes need to be done, and the first phase needs to be restarted. In short, the two-phase release voting process can significantly slow releases down, and therefore that in itself is a reason for a project, once it is ready, to want to move on and out of the Incubator. The Incubator phase is important to go through since it enables a community around a project to get to know each other and work together around releases of their shared project. However, as soon as it's clear that everything is working together reasonably well, the process begins of moving on to become an official Apache project.

The process entails a discussion on the project's dev mailing list. This discussion began in February 2019, it took some time, since we were also working on a release at the same time. After the discussion, a vote thread was started, which completed with around 60 votes all agreeing that NetBeans was ready to graduate, which enabled the vote around the same theme to be started among the members of the Incubator. There the vote passed, too, and in April 2019, NetBeans became an official Apache project.

A variety of small tasks then needed to be completed, mainly involving removing the text "incubator" from a variety of places. A press release was put together and published and, seamlessly, development continued, with many links being redirected to Incubator-free locations, for example, the mailing lists had the word "incubator" in them, and so on, the website had a range of disclaimers around incubation, and these were fixed and removed.

It had been a long process of 2 ½ years, though, all things considered, the process had been short and relatively painless. Though quite some code still needed to be donated from Oracle to complete the donation, in particular, the code related to C/C++ features, the community around NetBeans had been working together as an Apache project for quite some time, and graduation from the Incubator rounded off the process and completed the initial stages of settling NetBeans within Apache.

Beyond the Incubator

What is the road map of Apache NetBeans, now that it has left the Incubator? What features can be expected? And when? Well, on the simplest level, Oracle has not completed its donation, that is, there's quite some code, in particular in relation to C/C++ features, which are being audited and scrubbed, in Oracle. In other words, Oracle staff are looking at the code to be donated and determining whether that code really and truly belongs to Oracle and therefore whether Oracle owns that code and is, based on its ownership, able to donate that code to Apache. In some cases, after analysis, code may be found to be copied from elsewhere or reused from other repositories or technologies. Only after this kind of analysis is done can the code be handed over to Apache.

At the same time, a key driver for Apache NetBeans will continue to be new release of the Java Development Kit, that is, the JDK. As new releases of the JDK are made available, tools such as NetBeans needs to be ready to enable developers to work with those new JDK releases. Not only must NetBeans be able to run on top of new releases of the JDK, but the Java Editor must offer support, such as code completion and syntax coloring, when Java changes on the syntax level. That work in NetBeans is primarily done by developers from Oracle and constitutes the largest part of Oracle's commitment to NetBeans in Apache. For example, JEP-330 provides for the running of individual Java source files, outside the scope of a project, and support for this will be very useful in NetBeans for those teaching and learning Java, since whole projects will not need to be created to hold single Java source files. At the same time, Oracle Labs is focused on GraalVM, the new polyglot VM developed at Oracle, for which the tooling, in particular cross-language debugging, is provided in Apache NetBeans. In short, Oracle's commitment to NetBeans remains significant, especially now that there is a clear way forward via the Apache process that has taken over the governance and release management process from Oracle.

Aside from that, Apache NetBeans will deliver whatever its committers decide to commit. A lot of work is being done in the Gradle area, while more and more features are being added to the PHP support, too. Once the C/C++ features have been donated, expect to see developments there also, as developers making use of those features provide feedback, issues, and pull requests.

Summary

The most important message to take from this chapter is that Apache is "you," and Apache NetBeans will not exist without your involvement. There aren't magic pixies anymore developing NetBeans somewhere inside Sun or Oracle. Instead, there are individual contributors of all shapes and sizes, and you are needed to be part of the process. Is something missing? Now, for the first time, NetBeans is truly yours and you can, and in fact must, make it happen. We're all looking forward to your first pull request!

CHAPTER 13

Apache Infrastructure

Apache NetBeans is open sourced under the Apache Foundation. As such, becoming a part of the Apache NetBeans development community is quite easy, and there are many ways to do so. The Apache Foundation is based upon an easy environment for newcomers to come on board, and it is also intuitive for those who have been part of the community for years to contribute. There are a few key parts of the Apache Foundation infrastructure that play a role in participation within the Apache NetBeans community. The JIRA is an issue tracker that can be used by those in the community for reporting issues and also for tracking work that is to be done on a project. Apache uses Confluence, a project management site for the Apache NetBeans wiki. The NetBeans wiki is a dedicated resource for documentation of development and initiatives around the project. An open set of mailing lists is used to coordinate work. And finally, the most public focal point, the Apache NetBeans website is maintained by the community.

Even if you are not planning to work on Java code that is used to build the Apache NetBeans IDE, you can contribute by reading through mailing lists, contributing issues to the JIRA, helping to maintain Confluence, or the wiki, or dedicating time on the Apache NetBeans website. In this chapter, we will cover how to contribute to each of these areas that help to make up the Apache NetBeans community.

Apache NetBeans JIRA

The easiest way to participate in the Apache NetBeans community is to report bugs or provide enhancement requests. To do so, the Apache NetBeans JIRA is used. The JIRA can be accessed by navigating to the following URL in your favorite web browser:

```
https://issues.apache.org/jira/projects/NETBEANS/.
```

421

© Ioannis Kostaras, Constantin Drabo, Josh Juneau, Sven Reimers, Mario Schröder, Geertjan Wielenga 2020
I. Kostaras et al., *Pro Apache NetBeans*, https://doi.org/10.1007/978-1-4842-5370-0_13

By default, when the site is first opened, all OPEN issues are presented. The JIRA open issues are a great place to begin if you are interested in helping contribute to Apache NetBeans. Browse through the open issues and see if there are any that you may be able to resolve, or if there is something that peaks your interest (see Figure 13-1).

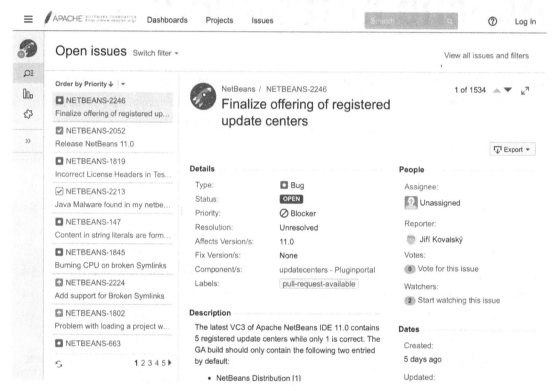

Figure 13-1. *Apache NetBeans JIRA – Open Issues*

To take full advantage of the JIRA, you must create an account and log into the system. Once you do so, then you will be able to add new issues to the tracker, if needed. You can also assign issues to yourself, comment on issues, or change the status of issues if you have the proper privileges.

To begin navigating the system, utilize the menu on the left-hand side of the screen (Figure 13-2). In that menu you will see there are options for Kanban Board, Releases, Reports, Issues, and Components.

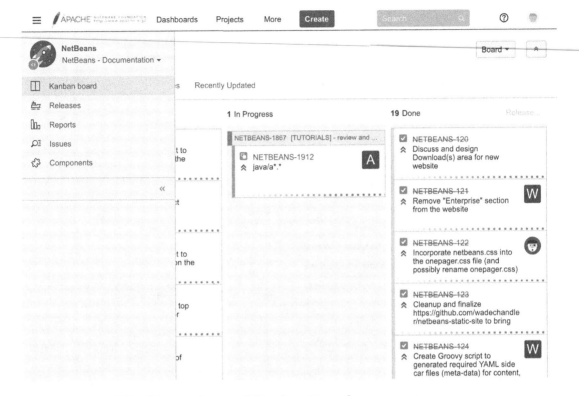

Figure 13-2. *JIRA Navigation and Kanban Board*

The **Kanban Board** is a nice display containing Open Issues, Issues assigned to yourself, and Completed Issues. If you click on one of the issues in the board, it brings up the issue in a pane on the right-hand side of the screen, allowing the board to remain visible. The board items can be dragged around, as you wish, allowing you to organize the board to your liking. A nice feature of the Kanban Board is that it works well on touch-based devices, allowing for easy dragging and dropping of the items on the board.

Next up in the menu is the **Releases** panel (Figure 13-3), which allows one to see a quick overview of the Apache NetBeans release status. The panel provides information about previous releases, as well as the next release in the future. When selecting the release, a balloon appears, which provides a quick summary of the issues.

Figure 13-3. *Releases Panel*

The **Reports** option provides a series of report options to present the issue tracker data in different ways. Many of the reports are configurable, providing a variable timeline of data. The report categories include Agile, Issue Analysis, Forecast & Management, and Other. Each category contains one or more different styles of report. In Figure 13-4, a Cumulative Flow Diagram of the issues is displayed.

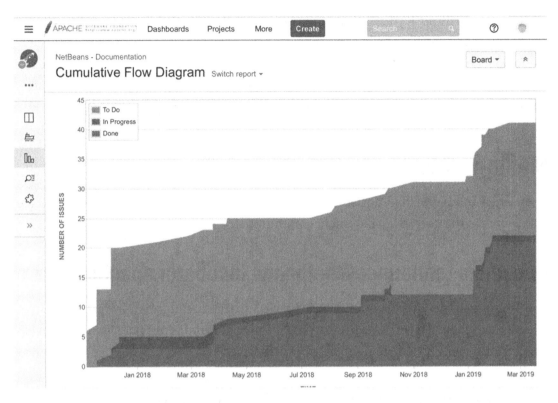

Figure 13-4. *Reports Option*

The **Components** menu option presents all issues grouped by the Apache NetBeans component. For instance, all of the Maven issues are grouped together and are easily accessible. Utilizing the Components menu, one can parse issues by component, making it easy to focus on support for one particular area with the IDE.

Apache NetBeans Wiki

Much of the documentation around Apache NetBeans resides within the wiki. The wiki is, of course, a series of online webpages that provide details and information on Apache NetBeans. The following URL can be used to access the wiki:

`http://netbeans.apache.org/wiki/index.asciidoc.`

The wiki focuses around an index of "recipe" style choices, grouped into sections, and each of the choices within the index covers a particular topic related to development. There are a number of ways to participate in updating and contributing to the wiki. For instance, if any processes have not yet been documented, the wiki is the correct place to do so. If you find any information on the wiki that is outdated or needs to be modified, you can help by making those updates. The wiki is a very important piece of the Apache NetBeans puzzle since contributors from around the world collaborate to make Apache NetBeans possible. Therefore, well-documented processes are essential for success.

Mailing Lists

There are a number of mailing lists that one can join to keep informed and communicate with others in the user or development communities.

Announce (announce@netbeans.incubator.apache.org)

The "Announce" mailing list is for those who wish to remain informed when new releases are made. This mailing list is typically low traffic and is designed as a high-level list to inform while minimizing the number of e-mails.

Users (users@netbeansincubator.apache.org)

The "Users" mailing list is aimed at the NetBeans user community. If you have a question pertaining to the usage of the IDE, then this is the place to go. Since this mailing list covers such a broad array of topics, it is encouraged to add prefix tags to subject lines, indicating the topic being addressed within the e-mail.

Netcat (netcat@netbeans.incubator.apache.org)

The NetCat mailing list is for those who are part of the Apache NetBeans NetCat testing and community acceptance program.

Dev (dev@netbeans.incubator.apache.org)

Those who develop Apache NetBeans should join the developer mailing list. This list is also targeted toward those who are committed to promoting the IDE via documentation, events, and tutorials.

Commits (commits@netbeans.incubator.apache.org)

If you wish to pay very close attention to the Apache NetBeans GitHub repository, then the Commits mailing list is for you. Members of this mailing list receive a notification each time a commit is made.

Notifications (notifications@netbeans.incubator.apache.org)

To closely follow the GitHub repository issues, comments, and pull requests, follow the Notifications mailing list. Each member of this list is sent a notification whenever comments are made on issues or pull requests are made.

Website

The most visible online presence for Apache NetBeans is the website. The website is one of the areas where just about anyone can get involved, whether it be someone very technical in coding or someone that is a very good editor … the website can utilize talents from all directions. The main Apache NetBeans website is accessible at the following URL: `http://netbeans.apache.org` and the sources that compose the website are available on GitHub: `https://github.com/apache/incubator-netbeans-website`.

The Apache NetBeans website GitHub repository actually contains sources for `netbeans.apache.org` and also `bits.netbeans.org`. The `bits.netbeans.org` site is dedicated to Apache NetBeans release documentation.

The best way to get started working with the Apache NetBeans website is to fork the GitHub repository and clone it to your development machine. To fork the repository, first log into GitHub with your account and then go to the Apache NetBeans website GitHub repository and click on the button entitled "Fork" in the upper right-hand side of the page. This will essentially create a copy of the repository under your own GitHub account. That way, if you make changes to the website, it will not affect the main Apache NetBeans website repository. It is important to note that changes published to the Apache NetBeans website repository are automatically deployed via Jenkins and integrated into the website. Therefore, if a change is committed, it will be made available for all to see. For this reason, it is essential to perform any work or modifications to the website within your own fork, and then create a Pull Request from your fork if you wish to have the work integrated into the main repository, and hence, published to the web.

Once your fork has been cloned to your machine, you can dig into the website sources. The website is primarily generated from Groovy templates utilizing a Gradle build and a tool set known as JBake to prepare the site. In the end, the website is statically compiled by running a Gradle build. There is also a Tomcat web server with the sources so that you can build and run the website very easily while working on it. Performing changes to the website is very easy to do by following the instructions located on the Apache NetBeans website GitHub page and within the README.asciidoc files that are packaged with the sources. In fact, there are such detailed instructions, I recommend reviewing the documentation before beginning to work with the website sources:

https://github.com/apache/incubator-netbeans-website/tree/master/ netbeans.apache.org

Making a Website Page Update

To get started, let's walk through the steps for making a simple change to the website, building it, and running it utilizing the embedded Tomcat server. There are no installations that will need to be made in order to build and run the site, other than having Java 8 installed on your device. The Gradle build will take care of downloading all dependencies required for the build.

There are different types of files that are used to collectively create the website. A series of asciidoc documents is used to formulate the website pages themselves, and Groovy Server Pages (gsp) are used for the templates. Let's assume that we need to make a change to the netbeans.apache.org main page. To do so, traverse inside of the netbeans.apache.org folder contained in the sources, and navigate to the src/content folder. This is where the main content of the website resides. Modify the website index page by doing the following:

1) Open up the index.asciidoc file in a text editor or within Apache NetBeans.

2) Make a modification to the page. In this case, I want to change the word "Participation" that resides within one of the cards on the index page to "Participation!" Go to line 39 of the index.asciidoc file and make the change.

3) Build the site by executing the following command from within the `netbeans.apache.org` folder within a command line or terminal.

    a. OS X and Linux: `./gradlew build`

    b. Windows: `gradlew preprocessContent bake`

4) Once the build completes, you can see the resulting output within the `netbeans.apache.org/build/bake` folder. Run the Tomcat server by executing the following:

    a. OS X and Linux: `./gradlew run`

    b. Windows: `gradlew run`

5) Once the Tomcat server is up and running, point your browser to the following site to see the resulting output: `http://localhost:8080`

To stop the server, press Ctrl+C from within the same terminal or command prompt, or issue the `gradlew stop` command from a terminal or command prompt in the `netbeans.apache.org` directory.

Making a Website Template Update

If you are interested in modifying the overall layout and structure of the website, then it may make sense to modify one of the templates that is used for constructing the pages. Templates can be modified by traversing inside of the `netbeans.apache.org/src/content/templates` folder. Each of the templates is constructed of a Groovy Server Page (gsp). These files can be opened and modified within a text editor or Apache NetBeans. The general process for modifying a template page is the same as those in the previous section. However, template modifications may span across a number of generated pages since a single template may be applied to one or more pages within the website.

Summary

As a community member, there are several ways to collaborate and help contribute to the Apache NetBeans project without even writing a single line of code. The issue tracker (JIRA) is the most obvious place to begin, by submitting issues if any are found, or writing answers and comments to help others in the tracker. The wiki is an ever-changing documentation site that is integral to the success of Apache NetBeans. Community members are requested to participate by adding documentation where it is needed or making updates to any documentation that has changed over the years. To take a more formal role as a contributor, work on the website and submit pull requests (PRs) to modify the site. In the end, any amount of contribution will go a long way toward helping to move the project forward into the future.

CHAPTER 14

The NetCAT Program on Testing

The Apache *Net*Beans IDE Community *Acceptance* *Testing* (NetCAT) program (`https://netbeans.apache.org/participate/netcat.html`) seeks to get early feedback on the main features and confirmation from the NetBeans community that the quality of the product makes it ready for the official release.

The goal of this program is to get active Apache NetBeans community members involved in testing the Apache NetBeans IDE development builds and providing feedback on product usability, quality, and performance. In return, these volunteers are given an opportunity to significantly impact the quality of the Apache NetBeans IDE. The NetCAT program is about *quality acceptance* and *not* about feature design. At the end of the program, you will be asked to submit a *Community Acceptance (CA))* survey in which you can express your opinion as to whether or not the new main features are ready for release.

Time Schedule

A typical NetCAT program takes around two months of activities, as described in the following table.

© Ioannis Kostaras, Constantin Drabo, Josh Juneau, Sven Reimers, Mario Schröder, Geertjan Wielenga 2020
I. Kostaras et al., *Pro Apache NetBeans*, https://doi.org/10.1007/978-1-4842-5370-0_14

Table 14-1. *NetCAT Program Activities*

Start Date	Description
2019-02-01	Preparation - schedule, pages, Synergy (3 days)
2019-02-04	NetCAT 11.0 invitation sent, participants start joining
2019-02-07	Synergy test run prepared
2019-02-11	Tribes updated, test assignments created (1 per participant), testing starts on *vc1*
2019-02-21	Request to switch to *vc2* sent
2019-02-25	1/2-way sync-up with tribe leaders
2019-03-07	Request to switch to *vc3* sent
2019-03-11	Community Acceptance survey launched for *vc3*
2019-03-18	Certification completed, blockers fixed in *vc4* or waived
2019-03-22	Community Acceptance survey closed and results published, satisfaction survey launched
2019-03-28	*Apache NetBeans 11.0 released*
2019-03-29	Satisfaction survey closed and results published, NetCAT 11 closed

How to Participate

If you would like to help NetBeans become the best IDE, simply subscribe to `netcat-subscribe@netbeans.incubator.apache.org` mailing list to get updates about the NetCAT program. The main communication channels are *JIRA* (`https://issues.apache.org/jira/browse/NETBEANS`) and the `netcat@netbeans.incubator.apache.org` mailing list.

You must also register yourself in the *NetCAT XX.0*[1] *Participants Wiki page* (`https://cwiki.apache.org/confluence/display/NETBEANS/NetCAT+XX.0+Participants`) or send an e-mail with the requested information to the NetCAT mailing list you subscribed to in the previous step if you cannot edit this Wiki page. You need to provide your availability per week and also one or more *tribe*s. We describe what a tribe is next.

---

[1]*XX.0* is a NetBeans version, for example, 11.0.

As a member of the NetCAT team you are expected to provide feedback on the functional areas (or tribes) you chose to focus on. Though it is perfectly acceptable to only evaluate milestone builds, we would truly appreciate it if you used and tested the daily development builds.

Finally, create an account in *NetBeans Synergy test case management system* (`http://netbeans-vm.apache.org/synergy`).

What Are NetCAT Tribes?

A NetCAT *Tribe* is a group of NetCAT participants focusing primarily on testing one particular functionality area of NetBeans. You declare which tribe you wish to participate in when you register in *Confluence* (see previous section).

Tribe members review and keep up-to-date test specifications for their functionality area, then perform full or sanity testing, and eventually provide either *Go* or *NoGo* recommendations according to a fixed schedule (see Table 14-1).

A list of tribes and what each tribe includes is provided in Synergy (`http://netbeans-vm.apache.org/synergy/client/app/#/tribes`). A summary is provided in Table 14-2.

Table 14-2. *NetCAT Tribes*

Prefix	Tribe
[ant]	Ant
[c/c++]	C/C++
[db]	Databases
[debug]	Debugger
[groovy]	Groovy
[gui]	GUI Builder
[jee]	Java EE
[editor]	Editor
[fx]	Java FX
[maven]	Maven
[php]	PHP

(*continued*)

Table 14-2. (*continued*)

Prefix	Tribe
[profiler]	Profiler
[python]	Python
[rcp]	Rich Client Platform (RCP)
[services]	Services
[unit]	Unit Testing
[vcs]	Version Control
[web]	Web Client

The first column in Table 14-2 denotes the subject prefix to use when you send e-mails to the netcat@netbeans.incubator.apache.org mailing list.

Tribe Leader

You may also choose to become a *tribe leader*. A tribe leader's main role is to distribute the functionality their tribe is focusing on among fellow tribe members to achieve maximum testing coverage and then coordinate the works. Such coordination could take an hour or two every week. The full testing is typically several weeks long and certification of the final GA candidate build just a few days. During these periods the tribe leader does the following:

- checks progress with individual members;

- keeps them motivated;

- helps them resolve potential issues;

- communicates with the *NetCAT coordinator*, particularly when obstacles arise;

- encourages the tribe members to verify fixed bugs.

According to each Apache NetBeans version's Release Criteria (e.g., `https://cwiki.apache.org/confluence/display/NETBEANS/NetBeans+11.0+Release+Criteria`), tribe leaders have two special privileges:

- They can label a bug with a **WAIVER** tag after reaching consensus within their tribe.

- They can label a bug with a **BLOCKER** tag after reaching consensus within their tribe. Only three such open bugs per tribe can be labeled this way at a time.

Additionally, it is much appreciated if tribe leaders organize a review of test specifications for their functionality and together try to update these if time permits *before* full testing.

NetCAT Coordinator

You may also decide to become a coordinator of the NetCAT program. As the *NetCAT coordinator* you will be responsible for the following:

- monitoring the progress of development and preparing the NetCAT schedule;

- updating the NetCAT schedule prior to start of the program;

- sending an invite message and promoting the program to assemble enough NetCAT participants;

- forming NetCAT tribes, finding their leaders, and supporting them throughout the program;

- maintaining Synergy (`http://netbeans-vm.apache.org/synergy`) (users, tribes, and test runs) to have development builds fully tested and Release Candidate builds certified;

- watching quality status and progress of stabilization through the JIRA bug dashboard (`https://issues.apache.org/jira/browse/NETBEANS`) and discussions on NetCAT mailing list (`netcat@netbeans.incubator.apache.org`);

- if needed, encouraging higher participation in the program by writing weekly status reports, organizing online meetings, creating online surveys, etc.;

- creating a final *Community Acceptance survey*, processing and publishing its results;

- helping get the approval from necessary Apache NetBeans stakeholders for the release;

- closing the program by creating satisfaction surveys among NetCAT participants, evaluating their activity, and announcing the best contributors.

If you feel you could do the tasks above and you can afford dedicating between two and five hours weekly to NetCAT coordination, please contact the NetCAT mailing list (netcat@netbeans.incubator.apache.org).

Synergy

Synergy (`http://netbeans-vm.apache.org/synergy`) is the test specifications and test run management system for the NetCAT program (see Figure 14-1).

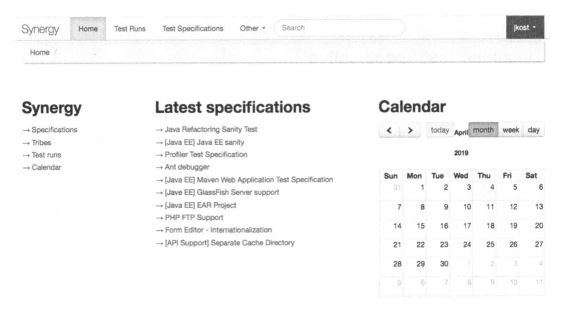

Figure 14-1. *Synergy home page*

In the preparation phase, you receive an e-mail from the tribe leader to review/ update one or more test specifications. Once the NetCAT program runs (see, e.g., Table 14-1), you are supposed to execute one or more of these tests, measure the time spent, and report any bugs.

Test Specifications

By selecting the **Test Specifications** menu item from Synergy's home page (see Figure 14-1), you are provided with a list of test specifications. Your tribe leader will have communicated with you a few days before the NetCAT program to assign you one or more test specifications to review.

An example test specification is shown in Figure 14-2. It provides you with a short description, the estimated execution time, and then the content.

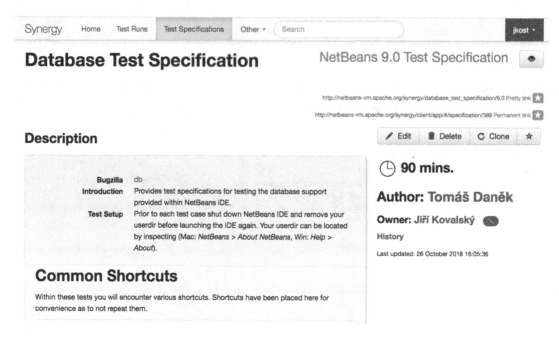

Figure 14-2. *A Test Specification*

A test specification consists of *test suites*. A test suite consists of *test cases*. A test case consists of a number of steps to execute and a number of results to expect (see Figure 14-3).

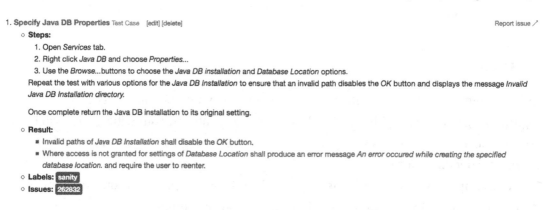

Figure 14-3. *A Test Case*

You may verify if existing bug issues are still valid, or report new issues by using the provided hyperlink. You are expected to modify the test cases to be inline with the version of NetBeans to be tested (e.g., update the steps with any modifications in the UI of the new version).

If you find any serious issues, you may inform the tribe leader.

Test Runs

When the time arrives according to the NetCAT schedule (see, e.g., Table 14-1), the actual testing is to take place. Your tribe leader will provide you the link of the Apache NetBeans binary to download for testing. Please don't compile NetBeans sources yourself, and use the compiled version for official testing.

In this case, select the **Test Runs** menu from the Synergy home page (see Figure 14-4).

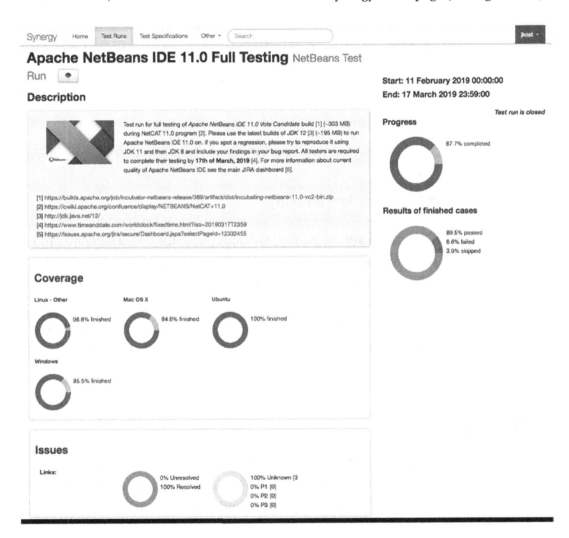

Figure 14-4. *A Test Run summary*

The NetCAT coordinator, together with your tribe leader, will have already updated this page and you should see an entry with your name, the Operating System that you mentioned in Confluence when you registered yourself, and the test specification assigned to you that now waits to be executed (see Figure 14-5).

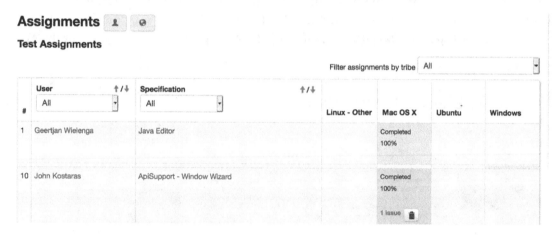

Figure 14-5. *A Test Run execution summary*

Click on the **Run** button to execute the test. You may pause the test at any time. You are informed of the progress and the remaining steps. You are given the opportunity to report any bugs in JIRA or skip some steps. Once you finish the test execution, the result is shown as in Figure 14-5.

At the end of the program, you will be asked to submit a *Community Acceptance (CA)* survey in which you can express your opinion as to whether or not the new main features are ready for release.

Summary

In this chapter we described the NetCAT program and how important is it before a new Apache NetBeans is released. We described the time schedule, how to participate, the tribes, the tribe leader, and the NetCAT coordinator, and finally how to do the actual testing using Synergy.

If you find it interesting and you believe you could participate, then don't hesitate to contact the NetCAT mailing list in order to ask to volunteer and actively prepare the next Apache NetBeans release.

CHAPTER 15

Apache NetBeans Sources Overview

As we have seen in this book, there are many ways to contribute to Apache NetBeans. You can help by writing documentation, blogging about NetBeans, participating in the NetCAT program, or even by fixing bugs and becoming an Apache committer.

In this chapter we will learn how to download Apache NetBeans' source code files. We'll learn how to build NetBeans, and we'll review an overview of the various modules and a high-level architecture of Apache NetBeans IDE itself. We shall also describe the procedure to fix bugs and contribute to the source code. So, fasten your seatbelts.

Download Apache NetBeans Sources

Since the donation to Apache, NetBeans has been stored in a git repository under Apache. Unfortunately, there are no separate repositories per module suite, as was previously the case with the mercurial repositories.

You may download Apache NetBeans sources in one of two ways:

- Navigate to Apache NetBeans website (`https://netbeans.apache.org/`), click on **Download** button on the top right and select the link that starts with *Source:* for example, *incubating-netbeans-11.1-source.zip*. Download the zip file and unzip it to a location of your choice. The download page provides instructions to verify the integrity of the downloaded files.

- If you have *git* installed in your machine, navigate to a location of your choice in your machine, and issue the following command from a DOS command prompt or a terminal:

  `git clone http://github.com/apache/incubator-netbeans/.`

© Ioannis Kostaras, Constantin Drabo, Josh Juneau, Sven Reimers, Mario Schröder, Geertjan Wielenga 2020
I. Kostaras et al., *Pro Apache NetBeans*, https://doi.org/10.1007/978-1-4842-5370-0_15

Build from Source

To build Apache NetBeans (incubating) from the source, you need the following:

- Oracle's JDK 8 or Open JDK 8;

- Apache Ant 1.10 or greater (`https://ant.apache.org`).

Once you have the Oracle JDK and ANT installed, navigate to the directory where you unzipped Apache NetBeans sources and issue the command:

`ant`

You will need an Internet connection as the build may download various artifacts from the Internet. Also note that the build will take some time to finish. Once built, you can execute the IDE by typing the following command into a terminal window on a Unix machine:

`./nbbuild/netbeans/bin/netbeans`

or on a Windows machine, by double-clicking on `netbeans.exe` or `netbeans64.exe`, where these executables are found in `\nbbuild\netbeans\bin`. You can further try running NetBeans with various versions of Java by editing `nbbuild/netbeans/etc/netbeans.conf` and setting the `netbeans_jdkhome` key to a JDK path in your system.

Congratulations! You just built and executed your own version of NetBeans!

Apache NetBeans IDE Architecture

Apache NetBeans is one of the biggest Apache projects (the second biggest one as these lines are written). While you can fix bugs without knowing the big picture, it helps knowing the architecture of each part if you wish to introduce new features. Knowing the architecture will help find your way around in the source code.

Apache NetBeans IDE has a modular architecture using the *Module System API* of Apache NetBeans Platform. Mastering the chapters in Part 2 of this book will help you write code to fix bugs and add new features or plugins to the IDE.

Apache NetBeans IDE consists of the following main components or clusters:

- **apisupport**: contains a number of modules that support NetBeans API. These are modules that support such things as Ant, Maven, Refactoring, and Wizards (see Figure 15-1).

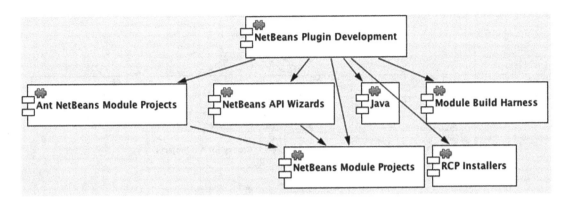

Figure 15-1. *API Support Module dependencies*

- **enterprise**: contains the JEE support (see Figure 15-2).

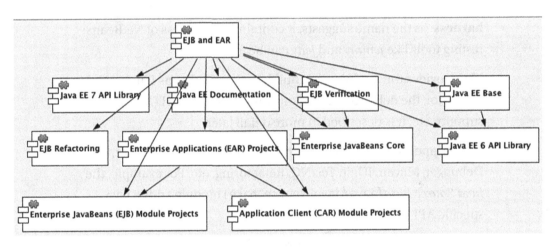

Figure 15-2. *Enterprise Module dependencies*

- **ergonomics**: dynamically enables IDE features on the fly, so the user never wastes system resources by installing full IDE distribution, but using only its subset.

- **extide**: contains IDE extensions like the ant support module and the **Tools | Options** dialog box.

- **extra**: provides JavaFX-wrapped libraries for the various operating systems.

- **groovy**: provides support for Groovy and Gradle (see Figure 15-3).

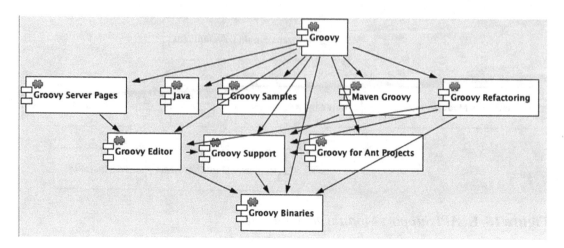

Figure 15-3. *Groovy Module dependencies*

- **harness**: as the name suggests, it contains the harness of NetBeans; testing tools like *jemmy* and *jelly* can be found here.

- **ide**: provides the modules that build Apache NetBeans IDE itself like the editor, the debugger, the languages support, DB, HTML and CSS support, etc. It is described in more detail later.

- **java**: support for the Java programming language and JEE, Ant, Debugger, Maven, JUnit, TestNG, Refactoring, etc. For example, the *Java Source Base* (java/java.source.base) module adds a Java-specific API to the IDE.

- **javafx**: JavaFX support (see Figure 15-4).

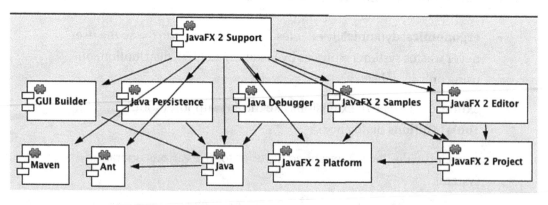

Figure 15-4. *JavaFX Module dependencies*

- **nb**: modules like branding, auto-update plugin center, welcome, deadlock detector, etc.

- **php**: PHP support (see Figure 15-5).

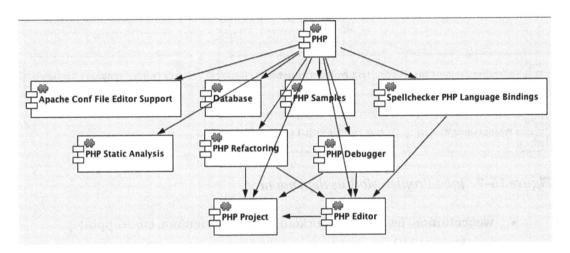

Figure 15-5. *PHP Module dependencies*

- **platform**: the modules that constitute the NetBeans Rich Client Platform (see Figure 15-6).

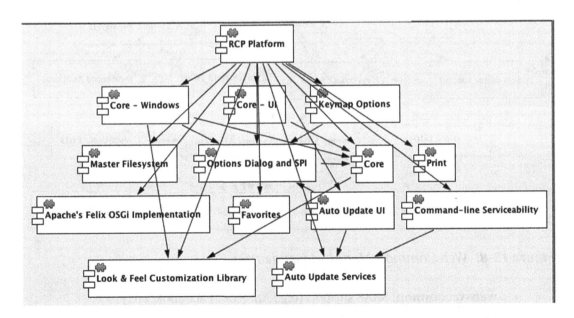

Figure 15-6. *NetBeans Platform Module dependencies*

- **profiler**: as its name denotes, the NetBeans profiler modules (see Figure 15-7).

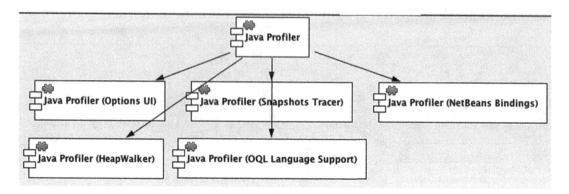

Figure 15-7. *Java Profiler Module dependencies*

- **webcommon**: JavaScript, Knockout, Angular, Selenium, etc., support (see Figure 15-8).

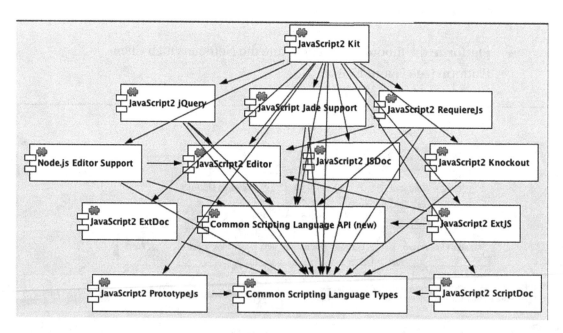

Figure 15-8. *Web Common Module dependencies*

- **websvccommon**: SAAS support (e.g., Amazon, Facebook, etc.) (see Figure 15-9).

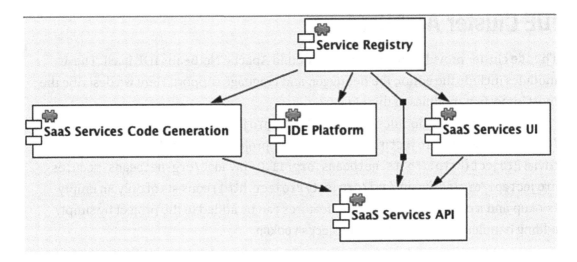

Figure 15-9. *Web Services Module dependencies*

The module to start with is *Bootstrap* (`platform/o.n.bootstrap`), and the class to begin with learning about NetBeans IDE source code is:

`https://github.com/apache/incubator-netbeans/blob/master/platform/`
`o.n.bootstrap/src/org/netbeans/Main.java`

Figure 15-10 shows this module's dependencies.

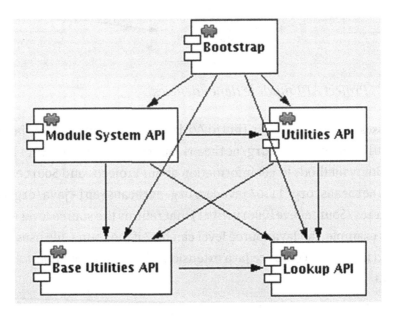

Figure 15-10. *Module dependencies of Bootstrap module*

IDE Cluster Architecture

The ide cluster provides the modules that build Apache NetBeans IDE itself. These modules include the editor, the debugger, and language support. Here we describe the most important modules of this cluster.

The *Projects API* (modules *Project API* (ide/projectapi) (see Figure 15-11) and *Project UI API* (ide/projectuiapi)) define how projects work in NetBeans. The most trivial Project (http://bits.netbeans.org/11.0/javadoc/org-netbeans-modules-projectapi/org/netbeans/api/project/Project.html) consists of only an empty Lookup and a project directory. More features can be added to the project by simply adding handlers for them into the project's Lookup.

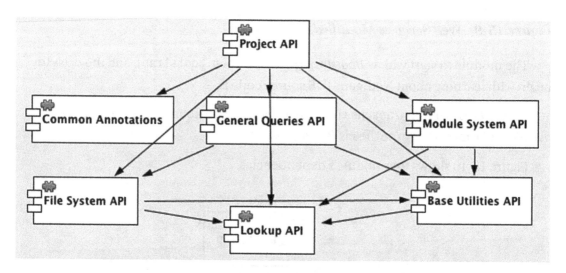

Figure 15-11. *Project API module dependencies*

Useful classes are ProjectUtils (http://bits.netbeans.org/11.0/javadoc/org-netbeans-modules-projectapi/org/netbeans/api/project/ProjectUtils.html) that provides utility methods to get information about Projects, and SourceLevelQuery (http://bits.netbeans.org/11.0/javadoc/org-netbeans-api-java/org/netbeans/api/java/queries/SourceLevelQuery.html) that returns the source level of a Java source file (for example, the Java source level can be 7 if the source file uses syntax that was introduced in Java 7). There are Java extensions to the generic *Project API* in module java/api.java.

The *Parsing API* (ide/parsing.api) (see Figure 15-12) is used for source code parsing (mostly in editor). It allows registering new parsers (http://bits.netbeans. org/11.0/javadoc/org-netbeans-modules-parsing-api/org/netbeans/modules/ parsing/spi/ParserFactory.html), defining some parts of the source code to be actually parts of embedded text in a different language EmbeddingProvider (http://bits.netbeans.org/11.0/javadoc/org-netbeans-modules-parsing- api/org/netbeans/modules/parsing/spi/EmbeddingProvider.html) and ParserBasedEmbeddingProvider (http://bits.netbeans.org/11.0/javadoc/ org-netbeans-modules-parsing-api/org/netbeans/modules/parsing/spi/ ParserBasedEmbeddingProvider.html) and running tasks on the outcomes of the parsers.

There are two types of tasks:

- ParserResultTask (http://bits.netbeans.org/11.0/javadoc/ org-netbeans-modules-parsing-api/org/netbeans/modules/ parsing/spi/ParserResultTask.html) is a SchedulerTask that processes the result of parsing automatically scheduled and run in a defined order.

- ParserManager (http://bits.netbeans.org/11.0/javadoc/org- netbeans-modules-parsing-api/org/netbeans/modules/parsing/ api/ParserManager.html) allows starting priority parsing requests for one or more sources and immediately runs user tasks on demand.

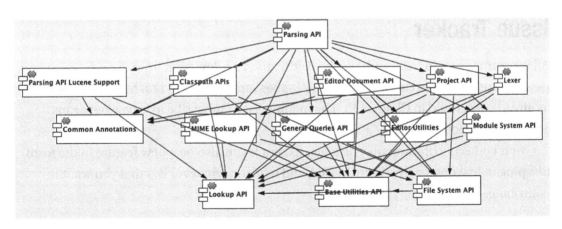

Figure 15-12. *Parsing API module dependencies*

The *Parsing Indexing API* (ide/parsing.indexing) is used for "indexing" (e.g., building a "global" index of anything that is important in the source files, so that queries like "which files use this class" can be done fast). Interesting classes here include:

- EmbeddingIndexer (http://bits.netbeans.org/11.0/javadoc/ org-netbeans-modules-parsing-indexing/org/netbeans/ modules/parsing/spi/indexing/EmbeddingIndexer.html), which gets a result of the parser, and can add whatever information it needs to the index.

- BinaryIndexer (http://bits.netbeans.org/11.0/javadoc/org- netbeans-modules-parsing-indexing/org/netbeans/modules/ parsing/spi/indexing/BinaryIndexer.html), which allows preparing an index for binary dependencies.

- CustomIndexer (http://bits.netbeans.org/11.0/javadoc/org- netbeans-modules-parsing-indexing/org/netbeans/modules/ parsing/spi/indexing/CustomIndexer.html), which is given simply the list of changed files, and can perform indexing in a custom way. Querying the index can be done through QuerySupport (http:// bits.netbeans.org/11.0/javadoc/org-netbeans-modules- parsing-indexing/org/netbeans/modules/parsing/spi/indexing/ support/QuerySupport.html).

Issue Tracker

All programs contain bugs and Apache NetBeans is no deviation from the rule. Bugs and new features are stored in JIRA (https://issues.apache.org/jira/browse/NETBEANS) as already described in Chapter 13. The mailing list to subscribe to is dev@netbeans. incubator.apache.org.

Your code contribution may be a bug fix, but it can also be a new feature in the form of a plugin. Just open a new issue in JIRA and work on whatever it is that you want to contribute.

Debugging Apache NetBeans

Whether you are fixing an issue or developing a new feature (plugin), sooner or later you will need to understand how your or NetBeans' code works or why it doesn't! Before you start debugging Apache NetBeans, make sure you have set the sources correctly.

Click on **Tools ➤ NetBeans Platforms** to display the *NetBeans Platform Manager* dialog (see Figure 15-13). You will see that there is one platform, *Development IDE*, already registered. This is the platform of the NetBeans IDE that you are running, for example, 11.1 if you run Apache NetBeans IDE 11.1.

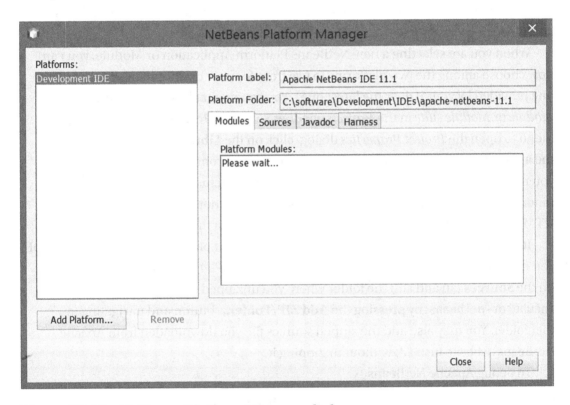

Figure 15-13. *NetBeans Platform Manager dialog*

However, you may wish, for example, to fix a bug in the latest sources update that you have downloaded and unzipped in a folder as explained earlier in this chapter.

As we already mentioned, when you build the sources, the output is stored inside nbbuild/netbeans folder. This contains a NetBeans IDE built from the sources, which includes a NetBeans platform, too. You can register that platform to your NetBeans IDE you are running by clicking on the **Add Platform...** button in the *NetBeans Platform Manager* dialog and selecting the nbbuild/netbeans folder from the *Add NetBeans Platform* dialog that opens (see Figure 15-14). You will notice that the **Next** button becomes enabled when you select the nbbuild/netbeans folder.

Click the **Next** button to move to the next step where you may optionally provide another *Platform Name* than the provided one (something like "Apache NetBeans IDE Dev (Build xxx-yyy)"; see Figure 15-15) and click **Finish**. You should now be able to see the two platforms in the *NetBeans Platform Manager* dialog.

Click on the **Sources** tab, click the **Add ZIP/Folder...** button and add the folder that contains the NetBeans sources (i.e., the parent folder of nbbuild) and click **Close** and **Close**.

When you are selecting a new NetBeans Platform Application or Module, you can now choose among the two platforms to use from for your development (i.e., either the one provided by your IDE or the latest one). You can do that by right-clicking on your *Module* or *Module suite* in the *Projects* window, selecting **Properties** from the pop-up menu to open the *Project Properties* dialog, click on the **Libraries** category, and select the appropriate *NetBeans Platform* from the respective combo box. In the same dialog, you many also customize which modules you wish to include and which not in your module suite (see Figure 15-16). For example, if you are not developing a JavaFX or HTML/UI application or plugin, just uncheck those from the list of modules.

If you don't wish to register a NetBeans development platform to your NetBeans IDE, you may simply add the latest sources. In the *NetBeans Platform Manager* dialog, click on the **Sources** tab and add the folder where you unzipped the sources, for example, incubator-netbeans, by pressing the **Add ZIP/Folder...** button and navigating to that folder. You may also add the zipped sources file you downloaded from Apache NetBeans' website instead, without unzipping it.

To debug Apache NetBeans:

1. Open an Apache NetBeans module that you're interested in debugging in Apache NetBeans IDE.

2. Place a breakpoint somewhere in the source code editor.

3. Right-click the module and choose **Debug**.

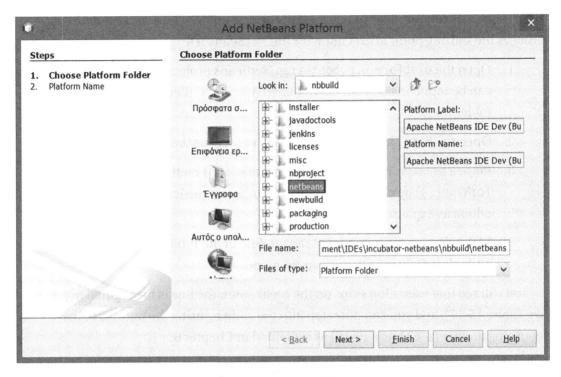

Figure 15-14. *Add NetBeans Platform dialog (Step 1)*

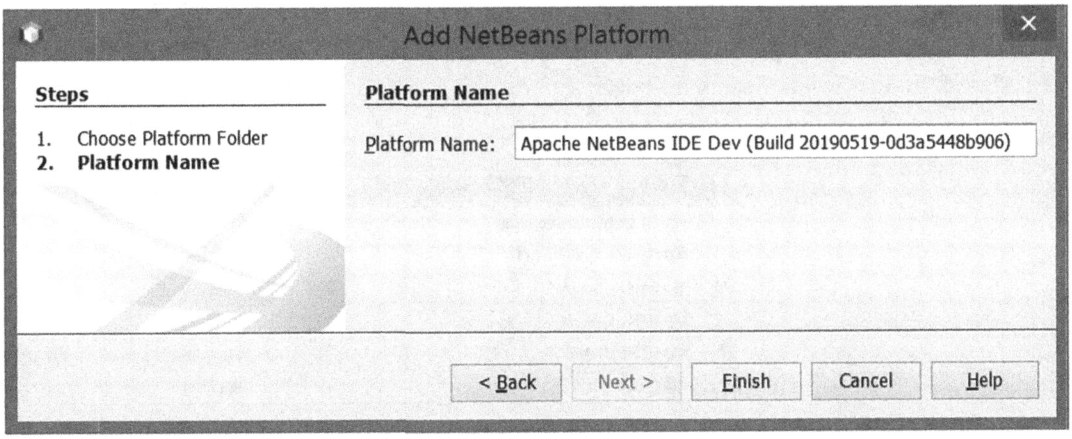

Figure 15-15. *Add NetBeans Platform dialog (Step 2)*

Let's see an example. Let's debug the *Bootstrap* module, which as we mentioned earlier, is the starting point of execution for the NetBeans IDE.

1. Open the `platform/o.n.bootstrap` NetBeans project, which can be found inside your downloaded Apache NetBeans sources folder.

2. Open the `Main.java` file found inside `src/org/netbeans` folder.

3. Place a breakpoint on the first line of the `main()` method (`Class.forName(…)`) by clicking on the line number on the left of the editor, as explained in Chapter 6.

4. Right-click on the `o.n.bootstrap` module in the Projects window and select **Debug** from the pop-up menu.

You will see that execution stops on the breakpoint, the line is highlighted in green (see Figure 15-17), and you can now step into the code by using the buttons of the debugging toolbar (see Figure 15-18) as explained in Chapter 6.

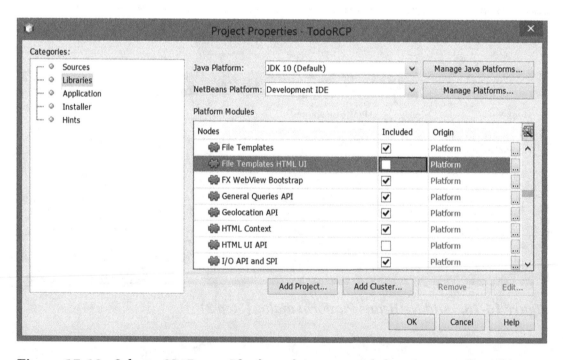

Figure 15-16. *Select a NetBeans Platform for your module suite as well as the required platform modules)*

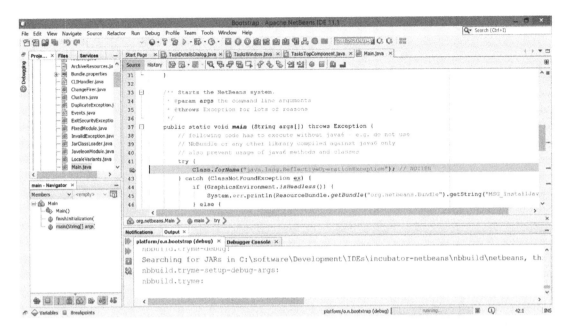

Figure 15-17.   *Debugging o.n.bootstrap NetBeans Platform module*

Figure 15-18.   *Debugging toolbar*

Commit Code

Once you have implemented and tested your modification, it is a good practice, not only to update the JIRA issue, but also to send an e-mail to the *dev* mailing list to inform others, get useful feedback, and maybe find potential testers. Once you are confident that your change is ready, issue a pull request to the master repo.

Summary

In this chapter you learned how to download and build the sources of Apache NetBeans IDE. You also had an overview of the architecture of the various components of Apache NetBeans IDE (which is based on Apache NetBeans Platform) and got an idea of how to commit your code back to the Apache NetBeans `git` repository.

Good luck and may the source be with you!

Index

A

Abstract Window Toolkit (AWT), 73
    Applets, 75
    GUI forms, 76
    GUI widgets, 77
actionPerformed() method, 244, 278
Actions global context, 190
Action system
    annotations, 244
    BAPI, 251
    BooleanStateAction, 249, 250
    CallableSystemAction, 252
    callback, 246
    categories, 246
    CookieAction, 252, 253
    DRY principle, 243
    enabled, 247, 248
    JComponent, 247
    shortcut keys, 246
    wizard, 244, 245
AddTaskAction class, 265
ANTLR, 357
Apache Incubator
    OpenBeans, 413
    incubation, 9.0, 414, 415
    incubation, 10.0, 416
    incubation, 11.0, 416, 417
    key milestone, 413
    source code, 413
    top level project, 413

Apache Maven, 16, 17
Apache NetBeans, installation, 5
Apache NetBeans 9.0
    Jigsaw support, 64
    JShell, 65, 66
    local variable type
        inference, 64
Apache NetBeans 10.0
    JDK 11 support, 67, 68
    PHP, 68–70
Apache NetBeans 11.0
    Gradle support, 71, 72
    Java EE 8 support, 71
    JDK 12, 71
Applets, 75
applyBindings() method, 239

B

BinaryIndexer class, 450
Blockchain, 342, 343
Branding, 336
Breakpoints, 130
    actions, 145, 146
    Apache NetBeans, 144
    AWT/Swing component, 151, 152
    class, 147
    comparators, 147
    constrains, 147
    dialog, 145
    exception, 148

Printed in the United States
By Bookmasters